# The Texture of Change

# NEW AFRICAN HISTORIES

SERIES EDITORS: JEAN ALLMAN, JACOB S. T. DLAMINI, ALLEN ISAACMAN, DEREK R. PETERSON, AND CARINA RAY

David William Cohen and E. S. Atieno Odhiambo, *The Risks of Knowledge*

Belinda Bozzoli, *Theatres of Struggle and the End of Apartheid*

Gary Kynoch, *We Are Fighting the World*

Stephanie Newell, *The Forger's Tale*

Jacob A. Tropp, *Natures of Colonial Change*

Jan Bender Shetler, *Imagining Serengeti*

Cheikh Anta Babou, *Fighting the Greater Jihad*

Marc Epprecht, *Heterosexual Africa?*

Marissa J. Moorman, *Intonations*

Karen E. Flint, *Healing Traditions*

Derek R. Peterson and Giacomo Macola, editors, *Recasting the Past*

Moses E. Ochonu, *Colonial Meltdown*

Emily S. Burrill, Richard L. Roberts, and Elizabeth Thornberry, editors, *Domestic Violence and the Law in Colonial and Postcolonial Africa*

Daniel R. Magaziner, *The Law and the Prophets*

Emily Lynn Osborn, *Our New Husbands Are Here*

Robert Trent Vinson, *The Americans Are Coming!*

James R. Brennan, *Taifa*

Benjamin N. Lawrance and Richard L. Roberts, editors, *Trafficking in Slavery's Wake*

David M. Gordon, *Invisible Agents*

Allen F. Isaacman and Barbara S. Isaacman, *Dams, Displacement, and the Delusion of Development*

Stephanie Newell, *The Power to Name*

Gibril R. Cole, *The Krio of West Africa*

Matthew M. Heaton, *Black Skin, White Coats*

Meredith Terretta, *Nation of Outlaws, State of Violence*

Paolo Israel, *In Step with the Times*

Michelle R. Moyd, *Violent Intermediaries*

Abosede A. George, *Making Modern Girls*

Alicia C. Decker, *In Idi Amin's Shadow*

Rachel Jean-Baptiste, *Conjugal Rights*

Shobana Shankar, *Who Shall Enter Paradise?*

Emily S. Burrill, *States of Marriage*

Todd Cleveland, *Diamonds in the Rough*

Carina E. Ray, *Crossing the Color Line*

Sarah Van Beurden, *Authentically African*

Giacomo Macola, *The Gun in Central Africa*

Lynn Schler, *Nation on Board*

Julie MacArthur, *Cartography and the Political Imagination*

Abou B. Bamba, *African Miracle, African Mirage*

Daniel Magaziner, *The Art of Life in South Africa*

Paul Ocobock, *An Uncertain Age*

Keren Weitzberg, *We Do Not Have Borders*

Nuno Domingos, *Football and Colonialism*

Jeffrey S. Ahlman, *Living with Nkrumahism*

Bianca Murillo, *Market Encounters*

Laura Fair, *Reel Pleasures*

Thomas F. McDow, *Buying Time*

Jon Soske, *Internal Frontiers*

Elizabeth W. Giorgis, *Modernist Art in Ethiopia*

Matthew V. Bender, *Water Brings No Harm*

David Morton, *Age of Concrete*

Marissa J. Moorman, *Powerful Frequencies*

Ndubueze L. Mbah, *Emergent Masculinities*

Patricia Hayes and Gary Minkley, editors, *Ambivalent*

Mari K. Webel, *The Politics of Disease Control*

Kara Moskowitz, *Seeing Like a Citizen*

Jacob Dlamini, *Safari Nation*

Alice Wiemers, *Village Work*

Cheikh Anta Babou, *The Muridiyya on the Move*

Laura Ann Twagira, *Embodied Engineering*

Judith A. Byfield, *The Great Upheaval*

Marissa Mika, *Africanizing Oncology*

Holly Hanson, *To Speak and Be Heard*

Paul S. Landau, *Spear*

Saheed Aderinto, *Animality and Colonial Subjecthood in Africa*

Katherine Bruce-Lockhart, *Carceral Afterlives*

Natasha Erlank, *Convening Black Intimacy in Early Twentieth-Century South Africa*

Morgan J. Robinson, *A Language for the World*

Faeeza Ballim, *Apartheid's Leviathan*

Nicole Eggers, *Unruly Ideas*

Mark W. Deets, *A Country of Defiance*

Patrick William Otim, *Acholi Intellectuals*

Daniel Magaziner, *Available Light*

Admire Mseba, *Society, Power, and Land in Northeastern Zimbabwe, ca. 1560–1960*

Ademide Adelusi-Adeluyi, *Imagine Lagos*

Jody Benjamin, *The Texture of Change*

# The Texture of Change

*Dress, Self-Fashioning, and History
in Western Africa, 1700–1850*

Jody Benjamin

OHIO UNIVERSITY PRESS
ATHENS, OHIO

Ohio University Press, Athens, Ohio 45701
ohioswallow.com
© 2024 by Ohio University Press
All rights reserved

To obtain permission to quote, reprint, or otherwise reproduce or distribute material from Ohio University Press publications, please contact our rights and permissions department at (740) 593-1154 or (740) 593-4536 (fax).

Printed in the United States of America
Ohio University Press books are printed on acid-free paper ∞ ™

*Library of Congress Cataloging-in-Publication Data*

Names: Benjamin, Jody, author.
Title: The texture of change : dress, self-fashioning, and history in western Africa, 1700–1850 / Jody Benjamin.
Other titles: New African histories series.
Description: Athens, Ohio : Ohio University Press, 2024. | Series: New African histories | Includes bibliographical references and index.
Identifiers: LCCN 2023057925 (print) | LCCN 2023057926 (ebook) | ISBN 9780821425466 (hardcover) | ISBN 9780821425473 (paperback) | ISBN 9780821425480 (pdf)
Subjects: LCSH: Clothing and dress—Africa, West—History. | Textile fabrics—Africa, West—History. | Clothing trade—Africa, West—History. | Africa, West—History—To 1884. | BISAC: DESIGN / Textile & Costume | BUSINESS & ECONOMICS / International / Economics & Trade
Classification: LCC GT1589.A358 B46 2024 (print) | LCC GT1589.A358 (ebook) | DDC 391.00966/09033—dc23/eng/20240402
LC record available at https://lccn.loc.gov/2023057925
LC ebook record available at https://lccn.loc.gov/2023057926

*The Texture of Change* is the recipient of the
Ohio University Press First Book Fund,
established by Gillian Berchowitz in 2018.

First-time authors are often pioneers in their fields, and their writing and research are crucial to understanding the critical issues of our time. The Ohio University Press First Book Fund sets out to make the process more equitable for African and Appalachian scholars as they seek to publish their first books.

For more information, please see ohioswallow.com/first-book-fund/.

# Contents

| | |
|---|---|
| List of Illustrations | ix |
| Acknowledgments | xiii |
| Introduction | 1 |
| *Chapter 1* Twelve Measures of New Cloth and a Magnificent Bubu Bamanan Kaarta between Sahel and Sea | 26 |
| *Chapter 2* Cotton Cloth in Western Africa Barafulas, Bafetas, and Piezas de India | 54 |
| *Chapter 3* Centering the Sahel in the Early Eighteenth Century Indigo Dyers, Precarity, and the Pull of the Falémé River Valley, 1730–1750 | 89 |
| *Chapter 4* The Politics of Dress at Saint-Louis during an Age of Islamic Revolution, 1785–1815 | 110 |
| *Chapter 5* Merchants, Maroons, Mahdis, and Migrants on the Upper Guinea Coast, 1795–1825 | 139 |
| *Chapter 6* Textures of a Changing Era Old Redcoats, Groundnuts, and Afro-Atlantic Missionaries, 1825–1850 | 171 |
| Conclusion | 194 |
| Notes | 199 |
| Bibliography | 225 |
| Index | 241 |

vii

# Illustrations

## MAPS

| | | |
|---|---|---|
| 0.1. | Map of western Africa | 4 |
| 1.1. | Map of the Sahel between the Senegal and Niger Rivers | 32 |
| 2.1. | Map of the region, including links with the Cape Verde islands | 57 |
| 3.1. | Map of the eastern Senegal River valley and the Faleme River valley | 93 |
| 4.1. | Map of the Senegal River valley | 114 |
| 5.1. | Map of the Guinea region showing Kankan in the hot, dry savanna | 142 |
| 6.1. | Map of the coastal Guinea region showing towns along the riverine coast | 179 |

## FIGURES

| | | |
|---|---|---|
| 1.1. | Equestrian figure, twelfth to fourteenth century | 29 |
| 1.2. | Equestrian figure, from the twelfth to the sixteenth century | 29 |
| 1.3. | Detail from Guillaume de l'Isle, *Carte de l'Afrique francaise ou du Sénégal* [...], 1727 | 34 |
| 1.4. | De l'Isle map crop | 35 |
| 1.5. | "Femme Bambara" in David Boilat | 41 |
| 1.6. | "Homme Bambara" in David Boilat | 41 |
| 1.7. | "Coussave [Kusaaba] or Blouse N'ajate Sego" | 42 |

| | | |
|---|---|---|
| 1.8. | Une armée Bambara en marche in Anne Raffenel | 50 |
| 2.1. | "Pano de terra / pano d'obra from Cape Verde" | 59 |
| 2.2. | "Habits des femmes de Kazegut / Clothing of the Women in Kazegut" | 61 |
| 2.3. | "Woman in coastal Senegal" | 69 |
| 2.4. | Indigo cotton garment, ca. 1659 | 71 |
| 2.5. | "Cavalry" ("Negro Cavalry") in René Claude Geoffroy de Villeneuve | 84 |
| 2.6. | "Soldier" ("Negro Soldier") in René Claude Geoffroy de Villeneuve | 84 |
| 2.7. | "Arrestation de M. Brue par ordre du Damel de Cayor, 1701" | 85 |
| 3.1. | "Mosque and place of assembly at Galam (Gajaaga)" | 95 |
| 3.2. | "A negro girl beating cotton rather than carding it" | 99 |
| 3.3. | "Image of Boulebane in Bundu" | 105 |
| 3.4. | Portrait of Ayuba Sulayman Diallo by William Hoare of Bath | 107 |
| 3.5. | "Negres de Bondu" | 109 |
| 4.1. | "Echantillons des Siamoises du Prince noir, deuxieme voyage," 1787 | 112 |
| 4.2. | "Manding Man" | 112 |
| 4.3. | "Letter from Boubou Guiobe to Mme Yaye Birame," 1776 | 113 |
| 4.4. | Images of Saint-Louis signares and marabouts, 1789 | 120 |
| 4.5. | Images of Saint-Louis signares and marabouts, 1796 | 120 |
| 4.6. | Images of Saint-Louis signares and marabouts, 1802 | 120 |
| 4.7. | European doll dressed in the style of a Saint-Louis signare | 123 |
| 4.8. | "Uniformes des Corps des Laptots de Goree," 1765 | 126 |
| 4.9. | African canoe paddling through surf, Gabriel Bray, 1775 | 131 |
| 4.10. | "Man with Walking Stick" | 132 |
| 4.11. | "Pretre sacrificateur / Sacrificial Priest" | 132 |

4.12. "Guerrier de l'Isle de Saint Louis / Warrior and Signare on Saint Louis" 133

4.13. "Woman in Senegal" 133

4.14. "Diai Boukari" 135

5.1. Detail from 1794 map of Sierra Leone and Bulama Island 144

5.2. "Costume of the Gambia" 147

5.3. Eighteenth-century alderman's gown 155

5.4. "Mr. Kizell Introduced by Couber to His Father King Sherbro" 160

5.5. "Female Clothing Styles, Sierra Leone, 1805" 161

5.6. "Temminee Wives, Sierra Leone, 1805" 162

5.7. "A Negro King in Monmouth Street Clothes with His Wives and Children" 163

6.1. "Bokari, the Kaartan guide" 175

6.2. "The Women at Timbo Drawing Water" 176

6.3. "Soolima Women Dancers" 176

6.4. Interior of a piazza in the *Illustrated London News* (October 25, 1856) 185

6.5. "Susu Women / Femmes Soussous" 191

*Illustrations* — xi

# Acknowledgments

The research for this book unfolded over many years and many miles. It could not have been completed without the many kindnesses I received along the way, including the generous support of colleagues, mentors, archivists, institutions, editors, family, and friends. For that, I am most grateful.

The book has evolved from a dissertation I completed in 2016. I would like to thank my dissertation committee members for their guidance and support while I was a graduate student and since: Emmanuel Akyeampong, Sven Beckert, Suzanne Blier, Caroline Elkins, and Judi Byfield. I am also grateful for the critical feedback and suggestions of scholars who engaged the work during a manuscript workshop in 2019: Michael Gomez, Edda Fields-Black, Jeremy Prescott, Rachel Jean-Baptiste, Ray Kea, David Lloyd, and Fariba Zarinebaf.

The idea for the dissertation and the book first emerged during summer visits to Mali in 2009 and 2011. I was there to study the Bamanankan language but was struck by the endless variety of textiles people wore daily in Bamako and that were for sale in the extensive mazelike passages of the city's *suguba,* or central market. I began to learn of the region's long and deep history of textile making and trading, which then led to research visits to Segu and Jenne. I would like to thank my Bamanan teacher and mentor Kassim Kone, and John Hutchison. I am grateful for the warm hospitality of Ibrahim and Madina Sanogo of Bamako. I'm deeply appreciative for the collegiality and support of the late historian Moussa Sow, of the Kati-based educator Maria Keita, of the scholar Ismaila Samba Traore, for the camaraderie of my colleagues Hamidou Fofana and Hamidou Kone, and for the research advice of Tal Tamari. I would also like to thank David Conrad for his mentorship and support, Joseph Hellweg, and colleagues in the Mande Studies Association.

I would like to thank many people in Guinea, such as El Hadj Ibrahima Fall, colleagues from the Julius Nyerere University of Kankan, especially

Abdulkarim Kourouma, Morike Sidibe, Namoudou Conde, Sidiki Kourouma, El Hajj Souware, Sory Kourouma. I'm also deeply grateful for the collegial generosity in Guinea of Nafadji Sory Conde, Saidou N'Daou, N'Daou Sangouye, Marie Yvonne Curtis, and Moustapha Keita-Diop of the Université Général Lansana Conté de Sonfonia in Conakry.

I appreciate the support of many colleagues in Senegal who have been generous with their time: Professors Boubacar Barry, Omar Gueye, and Babacar Fall of the Université Cheikh Anta Diop in Dakar; Maria Grosz-Ngaté and Eileen Julien, archivists at the Archives Nationales du Sénégal; Fatima Fall of the Centre de Recherche et de Documentation du Sénégal in Saint-Louis; Abdourahmane Seck; and members of GAEC in Saint-Louis.

Of those individuals who assisted me in France, I would like to thank Gaelle Beaujean, Sarah Frioux-Salgas, Helene Joubert, and Angele Martin of the Musée du Quai Branly in Paris; Krystel Gualde and Bertrand Guillet of the Musée d'histoire de Nantes; and the archivists of the Archives nationales d'outre-mer in Aix-en-Provence, the Archives départementales de Loire-Atlantique, the Archives de la ville de Honfleur, and the Musée de la Mode et du Textile in Paris.

I have been fortunate to participate in conferences on global history, dress history, and West African history, each of which encouraged me to expand my thinking in generative ways. I am grateful to Giorgio Riello of the University of Warwick and Beverly Lemire of the University of Alberta, who organized the "Dressing Global Bodies" conference in Edmonton in 2016; and also to JoAnn McGregor and Nicola Stylianou, who organized the "Creating African Fashion Histories" conference at the Brighton Museum and Art Gallery in the United Kingdom in 2016. I'd especially like to thank Sven Beckert and the Weatherhead Center for International Affairs, Research Cluster on Global Studies at Harvard University, for engaging with my work during meetings held in Saint-Louis, Senegal, and in Delhi, India. Thank you to Lorelle Semley and Rosa Carrasquillo, organizers of "Rethinking the Afropolitan: The Ethics of Black Atlantic Masculinities on Display" at the College of the Holy Cross. I'd like to thank Saheed Aderinto of Florida International University and Abosede George of Barnard College as well as the larger community of the Lagos Studies Association, where I have been able to engage with scholars thinking about West Africa in regional and global terms.

Fellowships from the National Endowment for the Humanities, the Hellman Foundation, the John Carter Brown Library of Brown University, the University of California Regents, and the University of California Humanities Research Initiative supported the completion of this work at various stages. More-recent collaborations with the Mellon Foundation–funded Humanities across Borders project (based in the International Institute for Asian Studies) with Aarti Kawlra and Philippe Peycam have helped advance a research agenda that also includes reimagining methodology and pedagogy in the humanities.

I am blessed to have a wide network of colleagues who have contributed in large ways and small to the development and completion of this work. I would like to thank my colleagues in the Department of History at the University of California, Riverside, including my emeritus History Department colleagues Sterling Stuckey, Ray Kea, and V. P. Franklin. I'm grateful for the collegiality across campus from Jasmin Young, andre carrington, Jade Sasser, David Lloyd, dylan rodríguez, Jeanette Kohl, Fatima Quraishi, Matt Durham, Savannah Esquivel, Yong Cho, Ruhi Khan, Andrea Denny Brown, Flip Tanedo, Worku Nida, and Yolanda Moses (emerita). A special thank-you to Rivera Library archivists Michael Yonezawa and Robin Katz, and to the Center for Ideas and Society, especially Georgia Warnke and Katharine Henshaw, who were so supportive during a fellowship year that was unfortunately disrupted by COVID.

I'd like to express gratitude to and solidarity with former colleagues at the Harvard University graduate program in African and African American studies: Carolyn Roberts, David Amponsah, Oludamini Ogunnaike, Armin Fardis, Tsione Wolde, Emmanuel Asiedu-Acquah, Lisanne Norman, Stephanie Bosch-Santana, Erin Mosely, Funlayo Wood, Kyra Daniels, and Boubacar Diakite. I found a second graduate school home at New York University and must shout out colleagues Laurie Lambert, Tyisha Maddox, James Cantres, Evelyne Laurent Perrault, and Larissa Kopytoff.

Thank you to my editors at Ohio University Press, and in particular to Jean Allman. Thank you for supporting this project and including it in the New African Histories series. Thanks and gratitude to Tyler Balli and to the copyeditor, Dana Johnson, for their patient and careful attention.

Thank you to colleagues who have engaged with my work or supported me at various stages of this research: Cherif Keita, Cheikh Babou, Leo Arriola, Martha Saavedra, Bruce Hall, Mhoze Chikowero, Corrie Decker, Yatta Khiazulu, Robert Vinson, Benjamin Talton, Nathalie Pierre, Colleen Kriger, Suzanne Schwarz, John Styles, Sarah Fee, Kazuo Kobayashi, Anka Steffen, Cliff Perreira, Chris Evans, Anna Arabindan-Kesson, Janet Goldner, Mohomodou Houssouba, Bernhard Gardi, Cameron Gokee, Sarah Zimmerman, and Carina Ray. At New York University: Madina Thiam, Robyn D'Avignon, Jennifer Morgan, and Abdulbasit Kassim. At UCLA: Jemima Pierre, Peter Hudson, Andrew Apter, and Ghislaine Lydon. At Stanford University: Ayana

Omilade Flewellen and Emily Osborn. And at the University of Chicago: Carole Amman, Karen Tranberg Hansen, and Elizabeth Fretwell.

Thank you to my mother, Carolyn Idalia Bryant, who first introduced me to books and has always encouraged my curiosity about our world. To the memory of grandfather Fred Bryant Sr., whose extensive library and record collection opened my eyes about the many different sides of the black world, and to my grandmother Joan (Jody) Bryant and Fred (Rocky) Bryant Jr. I would like to thank my parents-in-law, Prince Julius Adewale Adelusi-Adeluyi and Julia Adelusi-Adeluyi of Lagos, Nigeria. I'm so grateful for the many years of love and support we have shared. Thank you to Akin and Funke Ogunranti of Lagos and the entire Ogunranti family. I'm also grateful for the friendship and support of the Okonkwo family, Adamma and Chike, of the United Kingdom. Many thanks to Terence Taylor, of Brooklyn, New York.

I would like to record a special note of appreciation to departed teachers and friends, all of whom had a hand in shaping me as a scholar: Francis Abiola Irele, Paulin Hountondji, Calvin Hernton, Gloria Watkins (bell hooks), Georgiana Pickett, Bernard Harmon, Lynwood Mainor, Benjamin Israel, Rabbi Hailu Paris, and Gary Smalls.

And finally, to my wife and co-conspirator, Ademide Adelusi-Adeluyi—thank you for the love and laughter, and for your brilliance, inspiration, and support.

# Introduction

THE SMELL of charcoal smoke and grilled meat hung in the hot, dusty air, layering a pungent scent over the din of Bakel, a busy commercial port on the eastern Senegal River. On the water, canoes clustered around commercial boats, splashing and bumping against one another as people offloaded goods from vessels that had sailed the roughly five hundred miles upriver from the coast at Ndar/Saint-Louis.[1] On the muddy banks nearby, caravans of camels and oxen had arrived from parts of the Sahara, and dozens of commercial agents clustered around caravan leaders, conversing animatedly about deals. The cacophony of smells, sounds, and sights at the port was punctuated by these social interactions, forming a polyglot chorus and sartorial tableau: Groups of people mingled, speaking in a variety of African languages—Soninke, Fulbe, Hassaniya Arabic, Wolof, and Bamanankan—and dressed in an array of styles and vibrant colors—men in bright madder pants, women in indigo wrappers, others in plain white breeches and tunics, some in turbans, and some even in such foreign clothes as a cloak and little, round hat acquired from French soldiers.[2]

This was the frenzied and pluralist scene that French naval officer and explorer Anne Raffenel described taking place in 1847, outside the high walls of the French military and commercial garrison fort at Bakel, where Atlantic and Saharan trade systems interfaced. The fort, built in 1819,[3] had once been staffed by white French soldiers dispatched from the coast. But after they complained of unhealthy conditions leading to serious illness, officials replaced most of the Europeans with African soldiers, who were often commanded by mixed-race Eurafrican, or métis, officers, in the belief that they could better withstand those conditions.[4] The fort and adjacent town were located on a portion of the river that was a sort of fulcrum on the waterway's long arc east and then south, slicing through desert, Sahel, and then forest toward its source in the cool Fuuta Jallon Mountains of Guinea. Indeed, the fort was built there when the French could travel no farther upriver in 1818 due to low water levels. Raffenel's portrait of the pulsating port decades later speaks to the multiplicity of African actors and forces who had animated western African societies, cultures, states, and economies from the mid-to-late seventeenth century—when environmental forces, the end of the Mali Empire, and expanding European mercantile activity began to alter the region's social, economic, and political relationships—until the mid-nineteenth century, when European colonial powers were more firmly entrenched and an age of imperial global capitalism and African Atlantic diasporas were underway.

This book examines the contours of the social and cultural history of "western Africa,"[5] a broad region that encompasses contemporary Senegal, the Gambia, Guinea-Bissau, Guinea, Sierra Leone, and western Mali (see map 1), through the history of textile production, commerce, consumption, and the politics of dress. The time period analyzed here, from the turn of the eighteenth century through the mid-nineteenth century, has largely been defined historiographically by efforts to assess the impact of European imperial expansion and the transatlantic slave trade on western Africa, often in works of economic history or the history of a particular European empire in the region. More recently, historians have shifted away from this older emphasis on external stimulus or abstract economic processes to imagine the past through other lenses and on its own terms. This book contributes to that shift by using dress to instead center diverse African historical experiences and construct a narrative of regional and global history at this critical juncture from the inside out. I mine a range of sources on cotton, indigo, and textiles and explore dress as an expressive archive of historical self-fashioning and social change that can reveal much about how people experienced such changes wrought by warfare, slave raiding, Islamic reform, and Atlantic commerce. The history of textile making and trading in western Africa goes back centuries, with physical evidence of local weaving from the Bandiagara Escarpment in Mali dating to the eleventh century.[6] Significantly, the eleventh century was also the period in which Al-Bakri, the Arab travel writer from Moorish Spain, noted that in ancient Ghana only the king "and his heir apparent (who is the son of his sister) may wear sewn clothes [while all] other people wear robes of cotton, silk or brocade according to their means."[7] Thus the politics of dress had long mediated social, political, and commercial relationships between many types of people, such as rural farmers, herders, urban artisans, itinerant merchants, soldiers, clerics, and enslaved and ennobled people. Between the mid-seventeenth and mid-nineteenth centuries, I argue that people's choices in response to regional, political, and environmental conditions impacted commercial networks that coursed not only through western Africa but also far beyond it to shape an emerging global capitalism. But I also present the case for how different people within the region deployed textiles and dress to claim individual or group status in pluralistic societies experiencing revolutionary change. My focus on textiles and dress thus foregrounds and highlights an African historical experience in this period that was shaped by multiple forms of mobility, self-fashioning, and diaspora-making, and it does so over and above largely Eurocentric concerns with historical processes.

Forms of dress were strategic engagements with social life that in turn animated both African state-building projects and European imperial expansion through their respective commercial, political, and military agents. In resisting a tendency to think about the region through the lens of a single European nation and its imperial and colonial imperatives and activities, I focus on the often-polyglot populations living within western Africa's various state projects—from the Bamanan states of the Sahel, the Soninke-led polities of the Senegal River valley, the Wolof-speaking state of Kayor, the Fulbe states of Bundu and Fuuta Jallon, and several coastal city-states south of the Gambia River to Freetown, Sierra Leone—that manifested complex expressions of an African pluralism deployed strategically to advance particular social or economic objectives. This social process can be too easily homogenized, simplified, or simply ignored when viewed through the prism of macrolevel structural approaches. I read sources with a recognition of both the region's human diversity as well as what Boubacar Barry has called its "profound cultural cohesiveness,"[8] forged over centuries of interactions between its peoples.

In this book, I distinguish western Africa as the immense region west of the bend of the Niger River from the even larger geographical region of West Africa, which stretches eastward to Lake Chad in the north and, in the south to the riverine forests of the Niger delta region. Two-thirds the size of the continental United States, this larger West Africa is geographically and environmentally diverse, with many subregions and several economic cores, each of which experienced the historical transformations of the period in regionally specific ways.[9] In thinking about western Africa as a coherent space, I make comparisons and identify patterns across a broad

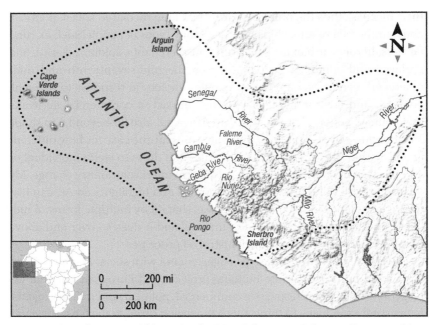

MAP 0.1. Map of western Africa. Map by Matt Johnson at Johnson Cartographic.

though historically integrated region that is distinct from other parts of West Africa or elsewhere on the continent. Western Africa is anchored by the expansive Fuuta Jallon plateau, from whose temperate elevations flow the region's three major rivers: the Senegal, the Gambia, and the Niger. This internal watershed also served as a transportation system, lending the region a geographical coherence that facilitated the extensive interactions of its people over a long historical trajectory.[10] The book covers the last quarter of the seventeenth century through the mid-nineteenth century as western African export economies shifted from Atlantic slave trading to cash crops and raw materials. Over the course of this period, some spatial shifts took place, as areas that had once been economic cores became hinterlands, and hinterlands became loci of economic activity.

But as the title of this book suggests, it contends with the textures of the historical experiences of the people who lived through the region's economic transformations and spatial shifts. I mean to emphasize the overlapping complexity and particularities of this large region through its peoples. This study moves between several disparate though related parts of western Africa.[11] It begins at the margins of the Atlantic coastal experience in the western Sahel near where the contemporary borders of Senegal, Mauritania, and Mali meet, with an account of the Bamanan-speaking polity of

Kaarta in the late seventeenth century. Kaarta's location at the geographical juncture of transatlantic and trans-Saharan commercial networks helps to situate them both, as well as the broader study, into a Sahelian context. Each subsequent chapter advances chronologically but also shifts to a different part of the region, beginning with the Gambia and the ports of Bissau and Cacheu to the south in the late seventeenth and early eighteenth centuries (chapter 2); then Gajaaga in eastern Senegal, near the confluence of the Faleme and Senegal Rivers in the early to mid-eighteenth century (chapter 3); Saint-Louis on Senegal's north Atlantic coast at the mouth of the Senegal River in the late eighteenth and early nineteenth centuries (chapter 4); and finally, the Rio Pongo on the Guinea coast in the early nineteenth century (chapter 5). This organization is meant to draw attention to continuities and contrasts across this broadly integrated region.

Dress regimes in western Africa not only varied across time and space; they were also differentiated by such factors as gender, religion, status, occupation, and age. While some clothing styles became associated with places—such as the clothing of merchant women at Saint-Louis—others were associated with, for instance, religious affiliation or occupation. A man wearing a long, embroidered cotton robe, red wool cap, and white turban would have been readily understood as making a claim to a Muslim identity—whether in Saint-Louis on the coast, Segu on the Niger river, or coastal Guinea on the Rio Nunez—and his dress carried expectations and shaped how others interacted with him. Even so, sartorial expressions among self-identified Muslims themselves could be quite varied. A few hundred miles south of Bakel, on the coast of Guinea, several African Muslim traders were described as partial to English trousers, shirts, and brimmed felt hats with tassels, which they occasionally wore as an expression of their contemporary affiliation to a global cosmopolitan world—an indication of the multiple economies of signification at play in the region.

These sartorial economies of signification are rich archives of the experiences of western Africans, whose lives shaped and were shaped by global flows of goods and people. For example, at a coastal port along the Rio Pongo in the 1850s, a wealthy African widow, discussed in more detail in chapter 5, received a visit from a group of Christian missionaries from Britain and Barbados. Descended from a line of Luso-African traders, Nhara Bely had lived her entire life steeped in a world of transregional commerce and cross-cultural diplomacy with men yet had always cultivated a respect for her own social power. She had grown wealthy from the commerce she had run with her husband, Louis Lightburn, an American slave trader from Charleston, South Carolina, who had died and left her the business. She stood on the veranda of her hillside compound dressed in fine, locally made cotton wrappers, a bright red head wrap, and heavy gold jewelry, presenting an image of fortitude and grit.

The trades in textiles and in human beings are deeply imbricated, as these markets stimulated each other through the exchange of textiles for humans and often through the labor used to grow cotton, spin thread, and weave cloth. Though their imperatives overlapped at times, neither trade was either reducible to or wholly dependent upon the other. The history of textile production, exchange, and consumption in western Africa situates the familiar Atlantic slaving economy within the wider context of other commodity exchanges from the Sahel in the north to the coastal tropical forests, while focusing attention on individuals, specific social groups, and subregional dynamics whenever possible. Western Africans were critical actors during this period of global integration through commerce, pursuing varied strategies of individual and group reinvention through mediation and incorporation of difference—thus contributing to the birth of the modern era. Textiles, I argue, allow us to contemplate change over time in western African societies in a way that gives voice and agency to a variety of western African perspectives in the history of global integration, to consider actors otherwise not seen, and to query the significance of their often-cosmopolitan character, as well as to critically examine their changing values and interests over time.

## WHY DRESS?

Many nineteenth-century ethnologists, missionaries, and colonial officials wrote about and collected African textiles and clothing. In chapter 1, I discuss garments such as the *kusaaba,* as well as an array of accessories and cloth samples that began to enter ethnographic museum collections of Europe and North America in the mid-nineteenth century. Archival inventories cataloged these objects as examples of African "industry" but exhibited them as ethnographic curiosities of timeless culture rather than as examples of "fashion," a term implying novelty and change.[12] This archival and naming process marked an object's transformation from the singular creation of skilled hands—crafted in a specific, dynamic context of culture and economy and meant to articulate a sense of place and particular subject position—into an inert trophy held out of time and space as a generalized representation of Africa. My interest in clothing lies in the possibilities it presents to transcend this dualistic constraint in thinking about the past in western Africa, to gainsay the idea that African modes of dress are merely traditional and thus represent a past undifferentiated across time and space. Instead, I read western Africa's history in this pivotal period through the prism of dress, adornment, and consumption across a variety of sources, engaging with historically contingent local ideas about the body, gender, ethnicity, and social status, and arguing dress to be fashion—a signifier of innovation, change, and claims making in western Africa.

Fernand Braudel defined *fashion* as a phenomenon that first appeared in mid-fourteenth century Europe, where increased wealth allowed the rich to alter and diversify the materials and tailoring of their dress in ostentatious displays to differentiate themselves from people of lesser means. Even among the rich, the habit of changing styles more frequently developed slowly for an increasing variety of reasons, Braudel argued, with the practice becoming widespread only after 1700. Wealth, then, was a precondition for the possibility of participating in what he called fashion. The poor lived entirely outside the world of fashion because, as he put it, they experienced "no wealth, no freedom of movement, no possible change. This was the fate of the poor everywhere. Their costumes, however beautiful or coarse, remained the same."[13] Though not all were poor in Africa and Asia, he also argued that dress in these places was less likely to change over time.[14] For Braudel, fashion was a social dynamic unfolding between European elites and those of the lower classes, who imitated the sartorial choices of the wealthy. He did not contextualize the source of European wealth as derived from Atlantic and Indian Ocean commerce. Nor did his framing allow that these global connections might also be transforming consumption habits and sartorial expression in societies across both regions.

Writing at the turn of the twentieth century, sociologists Georg Simmel and Thorstein Veblen articulated theories of fashion as a social phenomenon specific to Western societies whose elites were then flush with new wealth. Both men were working in rapidly industrializing societies fueled in part by expanding Western imperialism across Africa and Asia. Simmel, a German who studied the urban life of Berlin, argued that fashion functioned as a mode of differentiation between social classes, whereby the middle and lower strata of society imitated the dress of elites who, in turn, continually sought new ways to distinguish themselves sartorially from the masses. Simmel was influenced by the evolutionary theories of Herbert Spencer and Charles Darwin and viewed fashion as a dynamic social force driven by the tastes of elites in Western capitalist societies. This idea was not germane to most African societies, which, in this view, lacked conditions to support fashion except in imitation of colonial elites.[15]

Influenced by Darwin but also by Karl Marx, Veblen wrote *The Theory of the Leisure Class* as a critique of capitalism that analyzed the spending habits of newly wealthy American elites at the turn of the twentieth century, coining the term *conspicuous consumption* to describe elites' need for public displays of material wealth, often through fashion. Veblen argued that the lower classes endlessly sought to increase their consumption to gather esteem in the eyes of elite groups. Considering both the rich and the poor, Veblen theorized further that consumption in pursuit of social status, honor, or esteem in the eyes of others was a constant in human societies across time and space, which made it therefore a dynamic force driving historical change.[16]

Scholarship on dress in Africa entered a new stage with the 1965 publication of *Dress, Adornment, and the Social Order,* a collection edited by Joanne Bubolz Eicher and Mary Ellen Roach (later Roach-Higgins) on the social history of dress across the globe, which included Eicher's ethnographic research on the weaving industry and clothing practices in eastern Nigeria.[17] Eicher went on to extensively study textiles and dress in Nigeria, publishing research bibliographies and coediting volumes on dress. She then published important studies on the textile traditions of the Kalabari Ijo, documenting both their centuries-long engagement with global commerce on the Niger delta and the originality of their cultural productions.

Beyond the sociology of dress, archaeological studies have framed the temporal boundaries of cloth history in West Africa. Studies have analyzed the oldest surviving examples of wool textiles from eighth century Niger, spindle whorls uncovered near the ancient city of Dia on the Middle Niger River valley, and more than five hundred cloth remnants from the eleventh to eighteenth centuries recovered in the Bandiagara Escarpment in the Dogon region of Mali.[18] Archaeologists, museum researchers, art historians, and textile specialists have produced a sizable literature on West African textiles.[19] Historian Colleen Kriger, in a study of hundreds of cotton textiles from the Sokoto Caliphate held in museum collections in Europe and North America, identified a more substantial role for women in the large nineteenth-century cloth industry at Sokoto Caliphate in northern Nigeria than was previously known from witness accounts.[20]

Economic historians of West Africa, such as Antony Hopkins, Philip Curtin, and Joseph Inikori, have used textiles to historicize and analyze the workings of African industries and economies and to debate the impact of the transatlantic slave trade on their workings.[21] Marion Johnson mapped the use of cotton cloth strips as currency and produced a database of all trade goods exported from England to Africa during the eighteenth century, a scholarly contribution that confirmed the importance of textiles to British commerce in Africa at the peak of the transatlantic slave trade.[22] Within the context of French Empire, Richard Roberts highlighted important connections between colonial outposts in Pondicherry, India, where the French purchased indigo-dyed cottons called *guinees,* and Senegal, where guinees circulated as important commodities in a colonial market. Kriger carefully analyzed nineteenth-century garments and textiles from Nigeria as a basis for her comprehensive studies of the history of cloth making in West Africa, as well as of the histories of both cotton cultivation and British Atlantic trade in West Africa. Both Roberts and Judith Byfield carried the analysis of textiles' economic and social primacy into the colonial period, with Byfield using textiles to contrast the resilience of women in the indigo dyeing industry at Abeokuta with their economic marginalization by colonial policymakers. More recent interest in dress and fashion has produced a rich literature, including journals, encyclopedias, and edited collections from new research on most parts of the world, including Africa.[23]

Resonant with this recent work is an interest in the body as a key site of claims making. As Antoinette Burton reminds us, a focus on the body as a historical agent affords a view from inside political economies that offers evidence of power being asserted and challenged within those systems.[24] The bodies of individuals (even when their full biographies or interior lives remain obscure), and how those bodies are adorned, thus tend to index historical processes of gender, race, religion, and other types of identity claims. In the western African context, for instance, Rudolph Ware has focused on embodiment as an epistemological premise of Quranic schools, and he uses this fact as an interpretive lens through which to understand the unique character and historical trajectory of Muslim societies in the region.[25] Ware's approach to embodiment lends even greater salience, and more sharpened focus, to thinking about contrasts and comparisons between multiple communities of African Muslims across the region over generations, such as the Maninka-Mori of Kankan and the Tukulor of Fuuta Tooro or the Susu and Maninka clerics of coastal Guinea, who had direct and extensive contact with foreign traders settling in or near their villages.

I approach representations of dress and clothing within a variety of oral, written, and visual sources as an underexplored and embodied archive of social and economic aspects of both mundane daily life and extraordinary events. Textiles and adornments used to cover, reveal, protect, or decorate the body shaped experiences and conveyed information about cultural, social, gendered, and political priorities. As visual language, archival source, and memory, dress helps to critically explore a dynamic process of social relations between individuals, groups, and communities that unfolded in towns during the period covered in this book. This approach helps to broaden the historical analysis by considering a wide range of actors, such as women and girls of various backgrounds and conditions, peasant farmers, artisans, soldiers, clerics, merchants, military rulers, and enslaved people performing various kinds of labor.

My study of dress in this period of history in western Africa builds on the work of George Brooks, whose research on the commercial role of *signares* in Saint-Louis and on Gorée Island highlighted the significance of women entrepreneurs in coastal towns southward to Sierra Leone.[26] Philip Havik went further in his work on women traders in Guinea-Bissau, arguing not only that gender shaped their roles as cultural and commercial intermediaries but that many went beyond their roles as brokers to become matrons that controlled important economic, social, and political resources.[27] Given that Brooks and Havik have established gender as a critical element shaping commercial exchanges on the Atlantic coast, this book seeks to examine gender as an explicit or implicit concern for people in a variety of contexts and power relationships across the region as well as to heed the use of gendered metaphors to refer to people, places, or objects.[28]

Thinking through these issues has required drawing reasoned inferences and conclusions from close readings of sources, because the lives of women and girls are rarely ever extensively detailed in written documentary sources, whether in European languages or Arabic script. Similarly, in oral traditional sources, women are often mentioned or depicted within a limited number of representational tropes. These silences and gaps within the documentary and oral record have helped to obscure the roles many women laborers played in the regional economy beyond that of the coastal Eurafrican and African women most in contact with European merchants.

## SOURCES AND METHODS

References and depictions of cloth, textiles, and clothing are scattered throughout a broad range of written, material culture, visual culture, and oral traditional evidence, presenting a challenge in both locating those references and making sense of each within their medium and the imperatives of the text in which they are located.

Chapter 1 especially draws on oral history—most notably, the narrative of the bard Djeli Mamary Kouyate—to think about when textiles and clothing appear in the origin story of the Bamanan Kaarta and what meanings are thus conveyed by their inclusion at those moments. Kouyate's account was recorded in the 1970s, when scholars began to record, transcribe, and interpret more systematically a variety of oral traditions across a wide region from Segu on the Niger river to coastal Gambia and savannas from Guinea to northern Ghana. These oral sources generated considerable debate among historians and anthropologists about their utility and reliability as reflective of the past.[29] Many traditional oral accounts can be widely inconsistent on basic facts such as key figures and sequences of critical events, and this has led some scholars to discount their value as sources of historical knowledge. Others have argued that the complete rejection of these sources is unwarranted, which is the position adopted here.[30]

This book employs the three categories of analysis for oral tradition proposed by Michael Gomez in his recent study of the corpus of oral traditions concerning Sunjata Keita of ancient Mali.[31] These analytical categories allow us to distinguish between constitutive elements of the oral tradition and to assess their relative value in light of other sources (or lack thereof). They include, first, those historical claims that may be corroborated by independent sources; second, those that cannot be fully corroborated yet remain plausible in light of other evidence; and, finally, those that are didactic in nature, which is the case with Kouyate's narrative. Oral tradition in the last analytical category asserts the social and cultural context of events in an idealized form, thus providing a baseline for comparison with other evidence. I deploy this approach to examine oral traditional sources with an emphasis on the claims they make about social life both within families and between social groups identified variously through ethnicity, religion, status, or gender.

The core written documents for this study include British, French, and American shipping records, account ledgers, customs payments, commercial correspondence, and travelers' accounts, which provide the basis for discussions of cloth trading between Europeans and Africans as well as for patterns of consumption over time. For example, in chapter 2, I examine an early eighteenth-century memorandum by mercantile company director André Brue, which provided a detailed survey of French commercial activity across hundreds of miles to the inland markets of the Sahel and farther south to the tropical coastal region of Guinea-Bissau. Among other things, the document shows that the purchase and resale of African-made, indigo-dyed cotton cloths was an integral part of a multilateral, nested series of commercial exchanges between a variety of regional African markets—and that this was part of a wider commercial pattern that evolved over time.

In addition to these commercial records, I also draw on textile samples and pattern books of textiles marketed to West Africa, French- and English-language travel accounts by mercantile company agents or other visitors to western Africa, and a selection of more than two dozen visual images depicting individuals and scenes from the region. Eighteenth-century accounts by travelers and the correspondence of mercantile company agents often feature lengthy descriptions of the appearance, demeanor, and dress of people living in Saint-Louis, Gorée, or along trading routes to other markets. These passages were intended to inform readers about commercial possibilities, with details about dress practices and other social and cultural behavior that may have created a demand for textiles supplied by Europe.[32] Travelers' reports convey the perspective, preconceptions, interests, and motive of each writer, and these texts must be critically and carefully interrogated and contextualized. I draw on questions Tamara Walker posed in her discussion of eighteenth-century travelers' descriptions of enslaved Africans in Peru, asking, How did the visitors' expectations and ideas about Africans shape their perceptions about the clothing practices they observed? I examine published and archival sources not merely to reconstruct the facts they contain but to give particular attention to the variety of people, objects, and social contexts they portray. These evidentiary fragments generally do not permit the reconstruction of individuals with any depth and sometimes raise issues that cannot be resolved, yet taken together, they create a space for a multicentric history of the modern era.[33]

Beyond these written and material culture sources, I draw on a selection of more than two dozen visual images of Africans from the Senegambia and Upper Guinea regions. Produced between the eighteenth and nineteenth centuries, some were published in travel narratives and were based on direct observation, though this was more frequently the case later in the period. Others were created for inclusion in encyclopedic costume books, such as the twenty colored engravings of people in Senegal published in Canadian-born French diplomat Jacques Grasset de Saint-Sauveur's 1795 *Encyclopédie des voyages*. These images, like the travel writing, were imbricated in the process of European imperial expansion as part of a larger Enlightenment-era effort to "know" and categorize the (non-Western) world, which, in doing so, othered people and societies in Africa.[34]

In reading these images, I have focused on how they represent what Mary Louise Pratt called the "contact zone"—a geographic and temporal space in which people formerly separated from one another begin to interact, working across divergent worldviews and practices and often within radically asymmetrical relations of power.[35] In her work on clothing and adornment in the seventeenth-century Catholic kingdom of Kongo, Cécile Fromont takes this concept further with her notion of "spaces of correlation" in which she focuses on the cultural agency of people whose clothing choices "bring together ideas who belong to radically different realms, confront them, and eventually turn them into interrelated parts of a new system of meaning."[36]

Capturing this process of reinvention as it occurred in western Africa between the 1600s and early 1800s is one goal of this study. My approach to these images has been to carefully examine their content, then to consider the context in which they were produced and circulated, asking: Who are the central figures in the image? What are they wearing? How are they positioned in relation to others? Which figures appear frequently in these visual images, and which ones appear rarely? What representations of gender and status are evident from the image? How do these images compare to one another, to the written sources they accompanied, and to other evidence from the period?

In integrating material culture, visual culture, oral, and documentary sources, I have found useful the growing body of literature on material culture history that has resulted from interdisciplinary collaborations between historians, art historians, anthropologists, and museum curators. Historians working with material culture have been concerned with expanding the range of sources to include objects, not only as they were deployed for specific uses in particular contexts but also for the meaning people attributed to these objects over time and space. Historians' embrace of material culture sources is relatively new and follows the lead established by archaeologists, anthropologists, and museum studies scholars in analyzing how objects construct social worlds as people use them to express meaning, identification, and relations within their own lived context.[37]

With a focus on both African-made and imported cotton textiles, I approach the large historiography of the transatlantic slave trade in western Africa thinking about a diverse range of Africans making active choices as producers and consumers within specific temporal, spatial, and environmental contexts. By doing so, the analysis offered here extends a concern to move beyond the macrostructural and quantitative approaches prevalent in earlier historiographies of the transatlantic slave trade in Africa.

## HISTORIOGRAPHICAL FOUNDATION

Against the historiographical background of a period conceived and debated almost entirely in terms of the violent processes of Atlantic slaving, state formation, and resource extraction, I argue that the social life of textiles reveals histories of interconnectivity, cultural appropriation and translation, choice, constraint, and mutuality among western Africans and between them and the outside world. This book speaks to and reassesses some of these processes—by, for instance, underlining the importance of Indian textiles to European commercial aspirations in Africa during the eighteenth century and the development of industrial textile manufacturing in Britain within a competitive global cotton market. But it primarily seeks to extend the work of Africanist historians who have begun a wider reassessment of "precolonial" periods, by focusing where possible on individuals' experiences in a way that situates Africans as active social actors animating, responding to, and shaping global history. It works at a period that can meaningfully contribute to African, Atlantic, and African diaspora historiographies with fresh insights into the vibrant and complex social worlds of Africa before the advent of more formal forms of colonialism in the mid-nineteenth century.

Textiles have appeared in economic and social histories of Africa and the Atlantic for more than a century, but how textiles speak to African experiences and historical agency are often ignored or accorded attention only as they relate to economics, leaving unexplored what they can tell us about broader social and cultural dimensions. Textiles constituted a major eighteenth-century trade that linked African producers and consumers to exchange networks that were effectively global in scale. Commercial linkages between Europe, Asia, Africa, and the Americas across the eighteenth century established the "intimacies of four continents" and created the conditions for the birth of Western liberalism, which became a dominant ideology of modernity. In tracing liberalism's genealogy to this period, interdisciplinary scholar Lisa Lowe has shown how its abstract promises of universal rights, rational progress, wage labor, and freedom have often been discussed in ways that silence or disavow the global conditions that made it possible: namely, imperialism, settler colonialism, and plantation slavery.[38]

The seemingly disparate fields of African social and economic history, Atlantic history, and dress history are all still grappling, in different ways, with the legacy of late nineteenth- and early twentieth-century European colonial histories of Africa, which accepted only "monumental construction, literacy, and militarized political expansiveness"[39] as evidence of human achievement, or history, and thus preparedness for the promises of Western liberalism. Thus, for Africanists, the Sahelian empires of Ghana (300–ca. 1500 CE), Mali (1230–ca. 1600 CE), and Songhay (1464–1591 CE) loom large in the historical imagination of western Africa, chiefly as an artifact of colonial knowledge production. Findings made in the Sahel in the context of colonial conquest at the turn of the twentieth century—transcribed oral traditions, local chronicles in Arabic script, archaeological discoveries—provided empirical evidence that was mapped onto the positivist expectations of history that, for some, first served to validate notions of African history writ large.[40] Colonial administrators such as Maurice Delafosse, Charles Monteil, and Louis Tauxier produced voluminous studies and published primary sources that have influenced generations of scholars, but they did so as agents of a colonial state that embraced an ideology of progress they believed would ultimately be beneficial to Africans and to the wider world. Their work as historians was informed by nineteenth-century concepts about differential social evolution, some of which Raffenel articulated in his travel account with references to the physiognomy of the "African races" he encountered. The effect of colonial histories of Africa was to freeze African history at the point of the demise of these empires—which thus posited the categories of race, color, and culture in Africa as static and unchanging[41]—to reduce Africans to a Hobbesian state of nature that only the influence of European empires could cure, and to inhibit the study of African history between the seventeenth and nineteenth centuries.

The knowledge that colonizing historians produced about a historical "golden age" of Sahelian empires circulated in the metropolitan capitals of Paris and London as well as in New York and colonial capitals of the Caribbean and West Africa, where, against the backdrop of two world wars, African and African-descendant intellectuals, artists, and politicians began to articulate various responses to colonialism and the forms of repression affecting these populations. In the US, African-descendant intellectuals such as W. E. B. Du Bois and William Leo Hansberry promulgated knowledge about the empires of West Africa in their writing and teaching at historically black colleges to counter scholarly claims that Africa lacked history of any lasting significance.[42] In this context, Trinidadian-born and Oxford University–educated Eric Williams made a key intervention in the study of capitalism and British Empire. Williams published his classic study, *Capitalism and Slavery*, in 1944 while a professor at Howard University in Washington, DC. The book gave enslaved workers on Caribbean sugar plantations a central role in the emergence of Britain's Industrial Revolution, arguing that British planters reinvested profits from Caribbean slavery to expand the use of low-paid wage laborers in British factories.[43] Williams's thesis has provoked debates among economic historians of the transatlantic slave trade and of Africa ever since. Though transnational in perspective, Williams's research did not focus extensively on African societies or the experiences of Africans, instead linking forced African labor to larger processes. Some have argued his thesis even seemed to accept a now maligned gewgaw myth that imagined African consumers as passive dupes who were blithely seduced by "cheap," meaningless trinkets into selling precious human beings to their European trading partners.[44]

After decolonization across Africa and the Caribbean in the mid-twentieth century, the Cold War and the US civil rights movement provided the key context shaping questions, debates, and directions in African history. At the start of the Cold War, American universities, flush with funding from government and private foundations, embraced an area studies model for Africa that sought to position US scholars of Africa as uniquely objective because the country had "psychological distance" and "no territorial commitments in Africa," as claimed by the anthropologist Melville Herskovits, founder of the African Studies program at Northwestern University in 1948.[45] This shift of resources toward predominately white institutions marginalized the work of earlier generations of African-descendant scholars who viewed US racism and European imperialism in Africa as related phenomena and had placed the decolonization of knowledge about Africa at the center of their research concerns (rather than centering the more limited, though critically important, goal of decolonizing government and politics).[46] I situate my research and analysis of forms of African agency and self-fashioning in this black intellectual tradition of decolonial approaches to African history.

In the 1950s, as colonial governments established the first universities in places like Accra in the Gold Coast, Ibadan in Nigeria, and Dakar, Senegal, the African doctoral students who would be an influential generation of professors during the early years of postcolonial independence were already graduating from universities in Europe. The historian Abdoulaye Ly, having served in the French army during World War II, became the first Senegalese person to receive a doctorate from a French university in 1955, which he published three years later as *La Compagnie du Sénégal*. Like Williams, Ly produced a transnational economic history, but focused on Senegal, charting linkages between continents created by the slave trade and a nascent capitalism. Ly became a principal figure of the "Dakar School" historians, educating generations of students along with his colleague Cheikh Anta Diop, as part of a wider nationalist, anticolonial project to promote the "writing of African history by Africans."[47] In a parallel move, the Nigerian Kenneth Onwuka Dike, trained at the University of London, significantly advanced the study of anglophone African economic history by emphasizing questions of African agency and incorporating the use of oral sources. Inescapably, Dike discusses cotton textiles as a primary commodity exchanged for palm oil in early nineteenth-century Niger delta—along with iron bars, guns, brass manillas, and copper rods. But this pioneering study of economic history, *Trade and Politics in the Niger Delta, 1830–1885*, does not explore consumption and dress much further. Returning to teach in Nigeria, he introduced historical study of Africa into a colonial educational system that had previously emphasized European history and launched what became the influential Ibadan School of historians conducting research in West Africa.

Transnational economic perspective also informed the work of Walter Rodney, who trained a decade later than Dike and was also at the University of London on scholarship from his native Georgetown, Guyana. His *History of the Upper Guinea Coast, 1545–1800* argues that the Atlantic slave trade effectively expanded reliance on slavery among the largely stateless peoples in the region south of the Gambia River to Sierra Leone—a position vigorously contested by the British historian John Fage, American Philip Curtin, and others.[48] Their debates about the impact of the transatlantic slave trade on Africa fueled many publications and shifted scholarly research toward slavery in Africa itself through the 1970s and 1980s.

This was especially true in France, where Emmanuel Terray, Jean Bazin, Roger Botte, Claude Meillassoux, and Jean-Loup Amselle were among those who produced major studies influenced by Marxist theory on the structure, function, and reproduction of slavery and identity in Africa. Rodney's later historical work adopted the world systems theoretical framework to explain underdevelopment in contemporary Africa.[49] In Britain, leading economic historian Antony Hopkins and a field of other historians that included David Richardson and Marion Johnson were among those who argued that economic institutions in Africa were stronger and more adaptive than previously imagined. And, finally, the influential Nigerian historian Joseph Inikori took up some of the themes established by Eric Williams about the importance of the enslaved African laborers to the development of capitalism but also detailed the role of West Africa as an outlet for British-manufactured goods, particularly textiles.[50]

As these historical debates on the transatlantic slave trade and its potential relevance to contemporary Africa unfolded, a chasm gradually emerged between Africanist and Atlanticist approaches to the period. Confronted with the economic and political failures of many postindependence African states in the 1970s, Africanists increasingly found that questions of early kingdoms seemed less relevant to problems thought to be rooted in the more recent colonial past. Research in the field shifted decisively toward the colonial era while postcolonial African governments cut funding for higher education and research on the continent.[51] At the same time, the politics of the Cold War reoriented studies of black people of the Atlantic diaspora toward what Jemima Pierre has called a "domestic turn" that privileged national-level questions of "race relations" and a cultural nationalism interested in contrasting notions of African "origins" with modern forms of black identity.[52] Despite their overlapping genealogies and mutual influence, scholars researching in these fields increasingly drifted apart, with major debates and findings in one domain scarcely having impact on the other.

One outcome of a historiographical legacy that foregrounds national and transnational economic processes during the colonial and postcolonial periods at the expense of regional historical connections from the precolonial period has been the tendency to obscure individuals, the variety of ways people expressed themselves, and what this might reveal about their perspectives on the world. Their choices were consequential in shaping a global economy increasingly integrated by European and American capital. Kobayashi and others have made recent attempts to flip dominant frameworks of the period centered on European imperial expansion to ground analysis instead on the agentive role of Africans as producers and consumers whose choices were coeval with, and constitutive of, an emerging "modern" world.[53] I support such efforts to recenter African historical experience, but I also want to be clear that my use of the term *agency* does not seek to advance an explanatory economic theory that presupposes "rational choice," "self-interest," or "individuals." Rather, my interest is to bring focus to the contingent choices people made that sometimes leave traces in a fragmented archive and that add specificity, nuance, and complexity to our understanding of African societies of the past.

Such details open windows into social dynamics and changing tastes across western Africa. The literary scholar Simon Gikandi has pointed to the repressed linkages between the realities of plantation slavery in the Americas and the "culture of taste" that was performed and debated in Parisian philosopher salons and London's coffeehouses of the eighteenth century. Expressions of cosmopolitan thought, good taste, refinement, and sophistication in European metropolitan spaces were valued for their contrast with the vulgar milieu of slaving ports[54] around the Atlantic—despite their intimate connections to these ports.

However, as I examine in chapter 4, Saint-Louis was a vital cosmopolitan space of cultural interaction, where political and social relations were fashioned by patterns of consumption of a wide variety of textiles, apparel, and accessories. Written, visual culture, and material culture evidence from the period for ports from coastal Senegal to Sierra Leone, as well as oral sources from the Sahel, speak to the complex reality of the ways these ports were connected to the elite metropolitan spaces of bourgeois sociality, though these linkages often get elided. In African coastal trading towns, European merchants came to rely on the hospitality of their African partners, who often were fluent in multiple European and African languages and whose homes and sartorial choices often announced their participation in the global circulation of goods and ideas of their time. In western Africa, Eurafrican women known as signares represent perhaps the most well-known example of the coastal traders. Their culturally hybrid practices and material culture facilitated their roles as commercial intermediaries with Europeans.

An example of a study of such a hybrid culture can be found in *The Rise of the Trans-Atlantic Slave Trade in Western Africa, 1300–1589*, in which Toby

Green argues that the early emergence of the Kriolu language and a "creole" society in western Africa made the region an important site for the birth of the "economic and ideological currents associated with modernity."[55] In addition to language, the process of creolization in western Africa was marked by the development of mixed cultural practices connected to very early forms of economic globalization. Rather than being imposed from the outside, the two-way process of creolization and cultural change followed long-established patterns of accommodation and alliance building in western Africa stemming from migration and long-distance trade across ecological zones. He distinguished this historical process internal to Africa from the parallel development of the less flexible "classificatory typologies" of race that developed in European colonies in the Americas, which relied on enslaved African labor and the racism that legitimated the violence and expropriation of land and labor.[56]

Africans lived, experienced, and understood race in ways not defined by a Euro-American point of view. Historians of Islam in the Sahel have debated another discourse of race that was internal to the region and well articulated before the Portuguese first arrived by sea in the fifteenth century. This includes the racialization of space implied by the Arabic term *Bilad-al-Sudan*, "Land of the Blacks," a geographic region whose people and places Arab travelers and Saharan merchants wrote about in particular ways. These documents have allowed historians to trace over time an evolving discourse of blackness and anti-blackness among certain constituencies within the region and across the wider Muslim ecumene, wherein people defined as black became increasingly associated with "slavery, barbarity, ignorance and licentiousness."[57] Bruce Hall argues that "blackness," as defined in particular historical contexts in the Sahel, made people subject to enslavement or other legal liabilities from the perspective of some Muslims.[58] Rather than static and transhistorical, the claims different people made about race and "blackness" in the Sahel changed over time according to context. Countering this view, Mohammed Bashir Salau, in his work on plantation slavery in the Sokoto Caliphate during the nineteenth century, emphasized that social and cultural categories were more important than phenotype or biology in determining who was enslaveable there.[59]

Western Africa during the seventeenth and eighteenth centuries is unique in the Atlantic Africa region, where an internal Islamic discourse of race and blackness in the Sahel first converged with the discourse being generated within the context of Atlantic European Christianity. Following James Webb, a gradually expanding Sahara Desert during these centuries led to a gradual drift of pastoralist populations self-identified as *Bidan* (white) southward into better-watered land occupied by agriculturalists, defined by the former as *Sudan* (black).[60] The ensuing competition for land resources not only led to conflicts along the Senegal River valley and across the Sahel to the Niger River but also produced a written discourse about the meanings of race, blackness, and slavery. Ghislaine Lydon, historian of Saharan commerce, notes that the terms *Trab al-Bidan* (Land of the Whites) and *Bidan* are "problematic" self-designations for groups who are united by their use of the Arabic-based Hassaniya language. The terms refer more to a set of cultural practices than to skin color or physical features.[61]

Building on Salau and Lydon, and alert to the experiences and agency of Africans, I define race in this study as a set of socially and culturally constructed ideas and claims people make about themselves and others that change over time and across space and, as arguments about a preferred social order, are connected to forms of social power. These ideas and claims establish hierarchical categories and distinctions among people, which, although abstract and theoretical, have had real-world consequences as various people have drawn upon them to achieve particular outcomes, a process especially important to the history of slavery in the region.[62] This is not to overemphasize the salience of race as the most important defining factor for individuals whose experiences have been equally or even more determined by factors such as status, gender, language, lineage, religion, or occupational group. But it is to argue that there were multiple, sometimes conflicting, discourses of race and blackness unfolding in western Africa during the seventeenth and eighteenth centuries and that parsing those discourses is essential to writing about trade in cotton, textiles, and humans as well as to attending to the meanings of various claims making articulated through the politics of dress. The oral traditional account of Bamanan-speaking Kaarta, which I discuss in detail in chapter 1, contains a discourse about categorical social difference that presents an alternative view of race and blackness from that often presented in local histories written by Muslim scholars. In coastal trading ports and at interior markets where goods purchased from Atlantic markets circulated, the older Sahelian notions of race and social difference came into conversation with a set of different sensibilities and priorities being negotiated on the Atlantic coasts.

The Euro-American Atlantic discourse about race and blackness can be traced through correspondence, company memoranda, business records, published travelers' accounts, and other European-language documents of western Africa regarding the transatlantic slave trade. These documents were part of a process of knowledge production about Africa and Africans that unfolded as Euro-American commercial activity there transitioned from the mercantilist slave trading of the eighteenth century to the "free trade" imperialism of the nineteenth century. This discursive process of race making evolved dialogically with the dynamics of global commerce to shape the development of what Cedric Robinson called racial capitalism.[63] In drawing on this notion, this book attends to the multiple discourses of race and blackness at play in western Africa by considering how and when they appear in oral, written, and visual sources.

European travelers, merchants, naturalists, philosophers, and plantation owners outside continental Africa circulated ideas about its people and places and described them as others, racialized and timelessly yoked to tribe, custom, and the natural environment.[64] This discursive Africa was specifically unmodern, needing regeneration, and imagined as the object of abolitionist and later colonial intervention.[65] Against this backdrop, I have been drawn to the notion of the cosmopolitan as a way to explain evidence for how people in different parts of western Africa began to habitually engage diverse materials associated with global trade.[66] The combination of these elements articulated changing notions of spirituality, gender, and social status in the region between Saint-Louis and Freetown, whereby older notions of difference rooted in the Sahel came into conversation with newer notions generated by different dynamics circulating the perimeters of the Atlantic and Indian Oceans.

When we consider commodities such as textiles, consumption, and place rather than slavery in our approach to eighteenth-century western Africa, we arrive at a very different position than one of abstract arguments about "freedom," "civilization," and "progress," which were the concern of Europeans of the time and of too much scholarship since. We begin to account for a wider range of African historical actors, circumstances, and contingent choices beyond those associated with the predominant historiographical themes of the transatlantic slave trade, such as warfare, violence, and enslavement, and to integrate the social history of the region from a variety of perspectives into a larger narrative of global history. My approach foregrounds the capacity for reinvention and adaptation as a metric of this region's historical experience—in the face of an expanding inequality of global exchange.

By the early eighteenth century, European commercial exchanges in ports from Saint-Louis and Gorée to the Rio Pongo, Freetown, and beyond came to depend critically on textiles, mostly of cotton and silk and purchased in India, often with gold and silver bullion mined by enslaved Africans and Indigenous people of the Americas. In the West African Sahel, cotton cloths from India, just like cowrie shells from the Maldives, had for centuries reached markets overland by caravans of merchants traveling from Egypt who enjoyed direct access to Indian Ocean networks. When the Portuguese expanded commercial operations into the Indian Ocean in the fifteenth century, they learned the value of Indian cottons and cowrie shells in ports across the length of West and West Central Africa and began to import them heavily. Cowries were a major form of currency across West Africa, one of several that included cotton cloth, gold, salt, iron bars, copper rods, brass manilas, and livestock.

But more than mere currency, cowries, like cloth, became incorporated into a variety of daily uses as household objects, bodily adornment, and ritual costumes and practices across the region. Raffenel describes how cowries and other imported metals were incorporated into the clothing of young people undergoing ritualized circumcision. In public celebrations of this rite of passage he observed in a village in Kaarta, boys' clothing was complemented by a cowrie shell tied to their forehead, while girls were adorned far more elaborately, head to toe, with exaggerated amounts of jewelry all over their bodies. "Their arms, their ankles were so garnished with heavy rings that they seemed to have difficulty walking," he wrote.[67] For the two months of training, during which they were mostly in seclusion, the young women would be seen only by others dressed this way, in jewelry loaned to them for the occasion by "rich women" of the village. This fact reminds us, as Green has recently noted, that commodity currencies should not be narrowly thought of as instruments of capital accumulation but that their accumulation could serve symbolic and spiritual purposes as well.[68]

## OUTLINE OF CHAPTERS

The book opens not on the Atlantic coast but in the Sahelian interior, where the breakup of the Mali Empire and desertification of the northern Sahel were driving a period of migration across the Sahel and from the Sahel to coastal areas in the seventeenth century. In contrast to local Arabic sources, which depicted the Bamanan people of the Sahel as hostile nonbelievers, and European sources, which only note caravan routes in and out of Bamanan territories, Djeli Kouyate's 1975 oral history recounting the origins of the Bamanan states of Segu and Kaarta, a major regional polity controlling the movement of caravans from the Sahel to trading ports on the Senegal and Gambia Rivers, evokes a Bamanan worldview rooted in agriculture and the natural world. Cotton production and textile weaving emerge at key moments of Kouyate's oral tradition—where questions of belonging, social status, social relations in a pluralistic society, and state power are foregrounded. I also analyze that a kusaaba made in the region and preserved in a Paris museum collection tells us about not only the imperatives of French imperialism but also Sahelian meaning making and memory. Chapter 1 thus establishes three themes central to the book's argument: the role of textiles, particularly cotton cloth, as vectors of social and economic change over time; pluralism and the representations of social status, gender, and religious claims that emerge in pluralist western African societies; and the use of cloth and dress as expressions of social power and as a means for thinking about historical change.

With chapter 1 establishing connections of Sahelian states like Kaarta to global markets through Atlantic trading ports on the Gambia River and at Saint-Louis, chapter 2 takes a broader view of western Africa, demonstrating the ways in which several parts of it, from the Sahel to the Gambia River south to Portuguese-speaking Bissau, had become enmeshed in a global textile trade linking four continents. In addition to demonstrating the ubiquity of the cloth industry across the region, this chapter explores how the meeting of African and Euro-Atlantic economies of cloth trading produced a Euro-Atlantic discourse of race and blackness through the notion of *pieza de India,* a unit tied to enslavement and the monetization of enslaved bodies. Through the textile trade, we also see how Africans responded to attempts of European mercantile companies to impose monopolies by instead insisting on a right to what amounted to "free trade."

Chapter 3 focuses on indigo cottons in integrating regional exchanges. This industry depended on the labor of women dyers who are rarely considered as important economic actors in the historiography for this period, which, when highlighting women, tends to focus almost exclusively on merchant signares and coastal trade. It will discuss the implications of this gendered division of labor and regional dynamic in western Africa in direct competition from Indian-made indigo cottons imported by Europeans, plus new forms of consumption.

Chapter 4 explores the emergence of a reformist Islamic state at Fuuta Tooro along the Senegal River and its impact on the Atlantic trading community at Saint-Louis. It demonstrates the cosmopolitan nature of both coastal and interior market centers born of economic and political tensions between the interior Sahel and Atlantic coast. Looking beyond the role of Euro-African elites, the chapter demonstrates that *laptots,* or West African sailors, were important creolizing figures in the late eighteenth century, benefiting from their mobility within the region but also within the Atlantic and Indian Ocean perimeters.

The book shifts focus in chapters 5 and 6 to the Upper Guinea coast and its connections to the interior regions of Fuuta Jallon, the savanna, and Wasulu—where worldly figures such as Fendan Dumbuya, a powerful Susu

Muslim merchant, ran an extensive commercial business with caravans from the interior, settlers at Freetown, and itinerant traders from Britain, the United States, and colonial Cuba. These chapters show that the struggle to ban slave trading in the region produced new social relations in communities across this region where the textiles trade and evidence of clothing styles in archival and visual sources offer revealing insight. Chapter 6 examines a shift in the coastal political economy toward groundnut (peanut) exports, which was experienced across the entire region between 1820 and 1850. Accompanied by the expansion of West Indian missionaries' illegal slave trade, this period of relative prosperity reflected a social crisis—engendered by the conflict of competing agendas of colonial governments, missionary reformers, and local elites.

The book ends with the shift toward direct European colonial intervention in western Africa from the 1820s, which was accompanied by "scientific" explorations of the region. French naval officer Raffenel was to begin an official government mission to travel overland across the breadth of the African continent to the Horn of Africa on the Indian Ocean. The grandiose scheme—funded by the French navy, Academy of Sciences, Museum of Natural History, and Geographical Society—was intended to produce ethnographic, geographic, and commercial information to support imperial expansion into the region. This information-gathering mission took place in the context of the expansion of colonial territory on the eve of the jihad led by al-Hadj Umar Tal that was to resist increased French influence in the region.[69]

Leopold Panet, Raffenel's secretary, joined the expedition along with more than a dozen African service members. Panet was a Eurafrican[70] native of Gorée Island and cousin to a cofounder of the Maurel and Prom Company, a major Bordeaux-based trading concern on the Senegal River.[71] He was a member of a slaveholding class of African-born people of color on Gorée who the French were anxious to appease as calls increased for the abolition of slavery throughout the French Empire.[72] Perhaps to solidify his status and claim to compensation, Panet had conditioned his joining the expedition on being given an official government title. Among the others on the caravan were a native of Saint-Louis who was fluent in several languages and was paid 1,500 francs to serve as a *maître de langue* (interpreter), a traveling merchant, and a sandal maker known as Papa Segu, who regaled everyone with stories about the Bamanan town on the Niger River, hundreds of miles east.[73]

At Bakel, Raffenel procured a packhorse and fifteen donkeys to carry an assortment of goods intended as customary gifts and saleable items for purchasing subsistence along the way. The goods would have been known to have great material and symbolic value in the western African communities with which the French were familiar. There were some weapons—muskets, pistols, and long metal swords—but most of the goods were meant to adorn the body and delight the senses: silks, muslins, and guinees; eyeglasses, music boxes, and kaleidoscopes; mirrors and bells, along with beads of coral, amber, and glass; and brightly hued cashmere robes and neck scarves printed with colorful scenes of recent French imperial interventions in Algeria (1837) and Vietnam (1843).

Raffenel's mission to cross the Sahel from end to end fell far short of its outsize ambition. Several early misadventures seemed to foretell of trouble. Perhaps the most definitive was an encounter in the Kaarta village of Sanghe with a prince of the Kulubali clan, the Bamanan-speaking rulers of Kaarta. One morning, the prince arrived on horseback at Sanghe, summoned Raffenel to meet him and, without dismounting his horse, began speaking to Raffenel, first by recounting his lineage and personal achievements. He then announced he was soon to leave again on a military campaign and demanded Raffenel pay him ten lengths of guinee cloth, as he required fresh clothing for this mission.[74] Raffenel paid this tax, but it hardly satisfied the prince, who then made his meaning more clear. "You are here to cross Kaarta but your route is [now] finished. I know more about this than you do."[75] The prince rode away laughing, but it was not to be Raffenel's last encounter with the military force of Kaarta. A few days later, his caravan having traveled a bit farther, two Kaarta cavalrymen arrived to arrest Raffenel, obliging him to follow them to a fortified village where he was held for eight months before being released to return to Saint-Louis.

That the prince was able to extract this valuable tribute in the form of indigo cottons sourced from India demonstrates the material and symbolic value of cloth in exchanges that established status and power. It was but a Pyrrhic victory, however, that did not unsettle a pattern of consumption that had long since become an important commercial component of French colonial expansion in the region. This incoming colonial cloth economy sat uncomfortably with an older regional history of textiles and dress that continued to evolve within the colonial context of the nineteenth century and beyond to the present day. The dynamics of that longer history of textile making and dress appears across a range of oral, written, and material sources related to the Bamanan state of Kaarta that emerged in the western Sahel in the late seventeenth century.

# 1 ~ Twelve Measures of New Cloth and a Magnificent Bubu

*Bamanan Kaarta between Sahel and Sea*

> When the women saw the cloth [Sonsan] had made,
> The Maraka men never wove again for the Maraka women.
> Whenever a Maraka would ask a woman if it was time to do her weaving,
> The woman would reply,
> "If the Bamanan will do the weaving it is time to weave,
> But if somebody else is to weave my wool, I will wait.
> I will not give my wool to anyone but the Bamanan."
>
> —Excerpt from the epic "Sonsan of Kaarta," as related by Djeli Mamary Kouyate

> If you get me a magnificent bubu, a bubu fit for a great chief, I will impregnate it with such magic power that when Foulakoro puts it on, the town of Sonsanna will be yours!
>
> —Claim reportedly made by a marabout to Sonsan's rival, the ruler of Segu, as recorded in *Légendes historiques du pays de Nioro*

DJELI MAMARY KOUYATE was in the middle of telling the story of a seventeenth-century Bamanan farmer named Sonsan Kulubali who was living in a town of Muslim traders when the bard digressed. Kouyate, before continuing with his oral tradition, needed to share a series of philosophical observations that he ventriloquized through two small birds. He told how the birds fluttered irritatingly over the ears of a horse ridden by Soro Silamakan Koita, a wealthy and powerful warrior chief who lived near the

Sahelian border town of Nioro in the fifteenth century.[1] Nioro would later become a capital of Bamanan Kaarta, a powerful state that Sonsan helped to establish. As if prefiguring these major events, these birds animatedly discussed the grand reputation of a predecessor, Silamakan Koita:

> One said, "The great Soro Silamakan,
> He will become somebody in the world. The world is not a drum that lets a person dance twice to its beat.
> You must dance it right the first time,
> Whether your style is good or bad."
> "No! [the other replied.]
> Do not put all of your body into the world at once.
> The world is like a long warp thread in a loom
> with not enough people as woof threads to make a whole cloth."

Using the debate between the two small birds, a story within the larger story, Kouyate was also talking about the historical roots of Kaarta. Kouyate evoked the contingent, transient nature of life and suggested how, against this backdrop, people may perform great acts of courage against a world of indeterminacy, incompleteness, and limitation. This digression conveyed an additional layer of meaning to the oral tradition he recounted, which had been grounded in an understanding of Sahelian experience over a long period of time.

Blind from birth, the bard accompanied himself on a ngoni lute, tapping a beat on it as he plucked the strings to create sound clouds carrying the words that flowed out through him. Kouyate sat on a mat inside the rectangular compound of a household in Kolokani, Mali, located a few hours northeast of Bamako, in the Beledugu region, part of historical Kaarta. In the background of Kouyate's narration, women's voices occasionally can be heard over the pounding of mortar and pestle. A young male voice punctuates Kouyate's lyrical phrases, verbally affirming the veracity of the bard's most important claims with a sonorous *"Naam"* (Yes!). Musical interludes and narrative digressions peppered Kouyate's oral tradition, making time elastic and porous rather than linear and rigid. These shifts slipped listeners across temporal boundaries, between centuries and through anecdotes that establish context, continuity, and the gravitas of lineage and time. The djeli's evocation of Silamakan Koita as a powerful leader does this work, preparing the listener to hear the story of the life of Sonsan Kulubali, the Bamanan nobleman and farmer who would be remembered long after his death as an important forebear of the Bamanan state of Kaarta.

Kouyate's Kaarta origin story exists among a cacophony of fragmentary accounts that speak to the origins of Kaarta, including traditional oral

*Twelve Measures of New Cloth and a Magnificent Bubu*

sources, local chronicles in African *ajami* script or Arabic, and European commercial and travel accounts. These sources—along with visual images, sculptures, material objects, textiles, and clothing—convey layered, overlapping, and sometimes contradictory meanings attached to Kaarta and the Bamanan people. Their kaleidoscopic, discordant archival fragments resist the pretense of a singular totalizing narrative about the past. But read as a palimpsest, and with my attentiveness to where they diverge, converge, and overlap, as well as to the silences and gaps within and between them, these sources lead me to ponder what meanings they communicate.

The weaving metaphor employed by the second bird in Kouyate's digression is more than a mere figurative flourish. In jumping back two centuries to foreshadow the rise of Sonsan through the figure of Silamakan Koita, Kouyate and the oral tradition he was reciting were weaving the two together in the fabric of the story and, in the process, evoking the significance of textiles, of cloth, of cotton, and of a Bamanan worldview rooted in agriculture and the harnessing of the materials of the natural world, which I refer to here as *Bamanaya*. As a perspective, Bamanaya is partially defined in contradistinction to the view of Maraka and Fulbe Muslims, whose documents form the bulk of the locally produced written archive. Malian historian Moussa Sow defined *Bamanaya* as "a set of ritual practices and representations proper to non-Muslims; involving the use of herbs (*basiw*) and recourse to sacrifices on 'power objects' (*boliw*)."[2] I am using Bamanaya in this chapter to refer to a set of social values that includes notions of propriety and honor derived from a Bamanan worldview rooted in agriculture and a belief in the ability to manipulate the natural world through ritual practices. Celebratory assertions of Bamanaya appear within the oral tradition as fragments of evidence amid other discourses of power. Fleeting as these assertions may sometimes be, their existence suggests a counternarrative to more hegemonic written narratives that often discuss Bamanan people or Bamanaya, as a set of beliefs and practices, in negative terms.

Absent or disfigured in European sources and local chronicles, the significant place of cotton and indigo textiles in this agricultural worldview and the way that textiles conveyed status and power come to the fore in both oral sources like Kouyate's and in material artifacts from the western Sahel dating to the eighteenth century and before.

For instance, terra-cotta sculptures of men on horses testify to how cavalry had long been a primary feature of military and state power in the Middle Niger valley during the period of the Mali Empire (ca. 1230–1600). Delicately detailed figures of fired clay depict armed equestrians seated

FIGURE 1.1. Equestrian figure, Mali, Inland Niger delta, terra-cotta, twelfth to fourteenth century. Image courtesy of the James J. and Laura Ross Collection, New York.

FIGURE 1.2. Equestrian figure, Mali, Inland Niger delta, terra-cotta, twelfth to sixteenth century. Image courtesy of the Nelson-Atkins Museum of Art, Kansas City, MO.

high on horseback, whose straight-backed posture, dress, and armor conveyed power and authority (see, for example, figures 1.1 and 1.2). Dated between the twelfth and sixteenth centuries, the sculptures show riders wearing embroidered cloth breeches and vests, embellished cloths that hung from their waist to their knees, and head coverings anchored by straps over their protruding chins. They also carried such accessories as armbands with hunting knives and quivers to hold arrows. Male figures wore large bead necklaces, large earrings (possibly of amber, copper, or a precious metal), and bracelets around the arms and legs. The horses are generously adorned, too, with a necklace of bells, harnesses decorated with cowrie shells, and geometric motifs perhaps tattooed onto the animals' hips. Unearthed from lands between Jenne and Mopti in contemporary Mali, these figures suggest a wider sartorial landscape that was elaborate, differentiated, and aesthetically rich. It was a landscape that included the many Bamanan communities that had been subject populations within

*Twelve Measures of New Cloth and a Magnificent Bubu* ~ 29

imperial Mali but who later organized themselves into the two independent kingdoms of Segu and Kaarta under charismatic leadership during the seventeenth and eighteenth centuries.

References to dress and appearance constitute a rare but revealing sartorial archive, suggesting alternative seventeenth- and eighteenth-century western African histories of pluralism, authoritarian state power, and resistance to oppression. This archive raises several questions: At which moments do representations of cloth and dress appear in historical sources for early Kaarta, and what meanings are they used to convey? In what ways do they speak beyond words? What do forms of dress suggest about the self-fashioning of individuals and groups? What do these modes of negotiation, accommodation, and exchange reveal about the nature of power and change in the Sahel of this period? What do we make of a fragmented, often discordant archive, with its silences, elisions, conflicting perspectives, and layered meanings? This research on Kaarta draws attention to the role of the western Sahel in the early expansion of the Atlantic slave trade, which, with few exceptions, has been overlooked in histories that focus on the coast. I argue that textile production, exchange, and consumption already established in the western Sahel region helped to fuel networks connecting western Africa to parts of Europe, Asia, and the Americas. The moments and places in which textiles appear most prominently in sources for early Kaarta suggest that they were vital to the pursuit of social status, prestige, and symbolic power and thus mark important sites of contestation—both within and between communities. Textiles therefore mark a critical index of historical change and offer a window into the social and cultural histories of this part of the Sahel.

In the late seventeenth and early eighteenth centuries in the western Sahel between the Niger and Senegal Rivers, Bamanan-speaking communities occupied some of the best land for cotton agriculture, which they shared with Maraka clerics and traders as well as Fulbe pastoralists. The weaving and dyeing of cotton cloth was an extension of an agricultural economy attached to a centuries-long history of trade across ecological zones and ethnolinguistic boundaries. Within the Sahel itself, cloth manufacture intimately shaped the social and political landscape as producers conveyed local aesthetics in material forms that came to define status and power. Their work continued to mediate important social relationships, such as those between landlord and stranger; between noble, artisan, and caste groups; between Muslims and non-Muslims.

Paying attention to the making and selling of textiles allows us to contemplate the actions of various anonymous and skilled makers (spinners, weavers, dyers, embroiders, tailors) whose presence and voices are rarely otherwise recorded in historical sources but whose labor animated the social and economic life of their times. Their skill and their textiles were thus an important facet of Bamanan self-fashioning via Bamanaya. For the Bamanan of Kaarta, the exchange and wearing of these textiles was intimately connected to expressions of power and belonging among individuals, families, and communities in a pluralistic environment where dynamics were shifting under pressure. In the case of Bamanan-speaking peoples, we see that textiles were symbolically important to those seeking to dominate as well as to those resisting domination. Thus, material objects and oral sources that foreground textiles offer insights that go beyond those recorded in written texts.

In the following section, I locate the emergence of the Bamanan polities of Kaarta and Segu within the longer historical trajectory of Sahelian empires, in the ways they were imagined in European cartography of the period but also within the discursive tradition of West African Muslim intellectuals that refer to the Bambara in derogatory or othering language. The multivalent nature of these and other sources allows possibilities for understanding the nature of heterogeneous societies where people operated across difference. The goal is to problematize how historical sources of any kind allow only partial insight into a Bamanan past and to demonstrate how carefully parsed and contextualized sources offer insights and hold interpretive value. Despite limitations from the viewpoint of a Western epistemic lens, Kouyate's oral tradition constitutes an elastic archive able to transmit an alternative to the anti-Bambara discourse of written texts. Insight drawn from this aspect of the oral tradition helps to better contextualize the emergence of Kaarta circa 1650 (AH 1060) amid environmental crises, political instability, migration, human trafficking, and expanding global commerce.

In the last two sections of the chapter, I explore how textiles, as iterations of Bamanaya, are deployed in oral sources at moments of conflict and transition—conquest, diplomacy, and state making—as statements of self-fashioning. I begin with an examination of a physical garment, an indigo cotton *kusaaba* in a museum collection in Paris, the oldest garment of its kind. I explore the possible provenance and context for this garment archived in a Parisian museum as a history of colonial extraction and erasure but also as histories the garment itself archives of West African labor, technology, and aesthetics in a manner that goes beyond written evidence and spoken assertions. I then turn to how such garments show up in the oral traditions of the early Bamanan kingdoms as symbols of power, contested forms of

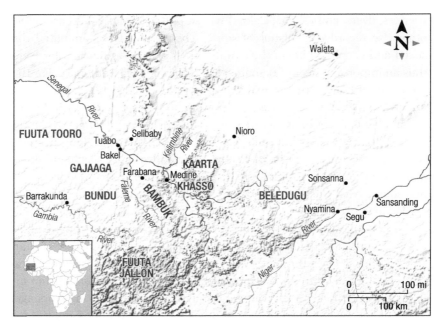

MAP 1.1. Map of the Sahel between the Senegal and Niger Rivers encompassing Kaarta, Beledugu, and Segu. Map by Matt Johnson at Johnson Cartographic.

self-fashioning, meaning making, and memory, especially in oral histories related to conflict between Segu and Kaarta in the mid-eighteenth century and to the power wielded by Biton Kulubali's son Dekoro.

In the final section of the chapter, I return to Djeli Mamary Kouyate's oral account of early Kaarta, which culminates with a late seventeenth-century slave revolt that brings Sonsan Kulubali to power over his Maraka hosts and establishes what would become known as Bamanan Kaarta. At the heart of this origin story are references to textiles—saving Sonsan from death and anonymity. Kouyate's mention of a slave revolt as a catalyst for state building also diverges from historical narratives about the proliferation of the fiscal military state model across western Africa, driven by plundering. Precarity and conflict existed alongside pluralism in deep cultural entanglements between Sahelian communities across boundaries of language, religious affiliation, and ways of living. Other explanations exist for the establishment of Kaarta, but the aim is to show how these various and divergent sources establish the context in which Sahelian farmers, weavers, dyers, and embroiderers animated a regional textile trade amid instability and global expansion between the late seventeenth and early nineteenth centuries.

## FINDING KAARTA AND DEFINING BAMANAN

Kaarta emerged as a polity in the late seventeenth century as the second of two Bamanan-led militarized states at a time when the hegemony of the Mali Empire was in decline.[3] Oral traditions, local chronicles, and European sources make divergent claims about the timing and circumstances that brought Kaarta into existence. This section seeks to locate the state and its people amid this fragmented archive. The founding rulers of both states descended from the same Kulubali lineage. Sonsan Kulubali was a distant cousin of Segu's first ruler, or *faama*, Mamari Biton Kulubali, and both were grandsons of Kalajan Kulubali. Segu, with its more favorable location on the Niger (Djoliba) River and more diverse economy, became the larger of the two states. The early Kaarta settlement was near the desert-side town of Mourdiah. Its political center changed over time to include the towns of Nioro, Guemou, and Yelimane. As political power in Segu passed out of the Kulubali lineage with the rise of Ngolo Diarra in the 1760s as faama, Kaarta's rulers claimed to be of more authentic Bamanan royal lineage than were those who would come to rule Segu.

Kaarta and Segu emerged during a period of political instability, environmental crisis, and migration throughout the region. Drought prompted people to leave the drier, hotter regions of the northern Sahel for the comparably wetter and cooler settings south. Many Soninke communities in Diafunu, a region west of Kaarta and home to one of West Africa's oldest clerical communities dating back to ancient Ghana, began an out-migration from their homes near the desert to travel south and east to the banks of the Milo River in Guinea. There they settled amid Maninka farmers to form the nucleus of what was to become the thriving clerical and market town of Kankan.[4]

Another major seventeenth-century migration took place at Maacina, many miles east of Diafunu, as communities of Muslim Fulbe traveled southwest to settle in the temperate plateau of the Fuuta Jallon. They were joined there by other Fulbe Muslim settlers who migrated south from Fuuta Tooro and Bundu in the same period.[5] They established mosques and Quranic schools to support the conversion of non-Muslim Fulbe and Jallonke residents. The migratory influx gradually transformed not only the demographics of the plateau but also its political economy, which was dominated by a clerical elite and expanding markets.

Fulbe pastoralists migrating south and west from Maacina brought distinct textile weaving practices with them that combined cotton and wool and incorporated a wider array of dye colors produced from local flora. The best known Fulbe textile associated with these migrations is the *kaasa*, produced in Maacina and adjacent areas west of Lake Debo and woven of sheep's wool and sometimes blended with cotton. These large loom-patterned strip cloths colored in reds, yellows, and black were used as blankets for sleeping but could also be fashioned as clothing. They circulated widely within the region. Bamanan, Maninka, and other groups wove similar blankets, which they called different names, such as *dampe*.[6]

Cotton was an important crop cultivated both in the Milo River region around Kankan and throughout the Fuuta Jallon plateau. Towns in the highlands also became known for producing fine indigo-dyed cotton cloths.[7] This process overlapped with and was informed by new opportunities and complications presented by Atlantic commerce and its global connections.

The emergence of two Bamanan-ruled states represented another form of upheaval: the rejection of Maraka Muslim rule amid the demographic shifts caused by migration. Sources written in European languages and in Arabic script that describe both polities also record the turmoil of the period. Bamanan-speaking areas of the Sahel generally appear in European sources and local chronicles of the seventeenth and eighteenth centuries in one of two ways: as large, densely populated spaces on the route of caravans or as hostile lands of nonbelievers who threatened clerical cities.

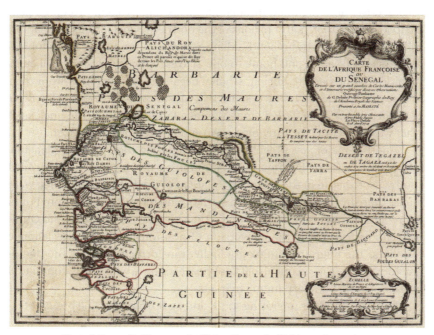

FIGURE 1.3. Detail from Guillaume de l'Isle, *Carte de l'Afrique françoise ou du Sénégal: Dressée sur un grand nombre de cartes manuscrites et d'itineraires rectifiés par diverses observations* (Paris, 1727).

34 ~ *The Texture of Change*

FIGURE 1.4. De l'Isle map crop.

Kaarta possibly already existed as a political community led by the Kulubali when the cartographer Guillaume de l'Isle created a series of maps of West Africa for Louis XIV on which their lands appear simply as "Pays des Bambaras"—Bambara Country. De l'Isle's title, "Map of French Africa or of Senegal" (figures 1.3 and 1.4), announced this document as an instrument of imperial claims making, surveillance, and extraction that has so often been framed agnostically by historians as French commercial expansion into the region. His map identified and located topographical features such as mountains and forests, the region's extensive riverine network connecting the Atlantic coast to gold mines a few hundred kilometers inland, and the proximate highlands of the Fuuta Jallon plateau. Its lines traced the boundaries of several territories defined as kingdoms, such as that of Alichandora, king of the Trarza Moors and whose lands were in contemporary Mauritania, where a forest of acacia trees produced a resin coveted by artisans in Europe. There were the Guiolof (Joloff) and Foules (Fulbe) on the Senegal River, the Bambuk on the Faleme River to the east, the Fuuta Jallon on the plateau to the southeast, and the Nalu on the Rio Pongo in the tropical south. Taken together, the dozens of place-names and ethnonyms represent a great effort to gather information, but they also document a regional coherence both geographical and profoundly historical.

*Twelve Measures of New Cloth and a Magnificent Bubu* ~ 35

The two Bamanan kingdoms' names do not specifically appear on De l'Isle's map. But the document records their significance and connection to the wider region through a striking form of visual language: a long, curved double line indicating the path of a caravan to and from "Bambara" Country (Pays des Bambaras). The route arches northward and westward toward Diafunu (Yaffon), curves south toward Nioro until it meets the Senegal River, where there was a French trading fort, and then continues south to the end of its path, at Barrakunda on the Gambia River, where British merchants traded. The map identifies Bamanan communities at a critical juncture connecting the markets of the Sahel riverine traffic along the two major riverine arteries linked to expanding Atlantic trade in the region.

The term *Bambara* (or *Bamanan*) has been a notoriously slippery referent for historians and anthropologists, as has been the Western notion of historical ethnicity in Africa generally.[8] The literal meaning of *Bamanan* in the Bamanankan language is "those who refuse [Islam]," although the people's engagement with Islam has been complex. Muslims continued to inhabit the towns within Bamanan-led Kaarta, often as merchants, and were advisers to and family members of its rulers.

Traders, travelers, and scholars used and recorded the term *Bambara*, often with great imprecision, to refer not only to the Bamanan but to a variety of other non-Muslim communities, such as the Kagoro, Senufo, Somono, Bozo, and Minianka.[9] The French learned about this part of the Sahel and its people indirectly from their commercial partners—Muslim Soninke and Fulbe merchants they engaged with at Gajaaga and along the Faleme branch of the Senegal River. It was likely through such encounters that the Fulbe-language pronunciation "Bambara" —for the people who referred to themselves as Bamanan[10]—became codified in French sources such as maps, commercial records, and travel diaries.

The meaning of *Bambara* also shifted in practical terms across space and over time as it was used by people in different colonial settings during the eighteenth century. The term began to evolve in the coastal settlements of Saint-Louis and Gorée and while it circulated in French overseas colonies such as at Saint-Domingue, New Orleans, and Isle de Bourbon (later Réunion).[11] In addition to social meanings constructed on the spot between people in Atlantic and Indian Ocean ports, *Bambara* was also defined in European and Arabic-script documents. Among the latter, the written opinions of Ahmad Baba (1556–1627) and Abd al-Rahman ibn al-Sa'di (1594–ca. 1655) stand out for their articulation of political boundaries and social hierarchies in the region not long before Kaarta emerged as a force to the southwest of the clerical centers of Timbuktu and Jenne. Such writings constitute an important local archive, but one that is, broadly speaking, hostile in tone and substance toward the Bambara, who are generally reviled as "pagans" and "unbelievers."[12]

An eminent scholar and jurist, Ahmad Baba famously criticized the association between race and enslavement, insisting that only "unbelief" rendered an individual enslaveable.[13] Baba articulated this view in reply to a query from a scholar from Tuwat, a desert oasis town on a Saharan caravan route, about whether it was permissible to purchase captives from south of the desert who claimed to be Muslim. Baba's response included an extensive religious ethnographic mapping of West Africa that identified communities as either Muslim (believers) or non-Muslim (unbelievers), also noting the timing and circumstances of each group's conversion to Islam. This ethnographic cartography mapped those from Timbuktu, south to the goldfields of Bambuk, west to Joloff, and more than a thousand miles east to Kano and Borno in present-day Nigeria. Closer to home were the Bambara, who Baba named as unbelievers and therefore legally enslaveable.

For Abd al-Rahman ibn al-Sa'di, author of the *Tarikh al-Sudan,* the Bambara represented a menace occupying lands just beyond "civilization" and needed to be suppressed.[14] Al-Sa'di was disdainful of the "pagan Bambara," who he said took advantage of the crisis caused by the Moroccan invasion of Timbuktu in 1591 to invade Jenne: "They sacked every territory, plundered every piece of property, and took free women as concubines from whom they had children who were raised as *majus*—God preserve us from this."[15] Bamanan depredations that al-Sa'di described took place amid a generalized chaos unleashed by the attack of the Moroccan army on Songhay-controlled Timbuktu and Gao. But the author conveys a particular scorn for the Bamanan as captors of free Muslim women who are reduced to concubinage and their children raised as non-Muslims. Here the meaning of *Bambara* appeared as a negation of *Muslim* and *free* and even a curse on future generations. He conveyed a similar sentiment when relating how Askiya Dawud, the Songhay ruler, harshly reprimanded an official for failing to reduce the number of "Bambara unbelievers" in his lands, observing that they had instead "multiplied" and "established themselves."[16]

A chronicle from Walata, a historic desert-side market town that was once a frontier outpost of the empire of Mali, portrays the Bambara in a similar vein, but also describes the Bamanan kingdoms of the eighteenth century as expansive powers that inspired fear and imposed "domination" on their neighbors. The *Fragment of Ancient Chronicles of Oualata* recorded that on the fourteenth day of Safar in AH 1160, or February 2, 1747, which was a Friday, a group of armed "Bambari" attacked a caravan of Walata merchants and put the caravan leaders "in irons." A few years later, in 1754 (AH 1167), the author noted that an army from Segu, led by Mamari Biton Kulubali, blockaded and destroyed the town of Sansa, or Sonsanna, which, according to Kouyate, had been so named by Sonsan Kulubali and which was still under the rule of his descendants.[17]

The Muslim authors of these documents expressed a worldview in which questions of belonging, social status, and difference were determined by one's proximity to Islam, and specifically to certain Arab and Berber patrilineages.[18] Perhaps as early as the fourteenth century, Arab and Berber pastoralist communities inhabiting the southern Sahara began to articulate these distinctions in the language of skin color. They began to define themselves as Bidan (white) in contrast to the Sudan (black) farmers to their south.[19] Despite their evocation of color, these socially constructed categories did not refer strictly to an individual's phenotype. Rather they correlated more to lineage (and religious affiliation), language, and occupational status. What the term *Bambara* referred to in these sources was not only a cultural and political community but a juridical category of persons who, as nonbelievers, were considered enslaveable under Muslim law. This debate of status and lineage, which reflects the hegemonic status of Islam, was thus part of an internal Sahelian discourse on race that preceded the arrival of European merchants on the Atlantic coasts in the fifteenth century but with which it later became entangled.[20]

The oral traditions of Kaarta and Segu also convey some of this debate. In Djeli Mamary Kouyate's narrative of Kaarta, Sonsan appears variously as a weaver, farmer, healer, and leader whose achievements are often contrasted with those of his Muslim neighbors. However, traditional oral sources offer perspectives that differ strikingly from those recorded in either European or local Islamic sources. Kouyate mapped the rise of Kaarta onto the life of Sonsan Kulubali, from his ancestry, birth, and youth—when a series of personal challenges revealed his unique qualities—to his emergence as a mature, charismatic leader, a defender of Bamanan values in the face of greed and corruption. Kouyate's perspective is rooted in agriculture and the ritual manipulation of the natural world.

However, like the archive of documents written in Arabic, African ajami, and European languages, the traditional oral sources for both Kaarta and Segu present limitations, with their narrow focus on elite lineages and on individuals whose exploits gained renown. There is almost no indication, for example, in the oral accounts of the trafficking of girls and young women who were carried in caravans of enslaved people that traversed the Kaarta region en route to Saharan markets, where there was a demand for them.

Instead, the representation of girls and women in oral tradition focuses on their roles as mothers, wives, and, occasionally, leaders and fighters whose actions ultimately support the achievements of heroic men.

The tone of these oral traditions is hagiographic and didactic. Sonsan is represented as a gifted, confident, and shrewd individual who overcame a series of challenges with charm, knowledge, and skill. In his dealings with a series of socially and ethnically differentiated others, both women and men, he benefited from not only these personal qualities but also the considerable good fortune that seemed to flow from them. When Sonsan's popularity fills his brothers with so much jealous rage that they make an attempt on his life, throwing him into a well and leaving him to perish, he is miraculously rescued by his mother and his sister, who use "twelve measures of new cloth" to pull him out.[21] After that, Sonsan was forced to abandon his childhood home, but this escape was blessed by his mother:

> Wherever you set your feet
> In place of where your brothers would find nothing
> May you always find good fortune there.[22]

It was under those circumstances that Sonsan had come to Dorko, the Maraka settlement where he would indeed find good fortune, so much so that he would later take it over. Sonsan won the favor of his new hosts in part by demonstrating his skills as a weaver and therefore his value to the chief of a Maraka village. Kouyate mentions that the chief's wives were instrumental in the decision to allow Sonsan to settle among them: "When the women saw the cloth [Sonsan] had made, / the Maraka men never wove again for the Maraka women." Kouyate continued to describe how the Maraka women felt about Sonsan's work on the loom: "If the Bamanan [man] will do the weaving it is time to weave, / but if somebody else is to weave my wool, I will wait."[23] From Kouyate's narrative emerges a Sonsan self-fashioned according to *Bamanaya;* he not only manipulated cotton into textiles that beguiled the Maraka women but also exhibited fearlessness as a leader and demonstrated great capacity for working the land, using his knowledge of local plants to heal.

Kouyate's narrative contains both hegemonic Islamic and counter-hegemonic elements. Much as he did with Silamakan Koita and Sonsan Kulubali, he conflates the names of important historical events and places of the western Sahel with equivalents in the history of the Hejaz, thereby aligning local geographies and history with the narrative of historical Islam. He refers, for example, to a battle at Kayes as the "war at Kaybara," making an allusion to the early Muslim conquest of Khaybar in the Hejaz during the seventh century. Later, he suggestively refers to the ancient city of Dia, considered the ancient heartland of the Soninke population, as "Medina, the capital in the Holy Land."[24] Individuals are described as having a range of engagements with Islam, from expressions of sincere devotion to open rejection of the faith. Similarly, there are references to a variety of its ritual practices, from performing daily ablutions and pilgrimaging to Mecca to consulting diviners, conversing with spirit jinn, and taking blood oaths.

Bamanan nobility were associated with agricultural and ritual control of land, hunting, and the military. Kouyate describes Sonsan Kulubali at various turns throughout his narration as a skilled farmer, as a healer knowledgeable about the curative properties of plants, and as a strategic military leader confronting an oppressive foe. Within their communities, Bamanan farmers cultivated the grains millet and fonio while specially trained hunters obtained bushmeat such as gazelles. They raised bees to produce honey, some of which was fermented to produce an alcoholic beer. Bamanan fondness for beer was anathema to neighboring Muslims, for whom consuming alcohol was prohibited.

Merchants occupied a secondary place among the Bamanan political elites, who taxed merchants trading in their towns. As French naval officer Anne Raffenel observed at a twice-daily market in Guemou, capital of Kaarta in the mid-nineteenth century, "The [market's] management was entrusted to a tax agent, selected by the king to collect a sales tax from the merchants for every sale they made and another duty from the buyers who paid in merchandise."[25] Nonetheless, merchants were essential for moving the products of Bamanan farmers to regional and transregional markets. Multiple currencies circulated simultaneously in Sahelian commerce, with iron bars, salt slabs, gold, textiles, and cowrie shells used for payment. In the late eighteenth century, Mungo Park described meeting a Bamanan man who had once been enslaved by Moors in the Sahara Desert but who was then living freely in Koulikoro as a prosperous cloth and salt merchant able to offer shelter to the Scottish traveler.[26] At the same time, the flow of imported textiles—especially indigo-dyed cottons, known commercially by the French as "guinees"—increased throughout the eighteenth century, as did their value as currency relative to that of iron bars.[27]

Among the most important agricultural products that Bamanan farmers cultivated were cotton and indigo, both long-established in the region. Their villages and towns south and west of the Niger bend were located just south of Maacina, one of the early centers of cotton production in West Africa.[28] The oldest textiles found in West Africa, dating to the eleventh century, were recovered from caves in the Bandiagara Escarpment nearby—hundreds of mostly cotton cloths woven with finely spun threads, some with classic loom patterns and others showing the skill of indigo dyers. But the practice of indigo dyeing is thought to be much older. Indigo from this region had long been trafficked in caravans across the Sahara to markets in Morocco, where the dye-colored threads were woven into Berber carpets made in the Atlas Mountains.[29]

In the Bamanankan language, *gala* (indigo) is associated with divinity, as in the names for the indigo plants *gala yiri* (divine plant) and *ma ngalaba yiri* (the Creator). In the seventeenth century, Bamanan artisans practiced several weaving and dyeing traditions, including producing patterns on the treadle loom and resist-dyeing with indigo. Skilled indigo dyers produced a dozen or more shades of blue from the unassuming green shrub, each shade with its own name and spiritual and cultural associations.[30] Bamanan women extended the practice of dyeing cloth to include dyeing cotton with leaves and fermented mud to produce the unique *bogolan* cloths with resist-dyed patterns that expressed their technical skill, philosophical worldview, and cultural knowledge.[31] Although Bamanan textile production and consumption are only intermittently referenced in an archive focused on

FIGURE 1.5. *(left)* "Femme Bambara" in David Boilat, *Esquisses sénégalaises: physionomie du pays, peuplades, commerce, religions, passé et avenir, récits et légendes* (Paris: P. Bertrand, 1853), plate 24. FIGURE 1.6. *(right)* "Homme Bambara" in David Boilat, *Esquisses sénégalaises: Physionomie du pays, peuplades, commerce, religions, passé et avenir, récits et légendes* (Paris: P. Bertrand, 1853), plate 23.

other matters, they animated the social and economic realities of daily life. Cotton, indigo, and textiles are thus important signifiers of Bamanaya and potent symbols of power, self-fashioning, meaning making, and memory.

## "A MAGNIFICENT BUBU": DRESS AS VEHICLE OF DIPLOMACY, STATE MAKING, AND SEDITION

A large, elegant indigo-dyed cotton robe, known in Maninka as *kusaaba* (see figure 1.7), is today stored inside a guarded vault of the Musée du Quai Branly, near the River Seine in Paris.[32] Visually striking, the robe stretches across the shoulders to eight feet end to end, with wide sleeves that hang almost as low as the robe's body. This was not a garment made for physical exertion but for elegance and display. It featured beautifully detailed, brightly colored embroidered motifs against a midnight surface: a red sun surrounded by widening circles of golden yellow and green stitched in shiny silk threads that wind outward into an orbit around the right chest area before bisecting a cross and ending at the neckline. A similar cross has been embroidered onto the left chest area, along with a bold-patterned curve in red, yellow, and green that continues over the shoulder to repeat the circular sundial on the back.

Looking closely at the kusaaba, it is hard not to imagine how this status garment came together through collaborative effort rather than the work of

FIGURE 1.7. "Coussave [Kusaaba] or Blouse N'ajate Sego" indigo cotton with colored silk embroidery, before 1850, ART569298 Photo Credit: © Musée du Quai Branly—Jacques Chirac / Art Resource, NY.

42 ~ *The Texture of Change*

a single artisan. It represents the combined labor of farmers, carders, spinners, weavers, dyers, tailors, and embroiderers: skilled men and women. Its body was constructed of several finely woven cotton strips, about five inches wide, that were stitched together so that the seams were barely noticeable. Its evenly dyed dark, almost black, indigo color showcased the technical ability of its artisan dyers and provided a sharp contrasting background for the motifs embroidered across it. The combination of structure and tailoring telegraphed grandeur and authority.

Embroidery in this region was often the part-time work of itinerant Quranic scholars, men who worked with student apprentices.[33] The striking geometric design motifs of the embroidery on tunics and robes are similar to those painted on the stucco facades of architecture in Walata, the desert-side town populated by Berber, Arab, and Soninke merchants and clerics.[34] The town was an ancient outpost of trans-Saharan commerce that had been continuously inhabited since the existence of the Ghana Empire. Local traditions claimed that Oualata, located north of Kumbi Saleh, had originally been settled by Bamanan farmers who migrated south sometime after the arrival there of Limhajib Berbers.[35] Caravans of commerce, as well as out-migrations of scholars educated in the mosques at Walata, continually animated traffic between the desert and the towns of Kaarta and Segu and the Senegal River valley. Embroidery on the kusaaba, as much as the garment itself, testified to such linkages.

This kusaaba has a long history in French museums. The precise provenance of the kusaaba has been lost, except that it came to France through the French navy, though it was likely woven in Senegal or perhaps along the Senegal River valley. In 1830, it was listed in the first inventories ever produced for the Naval Museum (Musée de Marine du Louvre), which featured objects brought to France from overseas. King Charles X created the museum by decree to showcase the "cultural achievements" of the Bourbon Restoration.[36]

What achievement did the museum's possession of this garment represent? Was it a diplomatic gift? Was it purchased in a market, and if so for how much? Was it perhaps commissioned by a colonial official? It was listed in a subsection of the inventory titled "Products of Industry" (*Produits de L'Industrie*) with almost two hundred other objects of local manufacture and everyday use, including gris-gris amulets, a bow and arrow and quiver, a small ebony tobacco box, a *laptot* sailor's hat, a *signares* headwrap, a wooden spoon, Moorish culottes, a Bambara flute, slippers from Segu, a marabout's tablet, a mortar and pestle, local soap, and a balafon.[37] Many of these objects have since been lost, as the collections moved between different institutions.

The kusaaba somehow survived these changes. When it came into the museum's possession, an archivist cataloged it as an odd mix of French, Wolof, and gallicized forms of local place-names: "*Coussave ou Blouse N'ajate-Sego—joussab en Fouta Galam des indig.*" *N'ajate*, the Wolof term for "embroidery," combined with the place-name Sego (likely Segu) seems to tell an origin story of at least the garment's inspiration, if not of the garment's manufacture itself: Segu embroidery. The next term listed, *joussab*, is another curious rendition of *khoussab*, while *Fouta* likely refers to the Fuuta Tooro on the Senegal River, and *Galam* to Gajaaga, adjacent to Fuuta Tooro in eastern Senegal. The archivist (or perhaps an informant) collapsed *Fouta and Galam* as if they were the same place rather than two contiguous regions. The multiple linguistic referents in the archivist's inventory testify to the wide circulation of these names across geographic regions that could imbue such a garment with the social currency of these places' reputation.

Such garments have long been produced and circulated in the region between Gajaaga on the Senegal River and Segu on the Niger River, where, in the Bamanan language, they are known as *lomasa* or *dloki ba*, and in Soninke as *lomanca*.[38] The archivist noted in the inventory that both the N'ajate-Sego and another textile in the collection, a blanket called *dampe*, "give a high idea of the industry of the Bambaras." Dampe, as they were known in Bamanan, were also made by Soninke and Fulbe weavers. Known as *koso wolani* in Fulbe and *damiya* in Soninke, these cotton blankets featured attractive patterns of alternating indigo and white checkerboard squares. The archivist's inventory noted the appealing aesthetic and technical skill that produced both the blanket and the tunic, but also trivialized with dismissive praise the rich cultural and historical context that produced them: "The weave, the dye and the embroidery of this garment make it known that in the interior of Africa there exist men for whom all of the arts are not entirely unknown."[39]

Like de l'Isle's map, the museum's inventory indexes French imperial imperatives; expropriating the cultural artifacts of the vanquished has long been a strategy of conquest that served to confirm the victory and to burnish the reputation of those in possession of them.[40] In the early nineteenth century, when the kusaaba entered the Naval Museum, this process was made explicit in the goal to make Paris an imperial capital. The museum had been established to educate the French public, including students, about the French navy and to promote advances in maritime technology at a time when France's overseas commerce was expanding again, producing economic growth after a generation of war. But these institutional displays, and the hundreds of other objects archived away from public view, perhaps never to be exhibited, invariably hid the forms of violence and exploitation endemic to the various modes of extraction, such as slave trading, general commerce, diplomacy, and scientific or religious missions, that ultimately brought thousands of objects from overseas to this museum repository of imperial conquest.

Though they offer compelling physical evidence of nineteenth-century West Africa, there is much that rare garments such as the kusaaba, stored in the museum vault in Paris, cannot tell us. Oral tradition and written sources offer some insight into the contexts in which people used them. Similar garments were mentioned in traditional oral accounts of both Kaarta and Segu. They occupy a significant place in the region's cultural memory, lending meaningful detail to historical narratives that emerge from moments of conflict or transition.

For example, in one account, an intricately tailored kusaaba was given a pivotal role in an oral account of the plot against Kaarta by the ruler of Segu, Mamari Biton Kulubali. In this version, conflict erupted between the two communities after the leader of Kaarta, Fulakoro, stopped a caravan from Segu conveying Biton's daughter BaSana, who was to be married off to a military subordinate in another town. Biton sought access to this town, with its market and ties to trans-Saharan commerce, and, like other political rulers and patriarchs throughout the region, used marriage as a tool in his state-building project.

Taken with the young woman's beauty, Fulakoro married her himself without consulting her father.[41] Once he learned of this, Biton responded by attacking Sonsanna. Fighters led by Fulakoro twice turned back these military attacks from Segu. Facing these initial setbacks, Biton turned to a group of Muslim clerics he relied on for spiritual assistance and strategic advice—an arrangement with a long history in the western Sahel, going back as far as ancient Ghana.

The marabouts debated several possible solutions before they settled on a scheme to distract Fulakoro by appealing to his vanity, occupying him long enough to launch a surprise attack on Sonsanna. For this, a finely tailored garment such as a kusaaba was needed. One of the marabouts said, "If someone were to give me a magnificent boubou[42] of a great chief, I will infuse it with such qualities that when Foulakoro puts it on, the town of Sounsanna [sic] will be yours!' Biton bought a resplendent boubou, pricked all over it with a needle and delivered it to the marabout."[43] The clothing needed to be beyond ordinary to appeal to the pretensions and vanity of a wealthy and powerful person. It was to be visually striking, appealing to the eye in a way that conveyed distinction—that is, "magnificent." Such a request suggests the quality of the textiles that local artisans were capable of crafting.

*Twelve Measures of New Cloth and a Magnificent Bubu* ∼ 45

Once a suitable garment was produced, the marabouts performed incantations over it, then arranged for a *jula* merchant to travel to Sonsanna to entice the Kaarta chief with it. *Jula*, a Manding word translated by some as "trader," refers both to individuals and to an ethnic group who were a ubiquitous presence across the region and played important roles in connecting distant markets in the eighteenth century.[44] The presence of a cloth-trading jula visiting Sonsanna would not have been unusual. That Biton promised to reward the jula merchant generously with one hundred enslaved captives shows not only the importance of slave trading in the political economy but also the high stakes of the gambit.[45]

Ultimately, the jula merchant succeeded in selling the "magnificent boubou" to the Kaarta chief. Seduced by the garment's extravagance and expense, Fulakoro purchased it, put it on immediately, and, in a short while, fell unconscious from the effects of the marabouts' incantations. By the time Fulakoro awoke the next morning, Biton's army had already launched the advance on Sonsanna, this time capturing the town and killing most members of the Massasi, as the lineage descendants of Sonsan Koulibali were known. The army transported BaSana and Fulakoro back to Segu, where Fulakoro, despite BaSana's efforts to protect him from her father's retributions, was killed.[46]

What is notable about this anecdote is not the degree to which this oral traditional account may be apocryphal but the way in which local textiles, tailored clothing, and ritual practices—all facets of *Bamanaya*—function as sites of memory for this major conflict between Segu and Kaarta. It shows cloth not only as an important binder between historical communities of the Sahel but also as a site of struggle between them.

Other oral accounts that relate to Biton Kulubali and his sons remember dress deployed as a language of state or authoritarian power. Biton died the year after the attack on Sonsanna, and his eldest son Dekoro became ruler of Segu.[47] Several sources describe this privileged firstborn as aggressive and cruel. Dekoro's character caused trouble even while Biton was still alive. Biton once had to defuse a quarrel between Dekoro and a key official, his *ton mansa*, who commanded an elite group of soldiers that had lost a battle. Enraged by this, Dekoro had the ton mansa whipped in front of his soldiers. When the ton mansa complained of this treatment, Biton removed the ton mansa from under the command of Dekoro to place him instead under that of Dekoro's brother, Bakari, who had studied in Quranic school at Jenne.[48]

In a further gesture of mollification, Biton sought to reassure the man by expressing his continued confidence in him and by gifting him 150 measures of silk cloth and a belt (*bila*) that was the symbol of cavalrymen. Textiles of woven silk had for centuries circulated throughout Manding-speaking

West Africa, where they were produced in both Dogon and Marka-Dafing communities known for their skills as weavers and traders.[49] At Segu, Biton used the gift of such a garment to convey an honor unique to the ton mansa and would serve as a visual sign of distinction among his soldiers, restoring some of the dignity lost through Dekoro's act of public humiliation.

Additional details of Dekoro's eighteenth-century life were embedded within a history of Kaarta narrated in the 1840s to the French naval officer Raffenel. Writing almost a century later, colonial official Louis Tauxier, in his study of early sources for the Bamanan kingdoms, dismissed parts of Raffenel's account as exaggerated. But he also found support for some of its claims in other local chronicles that describe Biton Kulubali's eldest son.

Dekoro was said to want to distinguish himself both from his father and his peers. He had become bored with the trappings of his wealth acquired from the numerous military campaigns in which he took part. He decided to have a wall constructed around the town of Segu that was to be ritually consecrated so as to offer supernatural protection to residents from outside attack. Dekoro ordered the bodies of sixty enslaved people to be buried in the wall's foundation, supposedly making the walls impossible to breach. The day appointed to begin construction of the wall was to be a public affair of state. Dekoro had each of the captives, both male and female, lined up around the perimeter of the town. Soldiers dressed the captives in six lengths of *riche etoffe* (fine cloth), as if for a festive occasion. Such a display was a familiar practice in which royals dressed their servants in finery when in public or for an affair of state as a sign of their wealth and social status. Praise singers dressed in their best clothing announced the arrival of Dekoro himself accompanied by musicians playing a balafon, drums, a flute, and silver bells. The white horse he rode was adorned with gris-gris amulets. He wore more cords of protective amulets over a *dloki ba* made of blue silk and embroidered with gold threads. On his head, Dekoro wore a hunter's cap that had been worn in battle by his ancestors, inscribing himself into sartorial semantics of a shared past with his viewers in which hunters constituted the noble class. He carried a musket inlaid with gold.[50] With the crowds watching, soldiers blindfolded the finely dressed captives who were then made to stand next to trenches around the town's perimeter. At a given signal, the soldiers slit a captive's throat and pushed the fallen body into the trenches. Each body was then covered with soil and stones before another corpse created the next layer to form the wall's foundation.[51]

Dekoro's actions were so excessively cruel that they provoked a revolt by those enslaved that turned the tables on the cruel sovereign and marked a decisive moment in the early history of Segu. A group of the surviving captives plotted to remove Dekoro from power and to make him pay for his abuses. They ambushed Dekoro the next evening after he had given his clothes to an attendant to take a bath. In this telling, the vulnerability of the sovereign's disrobed, nude body seems to foretell his impending demise, just as the excessively lavish textiles draped onto the bodies of the slaughtered captives seemed to declare his invincibility. The rebel captives forcibly restrained the king in his bath, then brought some of Dekoro's wives and children before him, tied together in a slave coffle. They threatened to kill them and use their bodies to build a tower at Segu at least as impressive as Dekoro's wall.[52] In Raffenel's version, the rebels later killed the royal, along with his wives and children, then installed someone from among their ranks as ruler of Segu. An account recorded by another colonial official, Robert Arnaud, notes that the rebels "strangled him with a strip of cotton [cloth]" and chased his family from the area.[53] The unusual sartorial details conveyed offer a remarkable snapshot of the political economy of symbolic power within the Bamanan kingdom.

## "COTTON, MAIZE, AND GOURDS": INTERCROPPING AS BOTH *BAMANAYA* AND A METAPHOR FOR PLURALISM

Kouyate's oral tradition narrates a Bamanan state that took shape through forms of accommodation and contestation between ethnically and culturally distinct communities. Its passages portray a certain synergy of knowledge and practice between these three distinct groups in the western Sahel—the Bamanan, Fulbe, and Maraka—and show both intimacy and contestation between Islamic and non-Islamic lifeways and memory. Kouyate reveals something of Sonsan Kulubali's character by explaining how, as a child, Sonsan not only was popular with children of his age set but even attracted the attention of an ethnically and socially diverse group of visitors to the family compound:

> Even if he was just walking through the village in the morning, even if he was on his way to wash his face,
> He would be accompanied by a group of friends, sometimes as many as ten of them.
> The Fula,
> The *numuw*,
> The *jeliw*,
> The *funéw*,
> The *garankéw*,
> The Kakolo,

All the strangers who come and go,
They stay at the house of Sonsan.

In Kouyate's account, Sonsan's cultural dexterity appears as a key to his success. After fleeing to the Maraka village, the Bamanan farmer begins to communicate with a Maraka jinn who encourages him to transform a field by planting "cotton, gourds and maize" that would secure his "destiny and fame." Following this advice, Sonsan once again exceeds his hosts' expectations by producing abundant crops, thereby gaining both status and wealth.[54]

Next, the Maraka jinn advises Sonsan to marry and tells him how to do so. Marriages and political alliances between linguistically and culturally distinct communities have a long genealogy in the western Sahel. So when the jinn urges Sonsan to wed the sickly daughter of a powerful Fulbe herder and warrior, there was ample precedent for it. Kouyate signals the father's importance by noting that when Sonsan arrives at the family compound, he finds four *djeliw* (bards) performing the *janjon* for him, a traditional praise song reserved for valiant warriors. "Janjon is not good for everyone. Janjon is sung for those who have faced danger," Kouyate intones.

The warrior, Alou Sangare, is incredulous when the farmer asks to marry the least attractive of his six daughters, Duba. "I do not ask even a piece of kola for her," he says in giving his consent. However, Sonsan sees an opportunity in the father's apparent lack of interest in Duba. He bathes Duba's sores and nurses her back to health with the help of the Maraka ancestor spirits, *jinnamagha* and *jinnamuso*. They provide him with medicine and instructions for her care. These acts of healing, drawn from a knowledge of the curative medicinal qualities of plants, are among several expressions of Bamanaya that appear throughout Kouyate's account. But significantly, Kouyate suggests something often absent in written sources: that these were also acts of collaboration with ancestors of the Maraka in spirit form, thus suggesting a mutual reliance and influence between communities.

After three months of care, Duba is completely rehabilitated. Sonsan returns with her to her parents' compound, but they do not initially recognize their daughter, so surprised are they by her transformation. For Sonsan, this achievement serves primarily to differentiate himself from his father-in-law as a purveyor of a distinctly Bamanan sense of honor. This account also presents a non-Muslim man marrying a Muslim woman and a Bamanan farmer marrying the daughter of a Fulbe herder, which counters a pattern found by some scholars of oral traditions in the savanna in which non-Muslim men do not wed Muslim women. It was the very outcome that so upset al-Sadi in his account, mentioned earlier, of Bamanan fighters attacking Jenne and forcibly marrying Muslim women. In the case of Sonsan, the Bamanan farmer insists on negotiating a bride price for Duba because, he explains, "I am not a Muslim. I will not take a wife without paying the proper bride price."[55] Kouyate's account has thus archived a complex layering of the history of Islam in the Sahel along with a politics of ethnicity, social hierarchy, and worldview.

Kouyate's account of Kaarta's origin story culminates with a crisis created when Sonsan's Maraka hosts capture fifty Bamanan men who were wandering nearby and tie "them together by their necks with rawhide."[56] The Maraka take the men hostage and chain them inside Sonsan's compound. In a powerful moment of recognition, Sonsan weeps at the sight of them. The captives wretched presence reminds Sonsan, now married and relatively wealthy, of his own difficult past of fleeing his childhood home to save his life. He says to them:

> You are Bamanan and I am Bamanan
> Yet they have captured you and imprisoned you in my compound
> This is the same kind of greed that brought me here
> If you see me weeping it is because I am reminded of my own suffering.

This moment reveals a surprisingly direct critique of slave raiding and trading. Sonsan's purported statement displays an element of self-reflection as well as compassion and humility. But it also makes explicit a sense of vulnerability that the Bamanan felt in relation to the Maraka: "If the Maraka

FIGURE 1.8. Une armée Bambara en marche in Anne Raffenel, *Nouveau voyage dans le pays des negres, suivi d'études sur la colonie du Sénégal* [...], vol. 1 (Paris, 1856).

decide to confiscate my property, they will do the same thing to me that they have done to you," he says. Sonsan and Duba take advantage of the captives having been chained inside their compound to conspire with them to overthrow the Maraka chiefs of the village. Sonsan is able to untie the captives and arm them with muskets before luring the village chiefs and their supporters back to the compound, where they are ambushed. Having surprised the unsuspecting Maraka chiefs, Sonsan forces them to surrender and name the village Sonsanna. Naming the settlement after himself was a form of taking possession of a space where Sonsan had once arrived as a needy supplicant. It was then to become a Bamanan stronghold from which, Kouyate informs, three of his sons left to establish settlements farther west and expand the territorial claims of Kaarta.

## WHAT THE WARP AND WEFT OF FRAGMENTARY SOURCES SUGGEST ABOUT CLOTH IN EARLY KAARTA

Jeli Mamary Kouyate's oral tradition thus concludes with an account of an act of refusal and one of creation. The revolt organized and led by Sonsan Kulubali and Duba Sangare against their Maraka hosts (and, for some, their enslavers) became the founding gesture of a new political force in the region. The revolt of Bamanan farmers, blacksmiths, potters, and weavers opposed the control of Soninke and Fulbe Muslim clerics and merchants. This revolt did not imply a rejection of slavery as a social and economic norm but rather a refusal of this group to be enslaved. The soldiers and armies of the Bamanan Kaarta state that was formed through this act of rebellion went on to operate as mercenaries who trafficked in captive people and whose exploits could tip the balance of regional dynamics. For instance, Kaartan mercenaries allied with the Denyanke of Fuuta Tooro and French traders of Saint-Louis to help defeat the Muslim reformer Abdul Qadir Kan in 1806, ending an expansive period during which Kan had abolished slavery for Muslims, as will be discussed in chapter 3.

Across this chapter, fragmentary sources in various media, languages, and forms of expression have attested episodically, and from varying perspectives, to how Bamanan Kaarta emerged in a pivotal location of the Sahel while the region's traditional commercial ties with the Sahara and Mediterranean North Africa weakened under the expanding influence of Atlantic maritime networks. The emergence of this state suggests both the Sahelian economies' commensurability and entanglements with the evolving global economy of that period.

The use of violence and warfare as modes of state accumulation and domination has also been examined by historians of early modern Europe, by Atlantic historians, and by Africanists writing about states such as

Asante and Dahomey.⁵⁷ At Segu, the alleged piling of adorned bodies in the foundation of the defensive wall was a variant of state power carried out as "spiritual terror," a term used by historian Vincent Brown to describe the spectacular nature of punishments that planters in Jamaica visited upon enslaved people as a form of social control. In Jamaica, beheadings and the public display of skulls and mutilated bodies paralleled the use of ceremonial state violence in the western Sahel that sought to reinforce submission and obedience among people coerced to pay tribute in grain or goods for protection.⁵⁸ Across the eighteenth century, state or colonial actors in both the Americas and in West Africa used authoritarian exhibits of spectacular death to exert control over laborers, and their excesses occasionally provoked enslaved or subject groups to revolt against the violent domination. In the western Sahel, this violent repression within Sahelian states was not then yoked to the production of mercantilist or nascent-capitalist profit, which was the rationale in the plantation economics across the Atlantic. Instead, episodic violence in the Sahel served to reproduce and continually recalibrate shifting hierarchies of social status and power among individuals and communities competing for resources in evolving circumstances.

Historical references to cotton and weaving in Kaarta reflect the important role textiles have long played in the political economy of the Sahel. Cotton was an important crop for the agricultural communities of the Sahel, who used it to weave cloth for household consumption and to exchange in markets for horses, salt, iron, beads, cloth, and other commodities. Textiles woven from sheep's wool and, more rarely, silk also circulated. And indigo was a vine that grew wild or was in some places cultivated and processed to add value, aesthetic appeal, and social meaning to local textiles.

Cloth mediated important social relationships. In both oral and written sources, garments made from local cloth are mentioned as instruments of statecraft and of subterfuge between competing factions of elites in the seventeenth and eighteenth centuries. The murderous behavior of Dekoro, for instance, demonstrates the convergence of the economies of cloth and slave making with a ritualized public expression of state power exercised on captive people. Dekoro demonstrated authority through his control over the lives—or rather deaths—of captives subject to his will. To blindfold his victims was to emphasize his control over their fate to the villagers viewing the spectacle. To announce his wealth and further confirm his immense power, he adorned their bodies with a surplus of cloth luxuries he had access to through warfare and plunder. These cloths were then buried in the foundation along with the corpses of the captives he had ordered killed and dumped into a mass grave in an orgy of gratuitous waste.

Traditional oral sources mention cotton, cloth, and dress in ways that go beyond the summary descriptions of the state in written documents. Cloth appears at pivotal moments in Djeli Mamary Kouyate's narrative of Sonsan Kulubali: when his mother uses twelve measures of new cloth to save his life, when his skills as a weaver won him powerful new patrons and a place to live, and when jinn advise him to plant cotton to secure his "destiny and fame." These episodes convey the importance of both cotton and cotton cloth to the memory of Kaarta within oral tradition.

Kouyate's oral tradition articulates a counternarrative to that recorded in written sources that describe Bamanan communities as dangerous, threatening, or uncivilized. Instead, what emerges is a heroic avatar of social values, rooted in Bamanaya, that allow him to navigate the region's fault lines of linguistic, cultural, and religious difference to build wealth and power for himself and his followers. Significantly, oral sources also convey forms of collaboration between individuals and communities otherwise thought of in ethnographic or nationalist frameworks as distinct, such as the union of the Bamanan Sonsan Kulubali and the Fulbe Duba Sangare. Even more suggestive are the allusions to the spiritual cooperation between Maraka jinn and Bamanan farmers such as Sonsan.

Technical collaboration between skilled artisans—weavers, dyers, tailors, embroiderers—is revealed in a rare cotton garment from the period stored in a French museum. The kusaaba, or khoussab, was constructed to convey the status and worldliness of an elite Sahelian wearer who, by donning the garment, also affiliated themselves to the fame of Segu, the town for which it was named. Its embroidery of bright red, yellow, and green silken threads displays patterns and symbols also found on the walls of buildings in the commercial border town of Walata and also in the designs of jewelry created by local silversmiths. The kusaaba is also thus an artifact of aesthetic diplomacy, cultural convergence, and commerce created within the Sahelian context that, sometime in the early nineteenth century, also came to represent new cultural contact with the Atlantic.

The following chapters focus on how cloth economies in other parts of western Africa converged with an expanding and evolving global commerce through the mid-nineteenth century. But they also show that the ability to deftly navigate social difference was a skill characteristic of many Africans who experienced social mobility in this period, whether gradually over time or through a sudden political upheaval, of which there were many, as the region increasingly accessed global goods through Atlantic connections.

# 2 ~ Cotton Cloth in Western Africa

*Barafulas, Bafetas, and Piezas de India*

MORE THAN a century before Bamana Kaarta emerged as a force in the western Sahel, imperial Songhay and imperial Mali dominated the region. The rulers of Mali and Portugal were in communication from as early as the sixteenth century. In 1534, the Mali *mansa* (king of kings) Mamadou II sent messages to the Portuguese king Joao III through Portuguese traders on the Gambia River seeking Portugal's assistance in turning back incursions of Fulbe and Tukulor armies led by Koli Tengela at Fuuta Tooro into the fertile floodplain of the middle Senegal River valley. Tengela's advances threatened to usurp Mali's control over the gold mines at Bambuk, a region located roughly between their respective centers of power.[1]

Since its inception, Mali's influence had at times expanded through military conquest but more substantively through the perambulations of its entrepreneurs, Mande-speaking blacksmiths, and scholar-merchants. They settled in villages and towns throughout the region southwest of the Niger River and its tributaries, and south as far as Sierra Leone on the Atlantic coast.[2] Their networks extended clerical education and trans-Saharan commerce trade in gold while also establishing the Manden language as a lingua franca and Manden culture as a hegemonic force in many communities.[3] Yet Mamadou II's diplomatic message suggests the fragility of Mali's hold over a region key to its strength.

The Portuguese responded by sending an ambassador, Pero Fernandes, to the capital of Mali to offer to conduct diplomacy between Mamadou II and Koli Tengela that might defuse tensions.[4] The Portuguese had long known of Mali, if not of this ruler, as an important supplier of the gold that trans-Saharan caravans had long transported to Mediterranean markets. Even as the 1530s were a period in which Portuguese traders obtained larger quantities of gold farther south through their commercial fort at Elmina on the Gold Coast, it is not surprising that Portugal also wanted to maintain diplomatic relations with this important older source of the precious metal in the Sahel.[5] Little else is known about Fernandes's actual visit to the capital of Mali, as it was mentioned only by the sixteenth-century historian Joao de Barros. If it did occur, the visit would have been a rare instance of a European traveling so far into the Sahel in this early period. In any event, such a diplomatic exchange also demonstrates how the politics and economy of the Sahel shaped the early development of Atlantic commerce in western Africa. Linkages between the Sahelian interior and Atlantic coast remained significant as Atlantic commerce expanded exponentially through the turn of the eighteenth century.

This chapter pulls back from the experience of Bamana Kaarta to show how several parts of western Africa from the Sahel to the banks of the Gambia River and from coastal Saint-Louis south to the coastal rivers of Guinea had become enmeshed in an expanding global textile trade by the late seventeenth and eighteenth centuries. By then, British and French mercantile companies had largely replaced the Portuguese in the region, and the primary focus of most Atlantic trade had shifted from gold to purchasing enslaved labor wanted for plantation colonies in the Americas. The commercial exchange of cotton cloth, however, was continuous throughout both eras and, if anything, became more important over time. I argue, on the one hand, that the region's already extensive production and exchange of cloth helped to forge links with expanding maritime trade networks in the seventeenth century in response to increased demands for enslaved labor in the Americas. Beyond their commercial exchange value, however, both local and imported textiles found their way into domestic settings and onto people's bodies, where they served to demarcate hierarchies of social status and identification in African communities. But the strength in western Africa of commodity currencies like cloth also meant the region was increasingly marginalized from global networks driven by the search for and accumulation of gold and silver specie.[6]

Beyond that, as Atlantic commerce intensified, this period was marked by a growing Euro-Atlantic emphasis on abstraction, quantification, administrative control, systematization, and acceptance of dehumanizing violence. This combination of factors began to powerfully shape early modern ideas about Africa, slavery, and slavery's association with "blackness." References to consumption and dress in a range of archival, visual, and material sources, however, suggest also that other narratives of African self-making incubated within the violence and inequality endemic to an economy of slave trading. In contending with archival fragments, this chapter shows that African self-making was rooted in the region's histories of mobility, creativity, and tolerance for cultural and religious pluralism.

In the first section of the chapter, I examine the spaces of market towns in Senegambia connected to not only Bamana Kaarta but the Portuguese islands of Cape Verde, where mobile merchants and traders from a variety of backgrounds interacted. Cloth emerged as a key commodity currency as well as a crucial symbolic marker of social distinction. Filtering into the region and coming up against older approaches to the accommodation of difference that characterized these spaces were more rigid European hierarchies of difference, particularly related to race. First Portuguese and then French and British interests, while recognizing and capitalizing on the regional trading value of cloth, pursued its trade to leverage their ability to purchase other commodities, including enslaved African labor. In the second section of the chapter, I chronicle how African-made textiles anchored European intermediaries in the regional cloth economy and connected it to the Atlantic economy; then, in the third section, I examine how the European tendency toward abstraction, quantification, and commodification produced fundamentally different notions of race and slavery to those already present in western Africa. From there, moving north to the Senegal River valley and the kingdom of Waalo, I examine the interactions of Maram Njaay, the senior wife of the *brak* (king) of Waalo, Ber Caaka, with French merchant Michel Jajolet de La Courbe in the 1680s, revealing women's active role in cloth production and trading as well as how their activity and agency shaped La Courbe's outlook on racial difference. I end the chapter with a discussion of the efforts of western African merchants and leaders to resist European attempts to establish monopolies on regional trade. Africans, already accustomed to an atmosphere of cultural pluralism, wanted to be free to choose their trading partners from among Europeans as well as other communities.

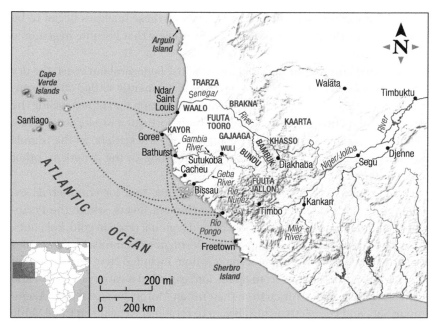

MAP 2.1. Map of the region, including links with the Cape Verde islands. Map by Matt Johnson at Johnson Cartographic.

## MOBILITY, CURRENCY, AND SPACES OF CORRELATION

From the late fifteenth through the early eighteenth century, economies of cloth were beginning to expand ties between western African communities and global trade networks. Market centers along the Senegambian coast and inland to the Kaarta Sahel linked up with the Atlantic trade running through the Cape Verde islands offshore from the West African mainland. These networks drew together a rich diversity of participants, including Portuguese New Christian and Luso-African merchants, Maninka and Fulbe villagers, and *djula* traders with connections as far away as the Niger River. They included British and French merchants as well as Portuguese based on Cape Verde, whose trade activities extended to markets in North Africa, Europe, the Americas, India, and the Indonesian archipelago. Across these spaces, cloth textiles had both material value as a commodity currency linking western Africa to the global market and symbolic value as key markers of social distinctions. As sartorial expressions changed from place to place across different local spaces of correlation, textiles signaled African self-making through communal belonging, local political economy, and the priorities of local elites. Mobility and flexibility within these spaces was

*Cotton Cloth in Western Africa* ~ 57

critical for accommodating difference, even as these qualities began to be confronted by the Portuguese Catholic worldview that became hegemonic on Cape Verde.

Located almost four hundred miles off the Senegambian coast, the dry and unpopulated rocky islands began to be permanently settled after Portugal claimed them in 1455 for use as a watering station for ships traveling the Atlantic. New Christian emigrants from both Portugal and Morocco were a significant presence among the population of early settlers, as the islands became a stopover for Portuguese ships traveling to the Americas, other parts of Africa, or Asia.

The islands quickly became a staging area, too, for commercial exchanges in ports along the Senegal and Gambia Rivers, where the Portuguese settlers tapped into a well-developed regional trade in gold, kola nuts, leather, textiles, and other goods. The Portuguese commissioned textiles from guilds of Jewish weavers, some of whom included New Christians and Sephardic Jewish refugees from Spain, and exported a variety of cotton and woolen cloths to West Africa from their urban Moroccan enclaves at Azemmour, Safi, and Fez.[7] Settlers also began to establish weaving on Cape Verde by relying on imported enslaved laborers from among Wolof, Maninka, and Banyun communities locally renowned for the quality of their textiles. Captive artisans farmed on plantations of cotton and indigo and wove textiles that the islands' merchants sold in coast African markets. Slave-produced cotton textiles on Cape Verde embedded themselves as a regional commodity whose exchange animated the larger transatlantic commerce in enslaved African laborers. They brought knowledge of weaving, spinning, and dyeing textiles from the mainland, working on African-made looms to produce narrow strips of cloth that were sewn together in the traditional manner to create larger pieces. Significantly, they produced dark indigo-dyed cottons known as *panos pretos* that were already in wide circulation on the mainland and which were similar to indigo-dyed *baftas* that began to be imported from India in the sixteenth century.[8]

Beyond this appeal to already-established consumer tastes, weavers on Cape Verde combined methods and aesthetic influences to create loom-patterned textiles that established new tastes. The island of Sao Tiago on Cape Verde became associated with the most highly prized cotton textiles: *panos de terra,* which were plain white or dyed a single color, or *panos de obra,* so-called and more expensive because of the great skill that went into producing their distinctive loom-patterned designs.[9] They were highly esteemed by consumers on the African mainland, who not only incorporated them into their prestige and ceremonial attire, but also used them as forms

FIGURE 2.1. "Pano de terra / pano d'obra from Cape Verde." Image courtesy of Instituto do Património Cultural—Museu Etnográfico da Praia, Cape Verde.

of bridewealth and currency.[10] The distinctive loom-patterned textile designs on panos de obra, for instance, show similarity to patterns on Alentejo textiles woven in Moroccan workshops and suggest both continuity and innovation of weaving traditions between Cape Verde and the North African Maghreb (see figure 2.1).[11]

By the late fifteenth century, Portuguese and Cape Verdean merchants had developed a multisided relay trade of goods between the Cape Verde islands and several western African ports. Salt or cloths woven on Cape Verde were transported to a network of ports such as Gorée, Kassang, Cacheu, Bissau, Rio Nunez, Rio Pongo, and Sierra Leone. They were exchanged in these ports for gold, ivory, or kola nuts. These goods were then transported to Senegalese coastal enclaves such as Rufisque and Portudal, where they were used to purchase other commodities, including enslaved people who might be transported to labor on Cape Verde or as far away as the Americas, where they were resold.[12]

African rulers facilitated these exchanges by offering protection to merchants who settled in coastal towns such as Rufisque, Portudal, and Cacheu and solidified their local ties through marriage to African women, who, via these unions, grew substantial wealth that stayed within their matrilineage. These merchants were known in Portuguese as *lançados*, or as *tungumas* in the Cape Verdean Kriol that had emerged by the sixteenth century. They were often the descendants of Portuguese men and African women.[13] Market centers from Kassang—the Mande town in Wuuli, on the north bank of the Gambia River and an outpost of the Mali Empire—to Gajaaga or Bamana Kaarta were spaces where people of contrasting backgrounds, worldviews, and value systems converged through the exchange of particular goods desired by both parties. The constitution of these spaces developed as a result of the mobility of goods and people over the course of the sixteenth and seventeenth centuries. Several coastal and riverine villages from Senegambia to Sierra Leone were home to increasingly linguistically, culturally, and

*Cotton Cloth in Western Africa* ~ 59

phenotypically mixed populations, some of whom maintained at least a notional affiliation with Cape Verde over many generations. This effectively made coastal western Africa an early site of "creole society" in an expanding Atlantic world that was beginning to feature multiple variations of them.[14]

By hosting these foreign merchants, rulers of coastal towns embedded themselves in commercial networks across four continents. New Christians especially had personal and commercial relations with family and partners in locales as far removed as Amsterdam in the Netherlands; Lima, Peru; and Goa, in southwestern India.[15] New Christian Manuel Bautista Perez drew on familial ties through an uncle, Diogo Rodrigues de Lisboa, who had relatives based in the Portuguese outpost of Goa who dealt in Indian cotton cloth, beads and spices. Between 1613 and 1618, Bautista organized the delivery of over fifty types of cloth to the port of Cacheu, with cottons from India comprising over half those trade goods.[16]

Traders like Rodrigues would have worked with Luso-African partners, important commercial intermediaries living in coastal towns. Luso-Africans made impressive contributions to the cultural and material landscape of the towns they occupied, including the unique architectural style of their homes and houses of worship and the material objects that filled these spaces.[17] Luso-Africans were multilingual and often culturally heterogeneous. Individuals had affiliations with multiple social networks, and their perceived identity and status might change as they moved from place to place or as time passed.

This followed a wider historical pattern in West Africa in which flexibility facilitated mobility and increased opportunity for people—such as the Mande blacksmiths who settled across the region between the Senegal River valley and coastal Guinea between the thirteenth and fifteen centuries or the Fulbe pastoralists who similarly settled among Bamana-speaking farming communities in the Wasulu region to form their own distinct traditions.[18]

Many western African coastal ports were deeply engaged with Atlantic Ocean and Indian Ocean trade networks—as evidenced by the architecture, material culture, diverse backgrounds, and sartorial styles of their inhabitants. For instance, at least one dedicated synagogue building in coastal Portudal was constructed in a local vernacular Portuguese style.[19] This structure added to the varied landscape of mosques, churches, sacred groves, and shrines that could be found in towns and villages through the coastal region south of the Gambia River. Already by 1701 at Bissau, there was both a small church and a convent building. Its congregation, according to André Brue, then director of the Senegal Company, consisted of "about one hundred fifty negro men and women, who call themselves Portuguese, though they are

FIGURE 2.2. "Habits des femmes de Kazegut / Clothing of the Women in Kazegut" in Jean-Baptiste Léonard Durand, *Voyage au Sénégal* [...] (Paris: Chez Henri Agasse, 1802). Image courtesy of the John Carter Brown Library, Brown University, Providence, RI.

quite of black complexion."[20] His evident confusion notwithstanding, what Brue observed about local parlance suggests that African discourses of race and ethnicity on the coast, as in the Sahelian interior, were less defined by phenotype than by lineage, religious affiliation, language, and culture.

Residents incorporated elements of Portuguese and Cape Verdean culture into local contexts. Unique foreign-influenced structures could be found even in villages with fewer Christians, such as on the nearby Bijagos Islands, where André Brue had been led by an elderly, gray-bearded chief to see a church, complete with chapel, benches, and a thirty-pound bell imported from Europe. The chief was not himself a Christian but had had the chapel built to attract European visitors to undermine Portuguese commercial dominance there.[21]

Economies of cotton growing, cloth making, and exchange sustained commercial linkages between the Cape Verde islands and the mainland during the seventeenth century. The regularity with which Cape Verdean merchants visited ports on the Gambia River, such as Kassang, was not incidental to this fact. At Wuuli, Africans not only bought Cape Verdean cloth but also exchanged local cloth for salt, kola, iron bars, brass basins, and other goods. The Wuuli region was a major producer of cotton, and it was also renowned for its cloth production,[22] which included *fataro,* a locally woven cloth. Farming cotton and making cloth were both labor intensive, requiring seasonal planning and organization at different stages. It was a process that favored those with sufficient social and material capital to attract and retain large groups of dependents to grow cotton and to weave it. In Wuuli, these actors included not only the mansa, or ruler, but lineage elders of villages and djula traders settled there whose networks transported enslaved people and circulated a range of other commodities across the vast region. Djula traders frequently viewed cotton farming and cotton weaving as central to their strategy of building larger and stronger communities, as cotton cloth was exchangeable for many other goods and could also be accumulated and stored over time to be used to make larger investments.[23]

Historian Al-Bakri first documented the use of locally made cotton cloth strips as currencies in two polities straddling both sides of the Senegal River in the Fuuta Tooro region in the eleventh century, noting that people also used sorghum, salt, and copper rings for the same purpose.[24] By the seventeenth century, the region was already a mature multicurrency environment where high-demand commodities such as iron bars, salt, cowrie shells, and gold dust as forms of standardized exchangeable value served to integrate commercial systems across the region. From the Sahara and Sahel to the tropical forest, they carried value dependent on the location and context. In the seventeenth century, as gold and silver from new sources in the Americas flowed into the coffers of European mercantile companies, who then spent some of it in India in exchange for cloth and spices, the widespread use of cloth currencies in the Senegambia was especially consequential in linking the region to a global maritime economy. It was so prevalent in the seventeenth century that the accounting books of slave trader Bautista showed enslaved people and other goods in mainland West Africa as purchased with locally produced cotton cloth money they called *panos,* possibly adapting the term from a similar one in local usage.[25] Further, Bautista incorporated the term into an early example of double-entry bookkeeping to make sense of complex transactions in different parts of the world; between 1613 and 1617, he used cloth "panos" as a unit of account for purchases of enslaved people in Guinea-Bissau and gold-backed currency for their sale in Lima, Peru.[26]

On the African mainland, Cape Verdean cloths served a variety of functions that went beyond their use for the compensation of labor or as exchangeable currency for other goods such as salt, rice, and game animals. For instance, cloths formed part of a dowry to codify marriage arrangements between two families or communities. They were also used as burial shrouds, and even here served as a marker of social distinctions, an average person served by perhaps a single cloth, whereas those of great wealth or authority accumulated as many as one hundred or more cloths for their interment, thus ushering them into death with the same prestige they enjoyed in life. Indian cottons, along with European linen and woolen textiles flowing into Atlantic ports in western Africa during this period, expanded the novelty and variety of cloth goods available to local consumers for such purposes, however they ultimately acquired them.

In these coastal port towns, foreign objects could be appropriated and repurposed into a local context, and local and foreign notions of prestige occasionally converged around particular materials or objects, such as felted black top hats. At Kassang, the Luso-African trader André Donelha witnessed the process of material appropriation when he encountered a powerful *satigi* (governor) sitting in an open-air mosque accompanied by many marabouts engaged in prayer.[27] The satigi sent a servant to tell the Cape Verdean visitor that he should sell the pants he wore—a pair of bulbous knee-length breeches made of crimson silk of the style common in seventeenth-century Portugal—because the satigi wanted to have his tailors use them to make a covering for his horse. That the satigi was concerned about embellishing his horse shows that it was an important symbol of his elevated status. The distinctiveness and attractiveness of a covering of crimson silk on the satigi's horse would have lent additional credibility and prestige to the authority he already enjoyed as a mediator of disputes.

The satigi lived in a home that also served as a communal court. It was architecturally distinct from others in Kassang because it was a two-story structure built in a square shape, rather than round, with wooden benches around the white-plastered walls of the building's perimeter.[28] On the day Donelha visited, he was allowed to witness the satigi conducting trials in the building, listening to accusers and defendants before rendering a decision. After that, the satigi led Donelha out of the building down a narrow path and through a door that opened into a courtyard where a few more two-story structures stood.[29] Mark finds the existence of these two-story structures evidence of the influence of Luso-African architectural styles in trading centers like Kassang,[30] but just as importantly, they indicated the wealth and ambition of the town's elite. In the courtyard, a large carved wooden chest from India sat against a wall covered with a locally woven and embroidered textile onto which were nailed the hides of lion and crocodile game killed by local hunters. Standing next to the chest, the satigi offered Donelha several gifts of local manufacture, including a spear with a brass blade, a knife with a leather sheath, a belt made of donkey skin, and two pieces of a fine variety of local cloth.[31] The satigi and Donelha conjoined multiple worlds through these exchanges in that courtyard: the worlds of Cape Verde, Portugal, and Asia combined with those of Islamic West Africa, Mande blacksmiths, hunters, weavers, and other artisans.

At their most basic level, of course, these textiles provided clothing for people, which meant that once worn, at least temporarily, they ceased to function as exchange currency. Instead, they transferred value to the wearer in the form of social currency. Many of the "soft currencies" that Africans used for commercial purposes in this period had this dual quality of exchangeable value and practical object. Cotton textiles, like glass and ceramic beads, cowrie shells, silver *pataque* coins from Italy or Germany, and iron bars and copper rods, were variously accepted in different western African markets. But at some point each passed out of circulation to be repurposed as clothing or adornment for the body or a weapon carried on the bodies of soldiers.[32]

Iron bars, supporting an industry of African blacksmithing, passed out of circulation when repurposed into farming tools or weapons. This means that the commodities African merchants acquired in exchange for their goods could produce value in multiple forms for multiple people over time, as both currency and usable object, and it is thus understandable how these exchanges must have been seen as beneficial, even advantageous, within the region itself.

But as these objects aged, their exchange value diminished over time until eventually they needed to be replaced altogether. The diminishing "purchasing power" of African commodity currencies marked a major contrast with currencies used in other parts of the Euro-Atlantic and the Indian Ocean perimeters, which were then flooded with an abundance of silver and gold mined by slave labor in the Iberian Americas.[33] These currencies, which were exchangeable in at least three of the four continents connected by maritime trade, retained their value across space and over time. It was as though the connection between European and African merchants made possible by the commensurability of their respective currency systems, oddly, also seemed to solidify the discontinuity of African economic currency systems from those of its global trading partners in this early period. Inequalities in the economic value of the currency acceptable in Africa over time and the accumulation of capital afforded to European merchant companies and slaveholders from the surpluses produced by enslaved labor in the Americas structured African Atlantic networks in lasting ways.[34]

Nonetheless, measures of cloth were a recognized standard across linguistically and culturally heterogeneous western Africa, but the value of cloth and textiles was also symbolic, and often both material and symbolic simultaneously. In the early seventeenth century, the English merchant Richard Jobson used the local cloth currency to negotiate with djula trader Buckor Sano, who arrived ceremoniously attired in his "best clothes" accompanied by musicians and an entourage of forty people that soon attracted a crowd of over two hundred. Arriving with an entourage was itself another assertion of power in that it must have conveyed a sense of clout by taking up space, increasing the number of witnesses and participants to the exchange, and telegraphing the abundant resources the djula merchant might potentially command. The two merchants negotiated over a couple of days, with Jobson inviting Sano and a few others to spend the night aboard Jobson's vessel docked on the river. After Jobson had provided an English gown for Sano to cover his sleeping body, Sano wrapped the garment about himself as he went ashore "in a manner of state" to announce to his followers how trade was to proceed. Sano chose a local cloth, possibly fataro, but Jobson referred to the textiles as "Negroes clothes,"[35] which would be the measure that determined how much bay salt Sano received in exchange.[36]

In the space in which these two strangers came to at least a temporary alliance for trading purposes, textiles were embedded with meaning on several levels. First, it seemed that Sano's wearing of the gown over his own distinguished garment was meant to publicly demonstrate to those assembled his satisfaction with this trading partner and set the stage for the actual bargaining and exchanges to proceed. Sano's choice of local cotton textiles as the "the staple commoditie to pitch the price upon, to value other things by," as Jobson describes it, suggested that Sano had an abundance of it with which to trade and that its exchange value was more advantageous to him than any other similar commodity to which he had access.

Whether on the coast or at internal crossroads, people brought together ideas, material goods, and practices whose radical combination sometimes suggested new social affiliations, changing power dynamics, or the recapitulation of established ones. Along with settlements of Mande-speaking djula and farmers, there were predominantly Fulbe-speaking villages that tended cattle but also engaged in cotton agriculture that fed into its economy. In the early eighteenth century, Francis Moore, merchant and factor for the English Royal Africa Company, observed of the Fulbe villagers along the Gambia that "they are very particular about dress, and never wear any other than white cotton clothes, which they make themselves."[37] The observation suggests this was a clerical community, as white cotton garments were usually associated with Muslim clerics and scholars. Moore's comment indicates how dress signaled communal belonging and the political economy of a particular village or community in ways that were quite specific.

As these sartorial expressions changed from place to place, they suggested the priorities of the local elites and the general disposition of other residents. At Ghinala, a major Biafada market town near Bissau on the Guinea coast, in the eighteenth century, Brue described a chief dressed all in black with a mixture of local and Portuguese-style garments, including a black cloth wrapper underneath a black Portuguese-style tailored coat, with black stockings, pumps, and a tall black hat. This assemblage likely reflected the town's close affiliation with the Portuguese and Luso-African merchants who readily purchased quantities of abundantly available kola nuts, which carried a mild stimulant for profitable resale in other African ports.[38]

In the late sixteenth century, André Almada noted the distinctive appearance of Luso-African *tangama* merchants, both men and women, who could be found traveling from Gambia south to Sierra Leone. He also observed the importance of their social ties within the local African host society: "Among these blacks, there are many who can speak our Portuguese language. They dress as we do, as do many black women of the advanced kind, known as *tangomas* [*tungumas*], because they serve the adventurers who go to those parts. These blacks, men and women, go with the adventurers from one river to another and to Santiago Island and other places. But our people do not take them without first obtaining permission from their fathers or their uncles."[39]

The regular mobility of merchants and villagers during this period engendered cultural flexibility on the part of those on the move and of communities receiving new settlers. But it is also evident in these early centuries of Atlantic trade that older regional patterns of accommodating difference were increasingly confronted with a less flexible Portuguese Catholic approach to difference that was hegemonic on Cape Verde as well as among Luso-Africans in coastal towns on the mainland. The story of André Donelha and Gaspar Vaz demonstrates the complex interplay between rigid Portuguese Catholic approaches to difference and the flexible, and indeed strategic, western African approach, and how textiles figured into both.

Donelha was born on Cape Verde, where he occupied an elevated social position but one still circumscribed from the highest levels within the Catholic social order of the island's society because, as a "mulatto" and a "gentile," he lacked purity of blood.[40] Little is known about his West African ancestry or whether he may have known or had relations with any of his mother's West African family or village. His writings portray the world through the lens of a sixteenth-century, Portuguese-speaking Catholic, viewing non-Christians in general, and Muslims in particular, as "infidels." Donelha, who traveled many times to the African mainland in the late sixteenth century, famously wrote about his visit to Kassang,[41] where he met a young Mandinka man whom he had known in Cape Verde as enslaved to one of his neighbors, a local tailor.[42] Baptized and known by his Christian name, Gaspar Vaz, the man had gained a reputation as a "good tailor and able buttonier" in Santiago before being emancipated and returning to Wuuli.[43]

Donelha expressed disappointment to encounter Vaz "dressed in a Mandinga smock, with amulets of his fetishes around his neck"[44] and asked whether this attire indicated that Vaz had renounced Catholicism. Whatever the circumstances of his enslavement in Cape Verde, in Kassang, Vaz was not a slave but the nephew of an elite elder man, the satigi discussed previously. Vaz denied being Muslim to Donelha, however, and professed instead to be an ardent Catholic.[45] He averred that he was dressed in a local-style garment only because of his relationship to his wealthy and powerful uncle from whom he might inherit wealth. To prove himself to Donelha, Vaz "took off his smock, beneath which he wore a doublet and shirt in our fashion, and from around his neck drew out a rosary of Our Lady—'every day I commend myself to God and the Virgin Our Lady by means of this rosary. And if I do not die, but come to inherit the estate of my uncle, I will see to it that some slaves are sent to Santiago, and when I have found a ship to take me I will go to live in that island and die among Christians.'"[46]

This vivid account written by one Luso-African about another shows the contingent nature of belonging in a coastal port town but also suggests that another frontier had emerged: one that defined linguistic, religious, and cultural difference in more absolute terms. Despite its striking details, it is difficult to take Donelha's description of this encounter completely at face value given the quite open hostility he expressed toward Muslims, which makes him seem predisposed to embrace such a story and to be incurious about alternate explanations. Donelha's antipathy toward Muslims may have been a device to endear himself to elite Portuguese readers, by whom he wanted to be accepted and for whom his account was written. In a similar vein, Vaz, who likely spoke Maninka as well as Kriolu, evidently tried to appeal to Donelha by displaying his familiarity with the Catholic mores of Cape Verde, and the level of concern expressed by Donelha suggested that he was correct to do so.

Slave owners on Cape Verde occasionally manumitted enslaved persons as an inducement for others to cooperate with the given labor regime in the possibility of eventually winning such relief, although the circumstances of Vaz's experience are unknown.[47] Whatever they were, it is not clear what issues might motivate someone to forsake inheriting significant wealth and social status from a family member in order to flee to the place

*Cotton Cloth in Western Africa*

of their former enslavement where they were likely to remain marginal to the dominant society. It is possible that Vaz concocted this story to flatter Donelha, who was a commercial partner, and in that sense, his layered garments might have been part of a routine strategy used to appeal to visiting merchants—thus mobilizing his knowledge of Cape Verde as a point of connection with potential clients.

During the visit, Vaz guided Donelha around Kassang, and helped him obtain the local price for goods, which was lower than that demanded of other foreign traders, for which Donelha expressed particular appreciation. Vaz's clothing reflected multiple allegiances and the nimbleness with which one might have negotiated the landscape of Kassang and the complex social dynamics around enslavement, religious affiliation, and belonging that were unfolding in the circulation of people between Cape Verde and settlements on the Gambia River in the early seventeenth century.[48] If Mande and other Africans could be captured into forced labor on Cape Verde or sold into the expanding Atlantic slave trade, this episode suggests some of the varied ways that these Africans constructed and navigated the starkly different social worlds that converged as part of that political economy.

### DEEP INDIGO: *BARAFULAS, BAFETAS,* AND *GUINEES*

From the late seventeenth century, global integration of western African economies was further advanced by French, British, and Dutch mercantile interests. Europeans adapted and procured western African currency commodities, especially varieties of cloth, that had high value either at other African trading ports or in markets outside of Africa. The high value of these cloths allowed merchants to ultimately acquire other valued goods, including gum resin and enslaved human labor, and thus the priorities of western African currency commodities affected the components of global trade networks, for instance, indigo plantations in the French Caribbean.

African-made textiles helped to anchor European participation as intermediaries in a regional cloth economy as vessels making several stops in African ports purchased textiles in one port that they resold in another. They were important to French East India Company director André Brue, who perhaps went furthest in this early period to pursue an expansion of the French presence in the Senegal River valley. Brue oversaw the construction of armed trading outposts Fort Saint Joseph on the upper Senegal and Fort Saint Pierre on the Faleme branch near the gold mines of Bambuk of the Sahelian interior—as well as conflicts with Holland and Britain for control of portions of the coastline.[49] He reported to company directors in 1702 that the regional carrying trade in locally made cloths along the Senegal River was "an important business to develop, as much for the cost advantages it gives us in the gum trade as for that of captives in Bissau."[50]

Trading port towns along the Gambia River such as Kassang, Borsalo, and Kantor sold a variety of local textiles to English and other European merchants, who carried them south to Sierra Leone, Sherbro, and the Gold Coast, where they were exchanged for slaves, ivory, or gold.[51] The French Huguenot slave trader Jean Barbot noted in the late seventeenth century that the merchants of coastal Senegal sold an "immense quantity" of locally made cloths to Portuguese, English, and Dutch merchants, who then in turn did a "considerable traffic" in trading them all along the West African coast. He complained that the French were disadvantaged because they lacked sufficient trading stations in the region.

Olfert Dapper reported that the most common cloths traded in western Africa were called *panos sake, bantans,* and *barafulas,* a remarkable claim, because each of these cloths had unique features that required more labor than plain white cotton, which also circulated.[52] The panos sake were made on a white background with eight bands of "couleur de feu" (color of

FIGURE 2.3. "Woman in coastal Senegal" (Negresse de la cote du Senegal) in Jacques Grasset de Saint-Sauveur and Sylvain Maréchal, *Costumes civils actuels de tous les peuples connus,* vol. 4. (Paris: Chez Pavard, 1788). Image courtesy of the John Carter Brown Library. Brown University, Providence, RI.

fire), presumably of bright red or yellow thread. Bantan cloths were made of threads that combined cotton with the fibers of the silk cotton tree, producing a fine weave comparable to silk.[53] And barafulas were indigo-dyed cotton cloths that came in a variety of hues.

Of these cloths, the barafulas were the most significant, not only because of their high value as currency when dyed to a dark indigo color but also because of how their circulation fed into overseas markets.[54] The Manden-language term translates loosely as "the work of Fula," the name itself signaling a complex cultural interplay between Fulbe and Manden populations. Barafulas, known in Fulbe as *soro* and in Soninke as *tama*, were a variant of dark indigo-dyed cloths traded across the Sahel to the coasts that also appeared in European account books as panos pretos or *toiles noires*.[55] Brue notes that French traders could purchase fifteen hundred to two thousand finished toiles noires each year at ports in the lower Senegal River in a good year "when the cotton bushes are not destroyed by locusts" and twice that amount, between three and four thousand cloths at upper river ports[56] in the Soninke Gajaaga region. It was through similar exchanges between African and European merchants at coastal trading posts that quantities of this black cloth traveled from around western Africa to other parts of the coast as far afield as Loango in contemporary Brazzaville in Congo, where a Dutch trader in the seventeenth century used some to buy a piece of ivory that weighed eighty-eight pounds.[57]

Figure 2.4 shows a cotton garment composed of narrow strips of loom-woven cotton sewn together side by side then dipped in a dye pit to produce a resist-dye pattern. It was purchased on the Atlantic coast near contemporary Benin by a German merchant, but it is believed to have been manufactured in the Sahelian interior—plausible because the networks of Mande djula traders circulated such goods over long distances.

Both barafulas and panos, which could be plain or dyed, also traveled on ships during the seventeenth century from Cacheu in Guinea-Bissau to Cartagena and Lima in New Spain, where they were used to settle debts and converted into gold-backed currency.[58] Green has pointed out that at least some of this cloth was likely traded by small numbers of free African and Luso-African traders who traveled aboard European ships. While some of the cloth later appeared on probate records of white colonists, some may have been consumed by free and enslaved Africans in those Iberian American ports.[59]

This shows that the output of weavers and dyers across western Africa fed into networks of commerce that carried them far afield as they integrated into a globalizing economy of the seventeenth century. These African

FIGURE 2.4. "Indigo cotton garment, purchased near border between Togo and the Republic of Benin before 1659." Weickmann Collection, Museum Ulm, Germany.

cloths joined a flow of indigo along maritime routes between the continents in the form of indigo-dyed cloths from India and indigo dyestuffs produced on Caribbean slave plantations for the European textile industry.[60] The number of "indigoterie" (indigo works) rapidly increased on several French Caribbean islands in the late seventeenth century until there were over two thousand such operations on Saint-Domingue in 1730, their output in great demand and producing an even greater profit than sugar.[61] The cultivation of indigo plants to make dye fed an expanding European textile industry as a source of new and better dyes and for experimentation with color fasteners and textile printing methods.[62]

At Saint-Louis, their trading post near the desert's edge, the French prioritized commerce in gum resin harvested from nearby acacia trees, which was highly valued for use as a mordant or color fastener for fabric dyes, as a tanning agent for leather, as a thickener for paint, and other purposes.[63] Even more than their use of African textiles, the French came to rely on indigo-dyed cottons from India to purchase resin from the Berber-Arab merchants who accepted them as comparable to local varieties of indigo cloths used for the same purpose.[64] Historians have stressed the importance

*Cotton Cloth in Western Africa* ~ 71

of the gum trade at Senegal, its value being greater than the trade in enslaved people in the late seventeenth century, and argued that the high profits to be made from selling it in Europe lay behind the "gum wars" a series of violent conflicts between France, Britain, and Holland for control of African coastal trading posts leading up to the Seven Years' War in 1754. During this period, indigo dyestuffs from the Caribbean and gum resin from western Africa were two commodities that helped to produce what Jutta Wimmler has called the "color revolution" in European textile making, which transformed the variety, range, and cost of textiles to average consumers in Europe.[65]

The combined importance of the gum trade to textile manufacturers in Europe and the already-established prestige and demand for indigo-dyed cottons in western Africa helps to explain the significance of Indian-made indigo cottons for Europeans trading in Africa at a critical historical conjuncture. Holland, Britain, and France each followed the Portuguese in establishing seaborne trade with Asia, initiating a relative flood of India-made cottons and Chinese- and Turkish-made silks into European markets, where they had an ever-increasing impact on consumer tastes, material culture practices, technology, and production. Indian cottons were popular in both Europe and Africa because of their relatively low costs, bright colors and patterns, and their colorfastness that allowed them to retain their color after several washings.[66] Indian indigo cotton cloths were also popular with consumers in the Netherlands, where their sales quadrupled during the fifteen-year period between 1674 and 1689, which suggests they shared an appreciation for the qualities of these textiles with consumers in western Africa.[67] To protect their respective textile industries, both Britain and France imposed laws to ban or limit the circulation of these Indian cottons but encouraged the reexport of these textiles to Africa, particularly for their use in purchasing gum resin and captive labor.[68]

Deep indigo-dyed cottons from India were traded under a variety of names—*bafetas, salampores,* or *guinees,* a kind of French marketing term for a type of cloth produced on the southern Coromandel coast of India, where they established a trading factory at Pondicherry in 1674, the same year that Nasir al-Din's death in western Africa removed a bitter opponent of French commercial activity there. The Indian indigo cotton cloths that came to be called *guinees* were the nearest approximation to the western African *barafula* or soro cotton textiles that the nomadic Berber-Arab merchants otherwise acquired from the settled agricultural villages south of the Senegal River. In western Africa, the brightness and colorfastness of the Indian cotton varieties were preferable to European-made versions, which at the time were not dyed to the same degree of brightness and were woven of cotton-linen blends rather than of all cotton.[69] Berber-Arab Moors enjoyed an advantage in controlling most of the southern Sahara's acacia trees—which secreted gum resin during the seasonally hot, dry Harmattan winds—by trading the resin coveted by the French for the prized indigo textiles that served as an important form of currency in the Sahel and Sahara. Enslaved people captured in Moorish raids on their farming villages were forced to extract the tree resin and later to transport baskets of it to riverine ports, or *escales,* where the resin was sold to European merchants. Thus, European competition for access to trade in interdependent parts of Asia, Africa, and the Americas began to link economies in different world regions in particular ways.

The early acceptance of Indian indigo-dyed cotton in particular suggests that these imports, circulating within a western African political economy with already-established consumer preferences, represented an especially lucrative opportunity for Moorish suppliers of gum resin. La Courbe described receiving one of these traders, Leydy, the mother of the Moorish king. She arrived accompanied by her daughter-in-law and several other women riding donkeys, with men walking alongside them. The queen mother informed the Frenchman that her son would soon send a large caravan of gum for trade and gave him a cow as a gift. La Courbe notes that this elder woman and most of her female entourage were dressed in garments of black "salapoury," a finely woven cotton cloth imported from India.[70] Only the female bard appeared differently from the other women, her clothing adorned with numerous amulets whose movements added to the music she made when the queen mother invited her to perform a praise song on a *ngoni* lute.[71]

## FROM CLOTH AS CURRENCY TO *PIEZA DE INDIA*

With the increasing European merchant traffic, coastal trading ports in western Africa became sites where multiple discourses of racial difference unfolded at once. Encounters between people there were increasingly marked by confrontation between preexisting patterns of cultural accommodation and the gradual development of new hierarchies. The former were characterized previously as cultural flexibility and pluralism but also were framed with reference to race and slavery in terms of lineage—evident in the story of André Donelha and Gaspar Vaz, driven by the search for profit from regional economies in Asia, Africa, and the Americas being connected through European maritime trade—or the reactions to them. European emphasis on abstraction, quantification, and commodification, seen in the abstraction of panos as units of value, also resulted in the abstraction of enslaved black bodies. Profit derived through this process of commodification was thus linked to the erasure of enslaved Africans' humanity.[72]

*Cotton Cloth in Western Africa*

Diplomacy, relationship building, and trust were key elements of commerce. European merchants were careful to follow social protocols and defer to people according to their status as they interacted with different societies in coastal ports. Yet despite the interpersonal dynamics of these face-to-face relationships, the accounting practices, recordkeeping, and correspondence generated from conducting the business of Atlantic trade also fed a Euro-Atlantic discourse of race marked by an even wider use of abstraction, quantification, and commodification of human bodies and labor.

Portugal enjoyed a rush of gold specie into its coffers from operations at its fort at Elmina on the Gold Coast in West Africa and, from the sixteenth century onward, from slave-worked mines in Brazil. This greatly increased amount of specie coins circulating through state officials and private hands led to greater numeracy of its merchants and the development of accounting methods.[73] Merchants moving between, or tracking the movement of goods between, different parts of the world, different forms of currency, and discrete social systems of value needed to calculate costs and estimate returns on their investments. Throughout West Africa, a wide range of currencies circulated—iron bars, copper, cowrie shells, salt, and white cotton strip cloth. But how to make the value of these various currencies comparable to the value of metallic currencies of Europe? Portuguese merchants in western Africa integrated locally widespread cloth currencies into their records, establishing a "pano" as a unit of value that referred abstractly to the value of a "piece" or measure of cloth.

They also began to use the term *peça da India* ("India piece," or measure of Indian cloth) to account for the numbers of enslaved individuals purchased in Africa and delivered to the Americas under the Spanish asiento licensing system.[74] The asiento contract used the term *peças da India*, or *piezas de India* in Spanish, as a unit of account and a measurement of value based on the estimated labor power of a healthy, able-bodied, African young male. This accounting metaphor made double reference to the cottons that first the Portuguese and later other Europeans imported from India for sale in Africa along with the bodies of captive people. The term is significant in the history of global capitalism because of how it, along with the practice of double-entry bookkeeping, was used by seventeenth-century New Christian merchants in western Africa, such as Manuel Bautista Perez at Cacheu in Guinea. Perez's language and method, derived from an adaptation to conditions in Africa, helped to link African currency value systems to European currency based on gold and silver specie.

The abstraction of the pieza de India precisely mapped the convergence of the economies of the Atlantic and Indian Oceans onto the bodies of enslaved African laborers through the medium and metaphor of cloth. The French also used the term. The Senegal Company's director Julien du Bellay defined a *piece d'Inde* in a 1724 company memorandum as "a strong and robust negro between twenty and thirty years old who has no personal defects. Sometimes we make up the piece d'Inde with a woman and two children, two negrillons (who are) thirteen or fourteen years old."[75] By calculating the value of a person based on the estimated profit to be earned from their labor, European merchants transformed individuals notionally into commodities in terms of units of labor power as a method to track expenses and profits. They also formalized methods to "count" human beings as less than whole, as fractions of a person based on an idealized measure. Women, girls, boys, and people in poor health or with signs of disease were counted as a fraction of a *pieza*, thus building hierarchical notions of gender and race into mathematical calculations of profit and loss. The Spanish crown taxed licensees by the number of *piezas de India* delivered to the Americas, which created an incentive to deliver more enslaved people who could be taxed at less than the full pieza rate, often younger captives, and thus yield higher profit.[76]

France held the asiento license to provide enslaved labor to Spain's American colonies between 1701 and 1713, after which Britain took over the contract until 1750, when the system ceased to be used.[77] These practices facilitated Atlantic commerce in Africa but also reflected merchants' and merchant company efforts to measure and "fit" trafficked populations of African captives into a gendered and ableist social order in which "blackness" became associated with the status of enslaved, of commodities, and of commodified labor. As Sylvia Wynter argues, the descriptive language and accounting techniques flattened culturally complex human beings into conceptual units of labor power while also animating a discourse that lowered the value of certain categories of humans. To trade in Africa, European merchants bundled varieties of imported textiles together with other goods, such as iron bars, brass basins, glass beads, muskets, and knives, to negotiate on ostensibly equal terms in African ports for captives, gold, and other goods. This shows the limitation of attempting to assess the impact of Atlantic commerce in Africa merely as a matter of tallying economic profits and losses over time. Beyond the relative outcome of specific commercial transactions, it is evident early on that western Africans were being pulled into discursive frameworks that calculated the value of African bodies in diminished terms. Such underlying discourses effectively worked to both shape perception and structure relationships as commerce increased throughout the eighteenth century and continued after the end of the slave trade through the colonial period and beyond.

Western Africans also had long engaged their own discourses about slavery and race that varied across space and over time. Sahelian notions of race were historically tied to Islamic distinctions between believers and nonbelievers, with greater status and "whiteness" accorded to those who could claim descent from people originally from central Islamic lands, while enslaveability and "blackness" were generally ascribed to nonbelievers.[78] In a major difference from the Atlantic world, where children born to enslaved mothers inherited slave status, people in western Africa followed the pattern of the wider Muslim world in which the status of children of Arab or Berber men and enslaved women acquired their father's status. This pattern shaped notions of race in a fundamentally different way over time, as it advanced a process of cultural Arabization and the expansion of Arab and Berber lineages. In contrast, the process across the Americas was marked by the exclusion of the children of enslaved African women and free European men from inheriting their father's status. Despite the long history of Islam in western Africa and before the arrival of the Portuguese, Muslim writers elaborated a discourse about the Sudan that, with a few notable exceptions, associated black people with slavery as well as with civilizational backwardness, cruelty, and ignorance.[79] In chapter 1, we heard a counternarrative among Bamana lineage heads that appears in the oral tradition. It opposes the civilizing discourse of Soninke, Fulbe, and other Muslims to posit the superiority of Bamana cultural values derived from agriculture. It is surely one of many that existed across such a diverse region of diverse peoples—some of which constructed alternative narratives that were defined by their rejection of enslavement (for themselves) and conversion to Islam.

Beyond distinctions of religious affiliation, lineage claims were even more widely relied upon to establish hierarchical relations between individuals and groups than color, phenotype, or any static notion of "ethnicity," which Mark and Green have shown to be a concept of Western anthropologists that was both foreign and anachronistic to western Africa in this period.[80] The ideology of lineage—wherein powerful groups sought to maintain or expand their strength through strategic marriages and alliances—helps to explain the process of making and remaking a given political and social order. The joining of two lineages was marked by a negotiated, two-way process of acculturation, informed by the particulars of the context and those involved. It was flexibility rather than adherence to rigid cultural religious dictates that facilitated the expansion of Mandinka populations from the Sahel to many areas throughout Senegambia and Guinea that began with the rise of imperial Mali in the thirteenth century. Green describes this earlier process, already well developed by the seventeenth century, as "primary creolization" to distinguish it from the similar process of "Atlantic creolization," which evolved in a different cultural and economic context.

WOMEN AS AGENTS: PRODUCERS, MERCHANTS, AND CONSUMERS

In the 1670s, the Berber-Arab marabout Nasir al-Din preached against the tyranny of local warrior aristocracies in the Waalo, Kajoor, and Fuuta Tooro regions.[81] He criticized the predatory raids on villagers that rulers sanctioned and the seizing and selling of captives from among the rulers' own populations to be enslaved by Christians. He declared a jihad whose goal was to establish a state organized by strictly observed Islamic legal principles. Popularly supported by villagers who were vulnerable to raids, al-Din attacked states along the Senegal River valley, including Waalo, whose ruler, Fara Kumba Mbodj, was killed in battle.[82] Al-Din installed leaders who were loyal to his opposition to Atlantic slavery (because it involved the selling of African Muslims to European Christians) but were not opposed to the enslavement of nonbelievers.[83] When al-Din was killed in battle with Hassani Arabs in 1674, the French seized the opportunity to support the return of traditional aristocracies to power in Kajoor, the Fuuta Tooro, and Waalo.[84]

That was the context in which the French merchant La Courbe, who was operating from the island of Saint-Louis, met in the 1680s with several members of the royal lineage at Waalo, where they were newly unconstrained from clerics in their dealings with Europeans. The meeting included two grown daughters of Fara Kumba, the former brak killed during the war, who were accompanied when they met La Courbe by two servant girls and a praise singer. The Frenchman noted how the two daughters were dressed in "beautiful black pagnes with white stripes, one of which served as a skirt that hung down to their feet, and the other they wore like a coat that dragged behind them in a long train, distinguishing them from people of a lesser condition."[85]

La Courbe got a sense of the source of some of that fine clothing when he was taken to pay a courtesy visit to the brak's wives, who lived in separate buildings around the royal residence. In entering the thatched-roof home of the king's first wife, Maram Njaay,[86] he found her "seated at the foot of her bed ... [with] five or six women around her, sitting on matts on the ground, who were spinning cotton. She stood as I entered. After I extended my hand and took off my hat, she bade me to sit next to her."[87] He found a similar scene in the home of each wife he visited.[88]

La Courbe's account of his time with the women in Waalo, especially Njaay, on the one hand, demonstrates that elite women were key agents in the production and trade of cloth and, on the other, shows how that agency unsettled La Courbe and shaped his outlook on racial difference. These fragmentary descriptions show that one of the principal activities of a seventeenth-century royal compound at Waalo was the production of wealth in the form of manufacturing cloth that would be used as currency. Across the region, spinning thread from cotton was the work of young girls and elderly women, just as women generally performed the agricultural labor of seeding, tending, and harvesting cotton. In most farming communities across western Africa, men did the labor of clearing fields, hunting large game, and weaving threads into cloths, as well as tailoring and embroidery. Elite women were key actors in the regional production of cloths, as they were able to use their access to enslaved or indentured labor to spin cotton yarn and to commission weavers and dyers to make finished cloth. Historians of the Atlantic trade have often focused on the role of male traders such as djula, who moved goods over long distances, but less attention has been paid to the agency of the women who were central to the production and distribution of cloth within the household and in regional markets.

Njaay had not been the primary reason for La Courbe's visit to Waalo, but nevertheless, she let him know of her own trading interests there. On a separate occasion, she came to visit La Courbe aboard his barge anchored in the river, accompanied by a large entourage of several women riding donkeys, followed on foot by about a dozen servants and two praise singers. Once aboard, Njaay and her attendants filled La Courbe's receiving room. "They were all dressed up in *pagnes* that they wrapped around their heads in turbans that also served as parasols," he wrote. "In removing them, they revealed a small cap made of striped cloth that is the mark of women of quality. Next, they removed the [upper] *pagne* to show themselves nude from the waist up, except for the queen, who remained entirely covered."[89] Njaay explained to La Courbe that having heard of his presence she wanted to see him for herself and that she had brought him a gift: a finely ornamented container, or reliquary, made of gold by Moorish goldsmiths, a costly object that, along with her fine dress, announced her as a person of means. Her companions added to this offering with gifts of local cloth and a baby goat. The women began to smoke from locally crafted clay pipes that had become popular among men and women across the Sahara and Sahel after Moroccans first brought tobacco to Timbuktu in the sixteenth century.[90] La Courbe indicated that he did not smoke, but the women's easy familiarity with the practice suggests the region had rapidly adopted a habit of smoking fed by the expansion of tobacco farmed on American plantations and sold into Atlantic markets.

La Courbe's visit lasted several hours. Maram Njaay and the women in her group peppered him with questions about the lives of women in France as they were served a dinner of meat and couscous, biscuits, and water mixed with honey.[91] The Wolof women asked about the beauty of women in France, their clothing, and the magnificence of the royal court. But they cared nothing more about these after hearing one claim that captured their imaginations: that in France, men only married one wife, a fact they agreed made those women fortunate.[92] As the visit concluded and they prepared to depart, La Courbe reciprocated their offerings with gifts of mirrors, fragrant cloves used to perfume the body (likely obtained in an Indian Ocean market), and beads of coral and glass that were used to make waist beads and bracelets and that also "served as the small units of the country money."[93]

The initiative taken by Njaay demonstrated her ability to establish commercial relations with foreign traders of her own account and, supported by a coterie of assistants and onlookers, was an expression of an elite woman's power within the otherwise male-dominated context of long-distance trade. There are no details of any specific trade relationship that developed because of this meeting aboard the French vessel, but the implication was that it would not be their last encounter. The authority that Njaay projected to La Courbe came from several factors, including her spousal relationship to the brak, her influence of decisions, and her ability to organize valuable trade goods, such as gum resin, to send to commercial partners of her choosing. The sultan queen had been born into a lineage considered royal so that some of her power extended from the symbolic significance that her followers gave to that fact.

It should be emphasized that Njaay and other women throughout the Waalo and Kajoor regions, which were still ruled by independent leaders, were *not* the signares of the French trading settlements historians have tended to focus on as cultural intermediaries of Atlantic trade and are discussed in more detail in chapter 4. Much historical writing about the signares has tended to focus on their mixed racial and cultural backgrounds in a way that obscures the participation of wider segments of the population in the same process of brokerage and the forms of cultural innovation that came out of it.[94] Indeed, it can obscure cultural exchange between Africans, such as the interactions between the Wolof and Moors that resulted in the production of fine objects in the workshops of the goldsmiths of Waalo.

Njaay's gift of a devotional object made of gold was a bold assertion of her religious subjectivity and her embeddedness in a material culture influenced by Moors and the wider Sahara and Sahel. This is further confirmed by references that Brue made about Njaay's husband, the brak, wearing a black-and-white-striped cotton garment made from *pagnes de Maures* (Moorish cloth) that glistened "like the most beautiful satin," as well as accessories made of Moroccan red leather, including a carrying case for the Quran and boots with metal spurs.[95] The notable finery and style of Njaay's clothing and that the exchange of items she and her mostly female companions purchased came from throughout Atlantic and Indian Ocean networks shows how women in Sahelian societies confidently asserted themselves in the context of global commerce in the late seventeenth century. The smoking of her pipe signaled a level of comfort with the foreign man who did not appear to intimidate her. It also demonstrated alternate gender norms from that of high-status women in France, who more commonly consumed snuff tobacco rather than smoking tobacco in pipes.

Maram Njaay sat at the top of a hierarchy of women throughout Waalo, both formally in her capacity as judge of other women's behavior but also informally as an ideal model for other women to emulate. Many likely were involved in trade on a smaller scale according to their means—not only spinning thread but engaging in a variety of artisanal labor, such as dyeing cloth and making pottery for household consumption as well as for exchange on outside markets. The women's involvement in trade locally near Saint-Louis was more extensive than that of local men who, except when they had one or two captives to sell, limited themselves to fishing and farming.[96] These women were frequently the primary sellers of textiles at local markets. In the 1680s, women from villages in Kajoor traveled downriver to Saint-Louis to sell goods they had procured at low cost from the interior, as La Courbe recalled:

> I entered the store where one trades. I found there several women from Bieurt and other neighboring villages who had brought hides, millet and *pagnes,* or cotton stuffs, because *it is they who conduct practically all the commerce* of Senegal; they have many captives who they send very far inland to buy the hides that they carry more than fifteen leagues on their heads or on donkeys; they buy them at very low prices.[97]

The agency of these women was unsettling to elite Catholic French men such as La Courbe. Their behavior defied his expectations of gender and sexual norms, and these complaints appear to have been added to a list of other critiques made of African mores. Though keenly observed, there is a general dissatisfaction or even hostility toward the societies he visited that courses through La Courbe's well-known account.[98] He took part in the expected diplomatic protocols, such as the exchanges with Ber Caaka and his wife, but La Courbe describes his general disdain for people of the region who he viewed as thieves, liars, and people interested in gaining unfair advantage in their relations with the French. He dismissed the practice of matrilineal succession in Waalo in prurient terms, suggesting that it showed lack of confidence "in the chastity of their women."[99]

He opposed a practice common at Saint-Louis, whereby French company men married local women according to local custom to facilitate ongoing trade relationships; he viewed these unions as forms of "prostitution."[100] It was under La Courbe's influence as director that the Senegal Company banned marriages between French men and African or Eurafrican women and sought to limit the amount of time women traders from surrounding regions could visit the island to conduct trade.[101] He complained that some of the African women traders "under the cover of selling merchandise, debauch our whites to get something because they do not make love without interest."[102] These relationships or coastal marriages between African women and French traders worried company officials in France who learned from La Courbe that their employees "used the most beautiful and the most precious of the Company's merchandise to satisfy and to assuage the luxury of these (female) fornicators."[103] This statement acknowledges the efficacy of the women entrepreneurs involved even as it also suggests certain ideas about race, gender, and sex that associated African women with a dangerous sexuality that was threatening to the goals of the financial monopoly the company sought to achieve. Despite this policy, many such unions continued through local marriage practices ("marriage à la mode du pays"), which is suggestive of how Atlantic and global maritime trade networks expanded beyond the agency of male African rulers and merchants, as both African and Eurafrican women seized opportunities as cultural and economic brokers connecting communities in the interior with a variety of goods sourced from Europe and Asia.

"FREE TRADE" IN WESTERN AFRICA

Women traders played leadership roles in the politics and economy of coastal trading towns from Senegal south to Sierra Leone, often in ways that contravened efforts by European mercantile company officials to impose monopolies, insisting instead on a version of free trade. Na Bibiana Vaz, for instance, a prominent merchant and elder in the Kriston (African Christian) community of Portuguese Cacheu, demonstrated the power of such women in their roles as commercial intermediaries and community leaders.[104] She led a successful popular revolt against a policy limiting all trade in the port to Portuguese vessels and forbidding commerce with other nations. Born to an African mother from the Pepel community of Cacheu, Bibiana Vaz was possibly related through her Cape Verdean father to the family that had enslaved

Gaspar Vaz on Cape Verde.[105] Already in advanced years, she had outlived her husband, Ambrosio Gomes, who had a similar family background and had become one of the wealthiest slave traders in the town as an administrator with the private Companhia de Cacheu. As a tunguma, she herself had grown wealthy through trading in enslaved people, kola, salt, and other goods. After her husband's death in 1679, Vaz secured access to his share of the business, expanded her own trading activities, and increased her prestige in the community. When the Portuguese sent a newly appointed governor to Cacheu to enforce the trade monopoly on its residents, Vaz had him arrested and held captive in Farim, a town miles inland and outside the reach of Portuguese authority, for more than a year. Other private traders, as well as residents in and near Cacheu, supported her act of rebellion. Vaz and her supporters sent a list of demands to the king of Portugal that included limiting the access of Portuguese and Cape Verdean vessels to the port without approval from local leaders and forbidding the Portuguese to trade with African groups other than the populations residing in Cacheu.[106] After a lengthy standoff, the Portuguese eventually captured Vaz, deporting her to Cape Verde to be tried for rebellion, although she evaded the most serious sanctions for her actions.

Similar conflicts over attempts to impose monopoly trade, the main goal of European mercantile companies, are mentioned in towns throughout the region in the written sources. These accounts show a pattern of openness of these communities to overseas commerce—a posture made more workable by the fact of a heterogeneous population already accommodated to an atmosphere of cultural pluralism—under certain broadly understood conditions. These conditions included the customary expectations of "landlords" to act as hosts to visitors and settlers, who were also then expected to abide by the duties of guests or newcomers.[107] It is this framework that explains why the leadership of these coastal communities, acting with the presumptive prerogative of landlords or hosts, reacted strongly against attempts to limit their ability to trade with anyone of their choosing and moved deliberately to undermine the control of trade by any single foreign actor.

In the early seventeenth century, the Wolof-speaking ruler of Bawol intervened to protect a community of thirty New Christians living in the coastal town of Portudal, south of contemporary Dakar. Lambaia prevented a group of Portuguese Catholics from violently attacking and expelling the New Christians from the town. He insisted that his town was "a market where all types of people had a right to live" and that he was the one to decide what behavior was accepted in the land he controlled and that anyone who defied his order would be beheaded.[108] It was a remarkable intervention that a ruler who was at least nominally Muslim rejected fratricidal conflicts over religion between foreign guests in favor of peacefully hosting a plurality of outsiders for the purpose of encouraging trade. Lambaia's actions helped to extend into the territory he controlled a trade diaspora that reached parts of North Africa, Portugal, and Holland. This action suggests an underlying ethos of tolerance for the existence of cultural difference, but it was also an exercise of a landlord's sovereign control of land occupied by "strangers" and guests.[109]

In the 1670s, after the French navy defeated and expelled the Dutch from their installations at Gorée and at Arguin on the Mauritanian coast, they also sought to sign exclusive commercial treaties with African rulers in several ports, thereby achieving full control of the northern Senegambia region. African merchants, textile merchants prominent among them, responded by refusing to trade under these conditions and migrating to other regions outside the French zone of influence at that time, such as Saloum, which had market areas on the Gambia River where British traders were active.[110] Francis Moore describes meeting Wolof cloth traders who may likely have come from an area with French-dominated markets to visit one such British trading operation:

> This day two Joloff people came to the island with some cloths to sell. The Joloffs make the finest kind of cotton-cloths, and that in large quantities: their pieces are generally twenty seven yards long, and never above nine inches wide; they cut them to what length they please, and sew them together very neatly, to make them serve the use of broader cloths.... I have seen a pair of cloths so fine, and so bright dyed, as to be worth thirty shillings sterling.[111]

Resistance to the imposition of European trade monopolies is most famously evident in the case of Lat Sukaabe Fal, who emerged in the late seventeenth century as the ruler of unified Kajoor-Bawol state, a robust version of the fiscal military state whose premise and structured relationships were not dissimilar from that of other states around the perimeter of the Atlantic and Indian Oceans. Like their peers in Europe, Asia, and the Americas, Kajoor-Bawol and other similar African states, like Kaarta and Segu, relied upon violence and warfare as a method of state accumulation, and a portion of its wealth was invested in preparation for recurring cycles of violence. Also like similar entities elsewhere, the authority of these African states was most cogently expressed by their power to punish their subjects with death or deportation. The scale, stability, and social and economic context of each of these African states varied considerably, but at a fundamental level, they were organized and structured in ways quite similar to that of their commercial partners.

FIGURE 2.5. Representation of soldiers' dress, published in "Cavalry" (Negro Cavalry) in René Claude Geoffroy de Villeneuve, *L'Afrique, ou histoire, moeurs, usages et coutumes des Africains: Le Sénégal* (Paris: Nepveu, 1814). Image courtesy of the John Carter Brown Library. Brown University, Providence, RI.

FIGURE 2.6. Representation of soldiers' dress, published in "Soldier" (Negro Soldier) in René Claude Geoffroy de Villeneuve, *L'Afrique, ou histoire, moeurs, usages et coutumes des Africains: Le Sénégal* (Paris: Nepveu, 1814). Image courtesy of the John Carter Brown Library. Brown University, Providence, RI.

In Kajoor, Lat Sukaabe Fal was part of a traditional Wolof aristocracy that had returned to power in the wake of the defeat of Nasir al-Din in the War of the Marabouts, just as had occurred with the Waalo. Fal relied upon renewed commercial ties to Atlantic commerce, but historians have credited him with going further by equipping more of his soldiers with muskets, thereby giving them an advantage over rivals, who he raided for captives and booty, making Kajoor the largest of the Wolof states for over a century. Fal used competition between European buyers to obtain higher prices for enslaved laborers and was angered by French attempts to limit British and Dutch participation in local markets. Leveraging his control over the coastal region between Kajoor-Bawol Saint-Louis and Gorée, he threatened the supply of local grain and meat to the French at both trading centers. He responded further to French attempts to impose a trade monopoly by ordering a group of his soldiers in the town of Rufisque to arrest the director of the Senegal Company, André Brue (see figure 2.7). Fal held Brue prisoner for a month and sent soldiers in canoes to burn and loot the French trading houses on Gorée Island.[112]

FIGURE 2.7. "Arrestation de M. Brue par ordre du Damel de Cayor, 1701" in Jean-Baptiste Léonard Durand, *Voyage au Sénégal* [...] (Paris: Chez Henri Agasse, 1802). Image courtesy of the John Carter Brown Library. Brown University, Providence, RI.

*Cotton Cloth in Western Africa* ⟶ 85

This standoff ended when the French paid a ransom in the form of guns, textiles, and other goods to release Brue. This protest action, and similar episodes in which Fal blocked trade, ultimately failed to achieve its main objective, but it did squeeze higher customs payments from the French for the right to trade, further strengthening the aristocracy. Fal's equipping his army of enslaved soldiers with muskets gave them a lethality that has contributed to the legend of *ceddo* soldiers, who are remembered by marabout historians as cruel drunkards who greatly expanded the violence and death in state-sponsored military raids on neighboring areas.

Despite the difference in perspective and objective between the European mercantile company officials and their African trading partners, these incidents also demonstrate that both sides shared similar understandings of political power, which allowed their interests to converge with these exchanges. Just as the ceddo soldiers were compensated with a portion of the valuables they captured during their raids, directors of the French East India Company allowed sailors and officers aboard their ships to privately trade a limited amount of goods as compensation and incentive to undertake potentially dangerous overseas voyages. Similarly, Fal redistributed the higher customs payments in the form of linen, wool, cotton textiles, amber, glass and coral beads, and other valuables he received to retain the loyalty of nobles and clients. These nobles likely included Muslim marabouts in the northern parts of Kajoor to whom he granted titles that reflected a protected status in exchange for their support in times of war and in administering the state in times of peace. Access to commercial goods helped him to manage the political relationships that had made him the titular head of a state that was linguistically, culturally, and religiously heterogeneous on the model of what might be called a "mercantile-military-clerical state." As he did so, he also achieved the ascendancy of his Geej matrilineage as the dominant power in Kajoor for over a hundred years.

FROM FREE TRADE TO THE COMMODIFICATION OF CAPTIVE BODIES

Lat Sukaabe Fal's revolt against the conditions of trade was not as exceptional as many public narratives of the transatlantic slave trade in Africa might suggest. There were many instances in which African rulers refused to conduct trade with their European partners—unless there was recognition of their control of the land and their prerogative to trade with whomever they desired. These actions show that they viewed themselves as equal partners and contested the right of the French and other European merchants to impose boundaries on trade relations in their land. These acts of resistance insisted on an African sovereignty and self-making that suggest a counternarrative to the one then taking shape in the Atlantic world outside Africa, where new meanings of race were then being constructed abstractly through the mechanics of global commerce. The incorporation of textile metaphors such as *pieza de India* into accounting language facilitated the abstraction and valuation of enslaved African bodies. Those meanings were being sedimented into a global division of labor taking shape.

The sartorial diversity described in towns across western Africa suggests a counternarrative of this period rooted in the varied backgrounds of residents and migrants drawn there in search of opportunity or the circumstance of enslavement. The black tailored Portuguese clothing, hats, and shoes worn by *tungumas,* merchants, and some Biafada chiefs on the Guinea coast offer an example of how people domesticated foreign imported textiles and cloth not only as expressions of affiliation to a Luso-Atlantic world but also as confirmation of their freedom of choice and assertion of status in relation to their peers and community. Wearing such clothing, however, did not preclude their commitment to pursuing their own interests even when these contravened the aims of mercantile company officials, as shown by the example of Bibiana Vaz. It is in this sense that these contingent choices were expressions of an African modernity that preceded an explicitly colonial context by one hundred fifty years. The sartorial diversity mirrored a certain tolerance for religious and cultural plurality shown by African rulers and chiefs throughout the region from Senegal south to the Guinea coast. Such tolerance was also reflected by their pursuit of free trade, an openness that ran counter to the imperatives of the officials of European mercantile companies who sought to establish exclusivity within defined borders.

Gaspar Vaz and Maram Njaay are examples of two Africans who, from their very different vantage points and social positions, sought situational advantages within a larger commercial and social context they did not control. Njaay did so through her diplomatic visit to La Courbe aboard his vessel, accompanied by an entourage of women dressed in fine clothes and expressing disappointment that the Frenchman did not share the women's contemporary taste for smoking a tobacco pipe. All these gestures, as well as her gift of a precious religious object, signaled a sense of equality she felt before him though he had not come to meet her, but her husband. Gaspar Vaz's comportment is less easy to read, although his apparent comfort in navigating the contrasting signifiers of Catholicism and Islam is striking. These and other examples show that the agentive sartorial choices Africans made within spaces of correlation were contingent, relational, and continually reinvented rather than emblems of fixed ethnic, "racial," or other group identities.

The global trade in textiles and the Atlantic commerce in human beings were deeply imbricated, as these markets stimulated each other through the exchange of textiles for people. As we will see in the following chapters, each of these processes unfolded alongside an internal African debate over Islam and enslavement that played out in different parts of the region. On parts of the Guinea coast, it was inflected by Catholicism and closely related to a Kriolu language and culture that emerged through trade between Cape Verde and western Africa.

In either instance, the rationale for western African participation in the Atlantic economic exchanges in this period is strikingly evident from the heavy importation of multiple forms of currency in exchange for the export of enslaved people of which textiles were primary, along with other African commodities such as gum resin, ivory, gold, and dyewoods. This is the same logic that obtained in Asia and Europe, where merchants accepted gold or silver bullion as currency in exchange for goods of all kinds.

The textiles imported into western Africa increased the amount of commodity currencies already in circulation that included varieties of locally manufactured cloth—feeding a process distinct from capital accumulation in Europe. They were exchangeable for other goods but also had second lives as useful objects, whether as clothing, accessories, or household items. The prevalence of these commodity currencies in western Africa effectively connected markets from the Sahel to the Atlantic coast, which explains why certain kinds of goods, such as indigo-dyed cottons, were in demand by African merchants.

But it was the prevalent use of cotton textile currencies—even more than other commodity currencies—and the wider consumer demand for cotton cloth across western Africa that were most consequential in forging linkages to Europe, Asia, and the Americas. They intersected powerfully with regional politics of consumption and sartorial display through which individuals expressed distinctiveness and social status. For all its inventiveness, however, this process was steeped in various forms of violence and inequality that held fast between groups such as the Berber-Arab and Wolof aristocracies in the Waalo near the Senegal River or the Fulbe pastoralists and Jallonke farmers of the Fuuta Jallon plateau. Such dynamics continued to unfold alongside, within, and against the pull of the Atlantic commercial currents. As a result, towns from the western Sahel to those of the Fuuta Jallon region and the Atlantic coast were spaces where multiple discourses of race and gender competed. The ones circulating in the coastal ports relating to creolization at the turn of the eighteenth century became but a recent addition to an already well-established pattern.

# 3 ~ Centering the Sahel in the Early Eighteenth Century

*Indigo Dyers, Precarity, and the Pull of the Faleme River Valley, 1730–1750*

THE STORIES of two young girls make legible the layered dynamics of status, power, and gender that animated the western Sahel in the early eighteenth century. The first girl, Niama, was the granddaughter of the Soninke *tunka*, or ruler, of Tuabo, one of three royal Soninke towns in Gajaaga near the banks of the Senegal River where the waterway bends south to branch into the Faleme River as it courses through the landscape of Bambuk that is rich with gold mines.[1] Born into the privileged circumstances of a royal household, Niama would have been well cared for and educated in Quranic schools. As a child she would have worn the locally dyed blue indigo and yellow *wolo* cottons reserved for elite members of her society. The adults in her household, both men and women, wore gold jewelry and were scrupulous about their appearance. Yet this was a period of widespread political and economic instability and thus precarity in the western Sahel, where competing branches of the Bathily ruling clan struggled among themselves for political titles within the gerontocracy while also engaged in several conflicts with Fulbe clerics downriver to the northwest at Fuuta Tooro and to the south in Bundu. War and commerce were often entangled, and from their settlements in the desert north of the river, Moorish cavalry opportunistically and periodically raided the towns and markets of Gajaaga, taking goods and people by force.

In 1745, when she was nine years old, Niama was captured during fratricidal warfare between competing branches of royal lineage in which members of her family were either slaughtered or sold into slavery. Transported by river to Saint-Louis, and then south to Gorée Island off the coast of present-day Dakar, Niama was eventually sold and transported overseas to the India Ocean island of Mauritius (Isle de France). Enslaved to a French East India Company employee, she was baptized Catholic as Marie Genevieve in accordance with the terms of the Code Noir and worked on a coffee plantation owned by the company.[2] Her enslaver Jean-Baptiste Geoffroy, who was much older than she, impregnated Niama when she was seventeen. She gave birth to a girl. Four years later, after having followed him to the Isle de Bourbon (Réunion), Niama gave birth to a second child by Geoffroy, after which he emancipated her. Their son, Jean-Baptiste, also known as Lislet, grew up on the island as a free person. He later went to school in Paris, where he eventually worked as a cartographer, meteorologist, and astrologer and in 1786 became one of the first mixed-race members of African descent in the French Royal Academy of Science. Niama's fate suggests the level of precarity in the western Sahel that could lead to this dramatic reversal of fortune for a privileged young person and reveals the fragility of an established order up until that period dominated by Soninke-lineage elites.

Less is known about the other girl in question: written sources do not name her, and her background remains undefined except in relation to her patron, Tunka Alimana, the political ruler of another Gajaaga town, Makrana. In 1736, the fifteen-year-old had been sent to work temporarily as a pawn inside Fort Saint Joseph, which was located just east of where the Faleme River flows into the Senegal River and adjacent to Makrana. As a pawn, the girl's labor was collateral for credit extended on a purchase—in this case, she was in the French official's employ until the tunka paid two pieces of imported cotton cloth (*toiles*). The girl was placed into the custody of a French clerk named Balmaure, but he soon left the fort to return downriver to Saint-Louis, leaving her to the general care of company officials inside the fort. At that point, Catin Jerome, the Eurafrican mistress of company director La Poupiere, took the girl as her own servant.

For a few months, she worked inside the French fort, which during the trading season typically swelled to a population of a few hundred people. A two-story defensive structure of about forty square meters (430 square feet), the fort contained several rooms on the ground level to store merchandise arranged around an open courtyard, and there were two large barracoon sections along the exterior walls that housed captives. On the upper level were rooms for the company director, his personal guards, and employees, including about sixty-five Europeans and more than twice that number of Africans who were both free and enslaved workers from coastal Ndar/Saint-Louis.

Though the young pawn was not a tunka's daughter, and thus there was no expectation of relative comfort or protection, it was nonetheless understood that she was *not* a captive and thus could not be sold and transported overseas.[3] However, Catin Jerome thought otherwise. For reasons unclear, she sought to break the customary pawn arrangement and return to Saint-Louis with the girl—which sparked something of a diplomatic crisis. Tunka Alimana vigorously protested, coming to the fort to insist that the pawn be left behind. Even after his demand was met, the incident left lingering tension between himself and the French merchants of the coast.

The stories of these two Sahelian girls from Gajaaga, one privileged and the other less so, underscore the generalized precarity of life for young women in the western Sahel and how that precarity mapped onto the overlapping intricacies of Sahelian political dynamics and long-distance commerce. The trade in enslaved labor for export across the Atlantic, for example, was nested within a series of other related transactions—diplomatic, financial, and sociocultural. These transactions were subject to mutually recognized rules and ongoing processes of negotiation. They were, however, also subject to disruption, for instance, through raids, ambushes, seizures, and other violent arrogations that violated ethical and normative market exchanges. French and British commerce in this region was constrained by Sahelian systems of credit and valuation as well as the fast-changing conditions of political and economic opportunity. In what ways did those Sahelian systems of credit and valuation and social systems map onto the body and labor of a young female pawn to overdetermine her fate? Or combine to expropriate the reproductive, physical, and care labor of the high-born Soninke daughter who, ironically, birthed a decorated scientist of the French Enlightenment?

Historians of this period, when they do write about women, tend to focus almost exclusively on merchant signares and coastal trade. Yet women throughout the region who labored as petty traders, potters, dyers, spinners, and pawns—as well as elite women who employed them—were integral to networks circulating currencies, commodities, and people through eastern Senegal. In much of the region, the production of indigo cottons depended on the labor of girls and women. This Sahelian world was a magnet attracting the economic and political interests of various peripheral groups, a circumstance requiring cross-cultural diplomacy. Women—as household managers, artisans, laborers, merchants, and elites—were vital to the centripetal forces driving the movement of people and goods.

Indigo and textiles were deeply embedded in the social and economic life of the region. Women laborers were critical players in local economies producing indigo cloth, while girls and aged women performed some of the more tedious tasks in textile production, such as harvesting and cleaning cotton and spinning thread. Under the centripetal pull of regional demand for indigo cloth, which could be exchanged for gold, enslaved captives, grain, and other valuable commodities, the choices of African consumers and market exchanges internal to the Sahel helped to shape the nature of textiles flowing between Atlantic and Indian Ocean ports. At the same time, the social and religious politics of Gajaaga were gradually being transformed. A convergence of factors saw a centuries-long hegemonic legacy of Soninke-lineage elites gradually lose power to ascendant Fulbe Muslim clerical groups.

In the first section of the chapter, I provide an overview of the significant indigo and cotton production in eighteenth-century Gajaaga and of how French trade in the region, conducted from Fort Saint Joseph, was predicated on good relations with Soninke rulers. I return to the story of the unnamed pawn at Fort Saint Joseph to explore the multiple claims made on her body and labor before focusing on the centrality of women's labor to the production of dyed textiles in Gajaaga and Bundu. Throughout, I illustrate how the dyed textiles produced by women and tailored by men communicated status and social belonging in the region. In the second section, I explore how Indian indigo-dyed cottons, in appealing to the tastes and preferences of Sahelian peoples, were crucial to French East India Company efforts to access both gold and captive laborers in eastern Senegal, pushing one agent to go so far as plotting to work with Bambuk and other neighboring rulers to undermine the Soninke tunka of Gajaaga. I end the chapter with the story of Fulbe cleric Ayuba Diallo, a slave-trading African Muslim merchant of some local renown for his own enslavement, manumission, circumnavigation of the Atlantic, and ultimate return to his homeland in Bundu. Diallo's 1734 arrest by the French on suspicion of commercial espionage for the British further illustrates not only the imbricated histories of the Sahel and the Atlantic slave trade as well as the economies of indigo textiles and enslaved persons but also how political instability in the western Sahel in the early eighteenth century, in part driven by European commercial expansion, resulted in a precarity that affected even those of high social status. Moreover, Diallo's own participation in the trade in humans and textiles—as well a painted portrait of him—speak to the role of textiles in western African self-fashioning.

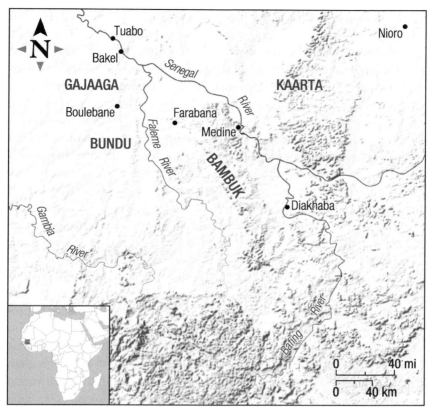

MAP 3.1. Map of the eastern Senegal River valley and the Faleme River valley indicating the proximity of Gajaaga, Bondu, Kaarta, and Bambuk. Map by Matt Johnson at Johnson Cartographic.

MAGNETIC FORCE: WOMEN'S LABOR IN THE
INDIGO COTTON CLOTH ECONOMY OF THE SAHEL

As one of the major dyeing centers in West Africa in the eighteenth century, the western Sahel, especially Gajaaga, was critical to an economy that integrated exchange networks of dyed textiles, salt, grains, and captured human beings bound for slavery. From the early 1700s, Fort Saint Joseph, and the colonial social world contained in its walls, marked Gajaaga as the easternmost point of the French western African trade network. Maintaining good relations with local elites was both essential to its success and difficult, given African suspicions of French interests. In early eighteenth-century Gajaaga, the labor of women in particular, as the story of the unnamed pawn further illustrates, was overdetermined by the broader economic and political tensions of the region, even as women and girls were central to the

*Centering the Sahel in the Early Eighteenth Century* ~ 93

production of dyed textiles and thus not only to the textile economy but also to the sartorial communication of status and social belonging in the region.

The western Sahel, especially the region connecting the Niger River and the eastern Senegal River, was historically one of three major centers of indigo dyeing in West Africa.[4] The others were in the predominantly Yoruba- and Edo-speaking areas of southwestern Nigeria and in the Hausa-speaking region of northern Nigeria. The cultivation and use of indigo in the western Sahel is thought to be much older than the earliest material evidence found for it thus far, which dates to the eleventh century. The proliferation of this artisanal industry across the breadth of West Africa made the region one of the most important centers of indigo dyeing in the premodern world. In the seventeenth and eighteenth centuries, the intensity and variation of the color blue obtained by West African dyers surpassed what was then attainable in much of Europe from the woad plant (*Isatis tinctoria*), which produced a less intense color.[5] Direct access to a range of dyestuffs—such as indigo, cochineal, camwood, and brazilwood—via trade with Africa, Asia, and the Americas, revolutionized European imperial textile production, driving demand for bright colors and necessitating new techniques to produce them on cloth.[6] By the late seventeenth century, enslaved plantation laborers on colonial Saint-Domingue in the Caribbean drove a flourishing industry of indigo production that continued to be more profitable than sugar on the island in the early eighteenth century. And indigo cultivation and processing were an early focus of French planters in colonial Louisiana during this same time, animated not coincidentally by the skilled labor of enslaved captives imported from Saint-Louis and the Senegal River valley.[7]

Across the much of the Sahel, people cultivated and processed the green leaves of the indigo plant into the potent blue dye that fed a regional commerce in dyed cotton textiles. The region of Gajaaga was at critical crossroads within this indigo cloth economy. The floodplains of the Senegal River valley were renowned for the cotton and indigo cultivated by residents for centuries, at least since they had been subsumed within the empire of Ghana. Arab travelers of the eleventh century described the towns of Silla and Takrur, both located along the Senegal River, as densely populated settlements where there was "almost no house without a cotton tree."[8] Muslim geographer and cartographer al-Idrisi observed in the twelfth century that these towns were animated by a regional network of exchange that began with salt mined at Awlil, a large salt deposit on the southern coast of Mauritania, then traded on boats to ports along the Senegal River to "Sila, Takrur, Barisa, Ghana and the other towns of Wanqara and Kugha as well as to all the towns of the Sudan."[9]

FIGURE 3.1. "Mosque and place of assembly at Galam (Gajaaga)" in Major William Gray and Staff Surgeon Dochard, *Travels in Western Africa, in the Years 1818, 19, 20, and 21* [...] (London: J. Murray, 1825).

Gajaaga's attraction as a resource-rich region of ecological transition remained important at the turn of the eighteenth century. It was anchored by the fertile floodplains of the Senegal River, which divided the reddish scrublands of the Sahel to the south from the drier sandy terrain to the north. In the lowlands of the floodplain, settlements of round, thatch-roof buildings dotted the landscape of date palms, baobab, and shea trees. The lowlands—vulnerable to both floods and raids from north of the river—were generally occupied by an ethnically heterodox mix of lower-status farmers indebted to more powerful merchants and the Soninke elite, including powerful chiefs and clerics, who lived in walled settlements, or *tata*, built on higher ground overlooking the floodplain and river.[10] Behind the walls, most towns had an open central area anchored by a mosque with roads or pathways leading away from it (see figure 3.1). The homes of wealthier djula merchants within the tata might feature the rectangular, flat-roof architecture of the Sahelian region along the Niger River valley, concretizing their cultural ties to larger towns such as Segu or Jenne.

Two branches of the Bathily lineage of Soninke had long dominated a series of settlements in early eighteenth-century Gajaaga and controlled all trade. Their cavalrymen led raids against vulnerable neighbors and political competitors—pillaging and imposing tribute payments on villagers.[11] In combat, their dress consisted of cotton tunics and trousers dyed a bright yellow color from a local plant called *tefe*. Gold earrings, gold bracelets, and two braids set with a gold ornament completed the uniform of an elite soldier. It was a color that symbolized their high social rank and recalled the yellow gold that was a source of their wealth and prestige.

The use of color in clothing to signify social belonging and social status in the case of elite Soninke warriors shows but one instance of an articulated sartorial world within the Sahel. Local cloth manufacture supplemented by imported textiles from Europe and Asia helped to supply communities

*Centering the Sahel in the Early Eighteenth Century* ~ 95

differentiated by a variety of users making, trading, and wearing textiles for distinct purposes. During the dry season, the market towns across Gajaaga received an influx of goods transported overland by djula merchants in caravans. The warrior elite of Bamana Kaarta allied with that of the Soninke to orchestrate this seasonal commercial traffic in captive human beings and consumable goods, such as salt, textiles, and grains. This alliance across linguistic, religious, and lineage lines had deep roots in the region's history. Yet it was one increasingly challenged from opposing sociopolitical alliances led by Fulbe clerics under the premise of Islamic reform.

The French East India Company built Fort Saint Joseph on the eastern banks of the Senegal River in 1700—not far from the Soninke royal capital of Tuabo, where Niama was born and grew up, and just west of where the Faleme River empties into the Senegal. To occupy and conduct trade at the fort, the French mercantile company paid the extant tunka an annual fee of five to six hundred *livres* in the early eighteenth century, and about twice that amount, or twelve hundred livres, in occasional gifts throughout the year.[12] For the French mercantile company, it was critically important to their goals of extracting profit from their long-distance, long-term financial gambit to maintain good relations with the Soninke tunka. Gajaaga was the easternmost interior region where the French sought to maintain a presence and was thus a critical node in a regional network of otherwise coastal trading posts from the islands of Saint-Louis and Gorée to Albreda on the Gambia River and further south at Sierra Leone. Commerce conducted in these ports was connected beyond western Africa to exchanges in French outposts in the Caribbean, the Gulf of Mexico, Canada, France, and the Indian Ocean. The town of Pondicherry, on the southeastern coast of India, was a particularly important site in this sprawling network because its weavers produced large quantities of textiles that the French East India Company ultimately transported to West Africa. In western Africa, the French supported the defeat of the Islamic reform movement led by Nasir al-Din that appeared to threaten their commercial interests. They paid weavers in India to produce a wide variety of cloths for export, including two varieties of indigo-dyed cottons, guinees and salampores, that were readily accepted by Africans at ports in Senegal.[13]

But this commercial expansion was not simply an anodyne matter of procuring and transporting a desired commodity to consumers in a distant location. The push of French and British mercantile company agents into Gajaaga and the adjacent gold mining area of Bambuk was accompanied by the violence inherent in slave trading and further destabilized the region. French gestures of diplomacy often collapsed from underlying tensions surrounding these high-stakes exchanges. A memorable example comes from the 1730s, when the company sent an engineer, Jacques Pelays, to negotiate permission to build another French fort at Neteko, in the center of the Bambuk mining region. Not only was Pelays unable to overcome the residents' suspicions of his intentions, he confirmed them. Backed up by dozens of African soldiers from the coast who had traveled with him from Saint-Louis, Pelays removed all pretense of disinterested commerce and attempted to seize power by declaring himself a ruler in Gajaaga. His actions sparked a crisis that ended only after a group of Soninke marabouts organized themselves to have Pelays killed.[14] After this, the French withdrew from the southern stretches of the Faleme River valley, limiting their direct access to gold mining Bambuk. Even so, successive company directors made the trip upriver from Saint-Louis seeking to repair the damage to their reputation caused by Pelays and keep trade ties open.

The population inside Fort Saint Joseph grew seasonally with the arrival of several dozen French and habitant traders and dozens of African laborers from Saint-Louis. It typically took a little more than two months for riverine convoys of vessels—armed, mobile trading communities—to make the almost-four-hundred-mile journey from the coast. As many as five hundred people looking for some commercial possibility or advantage, including sons and daughters of free families in Saint-Louis, could make the trip during market season.

A 1732 report presents a sociological portrait of the African laborers working for the company and offers a glimpse of the diversity of people driving an economy that was at once local, regional, and transnational in scope.[15] The report lists not only their names, thus capturing something of their cultural diversity, and ages of the 167 African workers in the French fort at Gajaaga, but it also categorizes them by company rank, religious affiliation, type of labor, gender, how much they were paid, and whether or not they spoke French. It lists other qualities, too, such as whether an individual was "good natured," good at their job, or an apprentice. In some instances, a laborer's social status as "free" (*libre*) is specifically cited: for example, "Demba Mody Libre" and "Amady Bouey Libre." Fifteen African Christians are listed with European or hybrid names like Claude Domingue, Francois Soliman, and Pierre Jara; they worked as blacksmiths, carpenters, masons, and cooks inside the fort. Ranging in age from nineteen to forty-five, the men are described as speaking at least a little French (with several listed as speaking "good French"), though they represented a range of linguistic backgrounds, including Wolof, Maninka, and Bamana languages, among others. Many of these Christian workers consumed bread and the alcoholic eau-de-vie with their meat rather than the millet and water listed for most other workers—another indication of how their lifeways had become influenced by the Euro-Atlantic goods and social practices on the coast. Non-Christian and "Bambara" men, with names like Pemba Bambara, Massa Nyouman, and Borom Dor, did similar labor as the Christians but were also interpreters (*maîtres de langue*), woodcutters, cattle keepers, sailors, and guards of captives held in the barracoons within the fort.

Twenty-eight "women, youth and female servants in the service of the Company" (*femmes, rapaces et raparilles au service de la Compagnie*)[16] are listed by name in the report's last two pages. Their jobs, unlike those of the men, are almost never mentioned (with the noteworthy exception of one woman listed as an interpreter). Instead, what is emphasized in the record was their socially recognized status as either a wife, a young male or female servant, or a free person. A few of the youth were two-year-old infants and toddlers up to five and six years old, while several were teenagers.[17]

The world inside the fort was a colony in microcosm in which people of varied levels of personal power and autonomy lived side by side. But the French and their allies, enslaved captives, and workers were all subject to trade conditions recognized and upheld by their African partners outside the fort, the Soninke tunka of Gajaaga. The struggle over the pawn featured in this chapter's opening illustrates the conflict that unfolded in the early eighteenth century between the French, the various tunka, and such neighboring competitors as Khasso, Fuuta Tooro, and Bundu.

Tunka Alimana of Makrana seemed particularly outraged that the signare Catin Jerome had attempted not only to return to Saint-Louis with the fifteen-year-old pawn but also to replace her with another captive girl in the fort to serve as a pawn for Alimana's debt. This suggests a complex relationship of these tunka to trafficking in captives with European Christians; they wanted to profit from this commerce, but in doing so, they also meant to reaffirm their authority and ability to control commercial transactions within their space. This included their power to determine and regulate the question of enslaveability and to protect an established social order. As a pawn, the young woman worked for Jerome, who took responsibility for managing the girl's labor from her partner La Poupiere. The pawn likely gathered firewood, carried water, and prepared meals, among other chores. She navigated a space in which captives held for transport to the coast were crammed into barracoons guarded by Africans from the coast. In wanting to take the young woman to Saint-Louis, was it Jerome's intention to eventually sell her onto an Atlantic-bound ship? Or rather to incorporate her as a laborer into her compound at Saint-Louis, which was a common practice?

Was Alimana's insistent claim on her body not also an implicit assertion of rights of access to her labor? The standoff was resolved when Jerome withdrew her claim to the girl and returned to Saint-Louis without her. Like Bibiana Vaz—the tunguma merchant farther south on the Guinea coast at Cacheu—Jerome was both merchant and cultural intermediary, but in this context there were limits to her influence. The work performed by this young woman of modest social rank was mundane and invisibilized within the archival record of human trafficking and high-stakes trading that took place inside the fort. This episode reveals the multiple, overlapping forces contesting for control of her body and her labor.

Women's labor was central to the economy of the western Sahel, notably in the production of dyed textiles in Gajaaga, which was an extension of the cycle of farming. Young girls and women were the primary agricultural laborers, responsible for seeding, weeding, and harvesting such crops as cotton, millet, sorghum, and maize. Cleaning raw cotton of seeds, detangling its soft white fibers, and spinning them into thread was the laborious work of prepubescent girls and postmenopausal women (see figure 3.2).

Spinners passed their work onto male weavers who, often working on commission from the senior wife of a compound, spun narrow bands of cloth from those threads on the horizontal looms most common in the western Sahel. Girls and women also harvested the unassuming green leaves of the

FIGURE 3.2. "A negro girl beating cotton rather than carding it" in René Claude Geoffroy de Villeneuve, *L'Afrique, ou histoire, moeurs, usages et coutumes des Africains: Le Sénégal* (Paris: Nepveu, 1814).

*Centering the Sahel in the Early Eighteenth Century*

cultivated *Indigofera tinctoria* plant and undertook the process of turning the plant leaves into a potent dyestuff. Beyond its use as a dye, herbalists, many of whom were women, also used the plant for medicinal purposes as an antiseptic and anti-inflammatory that could be applied directly to a wound.

The skilled labor of transforming green leaves into a blue dye and fixing the dye onto cloth required knowledge of plant species, fermentation, oxygenation, and other chemical reactions and processes to produce the desired color. To make the dye, workers pounded the green leaves of the plant in a mortar, mashing them into a paste they then shaped into balls. Left to dry, these balls were stored for later use by local dyers, and in some instances, they were sold in local and regional markets. When cloth was ready for dyeing, a craftworker dissolved the ball of dried leaves in a clay pot filled with water to which they added burnt plant ashes that increased the colorfastness of the dye. The solution was left in the sun to ferment for several days to produce the vat of dye solution.[18] It was then women and girls who plunged white cloth into the vats of dye in clay pots (produced by potters who were also generally female) to obtain the desired result—altogether a skilled, laborious process. Finally, the decoration of such cloth through resist-dye techniques was a specialized skill practiced by aristocratic women.[19] So while the production of cloth involved the labor of both women and men at different stages, girls and women made critical contributions to an industry of great social and economic importance.

Skilled dyers produced different shades of indigo—from pale blue to deepest indigo. These shades had distinct meanings for consumers. Of particularly high value was cloth with an intense deep-dyed indigo color. Sometimes referred to as "black" cloth, it had become a marker of status and prestige among Muslim clerical elites across West Africa, from Timbuktu to Kano.[20] This prestige item was also appropriated for wear by non-Muslim political elites such as the Bamana Massasi of Kaarta. Saturated with dye and striking to the eyes, this black cloth suggests a wider regional discourse of sartorial power, specifically, the generalized projection of social status linked to the accumulation and bodily display of clothing and accessories. The value of clothing came in large measure from the amount of skilled labor required to produce it.

Gajaaga's markets also served as transregional entrepôt where both plain white cotton as well as loom-patterned and indigo-dyed cloths were sent from surrounding regions, such as Bundu. It was one of the Soninke tunka who had first granted lands in a sparsely populated area to the Fulbe marabout and amulet maker, Malik Sy, in 1690.[21] In establishing a settlement at Bundu, Malik Sy attracted a group of clerics from the Fuuta Tooro to settle there. Boucard describes thriving settlements with abundant cattle, agricultural produce, and an active indigo dyeing industry. In time, their activities and linkages with a network of Quranic schools helped to establish its importance in an era of Islamic reform that would unfold over the next one hundred years.[22]

As the influence of Bundu expanded into the mid-eighteenth century, the labor of its women indigo dyers took on even greater significance for generating wealth as merchants traded finished indigo cloths for gold dust from nearby Bambuk. In the 1780s, Golbery observes, "The inhabitants [of Bundu] raise cotton with which they make very beautiful *pagnes* [cloth wrappers] that they dye black with the only pounded indigo that grows in that region, and that they sell to the Manden [of Bambuk] for one [quantity of] gold per piece." He also notes that merchant women in Bundu traveled, escorted by a few men, to Gajaaga markets to sell their wax, pottery, hides, and gold, going so far as to frame this commerce from Bundu as a kind of predatory conquest of this Maninka-speaking mining area, writing, "The Fula . . . have seized the trade in cloths [*pagnes*]" in Bambuk. These cloths were produced to different specifications for men and women buyers, with the lengths considered appropriate for women being three and one-half *coudees* long (a length measured from the elbow to the tips of the fingers) by three and one-half coudees wide, which was produced by stitching seven narrow bands of cloth together side by side. The versions for men were made up of wider stitched bands and were more expensive.

Despite recording these elements relating to the size and cost of these textiles, many details pass without mention, not only in Boucard's account but in most European travelers' accounts of the period. For example, several European travel accounts of the period celebrate the fine quality of African indigo cottons and even offer descriptions of how artisans made dye from the green plants. Yet there is little to no mention of the people performing the work. The expertise practiced by the women artisans and laborers who added value and meaning to white cottons remained opaque to eighteenth-century observers like Boucard—ironically, despite their evident preoccupation to acquire and record local knowledge and resources.

A CERTAIN SHADE OF BLUE:
THE BATTLE FOR MARKETS AS A BATTLE FOR COLOR

The principal actors in the making and dyeing of cotton cloth were girls and women; their skilled labor was integral to a regional economy of a primary good that had cultural and social implications. Their industry, however, was directly impacted by imported indigo cottons from India as well as by later imitations from Europe. Deeply dyed indigo cottons woven at Pondicherry, India, where the French built a factory and supported local weavers and dyers, early on became the primary kind of cotton cloth the French East India Company imported to Saint-Louis and other ports in West Africa. Indian dyers were especially gifted in indigo cloths, a quality they shared with Sahelian dyers and an aesthetic that pleased West African consumers. The French East India Company had its headquarters in Nantes, a commercial port town located near where the Loire River empties into the Atlantic Ocean. Merchants there benefited from the town's location and their commercial maritime ties to South Asia and transatlantic slave trading in Africa and the Americas. By some estimates, as many as half of all French slave ships traveling to Africa departed from Nantes. The company's activities in southern India were critical to its goals to increase its access to both the gold mines and captive labor markets of eastern Senegal. In India, agents purchased indigo-dyed cottons such as guinees, baftas, and salampores as well as other varieties of plain and printed cloth. In Nantes, the company organized the sales of these Indian cotton textiles to traders provisioning ships destined to West Africa.

By royal decree, these Indian cottons were banned for sale in France in a bid to "protect" local textile manufacturers. Nantes became a major center of the *indiennage* industry in which local textile makers were devoted to imitating the patterns and styles of Indian cottons made for markets in both Europe and overseas in Africa and the Caribbean. While French textile manufacturers were shielded from competition, the East Indian Company imported significant amounts of textiles into western Africa where there were no such limitations. In company correspondence from 1736, an agent specifically requests Indian bafta cottons (*toiles baftas*) "or Salempouris that must be dark blue to almost black with a violet or red eye that the shine gives them once they are well steeped in color."[23]

These specifications speak to the tastes and preferences of people across the Sahel, where similar goods already circulated. A deposition before a council of judges at the chamber of commerce in Nantes in 1767 demonstrates the importance of West African consumers in the nexus of interests extended to four continents. The focus of textile makers at Nantes and other French ports such as Rouen, seeking profit by manufacturing cloth for African markets, was to improve the quality of the indigo dye, specifically the intensity and colorfastness of the color it produced. The chamber's report found that imitations of the indigo-dyed cotton cloths made at Rouen intended for the African trade had not yet become competitive in many African markets because the quality of the dye was not to the liking of African buyers: "The dye is the part to which the Blacks are most drawn. We could hardly fool them or at least not twice with impunity. They take care of themselves in recovering once they have been imposed upon.... The necessity of a good dye is one more reason that the producers in the local textile dye industry should be exempt from taxes, entirely or partially."[24]

A note handwritten in small script at the margins of the main record of this hearing indicates that the intensity of the dye quality of Rouen cloth was thought to be about half that of similar Indian cloths and that the latter were the most in demand for the slave trade.[25] That reality explained the ongoing importance of Indian cottons to commerce in western Africa—although access to Indian markets was contingent upon interimperial warfare and extractive economies built to sustain imperial expansion.

By the 1740s, the French trading concession at Saint-Louis was again seeking to extend its presence from Gajaaga to other locations south along the Faleme River. Leading these efforts was East Indian Company representative Pierre David, the son of one of the company's principal investors, which indicates the personal financial interest David had in the outcome of the commercial venture he was managing in West Africa. In a scheme reminiscent of that of Jacques Pelays in the 1730s, David wanted to undermine the Soninke tunka of Gajaaga, whom he presented as an obstacle to expanding French commerce in the region. He believed that imported trade goods had become an important basis of tunka political power, alleging that they used their control over prices to manipulate neighboring communities in Bambuk and Khasso. David sought to undermine the tunka by seeking alliances among these neighbors, positing that in doing so, the French could gain an important commercial foothold in a gold mining town that may lead to even greater profits.

For the Maninka of Bambuk, the potential presence of the French not only meant possible protection from the raids of the neighboring Khasso; it also gave them access to imported Indian cottons; French- and European-made cottons, woolens, and linens; metalware; glass beads; and weapons and other goods—expanding the range of commodities available in their markets. But the development of such a scheme was not to be sustained. In 1746, David was named governor of the Isle de Bourbon, thousands of miles away in the Indian Ocean, where the French had established colonial sugar plantations worked by enslaved Africans. The movements of this son of a Paris-based financier between West Africa, the Indian Ocean, and Europe animated the deepening linkages between these global regions.

## MOBILITY, ENSLAVEMENT, AND SELF-FASHIONING OF A BUNDU CLERIC

Several years after the Pelays debacle but before Pierre David canvased the area, French company directors at Gajaaga found themselves in another controversy that brought trade between the French and Soninke to a halt for several months. The French were provoked that a Fulbe cleric from Bundu, Ayuba Sulayman Diallo, had traveled from a trading settlement on the Gambia River where the English were active to Bundu with an agent of the Royal African Company, Thomas Hull.[26] Diallo had intended to take Hull to Neteko, a vibrant center of the gold mining region of Bambuk, nestled at the base of the red stones of the Tambaoura Escarpment in western Mali. Numerous Bundu merchants traveled to Neteko seeking gold from its mines, which they acquired in exchange for other metals, such as brass manillas, silver coins, and jewelry, or for cotton "*pagnes* (wrappers) that the Bondu merchants brought to them in quantity."[27]

It is not clear what became of Hull's prospecting visit in Bundu. But the following year, in 1736, when Diallo traveled to Fort Saint Joseph on the Senegal River to collect a shipment of goods, the French arrested him on charges of spying on their commercial activities for the British. Diallo was a well-known figure, not just in the western Sahel but internationally as well. Not only was he the elite son of an imam at Bundu but he also had been enslaved in the Americas and spent time in England. In both places, his literacy and letter writing, as they did in Neteko, had attracted attention. Only five years before, the young prince had been captured by a British slaver on the Gambia River, transported to the British colony of Maryland in North America, where he was enslaved for three years, redeemed from slavery, transported to England once it was discovered he was literate in Arabic, and returned on a British ship to the Gambia River. Thought to be from the northern region of Bundu, Diallo's letters mention several towns throughout the Fulbe-controlled state, including Boulebane, which later became its northern capital.

He had been reunited with his family in Bundu for only a short while when he was arrested by the French and held at Fort Saint Joseph. This provocative act caused temporary unity among otherwise competing commercial interests in the region, drawing Soninke, Bundu, Jakhanke, and Arabo-Berber merchants into a standoff with the French that lasted several months until Diallo was released.[28]

At roughly thirty-four years old, Diallo's personal biography and perambulations narrated the overlapping histories of the western Sahel and the Atlantic world. He was related to the Torodbe clerics who first followed Malik Sy to Bundu in the late seventeenth century. His literacy was a clear sign of his privileged upbringing. He had received an elite Quranic education in Bundu,

FIGURE 3.3. "Image of Boulebane in Bundu" in Major William Gray and Staff Surgeon Dochard, *Travels in Western Africa, in the Years 1818, 19, 20, and 21* [. . .] (London: J. Murray, 1825).

where he learned to read and write Arabic along with Samba Gelaajo Jegi, son of the ruler at Fuuta Tooro who had been exiled to Bundu.[29] Literacy had conditioned his mobility around the Atlantic in the early eighteenth century. It was in support of some form of writing and reading that, in 1730, he had traveled from Bundu to a port on the Gambia River with two captive men he intended to sell to British traders in exchange for writing paper. Diallo and an assistant, however, were ambushed by a group of Maninka who captured them, shaved their heads and beards, and sold them to an English trader. He was then transported across the Atlantic and sold to a tobacco planter in Maryland.

There, it was again Diallo's literacy in Arabic that had attracted the attention and empathy of the colonists who eventually redeemed him from slavery. They learned Diallo could write after he had run away from his owner and was being held prisoner at a local jail. He penned a letter in Arabic to his father for help. His ability to write had functioned as proof of his exceptional background in a world in which literacy was a marker of social status that allowed him to be imagined outside the category of enslaveable in the colonial American context. His literacy and social standing continued to attract attention in England, where he was said to have penned three copies of the Quran from memory that he gave as gifts to well-connected aristocrats. Diallo was also introduced to aristocrats, such as Sir Hans Sloane, with whom he later corresponded about commercial opportunities for trading gum resin and gold dust in West Africa, and to members of the British royal family.[30] He wrote a letter to the Duke of Montagu asking him to redeem his friend

*Centering the Sahel in the Early Eighteenth Century*

Lamine Jay from slavery and to the naturalist Hans Sloane to encourage British interest in African commerce in gum and gold dust. His letters made him legible as an African Muslim of high social standing. Furthermore, he shared similar attitudes with them regarding Atlantic slavery and commerce.

Diallo sat for an official portrait (see figure 3.4) before returning to the Gambia in 1734. In the painting, he appeared as if light years away from that life experience he had recently endured. He perhaps had been stripped naked when forced onto the hold of the slave ship that carried him across the Atlantic Ocean. Later he would have been clothed in the coarse woolen raiment distributed to the enslaved, known as "Negro cloth." But in the painting, Diallo has transgressed that framing. He is represented stoically, with large bold eyes, a subtle smile, and a calm demeanor. He is dressed in the fulsome abundance of his robes in bright white cotton or silk with the red cap and turban of a Bundu cleric. A red leather pouch carrying a Quran hangs around his neck. It was Diallo who reportedly chose this clothing after the painter William Hoare asked how he wanted to appear. Diallo described the "country dress" of the clerical men of Bundu for the painter, but he also found an opportunity to challenge the painter, saying, "If you can't draw a dress you never saw, how can some of you painters presume to draw God whom no one ever saw?"

This trenchant critique adds another dimension to his strategic advocacy for himself and others through his written words, speech, and actions. It suggests that even while enslaved, and as he negotiated with the British and later with the French, he pursued an agenda that reflected the aims of the Bundu elite to whom he remained steadfastly attached. The tone of his statement suggests he centered his community and worldview on an equal footing with the British—including both those who had enslaved him and those who had not—and felt in a position to criticize the pretenses of European Christians who were his contemporaries. From this perspective, it is easy to imagine that his own experience of enslavement in British North America, together with his eventual redemption on the basis of his socioreligious status, did not alter Diallo's worldview steeped in West African Muslim traditions but rather may have confirmed it.

Back in Bundu, Diallo sought to take advantage of his relatively privileged position within that political economy that had once ensnared him. He involved himself in long-distance commerce in enslaved labor, indigo cloth, and gold—only to find himself once again detained after crossing an imagined and shifting political-commercial boundary.

In acting on their supposed right to defend their commercial interests against the British while in western Africa as guests of local sovereigns, French East India Company directors necessarily engaged in local politics

FIGURE 3.4. "Portrait of Ayuba Sulayman Diallo" by William Hoare of Bath. National Portrait Gallery, London, UK.

as well. The pushback from local rulers, as had been the case with Pelays a few years before, reasserted their ability to exert control over the space and to place limits on European commercial activity there. Not only was it the case that Diallo would have been well known and therefore his arrest been of significance to many people, the incident also raised the question of whether he, and potentially any other person of his status, had the right to trade with whomever he chose?

The standoff ended when Diallo was ultimately released,[31] but the underlying tensions were hardly resolved. We can see in this episode how

*Centering the Sahel in the Early Eighteenth Century*

Diallo's life experiences were imbricated simultaneously within the Islamic histories of the Sahel (in which the clerical community of Bundu was created within a larger context of Islamic reform and Fulbe political expansion) and the transatlantic slave trade (which he experienced directly as a captive and a broker). The textile and indigo dyeing industries of the region helped to fuel both Sahelian politics and the transregional linkages of the slave trade. It is likely that the commerce Diallo described to his partner in the Royal African Company involved selling the indigo cottons so abundantly produced in his homeland of Bundu to purchase gold in nearby Bambuk.

In Bundu, as in Gajaaga, women dyers and male weavers were part of a flourishing agricultural economy that supported the lifestyles of its most powerful residents (see figure 3.5), namely clerics such as Diallo who wished not only to access wealth but to pursue their ultimate goals of increasing the space of Dar-al-Islam in the region. Their work also became the focus of European mercantile company competitors who sought access to the region's wealth.

Like the examples of Niama, the nine-year-old Soninke tunka's daughter, and the fifteen-year-old pawn, Diallo's arrest offers further evidence that neither high social status nor custom could protect people from the disruptions and dangers of political instability, which was often linked to the politics of commercial exchange. If Diallo's choices can be construed as seeking to support himself and others in Bundu by seeking to take advantage of relationships he had developed with the British, they also reveal the limitations of such aspirations for African rulers and merchants of the period.

SAHELIAN DYNAMICS, GLOBAL IMPLICATIONS DURING THE EIGHTEENTH CENTURY

This chapter shows that spaces such as Gajaaga in the eastern Senegal River valley were defined by intersecting mercantile networks that connected overland and riverine traffic as well as by shifting internal dynamics driven by multiple competing interests. The painting of the Bundu scholar Ayuba Suleiman and the production of indigo cotton textiles by Bundu dyers and exchanged sold for gold reminds us that these Sahelian spaces, where wider regional discourses of sartorial power were articulated, were defined by the activities of competing economic and political interests. This process unfolded not only through the generalized projection of social status through the accumulation and bodily display of expensive (i.e., labor intensive) clothing and accessories; it also operated through the modalities of extractive labor linked to female bodies, as in the cases of the fifteen-year-old pawn claimed by the powerful elder man, and the Soninke princess, victimized by violent struggles for power, deported and enslaved thousands of miles away

FIGURE 3.5. "Negres de Bondu" in Anne Raffenel, *Nouveau voyage dans le pays des nègres suivi d'études sur la colonie du Sénégal et de documents historiques géographiques et scientifiques* (Paris, 1856).

from her homeland. In addition to these exceptional cases, there were thousands of girls and women agriculturalists—unnamed in written sources and scarcely dwelled upon in oral traditions—who daily farmed cotton, cleaned it, spun threads, and dyed cloth.

Within these distinct but overlapping and gendered economies of enslavement and patronage in western Africa, the exploitation of the productive and reproductive labor of young female pawns and enslaved people lay at the base of a hierarchical system in which privileged elites benefited firstly from profitable local commodities produced by dependent labor. Local dynamics of gender, status, and consumption were increasingly attaching themselves to Atlantic commercial networks during the eighteenth century. The intrusions of European mercantile companies into western Africa in the early eighteenth century exacerbated and accelerated this process driven by external demands for labor in the Americas and the Indian Ocean. Textile manufacturing was a key focus of mercantile interests in both Britain and France in the mid-eighteenth century. By 1756, competition in western Africa between the two countries exploded into an imperial war, the result of which saw expanded British influence in the region for the next two decades. It was a period that also witnessed a class of urban African elites in coastal Saint-Louis, in concert with those along the Senegal River valley all the way east to Gajaaga, develop further as powerful regional actors.

# 4 ~ The Politics of Dress at Saint-Louis during an Age of Islamic Revolution, 1785–1815

IN NOVEMBER 1776, five Senegambian sailors were aboard the British slaving vessel *Swallow* on the last leg of a multisite voyage from Saint-Louis, Senegal, to Barbados and Mississippi and back, when it was attacked by an American ship off the coast of the Bahamas. Upon the British ship's successful return to London, the sailors were each to have been paid one pound, six shillings per month for their work on the ship, which delivered ninety-three enslaved people to Mississippi. Instead, the Americans took the sailors as prisoners of war. They escorted *the Swallow* back to Providence, Rhode Island, a trading port town not much larger than the sailors' base of Saint-Louis on the West African coast.[1] The sailors' names—Jack Bamberry (Jack Bambara), Mamanly (Momeda) Sana, Alsimeer (Algema), Ganserry (Gansare), and Famsey (Tamsa)—suggest diverse ethnic and religious backgrounds resident in coastal Senegal. After holding the sailors for a few days at Providence, the Americans turned them over to the British at Newport.

As low-wage laborers on both sides of the Atlantic, these men navigated land and seascapes of enslavement, warfare, commerce, freedom, captivity, and debt before vanishing from the record. But in Senegambia, such laborers, even when dependent on powerful patrons, were also change agents who interfaced directly with a global flow of new commodities, distributing them to new markets, helping to establish consumer taste for particular goods, and shaping the material transformation of societies across the region.

The island of Saint-Louis was located at a major ecological and cultural crossroads. As a port town at the mouth of the Senegal River, it was a gateway from the Atlantic trading world to West Africa's Sahel, the biogeographic transitional region between the arid Sahara and its trading world to the north and humid savanna to the south, and it was home to a heterogeneous population of people from diverse ethnic, linguistic, and religious backgrounds. Sailors, known locally as *laptots* in French and as *lappato bi* in Wolof, were key agents in the production of this vital cosmopolitan space of cultural interaction. European merchants considered them indispensable to maneuvering vessels along the Senegal River the six hundred miles into the Sahel to reach large seasonal markets for enslaved captives, gum resin, cowhides, and gold. A regular daily presence in the island settlement and its adjacent river, laptots also sometimes labored on European ships to ports as far away and distinct as the Americas to the west and islands in the Indian Ocean to the east. The influence of laptots on the culture of Saint-Louis was matched by that of their patrons or enslavers, who were frequently Eurafrican *habitants*[2] of the city. They purchased large quantities of imported cloth from French merchants, then arranged for it to be ferried inland on their boats for resale at ports along the Senegal River.

Far from unilaterally imposing itself on a weaker population, the incipient European capitalism of late eighteenth-century Senegambia functioned within constraints produced by a nexus of overlapping economies—those shaped by regional reliance on slavery and slave trading along the Senegal River valley, the gendered nature of intergroup power relations across the region, the political dynamics of Islamic reform that opposed the enslavement of Muslims, and the prevalence of patronage and clientelism through hierarchies of kinship. By attending to questions of consumption and dress, I demonstrate the ways western African consumers actively engaged a global commerce in cotton textiles in the eighteenth and nineteenth centuries. Textile pattern books kept by European merchants trading in western Africa (see figure 4.1) contain physical evidence of the tastes of eighteenth-century consumers in coastal ports, adding a sensory dimension to the detailed lists in merchant account books of textiles imported in each port. Images of western Africans produced to accompany European traveler accounts are suggestive of how such imported cloth may have been worn by some, but

FIGURE 4.1. *(above)* "Echantillons des Siamoises du Prince noir, deuxieme voyage, 1787 / Sample Book of the Second Voyage of the Black Prince, 1787." Les Archives de la ville de Honfleur, France.

FIGURE 4.2. *(right)* "Manding Man" in René Claude Geoffroy de Villeneuve, *L'Afrique, ou histoire, moeurs, usages et coutumes des Africains: Le Sénégal* (Paris: Nepveu, 1814).

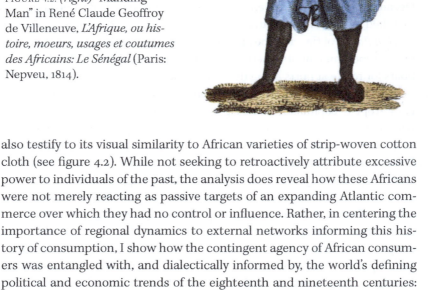

also testify to its visual similarity to African varieties of strip-woven cotton cloth (see figure 4.2). While not seeking to retroactively attribute excessive power to individuals of the past, the analysis does reveal how these Africans were not merely reacting as passive targets of an expanding Atlantic commerce over which they had no control or influence. Rather, in centering the importance of regional dynamics to external networks informing this history of consumption, I show how the contingent agency of African consumers was entangled with, and dialectically informed by, the world's defining political and economic trends of the eighteenth and nineteenth centuries: slavery and the struggle for abolition, colonialism, religious reform, and political revolution.

The emergence of global capitalism in this period was incited by locales and regions beyond Europe, including western Africa. Commercial exchanges in western Africa fed networks of capital exchange linking four continents, and it was western Africans who experienced its effects and shaped its direction and evolution. This period therefore was not defined solely by the loss, vulnerability, and victimization associated with slave trading, of which there was plenty. It was also shaped by the ambition, pleasure, optimism, and imagined futures implied by a wide range of other kinds of commercial and interpersonal engagements.

Along with other booty from the *Swallow*, the Americans captured four letters written by or on behalf of the Senegambian crew members carried on the British sloop's return voyage to Saint-Louis (e.g., see figure 4.3).[3] They give remarkable insight into the experiences of these sailors and the Eurafrican Catholic society of coastal Saint-Louis. The letters were all written by the same hand in a rudimentary, ungrammatical French on behalf of different senders, suggesting the limitations of literacy among ship workers, but they also testify to the literacy of some of their loved ones in Saint-Louis. The sentiments expressed in the letters demonstrate the intimacy of emotional ties among a diverse community of Saint Louisiens connected to overseas trade. One sailor wrote from the Mississippi River to his father, Francois Massa, to say he was sorry for leaving home without permission but wanted to reassure him that he was "doing well, thanks be to God." Another hoped to tell a friend he remembered from the Senegal River that he

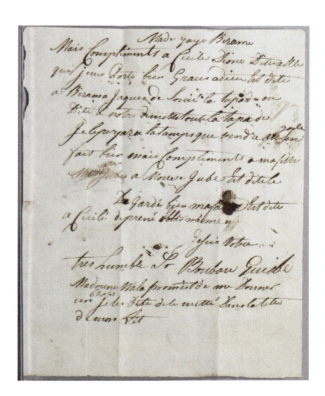

FIGURE 4.3. "Letter from Boubou Guiobe to Mme Yaye Birame." Documents from the Sloop *Swallow*, Providence, RI, 1776. Arnold Family Business Papers. Image courtesy of the John Carter Brown Library.

would consider him a brother "until the last days of my life." Boubou Birame Guibe wrote to Madame Yaye that she should greet another woman, Cuiba Sione Ditwaller, possibly his patron, to whom he would owe half of whatever he earned overseas: "Tell her that I am doing well thanks be to God. Tell Birama Jacques to put the tapa [*tapade* from Wolof for 'enclosure' or 'compound'] [in order] that I will pay for it when I come to Senegal. . . . Madoune Walo promised to give me some things. Tell her to put them at the head of my bed." A palpable optimism for life upon his return home stands in stark contrast to the grim circumstances of Guibe's maritime labor but also to many historical narratives about Africans in the context of Atlantic slavery that focus on loss, vulnerability, and victimization. The concern Guibe expressed from overseas about his tapade in Senegal suggests another perspective on many Africans' experience of the period as one also of hope and futurity. His expressed desire to contribute to the compound and access the material objects preserved within it demonstrate the ways in which sailors, merchants, and other Senegambians actively embedded themselves into the commercial networks through which people, goods, and raw materials from Europe, Africa, Asia, and the Americas flowed.

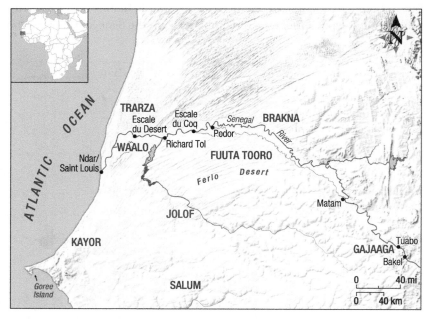

MAP 4.1. Map of the Senegal River valley connecting the towns of Gajaaga, Fuuta Tooro, Waalo, and coastal Saint-Louis. Map by Matt Johnson at Johnson Cartographic.

Urban slavery and slave trading by Eurafrican habitants and European mercantile companies, fueled in part by textile consumption, had long been the primary economic engines of Saint-Louis. The cultural flexibility of Eurafrican habitants, the mobility of sailors such as those aboard the *Swallow*, the prevalence of patronage and clientelism, and the impact of Islamic reform movements shaped the flow of goods from global markets to local consumers, who in turn had an impact on long-distance global exchange networks. Archival excavation of consumers' interactions with this flow of global goods, especially cloth, to local markets reveals the complex tapestry of people and competing cultural rationales of trade and consumption. But from the final decades of the eighteenth century, the moral legitimacy of slave trading as well as the sovereignty of Eurafrican habitants on Saint-Louis, was challenged on multiple fronts.

### HABITANTS AND TEXTILES IN SAINT-LOUIS: AFRICAN "COSMOPOLITANISM" AT THE GATEWAY TO THE SAHEL

Almost eight thousand people lived on the island of Saint-Louis at the turn of the nineteenth century,[4] diverse in religion, ethnicity, and language, including speakers of Wolof, Hassaniya Arabic, Serer, Fulbe, Bamana, French, and English. Located on the Atlantic coastline, just south of the Sahara and a major continental river, Saint-Louis became an urban community fed by the convergence of Atlantic and Saharan trades, both of which had their connections to Indian Ocean commerce. The island lay at the western outlet of a river flowing west six hundred miles from the market towns of Gajaaga, which were fed by caravan traffic from the Sahara and the Sahel. Eurafrican, or métis, *habitants* on Saint-Louis benefited as intermediaries between European merchants and the African markets of the interior, often by providing foreign merchants enslaved labor to transport goods along the river. They enjoyed political and economic primacy on the island throughout the eighteenth century whether under the aegis of either French or British mercantile companies. The wealthiest habitants, living in stone houses near a European fort at the center of the narrow island, were often Eurafrican women married or widowed to European traders with whom they participated in commerce. These signares often distinguished themselves by extravagantly combining several kinds of both local and imported textiles onto their bodies so that their dress projected not only wealth but a sense of cultivated taste to others.[5] Surrounding their homes in the central quarter were several blocks of stone buildings built along sandy streets and arranged in checkerboard fashion. Beyond these were thatched, circular, mud-wall homes clustered close together that housed a growing number of artisans, canoe men, and traders.

After an absence of two decades, the French retook the trading fort at the center of the town in 1779, returning in the wake of a yellow fever epidemic the year before that had weakened British forces on the island. The Eurafrican *habitant* merchant community abetted the French, hoping their linguistic and religious affinities as Catholics would lead to even greater prosperity. For two decades under the British, many *habitants* had continued to identify as Catholics but lived with neither a dedicated church nor the benefit of a priest.[6] In response, Christian *habitants* had met for Sunday worship, baptisms, and other ceremonies in the salon of the Thevenot family. Thevenot's salon contained a dedicated altar containing ornaments and vases of sacramental oils imported from France.[7] This room filled quickly during important services, with the overflow also fully occupying the courtyard outside. The Thevenot family patriarch had also served as "mayor," representing the *habitant* community's interest to the British governor beginning in the 1760s. In 1766, Thevenot wrote to the governor of Gorée to complain that his community had been without a Catholic priest for a number of years, requesting that one be sent to Saint-Louis because without a priest "errors and vices would multiply among us and we would become unworthy to be called Catholics."[8]

Along with their religious and linguistic affinities with French Catholics, however, the habitants pursued an economic and social agenda that was independent from that of French company officials, much less that of the French monarchy or later republic. On the one hand, the *habitants* would fight fiercely to protect their commercial independence, shrewdly declaring their loyalty to the French state while at the same time deploying revolutionary discourses of free trade against those wishing to subordinate them to mercantile company operations.[9] And on the other, they demonstrated a cultural flexibility that to some French observers undermined any notion of a shared Catholicism.

Habitants were already confronting opposition to their commercial slaving operations prior to the return of the French and the swell of French abolitionist efforts. Only a few years before the laptots aboard the British slaving ship *Swallow* were captured in 1776, Saint-Louis first learned that a group of Fulbe Muslim clerics had seized power in the Fuuta Tooro, an important grain-supplying region along the Senegal River. Fuuta Tooro lay between Saint-Louis, which did not grow its own food, and the largest markets for slaves and gold at Gajaaga to the east. The central floodplain region had long played a central role in the region's commercial and political histories since the days of ancient Ghana to the sixteenth century when Fulbe followers of Koli Tengela migrated from the Maacina region of the Middle Niger

River to settle on the middle Senegal River valley in large numbers, transforming its demographics.[10] They established the Denyanke rule of Fuuta Tooro that, because of its engagements with Atlantic slave trading of local people, including Muslims, had once engendered the ire of clerical reformers in the late seventeenth century, and again more forcefully a century later.

The expansion and "reform" of Islam across the western Sahel and the Senegal River valley shaped the context and the rationale for the region's engagement with global commerce well into the nineteenth century—a fact that historians who have been focused on the expanding influence of European capitalist and imperialist interests have glossed over. Combining the diverse interests of peasants and clerical elites, the Tukulor state under Qadir Kan emerged as a countervailing force against which the Euro-Christian dominated society of Saint-Louis defined itself. But Kan's Fuuta Tooro stemmed from a longer trajectory of Islamic reform movements in western Africa and from a more immediate competition with Hassaniya Arab- and Soninke-controlled areas for limited resources, rather than merely as the result of its conflict with Christian Saint-Louis over slave trading. This broader context connected the Fuuta Tooro and Fuuta Jallon with the distant Sokoto Caliphate in northern Nigeria (1804) and broadly impacted political relations between Muslim and non-Muslim populations across the Sahel. In the Senegal River valley, the influence of Islam, supported by the mobility of itinerant Muslim merchants who could move freely throughout the region, continued to expand even as French colonial and cultural influence gained strength from its Atlantic coast base, creating a dynamic between the coast and interior that had profound implications for the history of consumption and fashion.

In the 1770s, Qadir Kan blocked French and habitant vessels traveling through his territory to Soninke markets at Gajaaga to protest the enslavement and sale of captive Muslims to the French. He relented only after negotiating both higher customs payments—usually rifles and indigo-dyed cotton cloth from India—from commercial convoys as well as the right to inspect slave coffles to ensure that no Muslims were among those being trafficked. This negotiation shows Kan's interest not only in reinforcing his state's ability to commit violence but also in enacting softer forms of power through the stockpiling of a commodity that could be spent as currency, distributed as diplomatic or interpersonal gifts, or resold to generate surplus resources for himself or close associates.

British abolitionists hailed the actions of the Fuuta Tooro clerics and Kan as proof of African resistance to an immoral trade, and indeed, this jihad, the Torodbe reform movement, represents a critically important West African

Muslim discourse on slavery and abolition that has often been ignored or underappreciated by historians focused on its Euro-Christian counterpart in the Atlantic;[11] however, as I discuss later, the reformers' concept of abolition and emancipation was limited in scope to believers and was not embraced by neighboring groups. Even as the new French merchant colonial state successfully implemented reforms within its territory in 1779, the region's wider political economy remained entangled with enslavement, slave trafficking, and expropriation of the labor and produce of weaker populations.

Resistance from such powerful actors as the Torodbe clerics meant that the potentially lucrative river trade could be volatile and politically fraught. In the 1790s, commerce on the river was frequently interrupted for short periods because of violent battles or standoffs between African polities, disputes between Africans and the French at Saint-Louis, and battles between England and France as part of the Napoleonic Wars, some of which played out in Senegal. In this context, consumers at Saint-Louis were enmeshed—along with those in western Europe, Asia, and the Americas—in the global circulation of consumable goods that was unpredictable and subject to commercial disruption, delays, and other impacts of political instability. Nevertheless, these Atlantic imports of textiles, beads, hats, tools, cooking implements, iron bars, cowrie shells, alcohol, guns, and gunpowder augmented and diversified an ongoing commerce through trans-Saharan caravans reaching interior and desert-side markets, such as the one at Gajaaga.

At the convergence of those two broadly different political economies— one European, Christian, and Atlantic Ocean / maritime in character, and the other African, Muslim, and Sahelian / Saharan—were the successful merchant women habitants, or signares. Like most habitants, they spoke French, and some were also literate in the language. Still, many of them spoke Wolof in their homes. Their dress on Saint-Louis, though distinguished by expensive imported textiles and local cloths, was similar in style to that of Wolof women on the mainland. They wore tall headwraps similar to those worn by other local women and beads around their waist that clicked as they walked in the same manner of Wolof women.[12] Wealthier signares became renowned for their public displays of finery, with copious amounts of gold jewelry adorning themselves and their servants, whose presence extended the nonverbal message of status. As their party walked through town, the servants shaded the signares' path with a parasol to block the sun.

Signares and other habitants were often associated with a religious and cultural pluralism that acknowledged and participated in both Muslim and Wolof practices. Dominique Lamiral (1751–1800), a mercantile company agent living on Saint-Louis in the 1780s, wrote that there were some who after Mass went to "'do the Salaam' (i.e., Muslim prayers) and they pray with the same fervor to Jesus Christ and to Mahomet."[13] Many joined celebrations of the Eid festival, known locally as Tabaski, wearing protective "gris-gris" amulets, and followed Wolof naming practices for their children.[14] Some French observers viewed such mixing of religious and cultural practice merely as flawed, even debased, versions of both Christianity and Islam. This alleged corruption and the European response to it was an important element in developing eighteenth-century European racial discourse about Africans.[15] It was but a further indication of a lack of civilized order that was perpetuated by the predations of slave trading. However, this culturally flexible posture that actively integrated divergent and apparently incongruous elements reveals the habitants as West African "cosmopolitan" figures[16] contemporaneous with, yet entirely distinct from, those of metropolitan Europe. In the philosopher salons of Paris, as Simon Gikandi has argued, good taste, refinement, and sophistication were measured in the performance of their difference from the vulgar milieu of slaving ports.[17] By contrast, the cosmopolitanism at Saint-Louis was expressed in the way people combined and displayed myriad and sometimes incongruous materials—including textiles, jewelry, amulets, and novel objects such as umbrellas—into a where the realities of slavery and slave trading were more proximate to the lives of social elites.

Eighteenth-century engravings of life at Saint-Louis published contemporaneously depict socially entangled and hierarchical relationships between Christian signares, Muslim marabouts, and soldiers, who were often enslaved labor of signares or mercenaries. And in these artworks, textiles were central markers of these relationships. The central focal point of an image published in Lamiral's 1789 account (see figure 4.4) features a signare and a marabout engaged in conversation while a female servant, an infant child, and a rifle-bearing man watch from either side of them. Both the marabout and the signare are visibly distinguished from the onlookers by the abundance of textiles covering their entire bodies from their necklines to their ankles. Wearing a long robe, and holding the signare's wrist, the marabout appears to be draping a dark-colored cloth, perhaps a prized indigo guinee cloth, over the signare's shoulder. The servant, adorned with strands of ornamental beads draped over her bare upper torso and wearing necklace and earrings, stands behind the signare holding an umbrella over her matron's head as she faces the marabout and the armed soldier standing behind him. As though physically embodying their commercial acumen, signares often draped themselves in ample garments and accessories—multiple

FIGURE 4.4. Images of Saint-Louis signares and marabouts published in Dominique Harcourt Lamiral, *L'Affrique et le peuple affriquain considérés* [...] (Paris: Dessenne, 1789).

FIGURE 4.5. Images of Saint-Louis signares and marabouts published in Jacques Grasset de Saint-Sauveur, *Encyclopédie des voyages: Contenant l'abrégé historique* [...] ([Paris], 1796).

FIGURE 4.6. Images of Saint-Louis signares and marabouts published in, Jean-Baptiste Léonard Durand, *Voyage au Sénégal* [...] (Paris: Chez Henri Agasse, 1802). Image courtesy of the John Carter Brown Library.

pieces of chintz and muslin cotton from India, taffeta from China, and local woven cloths and embroidered varieties, all accentuated with gold jewelry fashioned by local goldsmiths, strands of beads of amber, glass, and coral, and leather slippers from Morocco.

In a second image (figure 4.5) set against an identical backdrop of a thatch-roofed building and a stylized palm tree, a Senegalese man and woman kneel before a marabout who lays his hands on their heads and appears to be praying over or blessing them. Here, the plain white color of the marabout's long robes contrast with the colored garments of the supplicants to distinguish his clerical position and role from that of others. Appearing a few years later in the narrative account of French Senegal Company director Jean-Baptiste Durand, a third image (figure 4.6) builds on the same visual tropes, featuring the additional figure of a second female laborer (identified in the image caption as an enslaved subject) poised behind the marabout, carrying an infant on her back and a package on her head. Walking next to her is a soldier carrying a rifle over his shoulder, an assegai in one hand, and a machete hanging from his waist.

Together, these images locate the relationships between signares and Muslim marabouts at the center of economic and political life in Saint-Louis—at least as imagined by French male travelers and engravers who created these representations based on their reports. Signares navigated within the limitations of a Wolof society that was patrilineal and hierarchical but that afforded them the ability to conduct commerce as well as to own and inherit property. These engravings envision them as principal agents in a coastal society immersed in a Euro-Atlantic world alternately aligning with or confronting local male Muslim authority. The artistic renderings display a kind of visual ethnography that communicates the gendered nature of cross-cultural exchanges and commercial relations that structured coastal society.

As elite members in a larger community of free Africans, signares had some influence over wealthy merchants or company officials seeking to carry out state orders in Senegal, as they were often their lovers or wives. As slaveholders, they also provided European sailors and general laborers sexual access to enslaved girls in their households and later absorbed children produced from those relationships into their households. Through these gendered and sexual negotiations of power, they interacted with the French as coeval host-partners in commerce rather than as colonial subjects—and it was this relationship that was at stake in struggles over abolishing the slave trade and control of access to interior markets. As historical sources, these images further suggest that those at the apex of Saint-Louis society excelled at navigating religious and cultural difference in ways that allowed them to create wealth and power. Though by the 1830s signares lived according to the French civil code,[18] they were also known to modify that code to fit local understandings and to dispense with some European social mores on occasion.

Cloth and textiles were key markers of signares' elite place in Saint-Louis society and evidence signares ability to navigate difference, strategically adopt fashion to fit the local context, and signal their social standing. Their signature tall head wraps—a local distillation of an eighteenth-century trend among elite French metropolitan women for large wigs and turbans—were meant to trumpet their exceptional social status. They were made using imported cloth and ribbons intended to convey the leisure of the wearer but were localized with an artfully arranged style that became uniquely associated with Saint-Louis. Lamiral described them as resembling "a tiara with a triple crown" meant to indicate that the wearer was not a commoner who carried items on her head (see figure 4.7).[19]

Signares not only promoted forms of metropolitan and hybrid fashion but also participated in a wider regional textile economy in which cloth was both an exchange currency and a powerful personal expression of taste, social status, and belonging. Often, cloth circulated through mechanisms of patron-client relationships that organized the transport of connected distant markets and brought loom-patterned Cape Verdean cloths over long distances to reach individual buyers in Gorée Island and Ndar/Saint-Louis. Moreover, dress was a medium of expression in the performance of power and status lubricating commercial negotiations. The sources suggest something of the slipperiness of social identification in which personas could be made and unmade through dress according to the context. Lamiral wrote with equal parts outrage and marvel at how some redistribution from the market to local people occurred as he saw it. He described an Arabo-Berber chief who was as "badly dressed and poorly fed" as the poorest of his subjects. On a trading day, the chief would turn up with an entourage all dressed in beautiful robes made of *pagnes,* a locally woven strip cloth. If the chief had none of his own, he would borrow some from a signare who, as matron of a household, might have acquired varieties of textiles and garments to be worn on special occasions. Negotiating prices, the chief would "march about with gravitas, look around with a disdainful air, and have [Lamiral's] words repeated to him by two interpreters even though he has well understood."[20]

Having obtained an acceptable amount of goods in part through his sartorial performance, the unidentified chief and his entourage returned home where, as Lamiral saw it, social distinctions appeared to fade away. Those

FIGURE 4.7. European doll dressed in the style of a Saint-Louis signare, likely donated by the abolitionist Victor Schoelcher in the late nineteenth century and refurbished in the late twentieth century, AR6192273 Photo Credit: © Musée du Quai Branly—Jacques Chirac / Art Resource, NY.

once referred to as "slaves" were now free enough to eat from the same bowl and smoke from the same pipe as their chief. Also, the Moorish chief would quickly distribute goods just obtained from the French—textiles, gunpowder, guns, and accessories worth "40 to 50 thousand French livres"—within an hour or so: "When the chief had given it all away, if his people were still not satisfied, they would take even his shirt, saying to him, 'you can still give up the shirt, the whites will not refuse you something to wear.'"[21]

Lamiral's description points to the existence of a social contract among the Hassaniya Arabic-speaking groups, wherein recognized leaders owed their status in large part to their ability to both protect and provide for their followers. Certainly, this was the case with the Trarza military chief el-Kawry, described separately at length by Lamiral, who arranged a customs payment of indigo cottons from the company for several subofficials, who also in turn likely redistributed goods to their own circles of dependents.

Arabo-Berber communities consisted of nomadic pastoralists. They settled in tent camps near the river when commercial traffic increased, then relocated north into desert camps. Lamiral's characterization of his Arabo-Berber partner—as a despot and a thief—fit a broader orientalist worldview that also animated a racial and gendered transatlantic discourse about Africans amid struggles over slavery and abolition. Lamiral was critical of a gender division of labor that allegedly reversed the dominant European Catholic patriarchal order. He claimed that among these pastoralist groups, women did the lion's share of both the daily household and artisanal work, while men, except when engaged in warfare or tending to herds, did "nothing but sleep and smoke a pipe."[22]

Lamiral had a clear stake in these debates. He was a self-interested advocate of the slave trade, and he was bitterly opposed to abolitionists like Abbe Henri Gregoire and Thomas Clarkson. His work on Africa also consciously fed an evolving eighteenth-century discourse among European naturalists seeking to establish a typology of human "races," as is clear by his reference to the influential work of Georges-Louis Leclerc, Comte de Buffon.[23] He describes Africans as technologically less developed than their peers elsewhere and opines that the alleged reality might represent a permanent condition. At the same time, Lamiral grudgingly acknowledges the diversity of locally manufactured textiles and their high aesthetic appeal. He wrote that Fulbe women appeared to him as West African embodiments of Greek goddesses, "their wrappers made of light and floating muslin that they made themselves, and that resembled the belt of Venus." When it came to indigo-dyed cottons, Lamiral avers that African dyers produced "the most beautiful color. Our most beautiful guinees from India are less vivid and less azure. They don't just make single-colored cloths. They also know the art of making patterns and designs."

In western Africa, ideas about status, hierarchy, and race, whether Euro-Atlantic or African, were complex. These eighteenth-century Euro-Atlantic ideas did not operate on a tabula rasa, as Bruce Hall has shown. Rather, they overlaid or competed with an older regional discourse within the Sahel about racial difference, one that was not organized around phenotype and skin color but rather around notions of lineage, genealogical descent, and proximity to a Muslim Arab ancestor or notable Muslim scholar.[24]

As discursive claims, they did not predict or determine how particular people actually lived. But they offer clues to the likely priorities, motivations, and concerns of the diverse historical actors interacting in this context and who thereby shaped the historical meaning of these ideas in practical terms. Beyond judging the merits of Lamiral's claims, we can see in his account and in similar observations by foreigners that commercial relations between various social groupings in and around Saint-Louis were gendered, could be expressed in material form, notably through textiles, and carried certain expectations of reciprocity. In the heterogeneous Senegal River valley, dress mattered as an important though contingent means of self-assertion that drew from its connections to a commodity flow through networks that spanned two ocean perimeters. At the same time, these social relations were embedded within, and perhaps helped to obscure, a larger process of colonial extraction that ultimately would not rebound to the region's benefit.

## SAILORS AS SELLERS AND CONSUMERS ALONG THE SENEGAL RIVER VALLEY

Maritime-related activities were a primary aspect of daily life in Saint-Louis. Seasonal commerce along the river was an essential part of business because it was how local merchants accessed goods for export overseas—enslaved captives, gum resin, gold—and for local sustenance, as there was no agriculture on the island, which imported its grain from Wolof- and Fulbe-speaking regions of the mainland. Women and girls constituted most of the island town's enslaved population, working in households pounding millet in mortars that fed both the town's residents and enslaved captives being held for shipment overseas.

About 40 percent of the African men residing in Saint-Louis were laborers in the river trade, including riverboat captains, language interpreters, and canoe builders.[25] Most common were the laptots, derived from the Wolof term *lappato bi*, meaning "interpreter" or cultural translator.[26] By the end of the eighteenth century, the term was used loosely to refer to a class of common laborers, sometimes with specialized skills, that were mostly enslaved to Saint-Louis's signares or habitants. It remained the case, however, that free Muslim migrants from the mainland could also be found among those working as laptots in Saint-Louis, where they lived seasonally and returned periodically to their villages in Waalo or Kayor. Also counted among the laptot ranks were sons of ruling elites from inland states who resided temporarily at the French fort to gain experience in conducting commerce.[27]

Thus, there was considerable difference in the backgrounds, individual qualities, and circumstances among laptots. A 1765 image (figure 4.8) of laptots working for the governor of the French colony on Gorée Island presents a visual map of social hierarchy between Eurafrican and African, gourmets and laptots, "free" and enslaved, through a typology established visually by observable differences in their uniform clothing. Reading from left to right, top to bottom, the image presents a "free mulatto" (Euro-African) captain dressed in a French military officer's uniform with a tricorn hat as the highest-ranking officer of the corps, positioned over a free African; both these men were placed figuratively above the two enslaved men pictured below. There, an African "gourmet" is shown to be both Christian and enslaved but also given the title of "corporal" with superior rank and authority (symbolized by the rifle and bayonet the man holds) over laptots,

FIGURE 4.8. "Uniformes des Corps des Laptots de Goree," 1765, non-cote. Archives Nationales d'Outre-Mer, Aix-en-Provence, France.

126 ~ *The Texture of Change*

such as the one to the right, identified as a "captive," or Muslim slave, and the only man of the four depicted without a weapon. The freemen appear to be wearing European stockings and boots, while the lower-status laptots are barefoot.

These images suggest that eighteenth-century French discourse about western Africans conflated notions of "freedom" and high social status not only with Africans' religious identification as Christian but also with their assimilation to European-tailored clothing styles, which functioned as an outward sign of a more thoroughgoing attachment to European cultural ideals and even biological proximity to Europeans. Lamiral identified gourmets on voyages to Gajaaga as "free" men given key positions such as helmsman or pilot, whereas those designated "laptot" were slaves who performed more arduous tasks. The higher-status company officials accorded to "gourmets" at Saint-Louis, or to Christian-identified Africans in general, helped to distinguish the island society's evolving social structure from that of its neighbors.

Some laptots enslaved to habitants were considered *captifs de case* and could not be sold overseas without social sanction. Their distinction from *captifs de traite,* who were acquired through capture or purchase, was that they were born in their owner's household and were being incorporated as lower-status members of their owner's lineage. Their value, then, derived from reproducing and expanding the owner's lineage. This proscription against the sale of house-born slaves into a market cannot be explained as a response to the Atlantic slave trade per se but rather preceded it as a historical practice among stratified ethnic groups such as the Wolof, Fulbe, Soninke, and Bamana along the Senegal River valley. Its existence shows how the Atlantic economy of slave-based plantation agriculture in the Caribbean, the engine of an emerging capitalism, was fed by exported African labor, but at the same time, it effectively sustained a lineage-based slaving system in western Africa that was focused not solely on producing surplus for a market but also on reproducing social hierarchies.

Laptots typically owed part or most of their earnings to their patron but were often permitted to trade on their own behalf as a form of compensation. Although enslaved, some individuals rose in status over time and could be placed in positions of authority over others. In the late 1780s, most unskilled laptots earned three iron bars a month. Several categories of skilled laptot laborers earned significantly more, including a maître de langue, paid twelve bars a month; a carpenter or master mason, ten bars a month; a caulker, six bars a month; and a baker or shepherd, five bars a month.[28] On commercial voyages upriver, women also labored as cooks and launderers. Like the men, they were permitted to trade for themselves, and some likely parlayed success in this activity into acquiring significant income and even purchasing their independence. Although reflecting only a portion of the economic activity that year, the document suggests differentiation of earning capacity across the population that can be obscured by a focus on their status as enslaved people.

The precise ways that those laborers may have spent or redistributed possible surplus income is difficult to document with any specificity. Rather, the capacity of such common laborers as economic actors and consumers must be inferred from anecdotal evidence showing the multiple opportunities presented to them while buying and selling on long journeys to the interior and back. Company officials occasionally complained of laptots taking excessive liberties with their independent trading of company goods that were never accounted for, or of allowing enslaved captives purchased with company goods to escape, thus cutting into profits. Many laptot sellers traded salt for goods on the river. With access to imported cloth, especially indigo guinees, laptot sellers could obtain a range of other goods, from food such as grain or goats to local cloths or gold dust, thus animating a wider economy. Saugnier notes the company generally turned a blind eye to such behavior because it feared the possibility of a labor strike.[29]

Laptots were reportedly known for abusive behavior toward villagers in places where company ships stopped to trade. Such claims about strikes, theft, and contraband indicate the conscious behavior of those laptots, whether enslaved or free, who were aware of their power within social and economic systems larger than themselves and who strategically sought to extract material benefit from their location within those systems.

The maneuverings of petty traders informed the circulation and distribution of goods within the region in ways that went beyond formal structures of capitalist exchange that imagined individualized transactions between a seller and a buyer using fixed currency in a market. Historians have moved beyond earlier characterizations of barter exchanges as "simple." There is increasing recognition of its complexities, such as the role of illicit trading and even theft in steering commodities to consumers, especially nonelites who would not have otherwise gained access to them.[30] As entrepreneurs, laptots extracted benefits from operating between the profit-driven demands of European mercantile companies and the patronage systems of African rulers and patrons.

Charles Scipio, a riverboat captain and successful African resident who spoke Wolof, Bamana, Fulbe, Arabic, English, and French exemplified the process. Scipio won prestige through his military and commercial exploits in the river trade. Migration is a critical part of Scipio's biography. He is thought to have originally come to Saint-Louis in the 1760s when the British occupied the fort, as a captive from the Bamana-speaking lands east of Gajaaga. By the 1780s, Scipio was commander of a force of laptot crew members on a convoy to Gajaaga led by the French slave trader Saugnier. The account demonstrates how Scipio's linguistic, diplomatic, and fighting skills were indispensable even for an otherwise ill-fated convoy repeatedly beset by accidents that endangered its vessels, merchandise, and crew members. Local rulers often claimed property or taxation rights over shipwrecked, unauthorized vessels grounded on their territory. Saugnier's convoy was confronted by such claims during the journey to Gajaaga and back at least four times—by the Trarza chief Ahmet Moctar; a ruler of Bakel; his overlord, the Serakhule tunka at Gajaaga; and even opportunistic Fulbe soldiers at the Fuuta Tooro.[31] Considering the high season traffic on the river of dozens of commercial vessels owned by both European and habitant merchants, these seizures could amount to a significant stream of goods exiting the market into the stocks of powerful or opportunistic entrepreneurs. Mercantile company officials usually characterized such actions as simple theft, but they were also another mechanism through which, by claiming sovereign control of terrain, imported goods circulated into the region.

Midway through the voyage, Saugnier discovered that the bales of indigo cotton cloths he intended to exchange for enslaved captives at Gajaaga contained serious flaws. Many were unevenly colored, of poor quality, and virtually unsalable, representing a major loss for the entire venture. The guinees had been imported to France from southern India to be dyed and reexported to Africa. Rushing to participate in a seasonal trade and turn a profit, bundlers in France sold them to Africa-bound ships at discounted prices, perhaps oblivious to the fact that the cloth's value to African buyers lay in the finishing, without which the cloths were worth little. The telling detail that imported white cottons from Asia were dyed in France rather than in India already suggested their dubious prospects in western African markets. Africans admired such cloths for the intensity of their dark blue or black color, with a coppery red sheen visible on the surface produced from the oversaturation of added starch. Indigo cottons were a well-established product of the West African weavers and dyers for centuries, with some subregions famous for the quality of their output, such as villages and towns in Gajaaga and along the Niger River, with perhaps the largest centers at Jenne and Timbuktu.

For French mercantile company officials, the price, quality, and source of the indigo guinees imported into Senegambia were a cause of regular concern. From the perspective of African consumers, the insistence on the quality of the dyed cloth may have been a reflection of its value not only as protective daily clothing but also as an exchangeable currency in regional markets. Textile manufacturers at Rouen and Nantes seeking to compete in the region endeavored to reproduce better quality indigo-dyed cloths throughout the eighteenth century, but African consumer demand favored French reliance on manufacturing at Pondicherry in southern India, with buyers preferring cloths from there well into the nineteenth century.[32] This is one way that African regional demand structured a wider external economy that was global in scope.[33] A 1786 memo from the French Senegal Company confirms Saugnier's observation of a clear preference for the Indian cottons, indicating that French-manufactured copies of indigo cotton cloths from India, even though significantly cheaper, were "impossible to employ for commerce in Senegal, especially for the gum trade and even less so as presents or customs payments. Only superior quality guinees from India are required."[34]

In Saugnier's case, it was the laptot Scipio who successfully traded 120 pieces of the guinee cloth salvaged from the damaged lot by traveling upriver with a small crew to markets at Tambaakundaa while the Frenchman stayed behind as the guest of the tunka. And it was again Scipio who later maneuvered Saugnier out of a bind, recovering some of his merchandise from the tunka when the latter tried to claim them. Scipio had gained a reputation at Gajaaga as a shrewd and charismatic leader. Saugnier reported that at one point, Scipio confronted the tunka by declaring that the tunka's sovereignty ended at the land's edge, whereas Scipio's own was on the river, and that he "was not of the disposition to be enslaved by a black king."

Such a bold statement suggests the social disruption incurred and that an enslaved laptot might achieve social mobility by allying with a powerful sponsor (in this case, a powerful foreign sponsor) to protect himself from hostile enemies. Thus by the 1790s, having distinguished himself in several commercial convoys to the interior, Scipio had become a respected member of the habitant community who signed his name to petitions, such as the one demanding that habitants' right to trade on equal terms with mercantile company ships be protected by the metropolitan government.

In turning from their roles as commercial agents to those as consumers, laptots returning from a successful months-long voyage were said to celebrate in Saint-Louis in fine clothes purchased at interior markets: expensive kusaaba and brightly colored, wide cloth belts embroidered with wool or silk,[35] both specialty products of Gajaaga. This shows not only that regional "fashions" circulated within western Africa but that in Saint-Louis they contributed to a polyrhythmic interplay between discrete discourses of social meaning, value, and status. Rare mentions of *habitant* men suggest many wore imported European breeches, shirts, and waistcoats. Higher-status laborers like Scipio, even those who remained enslaved, may have appropriated such garments to embody and distinguish themselves from younger or less storied men. But larger numbers of these laborers worked for Eurafricans or Africans and had little contact with Europeans, who were a small and often transient minority of the island's resident population. Many would have had little access to tailored European garments but some access to individual articles or to lengths of cloth purchased in the market or received as payment for goods or services. They dressed in local rather than European styles, wearing breeches known as *dhiata* and loose tunic-like boubou, also called *mboube*.[36] Even more basic were locally made white cotton shirts, breechclouts, and white caps like those worn by the African sailors standing upright as they paddled on the open seas that Gabriel Bray depicted aboard the British ship *Pallas* during a stop in Saint-Louis in the 1770s (figure 4.9).

In 1796, Jacques Grasset de Saint-Sauveur, a Canada-born former French diplomat, published twenty-five etchings of Senegambians drawn from traveler accounts (see figures 4.10–13).[37] The *Encyclopédie des voyages* featured sixty-six engravings depicting a wide range of men and women in different parts of Africa, from Egypt and the Maghreb through parts of West, West Central, and southern Africa. It was part of a wider series that

FIGURE 4.9. African canoe paddling through surf, Gabriel Bray, 1775 © National Maritime Museum, Greenwich, UK.

*The Politics of Dress during an Age of Islamic Revolution, 1785–1815* ⁓ 131

included collections on dress among Indigenous populations of the Americas, Europe, and Asia. In his introduction to the work, Saint-Sauveur notes a particular taste for fashion in Saint-Louis, stating people's desire to distinguish themselves in society resulted in frequent changes in taste and clothing styles: "The young people that want to [be attractive] have their tunics and breeches painted with bands of colour, flowers and with other lovely designs." His images of Senegambians depict forms of sartorial creolization as people combined elements of dress, such as men wearing striped or red sashes with fringes or a tricorn felt hat, and detail how those in traditionally proscribed social roles, such as praise singers or herbalists, created novel assemblages from diverse goods within their reach.

FIGURE 4.10. "Man with Walking Stick," representations of people in Senegal in Jacques Grasset de Saint-Sauveur, *Encyclopédie des voyages: Contenant l'abrégé historique* [...] ([Paris], 1796).

FIGURE 4.11. "Pretre sacrificateur / Sacrificial Priest," representations of people in Senegal in Jacques Grasset de Saint-Sauveur, *Encyclopédie des voyages: Contenant l'abrégé historique* [...] ([Paris], 1796).

FIGURE 4.12. "Guerrier de l'Isle de Saint Louis / Warrior and Signare on Saint Louis," representations of people in Senegal in Jacques Grasset de Saint-Sauveur, *Encyclopédie des voyages: Contenant l'abrégé historique* [...] ([Paris], 1796)

FIGURE 4.13. "Woman in Senegal," representations of people in Senegal in Jacques Grasset de Saint-Sauveur, *Encyclopédie des voyages: Contenant l'abrégé historique* [...] ([Paris], 1796).

## ISLAMIC REFORM IN WEST AFRICA DURING THE AGE OF ATLANTIC REVOLUTIONS

During the years marked by imperial warfare between Britain and France and the eventual British decision to ban slave trading for its subjects, residents of Saint-Louis felt pressure from multiple directions. Commerce with the island was blockaded multiple times, whether from British ships on the Atlantic or from African forces refusing passage along the river to the interior.

Unlike the Euro-Christian commercial center at Saint-Louis, the Torodbe movement had extensive regional networks that connected Quranic schools in parts of Mauritania to the Kayor region south of Saint-Louis, to Gajaaga and Bundu in the east, and the Fuuta Jallon plateau a few hundred miles to the south. Rudolph Ware has persuasively argued that these movements emerged out of a centuries-old ethos of West African Islamic intellectual tradition that idealized various forms of embodied knowledge, from practices of corporal discipline such as fasting to the conception of the faithful memorizing the *Quran* as the physical vessels, guardians, and protectors of the Book and its teachings.[38] Torodbe reformers emphasized values such as piety, personal humility, and keeping distance from political power. In this view, the eruption of the Torodbe-led revolution stemmed from the belief that the enslavement of Muslims violated not merely the rights of individuals but core affirmations of the faith and therefore must be opposed.

Qadir Kan's worldview and social agenda were shaped by his lineage and scholarly background, which connected him to some of the most important scholars and Muslim holy places in western Africa.[39] Elevated with the title *almaami* (imam), he expanded the building of mosques and Quranic schools as a basis for the society he envisioned. Part of that vision must have been pursued by clerics and other Muslim elites who were purveyors of particular forms of dress—including styles covering more of the body and cloth made of plant fibers rather than animal skin or by-products (as an example, see figure 4.14). Their shaping of regional taste and consumer needs must be considered a factor of commercial dynamics.

But as a strategic response to the enslavement of Muslims for sale into overseas markets, Kan's embargo of trade with Saint-Louis did not fit neatly with the discourses of either the European slavers or the European missionary–inspired abolitionists. Kan's outrage at the enslavement of Muslims did not speak to the enslavement of non-Muslims, who continued to be legally enslaved. The sources are notably silent on whether this abolition extended across gender lines to include the manumission of enslaved

FIGURE 4.14. "Diai Boukari" in Gaspard Théodore comte de Mollien, *Travels in the Interior of Africa, to the Sources of the Senegal and Gambia: Performed by Command of the French Government, in the Year 1818* (London: H. Colburn, 1820).

domestic female laborers or concubines. Nor was his conflict with the French a complete rejection of commerce with Europeans. It was closer to an apparent attempt to contain and to regulate such exchange by harnessing it to his project of Islamic reform. Boubacar Barry has noted that in taking power Kan adopted several ceremonial customs from the Fuuta Jallon, Fulbe neighbors to the south to whom they were connected, and also retained some symbolic traditions of the Denyanke as a form of blended state craft.[40] While he appointed imams and local officials in villages throughout the Fuuta to collect taxes from farmers and pastoralists for his administration, there were also instances where he did not replace local leaders and instead worked through them to carry out his aims.[41] Thus the Fulbe-led clerical revolution was attentive in a variety of ways to the diverse cultural and political interests within the territory they controlled.

The importance of this balance is best reflected in a now epic confrontation with the *dammel* (king) of Wolof-speaking Kayor in 1796, when Kan's army was routed during its attack and Almaami Kan himself was captured. The defeat marked a turn in the fortunes of the Torodbe state and the history of Kayor, the polity immediately inland from Saint-Louis that controlled villages along the coast between Saint-Louis and Gorée. Possessing a cavalry and army of about five thousand, Kayor had attempted its own boycott of French trade in 1788 and 1789. Traditionally, the dammel, as ruler of Kayor, was nominally Muslim, but his authority derived not from clerical education but from his kinship claims to a noble lineage. They were known to appear in public on horseback, magnificently dressed in garments of local manufacture with ample sleeves and proportions, along with silver adornments and feathers incorporated into their headwear. According to Clarkson, the dammel provided uniforms for the ceddo soldiers of his army, which were locally woven cotton garments of a light brown color made with local dyes.

Clerical communities were spatially and politically isolated from power in Kayor, this spatial configuration centuries-old in West Africa, and members of the Kayor nobility were not permitted to intermarry with clerical families. Nevertheless, two important Quranic schools at Pir and Kokki flourished in Kayor, drawing multiethnic, multilingual cohorts of students from around the region to study with renowned scholars there. Kan himself had once studied in both places, a period when he is said to have learned to speak Wolof and studied from a Wolof-speaking scholar at Kokki, Matar Ndumbe.[42] By the time Almaami Kan had come to power and brought his Torodbe movement to Kayor, he would have been well aware of the sympathy for the wider reforms likely found in these clerical communities. Condemning the dammel as drunkard and apostate, the almaami sent messengers to Kayor demanding that he cease drinking the trade liquor eau-de-vie and all alcohol, shave his head, and wrap it in a white turban as symbols of his submission to Kan's authority. Viewing this as an infringement of his sovereignty, the dammel's army resisted Kan's forces with much brutality and scorched earth, sending captured fighters to slavers at Saint-Louis. The dammel held the defeated almaami captive for three months before allowing him to return to the Fuuta Tooro.[43]

Several months later, Scottish explorer Mungo Park heard an account of the events near the foothills of the Fuuta Jallon plateau, hundreds of miles to the southeast, where local praise singers proclaimed the dammel's actions.[44] Qadir Kan returned to his capital, recouped his forces, and the following year, his army launched eastward, but the loss at Bukooy initiated a period of decline in Kan's power and increasing challenges to it through his eventual death in battle in 1806. The symbolism of the white cotton turban mentioned by Lamiral represented a debate and struggle internal to distinct African constituencies engaged in both Atlantic and trans-Saharan commerce. This debate had material ramifications, as wearing the turban was meant to imply an accompanying shift in behaviors, including in patterns of consumption, personal comportment, and dress that might become common throughout Kayor.

## THE EMBODIED COSMOPOLITANISMS OF THE SENEGAL RIVER VALLEY IN THE EARLY NINETEENTH CENTURY

This chapter has shown that African laborers, such as laptots, cooks, and grain pounders (*pileuses*), animated global commercial linkages by also working as petty traders on convoys along the Senegal River valley. With the advent of mass-produced cottons, consumers along the Senegal River valley continued to prefer Indian cottons as a primary import. Further, colonial ambitions were subject not only to control over adequate farmland but to labor to work on it, both of which remained elusive to the British within the context of the competing African interests in and around Saint-Louis. "There can be no doubt that cotton and indigo and many other articles of colonial produce could be cultivated advantageously in the vicinity of Senegal," wrote the British lieutenant governor Charles Maxwell in 1811. "Indeed a considerable quantity of cotton is gathered for the manufacture of cloths both in the settlement and in the native villages and is obtained at a very cheap rate. The character of the natives is too indolent to form any reasonable hope of their being ever cultivated by them for exportation."[45]

These farmers made themselves intractable for the purposes of colonial labor projects. But Maxwell's statement suggests that a vibrant commerce in local textiles remained out of the control of British colonists even as consumers in Senegal had access to the foreign textiles being imported by Britain. In Saint-Louis, this economic complexity was matched by the social intricacies of a multiethnic, multilingual population existing within overlapping discourses of law and custom. In that environment, the seeming cultural fluidity of signares and other habitants, evident in clothing styles and social practices remarked upon by observers, was not a failed attempt at imitating European norms, but an embodied material expression of the island's social landscape. It extended a wider pattern of cultural pluralism practiced by African elites in a variety of contexts throughout the region.

The cultural ecumene of early nineteenth-century Saint-Louis was cosmopolitan in its embrace of overseas and regional influences but in ways that may have confounded the ideological expectations of their contemporaries in both Paris and the Fuuta Tooro. Africa-born habitants protected their access to foreign sources of wealth and imported commodities by allying with European trade partners. Yet for many, this did not foreclose the possibility of alliances with Muslim or other Africans, which they also cultivated. This polyglot African coastal society developed a preference for specific goods such as indigo-dyed, check-patterned, or painted Indian cottons; British woolens and linens; printed French *indiennes;* coral and glass beads; Maria Theresa silver dollars (used to make jewelry); and brass buttons from Birmingham, England—all of which became incorporated into forms of local dress and bodily adornment.

The circulation of these goods throughout the region was highly uneven, with different segments of the Senegambian population accessing them only through proximity to certain elite actors or centers of power and wealth. Their adoption as clothing, whether in combination with local textiles and accessories or not, articulates the history of fashion in Senegal at the dawn of an era understood as a prelude to a colonial project associated with delivering civilization and modernity. Into the nineteenth century, dress mediated the countervailing forces of an expanding colonial power from the coast and the expanding influence of Islam from the Sahelian interior—a process informed by a longer tradition of tolerance for cultural pluralism. It is an embodied history of social and economic relations, which reveals multiple premodern forms of cosmopolitanism in West Africa linked to the global circulation of people, goods, and ideas.

After Napoleon's defeat at Saint-Domingue in the Caribbean and ultimately to the British in Europe, the French returned to Saint-Louis once more, having agreed at the Congress of Vienna in 1815 to ban the slave trade. A new generation of French merchants, organized in small private firms rather than under a state-backed mercantile company, again took up the idea to develop an agricultural colony worked by paid laborers as an alternative to the slave plantation economies of the Americas. They imagined that plantations of cotton and indigo would become the basis of a new colonial economy, feeding other parts of an imperial network. But these efforts to draw the multifaceted, overlapping economies of the region into a single capitalist industrial and financial system controlled by Europe would not so easily overcome the complex realities of western Africa.

## 5 ~ Merchants, Maroons, Mahdis, and Migrants on the Upper Guinea Coast, 1795–1825

THOMAS COOPER found himself one sweltering evening in 1796 hosting three European visitors in his home in Dominghia, a trading port town near where the Rio Pongo flows at its widest girth into the Atlantic Ocean. Four years earlier, Cooper had been one of the "Black Poor" of London and had come to Freetown. He had since come to the Rio Pongo accepting an opportunity to operate a trading factory in the area on land rented to the Sierra Leone Company by a local Susu chief, Mungo Kerefa, later named Freeport. The company hoped that Cooper's activity at Freeport might generate valuable produce to support the colony at Freetown, Sierra Leone. As company agent, Cooper occupied an unenviable position. Of African descent, he was the settler face of the company's missionary-driven push into the region with its agenda to end slave trading, develop alternative commodity commerce and, eventually, offer missionary education. Freeport sat downriver from several trading posts operated by British, American, African, and Eurafrican merchants, who sought to continue slave trading and viewed the company's activities as impositions on their sovereignty.

Over a meal of wine and biscuits, Cooper told his visitors a story about the daring escape of three enslaved women from their enslaver's compound not far away. The three women, together, had been held on the coast for several months after being purchased in the Fuuta Jallon. There, they had been put to domestic work for the trader's wives while he waited for an opportunity to sell them to an arriving ship bound for the Americas in exchange for its trade goods. On their third attempt, three of the women (the fourth was pregnant, which made her flight difficult) made their escape after one dressed herself in the best of her mistress's clothes, garments that she had likely washed many times and carefully observed. Thus disguised as an elite woman, she presented herself to those they met on their way as a wife of the powerful Fulbe ruler of the Fuuta Jallon, Almaami Sadu. She and her two assistants had visited the coast and were returning to Timbo, the capital town of a Fulbe clerical state that had grown wealthy and powerful from conquest and slave trading.[1]

Though Cooper told the story of the three women as an allegory against the slave trade, it also reveals that in the same period that laptots, Eurafrican habitant signares, and Islamic reformers were influencing a politics of dress and consumption in Saint-Louis, hundreds of miles north, the imperatives of a different western African economy of dress and consumption fanning from the interior highlands of the Fuuta Jallon along the many paths and rivers flowing to the Guinean coast between the Rio Nunez and Freetown was also shaping the integrated global trade in enslaved persons, textiles, and other goods.

This story of an escape to Timbo may or may not have been apocryphal, but it likely served to remind its listeners of the clerical state of Fuuta Jallon, the prosperous, temperate plateau region that was just a few days away on foot. Cooper's refugees would have blended into a flow of regular foot traffic on paths between the coast—where a patchwork of Susu-, Baga-, and Maninka-speaking towns and villages shared space with foreign traders settled among them—and the plateau region controlled by a centralized state of Fulbe clerics. Their escape from the coast took place within a context in which slavery and slave trading were important features of a regional political economy also informed by resistance, marronage, and discourses of religious revival and abolition. The women's clothing, along with their bodily adornments, language, and physical demeanor, would have supported their performance of social status, belonging, and claim to the protection of a powerful figure such as the almaami of Timbo. These factors worked together to facilitate the women's movement across a landscape marked alternately by episodes of warfare, diplomacy, and détente.

This chapter examines the ways in which consumption, dress, and material culture mediated social and political hierarchies across a network of

Muslim notables, among the enslaved and those in maroon villages, among the formerly enslaved settlers from the Americas, and among Eurafrican coastal elites who settled in towns and trading villages like Dominghia. It argues that expanding missionary and civilizationist discourses and economies at the turn of the nineteenth century—both African Muslim and European Christian—led to a new politics of dress in which people drew sharper lines of distinction between individuals and groups, solidifying affinities between others. These dynamics also created openings for marginalized others such as women and ethnic minorities to effect social mobility as they navigated the overlapping and contradictory discourses of abolition, antislavery, antiblackness, anticolonialism, and religious reform.

That the enslaved women escaped by fleeing to Timbo and thus *into* the lands controlled by another slaving power suggests both the ubiquity of slavery and the multidirectional ways Africans sought to protect their interests within available constraints. It also suggests the multidirectional binds African women of the region faced in pursuit of their own safety and well-being. Cooper's story of their escape draws attention to the myriad ways in which dress mediated social interactions and physical mobility in the past: when deployed strategically, it enabled people to make particular claims of identity or authority—temporarily, opportunistically, or even subversively—to effect a desired outcome. In the women's case, clothing facilitated physical mobility that might otherwise have been difficult to accomplish, allowing them to move inland from the coast, where foreign traders held sway to areas controlled by the theocratic state. It is likely that a larger set of factors also mattered, including variables such as hair, grooming, body posture, forms of speech, and even knowledge about current events and details of the almaami's life, all of which would have been important to their performance.

The chapter starts with a social and political geography of coastal Guinea, parts of which were dominated by Fuuta Jallon and its Fulbe clerical state but also by several competing actors. These included diverse foreign merchants—most notably formerly enslaved Africans and descendants from the Americas—and inland Muslim merchants with ties to the savanna, who were drawn to the lucrative coastal trade that revolved around slave economies, as well as local headmen and British abolitionists. In the sources relating to many of these notables, the textiles produced, imported, and exchanged along the Guinea coast operated locally as displays of status, values, wealth, and authority. The second half of the chapter examines the contours of the local politics of dress and the importance of nonlocal styles to fashioning and performing status and authority in the context of growing reformist and civilizationist discourses.

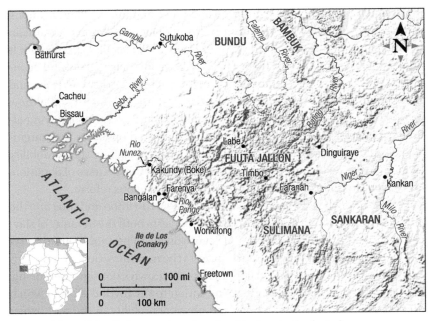

MAP 5.1. Map of the Guinea region showing Kankan in the hot, dry savanna to the northeast, major towns of the Fuuta Jallon on the cooler plateau, and towns along the tropical forested riverine coast from Bissau to Freetown. Map by Matt Johnson at Johnson Cartographic.

First, I focus on one local trader, Fury Cannaba, and what his sartorial hybridity meant in the context of both British abolitionism and Islamic reform movements, whose agents interpreted it in different ways. Second, I examine powerful merchant Fendan Dumbuya and what is revealed about his own state-building ambitions through his military defeat of a community of self-emancipated people at Yanghekori, as well through the public non-Muslim sartorial performance of a Maray—a former slave turned mercenary—for Dumbuya. Third, I examine black Loyalists and other Western or Western-influenced figures along the coast of Guinea and Sierra Leone and their choice of tailored Western garments as signs of their faith, morality, and aspirations. I end by looking at a pointed rejection of this Western sartorial regime on the eve of more formal colonial economic interventions in the area.

## MUSLIM NOTABLES AND COSMOPOLITANS CONNECT THE COAST TO THE PLATEAU AND WIDER REGION

The social, political, and economic geography of coastal western African that Cooper knew from his base in Dominghia was filled by a dense and

142 ~ *Texture of Change*

heterogeneous collection of regional African rulers, Eurafrican merchants, local headmen, European colonial company officials, and their agents and allies. Though slavery and the slave trade were central to the economic, political, and social world of the area, investment in and attitudes toward it varied, making for a complexity of interests vis-à-vis that economy. Broadly, though, what emerges from the sources from this area in the late eighteenth and early nineteenth centuries, in addition to the social and political complexity, is a sense of the role that textiles played in communicating wealth, status, and authority along the waterways and in the communities connecting the Fuuta Jallon to the coast.

One of the major nodes of the coastal geography linking the highlands to coastal centers such as Freetown, Wonkifon, and Dominghia via aquatic avenues such as the Rio Nunez and the Rio Pongo was the plateau capital of Timbo—where the runaway women Cooper spoke of claimed they were trying to reach. The capital was home to a Fulbe clerical state with Almaami Sadu as its head. This state had emerged decades before as a multiethnic reform movement opposing what it viewed as the corrupt governing practices of Jallonke leaders. By the early nineteenth century, authority in the centralized state was more closely identified with two Fulbe lineages whose leaders themselves had, by many accounts, become corrupted by the growing wealth and power they derived from conquest and slave trading. Almaami Sadu and his successors were but a few among a wider constellation of Muslim notables in towns across the savanna, plateau, and coast. They were ethnically and linguistically diverse and preached differing theological interpretations of Islam as well as maintained varied political relations with the Fulbe state. They were generally literate, well informed, and wrestling with the many contradictions of their societies.

Timbo was a walled town of about several thousand people in the 1790s, with residents living in mud-walled, thatch-roof homes along streets that extended from a central courtyard and mosque near the town's entrance (see figure 5.1). The ruler's compound was in a quarter behind the mosque. It was protected by mud walls, and its central courtyard featured an enormous square tower purportedly modeled after a tower that a Fulbe ruler had supposedly once seen on a trip to England.[2] While this claim is not possible to confirm, the idea that such a structure might have been constructed based on an eyewitness description by an African who had visited England and returned to Timbo announced the town's cosmopolitan attachment to a wider world. This architectural curiosity at the center of the Fulbe ruler's compound was just one of many indications of how the town and its people were enmeshed by the long-distance circulation of people, goods, and ideas.

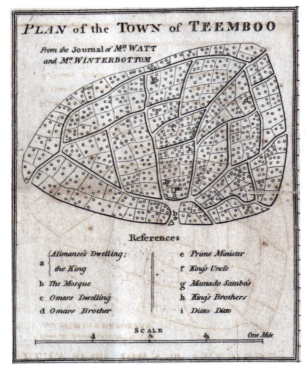

FIGURE 5.1. Detail from 1794 map of Sierra Leone and Bulama Island in Carl Wadstrom, *Observations on the Slave Trade, and a Description of Some Part of the Coast of Guinea, during a Voyage, Made in 1787, and 1788* [...] (London: James Phillips, George-Yard, Lombard-Street, 1789).

That textiles arrived in coastal Guinea alongside rice, salt, and other goods via this global trade, circulated widely in local markets, and eventually found their way to the highlands signaled the sovereign status and authority of the Fulbe state—operating as a diplomatic force equal to European powers by the mid-1790s—and its elites. Members of the almaami's court and household would have readily recognized and received the diplomatic gifts of English scarlet wool and Indian cotton chintz delivered by a delegation from the British colony at Freetown led by James Watt in 1794. Watt had worked as an overseer on slave plantations in the Caribbean colony of Dominica. Since arriving in Sierra Leone a few years earlier, Watt had been tasked with managing workers on a farm on the Bullom Shore that grew cotton, sugar cane, tobacco, coffee, and rice to support the colony at Freetown. Having gained a reputation as an able negotiator with landlords on the Bullom Shore, the colonial governor Zachary Macaulay charged Watt with a diplomatic visit to the Fuuta Jallon to secure regular commercial exchanges between the plateau and the fledgling coastal settlement. The gifts of clothing rejuvenated the dress of some Fulbe notables, whose robes Watt described as being "of fine flowered muslin, though now worn almost to rags." These gifts from a European thus symbolized the renewed potential of Timbo under Sadu.

The wealth and authority Timbo enjoyed by 1794 were the product of the stability Sadu's military leadership ushered in following a military challenge by Konde Birama of the Wasulu region in the 1780s, which destroyed much of Timbo's infrastructure and killed or displaced many of its residents. After Sadu became almaami in 1794, he used his power to exhibit his authority and safeguard the state's economic might, aggressively confronting European traders on the coast who angered him by paying lower prices for captives trafficked by Fulbe caravans. He imposed a trade embargo, refusing all commerce with foreign traders "from Cape Verga to Cape Mount," a claim recorded by Watt that likely exaggerated the scale of Timbo's actual influence but nevertheless does give an indication of the imagined power of Fuuta armies in the region. In contrast to the ban at Saint-Louis imposed by Almaami Qadir Kan to the north, Almaami Sadu at Timbo sought not only to protect the slave trade (rather than to abolish it) but also to keep as high as possible the prices paid for enslaved captives.[3] When traders offered only 120 irons bars per captive, Sadu reportedly forbade any trade at all until the price climbed back to his desired 160 bars.[4] Despite reports that not everyone respected the embargo, Sadu's ban did push the price back up to 150 bars per captive after a few months, which demonstrates the strength of his authority during this period. Religious revival at Timbo helped to legitimate the state's trafficking in captives from its wars and raids of its non-Muslim neighbors. Such trafficking was critically important to its economy and the political power of the clerical state, which Watt's gifts of textiles symbolized.[5]

Despite the economic and political might of Timbo, on the coast, in the surrounding savanna, and even in some areas within the Fuuta Jallon itself, there were a number of others with competing interests, some of whom did not participate in the slaving economy, did so on a smaller scale, or even actively resisted it.[6] Enclaves of marronage, where self-emancipated peasant farmers settled in separate areas sometimes protected by walls, could be found throughout the region from the Fuuta Jallon to the coast.[7] Adding to the heterogeneous populations residing on the coast were newcomers like Cooper, one of several thousand African-born or African-descendant settlers who had come to the region black Loyalists who had been resettled in London or in Nova Scotia following the American Revolution, along with some free black people from the Caribbean. Most of the returnees lived in Freetown, but Cooper was among a smaller number who settled near the Rio Pongo. In its first two decades in the region, the Sierra Leone Company supported plans of the Church Missionary Society to build missionary education for children in the Rio Pongo by trying to establish trade outposts and relationships with local partners that might supply the colony with food or trade goods.[8]

The commercial towns of coastal Guinea were different from Saint-Louis, where most foreign merchants were French and rarely settled in villages on the mainland or in the interior. In Guinea, however, foreign merchants of more diverse European and American origins settled in numerous villages along multiple rivers flowing from the interior to the Atlantic coast north of Freetown. Foreign traders and African migrants to the coast anchored themselves in coastal communities by marrying into local families, a long-established practice in western Africa that signals gender and sexuality as critical to shifting social and commercial relations within the larger context of Atlantic slaving and the emergence of legitimate commerce. As guests of local African landlords and married to local women, foreign and migrant men on the coast maintained households and clients who supported and protected their local operations. Children from these relationships inherited these households to become part of an expanding privileged, slave-owning class of Eurafrican merchants. Both before and after British abolition of the slave trade in 1807, many "illegal" foreign traders—English, French, Spanish, and American—took advantage of the serpentine coastal waterways and mangroves to evade Sierra Leone Company officials.

Eurafrican and African merchant women were also key players in this region, both as wives of foreign traders and in their own right. They used their influence to mediate between the fledgling settlement at Freetown, those with slave-trading interests along the rivers, and Maninka- and Susu-speaking Muslim clerical towns on the coast, all of which competed for inland caravan and overseas maritime trade. In one image of Banjul, Gambia, from the early 1820s (figure 5.2), a Eurafrican signare faces a Maninka headman at the center of a small group of people, recalling the way similar figures appear as central figures of social life in images of Saint-Louis. Wearing brightly dyed indigo robes and a white cloth turban adorned with red embroidery, the headman carries a curved machete, gesturing toward the signare. His indigo robes represent simultaneously a traditional African aesthetic and an eighteenth-century modernity fed by the global circulation of indigo cloth as a luxury commodity. The signare is depicted as a fair-skinned woman dressed in bright yellow robes, the abundance of cloth covering her entire body from neck to ankle and draping lavishly from her limbs. The heavy jewelry about her ears and neck; a tall, conical turban; and the imported umbrella she carries convey the impression she makes as a person of means. In contrast, a woman in a more plainly colored wrapper carrying an

FIGURE 5.2. "Costume of the Gambia" in Thomas Edward Bowdich, *Excursions in Madeira and Porto Santo during the Autumn of 1823, While on His Third Voyage to Africa* (London, 1825).

infant on her back and a basket on her head passes behind the two central figures, as does a red-turbaned man carrying weapons or tools.

Indigo-clad Maninka headmen proliferated along the Guinean coast south of Banjul during this period, competing with one another in their separate interactions with caravans from the interior. For instance, Maninka-speaking settlers from the Bate region of Kankan migrated in the eighteenth century to found the coastal clerical town of Forecaria located between today's Conakry and Freetown in Sierra Leone. The ancestors of its headman in the early nineteenth century, Almaami Daouda Toure, were said to have welcomed successive arrivals of additional Maninka-speaking settlers from the savanna to Forecaria, including the Dafe from Woulada and the Cisse and the Soumah from Bate and eastern savanna.[9] This process of migration and settlement in the eighteenth century was more important demographically in areas on the Guinea rivers' coasts than it had been at Saint-Louis or on the northern Senegambian coast. There appears to have been a greater diversity of local peoples who acted as hosts for the coastal newcomers, who were often Maninka speakers from different parts of the savanna. The western coast was a "hinterland" from the larger populations and the bigger markets of the savanna, which had been previously oriented northward to

*Merchants, Maroons, Mahdis, and Migrants on the Upper Guinea Coast*

trans-Saharan trade and were then only gradually drifted toward more emphasis on the coast.[10]

Wonkifon was another important town in the region. Swallowed up today by the sprawling city of Conakry, Guinea, the town of Wonkifon sat at the edge of a river flowing south to the Atlantic and benefited from caravans it received from the Fuuta Jallon. By the early nineteenth century, Fendan Modu Dumbuya was already a wealthy senior man in Wonkifon. He was the scion of a merchant who had migrated to the coast from the gold mining region of Bambuk, settling in the 1750s in Kissi, which was Susu speaking but already home to a number of family members also from Bambuk. This was part of a larger migration of Maninka-speaking Muslims drawn by Atlantic trade opportunities from savanna settlements north and northeast of the forested coast. The elder Dumbuya was said to have trafficked between Bambuk and the coast in enslaved people, ivory, and gold, which he exchanged for imported European scarlet wool (often sought after by African buyers for the vibrancy of its color), imitation coral beads, a local African cloth called *arunku,* and (likely) salt.[11] Fendan Dumbuya likewise capitalized on the coastal trade, controlling several trading villages where hundreds of enslaved laborers grew rice, tobacco, and, notably, cotton on his land for sale to European, American, and African buyers.[12] Unlike Sadu at Timbo, Dumbuya was not a political ruler of his home settlement of Wonkifon, where, as a Maninka Muslim migrant, he remained an adviser to the Susu lineage head of the town.

In good years, Fendan Dumbuya could organize a caravan of up to one thousand to sell his produce and imported goods in the interior savanna, and one of his agents—a Baga man named Thomas Williams, who had been to Liverpool and spoke English—sold his rice to European and American ships that stopped at the Iles de Los, facing present-day Conakry. Dumbuya informed a British naval officer visiting Wonkifon on a diplomatic mission in 1802 that enslaved laborers working for him between Wonkifon and other territories were producing "100 tons of salt and 100 tons of rice" annually along with "360 beyles" of cotton and a "considerable quantity" of coffee.[13] These quantities are difficult to measure in contemporary terms, but Dumbuya's comments suggest the scale of his operations and also place an emphasis on commodities that were desirable in Europe, such as coffee. They also suggest that Dumbuya's laborers produced both crops for export, such as the "beyles" of cotton and coffee sold to Europeans, and commodities for sale within the region, such as salt and rice. Cloth was a critical trade good in this context, as Dumbuya sent inland his weavers' output as well as what he imported from Europe and Asia to markets at Benna, the Fuuta Jallon,

Solimana, and elsewhere in exchange for enslaved captives, gold, ivory, and cattle. Perhaps even more explicitly than was the case for the Fuuta Tooro and Bundu, the available sources in this region suggest that the production of Dumbuya's agricultural estates were organized for "long-distance" markets and looking to expand. Even the settlement's location—along a river that opened to the Atlantic Ocean but far enough inland to facilitate exchange with land-based traffic from the interior highlands—suggests its role as an entrepôt. Some Fula herders reportedly believed their cattle preferred the salt panned on the coast by suppliers like Dumbuya to the rock salt available from desert sources.

Evidently successful in commerce, Dumbuya was also a scholar of the Quran and corresponded with foreigners by using scribes to compose his thoughts on paper in European languages, signing his name in Arabic[14] and receiving foreign guests in the roomy apartments of his compound, where he served them on English-made pewter and imported chinaware.[15] He had great influence beyond Wonkifon to a number of towns and villages between the Iles de Los and Freetown, where his children or younger relatives were positioned as either headmen or the wives of local chiefs. One of his sons, Dala Modu Dumbuya, managed a fleet of canoes that became a dominant presence along a north–south Atlantic coastal corridor between the Iles de Los and Freetown,[16] trading rice, salt, and other goods.

In pursuit of commerce, Dumbuya had developed a friendly rapport with governors at Freetown and became a reliable source of information on local matters for the company. Dala Modu moved with a group of family and clients to Freetown in 1799 and later came to the company's aid after a group of Nova Scotian settlers and Temne chief King Tom led a failed attack on the settlement in 1801.[17] As the Sierra Leone Company struggled from the 1790s to establish itself as an abolitionist outpost at Freetown within a few hours' canoe ride from Wonkifon, two of his adult sons, Momodu and Dala, were active agents there working with the British and African American settlers as traders and linguists. These actions and relationships indicate that the Dumbuya clan confidently viewed themselves as independent partners of the Sierra Leone Company, willing to support it as a means of ensuring ongoing business with this new neighbor. The Church Missionary Society initially considered establishing an outpost at Dumbuya's Wonkifon but later backed off the idea, citing the prevalence in the town of Quranic schools run by "Mandingos" who would object to the presence of Christian missionaries among the Susu.[18] Dumbuya's trade with Freetown in the early nineteenth century was but a recent extension of decades of experience with caravans from the interior and with other

*Merchants, Maroons, Mahdis, and Migrants on the Upper Guinea Coast* ⁓ 149

Europeans on the coast. It was still defining its relationship to the abolitionist goals of the new experiment at Freetown.

Dumbuya expressed interest in possibly adopting new technology that would support increased commerce, if Freetown could arrange it. This included an offer that Dala Modu might travel to Britain for a period of study and later return with a "black Overseer of good character from the West Indies, if such a one could be engaged on liberal terms for a certain period." He communicated his desire to have an English loom and an English weaver and also to adopt the West Indian mode of cultivation on his estates, especially with regard to cotton and coffee.[19] This plan, which never came to fruition, was an audacious vision to expand local textile production with new technology and to deepen the local industry's ties to Atlantic slave trading and plantation cash crop economies of the day.

The account book of a French slaving vessel, *La Bonne Amitié*, provides some direct evidence of Dumbuya's purchases from European traders at the Iles de Los in 1786. The ship had originated at Honfleur in France's Normandy region, which was a main outlet for the large textile industry at nearby Rouen, producing cotton and cotton-linen blended cloths for Africa-bound slaving ships as well as for markets in Europe. In the end, *La Bonne Amitié* carried over three hundred enslaved people from the Guinea coast to the Caribbean port at Les Cayes, Saint-Domingue, just a few years before the first revolts of enslaved plantation workers that launched what became the Haitian Revolution.[20]

According to the ship's account book, Fendan Modu purchased some of nearly every type of the eighteen different textiles carried aboard the vessel.[21] The largest amounts included fifty-nine silk handkerchiefs, forty pieces each of indigo-dyed guinee cloths from India and Switzerland, and twenty pieces of so-called "Siamoise" cloths from Rouen. With each "piece" of cloth effectively measuring several yards in length, it is likely that this amount of textiles could have served hundreds of people. He also bought significant numbers of French-printed imitation indiennes, linens called *bretagnes*, and the Indian-made cottons, *chasselas*; plus, smaller quantities of several Indian cloths, such as *limeneas, bajutapeaux, neganepeaux,* and *nicanies*. The majority of his purchases from *La Bonne Amitié*, which were not textiles, are equally revealing of the diverse material interests of consumers in Wonkifon or others reached through the town's commercial networks. These included large quantities of the French-made alcohol eau-de-vie, varieties of glass beads, four hundred iron cooking pots, a couple dozen swords, copper basins, two reams of paper, fifty guns, bullets (*pierres a fusil*), and gunpowder. Dumbuya would have stored these valuable goods in his factory on the Iles de Los before they were carried to the mainland to be sold or to be redistributed to family and clients. The imported textiles filling coastal African warehouses fed an expanding and elastic African consumer base, providing more options to African buyers and supporting existing textile production rather than diminishing it through competition.

Adam Afzelius's description of festive public observances marking the end of Ramadan in Maliguia, a town of whitewashed stone buildings set inland from the river of the same name, provides some sense of the way textiles, both locally made and imported by merchants such as Dumbuya, communicated influence, rank, and power. His observances featured a procession of two to three hundred men in brightly colored "Mandingo clothes"[22]—the loose-fitting, embroidered garments favored by male authority figures, merchants, and clerics—parading to an open-air mosque, where they sat on reed mats for a public service. Some of the men were armed with guns and others carried a kind of machete sheathed in a leather scabbard frequently worn by Maninka men. These leather scabbards were made by local specialists among the Kuranko, another people who were migrants to the coast and often worked as servants and craftsmen to Maninka benefactors. The procession was led by the local headman and top cleric, who were dressed all in white with their heads wrapped in white turbans. Seated behind the crowd of men were about fifty women, their heads covered in white cloth veils, and some children without mats of their own were seated on the ground.[23] The scene suggests some of the ways that textiles produced, imported, and exchanged along the Guinea coast became incorporated into local displays of social status, social values, wealth, and authority.

### SARTORIAL HYBRIDITY AND MAHDIST REFORMS

British officials at Freetown also note the importance of textiles and dress in displaying status and authority in Sierra Leone, where they, like in the Fuuta Jallon and at Wonkifon with Dumbuya, pursued diplomatic and commercial relationships with several Muslim notables across the region to the south. Their pursuit of these relationships was a bid both to shore up the fledgling colony's viability by securing reliable sources of food and marketable commodities and to advance the abolitionist vision of its founders. They discovered, however, that their moral and civilizationist influence in the colony had competition from a self-proclaimed Mahdi, a reformer preaching a purified Islamic practice. These competing religious reform agendas clashed over the meaning of Western fashion and its adoption by regional leaders. Thus, even local expressions of status and authority, inflected by competing visions of what those expressions meant, influenced consumption and therefore global trade in textiles.

In 1795, Governor Macaulay dispatched two representatives, James Watt and the accountant John Gray, to survey commercial possibilities for camwood, ivory, and cattle north of Freetown along the Kamaranka River, especially with Fury Cannaba, one of the region's most prominent traders. Along the way, Watt and Gray passed a series of trading towns controlled alternately by African-, Eurafrican-, and European-headed trading families tucked along the serpentine rivers and creeks of the coastal mangroves. It was a landscape marked by the productive labor of enslaved people, who animated the small farming and trading settlements. Laborers at one town, Patungwa, which Watt reported meant "town of slaves" (possibly in Susu), produced great quantities of rice. At another town, Walla, women laborers were especially visible: "On walking about the Town we found all the Women busily employed. Some were preparing the Bamboo Palm to make baskets and matts. Some were weaving the matts and making dish covers others were preparing and burning the plantain stocks to make soap, while there were others again spinning cotton so that of the females there were none idle."[24]

While this labor was of great interest to abolitionist officials looking to secure economic relationships in the area, indications of an active English influence were also already present in the region. For instance, several towns' headmen were Africans with English names, like Tom Walker and Jack Ryan, as well as hybrid Susu-English combinations like Pa Woney, which suggests the impact of the presence of British merchants that overlay earlier waves of Portuguese influence. Tom Walker, for example, described as "a black man [who] speaks tolerable good English,"[25] was headman of a settlement of about two dozen houses set on a rise above the mangroves along the Kamaranka. As a headman, Walker had helped the British when Freetown came under French attack in 1794 by sheltering another Briton, David Ford, during the attack. His presence, along with that of others like him, added to the cultural complexity and richness of early nineteenth-century coastal societies in Guinea and suggests a certain receptivity to British, and perhaps abolitionist, influence.

However, they were relatively minor figures in the region compared to headmen and merchants such as Cannaba, who controlled a large trading operation across several towns where enslaved people panned for salt, grew produce and cotton, and raised cattle.[26] Like Dumbuya, Cannaba had Maninka roots with ties to the savanna interior. As a wealthy merchant in an area populated largely by the ethnically distinct Bullom people, Cannaba was a powerful man who kept track of sales when a caravan from the interior arrived in his towns north of Freetown selling rice and camwood. He also presided as judge in cases brought to him in which his decision might determine whether a person lived, died, or was sold to slave merchants. On meeting him, Watt and Gray presented Cannaba a gift of printed chintz and a case of gin, fine gifts any refined Englishman would have appreciated.[27] Indeed, Gray's description of Cannaba could also have been of an English merchant: a man of about seventy years of age with a "yellowish" complexion and dressed in a gold lace hat, matching waistcoat, ruffled shirt, and "a pair of country cloth trowsers, with stockings on his legs and shoes on his feet." In his home, Fury Cannaba displayed the gift of an earlier visitor, an agent of Bance Island, Captain James Bowie: a brass-barreled gun mounted with silver onto which his name was engraved. Such an object was a reminder of Cannaba's extensive dealings with the English, principally those engaged in slave trading. Nevertheless, he was open to opportunities raised by the abolitionist company's proposal to establish a trading post at one of his towns, Robaina. By the mid-1790s, Cannaba already had an intricate connection to the company's missionary ambitions, as one of his nephews, John Naimbanna, had spent two years in England before returning to Freetown with high expectations for his future, only to fall ill and die within weeks of his arrival.

Published accounts of this tragic story have preserved telling details about the experiences of young western African elites at home and in England at that time and about how clothes symbolized status in western Africa. Naimbanna left for England in 1791 wearing and carrying with him clothing that had been gifts to his father from French and English traders: an old blue cloak bound with broad gold lace, a black velvet coat, a pair of white satin breeches, a couple of shirts, and two or three pairs of trousers. Once in England, he learned to read and write the language and do basic math. His general exposure to English society included visits to Saint Paul's Cathedral and to the Houses of Parliament, where he heard debates about the slave trade. An engraving of Naimbanna in England depicts him wearing the waistcoat, jacket, breeches, and hat of a gentleman as another man appears to handle a horse.[28]

In the wake of his tragic death, colonial Freetown's ongoing pursuit of commercial and diplomatic relationships with Cannaba, the young prince's paternal uncle, shows the intricacy of the ties between African and European merchants and the extent to which Cannaba valued consumer goods, particularly textiles and accessories. Cannaba responded to the visit from Gray and Watt in part by sending them back to Freetown with a list of goods he wanted them to procure for him there, a list that reveals something of the material culture and preferences of Cannaba's town and its elite. Cannaba asked them to send "sugar, butter, cheese, flour, ear rings, small bells, manillas, one dozen Windsor chairs, a French horn, nutmeg, a tea kettle, a gold-laced hat, a gold-headed cane (with no alloy in it), coral, and an Alderman's old gown."[29]

It is easy to imagine that with Cannaba's request for a gold-headed cane and the alderman's gown, a voluptuous garment of a striking color that signaled political status in its English context (see figure 5.3), he was seeking to appropriate "ready-made" foreign objects to further his own agenda for wealth and power in local terms. The items Cannaba is reported to have requested (as well as the garments he was reported to have worn) reflect an eclectic, cosmopolitan taste for foreign luxuries, including food, spices, furniture, accessories, and clothing.

However, descriptions of him also suggest a different persona from that of Fendan Dumbuya, a few dozen miles north. Unlike Dumbuya, Cannaba is recorded as being dressed in Western clothing, although with a unique combination of items that reflected a local African sensibility and a style that was not a mere copy of English dress. As powerful figures in their respective communities, both Dumbuya and Cannaba projected their status in part through their public display of clothing that was not available to many commoners. The examples of Dumbuya, who dressed in the embroidered cotton robes common to Muslim scholars, and Cannaba reflect the diversity of sartorial approaches among coastal Muslims, as each person drew from differing visual vocabularies to project their status, cosmopolitan ethos, and openness to trade with all foreign comers.

Coastal traders such as Fury Cannaba and Fendan Dumbuya, in providing goods for their respective lineage affiliates and clients, competed with one another for commercial position in terms of attracting caravans from the interior and cultivating relations with Atlantic traders. Gray and Watt seemed optimistic about the company establishing commercial linkages with Cannaba, noting his ability to access cattle, salt, straw mats, and baskets, which laborers in his towns produced in significant number. Gray also speculated that Cannaba, though he was an observant Muslim, might possibly be persuaded to convert to Christianity and thus perhaps also to cease slave trading and employing slave labor, if engaged by missionaries. The reason Gray gave for this assertion to his superiors was that Cannaba, though wealthy and powerful, was an insincere Muslim who only put on a show of religious pretense "to gratify his own pride, and to dazzle the eyes of his people" and thus a sham figure who drank gin in private, deceiving the

FIGURE 5.3. Eighteenth-century alderman's gown in Auguste Wahlen, *Moeurs, usages et costumes de tous les peuples du monde, d'après des documents and authentiques et les voyages des plus récents* (Bruxelles: Librairie Historique-Artistique, 1843).

people of his town. This claim must be measured against the longer record of eighteenth- and nineteenth-century European discourse about West African Muslims that portrayed them as improperly and inauthentically adhering to the tenets of the Islamic faith. If Cannaba consumed alcohol privately, it said as much about what the English were trading as it did about his own individual faith or sincerity as a community leader. In any case, such drinking would have been part of a complicated set of responses to the trading environment evolving around him.

British abolitionists were of course not the only actors on the coast who were preoccupied with fervent religious ideological discourses of civilization promoting social, economic, and sartorial reforms in western Africa. The turn of the nineteenth century on the Judeo-Christian calendar was the thirteenth century for Muslims, who were anticipating the arrival of a God-sent messenger, or Mahdi, to redress injustices and renew the faith worldwide. In the 1780s, a self-proclaimed reformer, who the available sources name only as "Fatta," arrived at the head of an army that had marched hundreds of miles from the interior, gathering converts and conscripts along the way, on a mission to expand and to "purify" the practice of Islam throughout the region.[30]

The Mahdi's arrival threw the coastal rivers region into social crisis, with several European traders sending him gifts and seeking to remain in his favor. Dumbuya felt obliged to send to the Mahdi a *bonya* (customary gift) worth thousands of iron bars (about 650 pounds sterling) and to crawl on his hands and knees into the Mahdi's presence as a sign of submission.[31] The Mahdi's critique of the supposed laxity of Muslims in villages across the region and of the supposed offense of non-Muslim religious practices—both African and Christian—were reflected in his critique of immodest or inappropriate clothing.[32] This charge is interesting in that it reveals how coastal Africans' adoption of tailored European clothing, taken by missionaries as an embrace of civilized modesty, was viewed by some Africans as a form of apostasy and therefore to be rejected.

To signify submission, Mahdi's followers were required to change their style of dress to a simple, standard uniform of a cotton garment dyed yellow with a local bark—a visual rebuke to the more varied choices then commonly in use by coastal Muslims. The Mahdi's claim of invincibility was successfully challenged with fatal results when he was bludgeoned two years later in 1785.[33] The Mahdi's unsuccessful maneuver reveals how clothing—in this case, locally grown and produced cotton garments—represented an imaginative expression of power contested by various actors and groups of actors on the coast.

## AGENCY OF THE ENSLAVED: VILLAGES, MARKETS, AND SOLDIERS

Around 1783, a group of enslaved household and farm laborers in and around Dumbuya's Wonkifon took advantage of the local militia being away to escape to the nearby Yanghekori hills.[34] Infighting among the Susu and Maninka slaveholders from whom they fled forestalled efforts to immediately put down the rebellion. The rebels used the delay to fortify their settlement, surviving for thirteen years under the cloud of a tenuous truce with their erstwhile owners. In time, the community at Yanghekori became a magnet for other laborers on the coast fleeing enslavement, swelling its population to a few thousand. To sustain themselves, they planted extensive fields of rice and cotton outside the walls. Dumbuya engaged in a war of attrition with the rebels, his former laborers. For as long as the fortified settlement at Yanghekori remained independent, it effectively joined a constellation of small polities—some headed by Africans, others by Eurafrican and European merchants—seeking to provide for themselves and to produce wealth through the control of land and labor and the exchange of cotton and cloth.

The participation of these self-emancipated captives, dislocated from their original communities but choosing to make new communities within the narrow opportunities open to them, demonstrates that the process of African self-fashioning in this period extended well beyond the prerogatives of African elites. In the Benna region, a formerly enslaved man called Mambee established a settlement of about six hundred formerly enslaved men and women followers that was still inhabited in the late eighteenth century.[35] Another maroon settlement, Fula Coundingi, was established on the Capatches River.[36] Gordon Laing's record mentions Kondeah, a settlement of formerly enslaved people established north of Timbo in the Fuuta Jallon who repulsed repeated attacks from both the Fuuta Jallon state and Solimana.[37] In 1794, a map of the Sierra Leone peninsula published in a company report indicates the location of a town southwest of Freetown called simply "Town of Runaway Slaves."[38]

These towns and their inhabitants were under constant threat, however, the settlement of Yanghekori coming to an end in 1796. The Mahdi Fatta's reform movement had the unintended consequence of uniting Muslim merchants on the coast in opposition to him and his preaching, momentarily setting aside their differences and competition. Their combined force of 2,500 fighters waged a five-month siege that finally ended when the last rebel leader, called Dangasago, was captured after being lured outside the settlement walls on false pretenses.[39] Victorious at last, the elder and junior Dumbuya men shared the spoils with the Susu slaveholders they partnered with in attack. They sold off some captives, who numbered in the hundreds, and put others to work for themselves. Defeating the rebellion seemed to destroy a symbolic threat to a social and economic order on the coast.

Even with their ultimate defeat, the revolt of Yanghekori and other settlements of self-emancipated people underline the highly competitive and fluid nature of coastal society where a range of agents—individuals, small corporations, and large states—grabbed openings to advance their interests as much as possible. These breakaway communities faced the organized repression of slaveholding chiefs and merchants whose fighting forces were populated with coerced and enslaved soldiers, including the Maray, a class of elite, professional warriors from Solimana with specialist skills that reportedly made them fearsome. Dumbuya brought Richard Bright to a central plaza at Wonkifon to view the public performance of a Maray, a masked dancer who appeared at the center of the crowd carrying a sword and performing martial moves intended to display his strength and agility.

> His dress consisted of a close jacket with sleeves and pantaloons of a uniform color being a rust brown marked with black annular spots. His head and face were completely covered with a hood, the forepart of which was made of scarlet cloth ornamented with rows of cowries and provided with sight-holes encircled with the same kind of shell. The scarlet was tipped with fur. . . . His waist and ankles were encircled with leathern belts to which small bells were fastened which sounded as he moved.[40]

Such public displays also suggest how Dumbuya and other coastal Muslim leaders drew not only on the labor of non-Muslims but also on the visual power of their self-expression and self-representation to enact their own state-building projects. This Maray, redeemed by Dumbuya from a prior enslaver, became a mercenary working in military campaigns against his new patron's enemies. The irony is that high-status men like Dumbuya relied upon enslaved men under their control to win military campaigns against those who had escaped their grasp, such as those at Yanghekori. Maray were entitled to a larger share of the spoils of war than average soldiers, but it was their fighting prowess that gave Dumbuya the right to wear the white turban, elevating his prominence within the region.

## CONSUMPTION AND DRESS OF BLACK SETTLERS, EURAFRICANS, AND ELITE AFRICANS

The migrants to Sierra Leone from London were joined there by hundreds of formerly enslaved people who had fled American colonies like Georgia and

Virginia during the Revolutionary War, escaping on British vessels to Nova Scotia before later relocating to the British colony at Freetown. Led in part by the spirited preaching of their own Methodist and Baptist preachers, they contributed to the overall revivalist spirit of the period, especially with their embrace of the tailored, Western garments that were the external symbol of their faith, morality, and future-oriented aspirations.[41]

Some of these settlers had indeed left this region of West Africa as young people. Several were Kuranko natives who had once been sold at nearby Bance Island. One settler reportedly reunited with her mother who had been enslaved to a Temne chief. Another settler, Frank Peters, reportedly returned to the village of his birth after having been enslaved in South Carolina.[42] John Kizell returned not only to where he was born on Sherbro Island,[43] south of Freetown, but in 1811, became president of the Sierra Leone Cooperative Society, which sought to compete with European traders in the region.[44] His transnational life experiences supported his pivotal role in the emerging coastal society: once enslaved in Charleston, South Carolina, Kizell fought with the Loyalists during the Revolutionary War, relocated to Nova Scotia where he learned to read and write, and later returned to Sherbro with his wife, Phillis, and three children.

Kizell distinguished himself as a mediator between warring factions in the region while also advancing the broader antislavery aims of the Sierra Leone Company. He pursued a political vision that supported Freetown's goals to abolish the slave trade and that viewed Sherbro as a viable home for African Americans, lobbying the British and American governments as well as the Sherbro ruler to support such a venture.[45] Having fled South Carolina a generation before during the American Revolution, Kizell was advanced in age when two white American missionaries arrived in Sherbro in 1818 seeking land on which to establish a settlement of formerly enslaved African Americans. It may be Kizell shown standing between the ruler of Sherbro and his son, Kong Couber, who is introducing the missionaries to the king in an image (figure 5.4) in *Africa Redeemed*, a publication meant to promote the resettlement of African Americans in Liberia.[46] Kong Couber is depicted wearing a tailored European-style shirt and jacket, while the seated king is wearing a British naval cap on his head, his body draped in a large robe with fringes that might be an imported alderman's gown or a locally tailored cloak. He is grasping a metal-tipped scepter in one hand and a horsetail whisk in the other. This combination of foreign and local elements conveys a unique expression of power and status not imitative or derivative of foreign examples but consequent of the specific historical dynamics of Sherbro itself.

FIGURE 5.4. "Mr. Kizell Introduced by Couber to His Father King Sherbro" in *Africa Redeemed: Or, The Means of Her Relief Illustrated by the Growth and Prospects of Liberia* (London: J. Nisbet, 1851). Manuscripts, Archives and Rare Books Division, Schomburg Center for Research in Black Culture, The New York Public Library.

Most settlers, if not all, arrived infused with an evangelizing ideology formed by their experiences of British Empire in North America, which shaped their expectations of how to live as "free" civilized (and civilizing) Christians in Africa. In Freetown, they built clapboard homes for themselves, unlike the thatched structures of wattle and daub built by Africans. They mostly wore Western clothing and established a reliable consumer base for American products, such as tobacco, rum, and molasses. Descriptions of clothing worn by Nova Scotian settlers at Sierra Leone suggest their ongoing attachment to the tailored styles and accessories common in British North America. One British observer, Francis Spilsbury, remarked that Nova Scotian women dressed differently from women on nearby Gorée, who commonly appeared in a loose-fitting chemise over a cotton wrapped around the waist. By contrast, among Nova Scotians in Freetown, "the fashion of the women's cloaths somewhat resembles the costume of a Welsh girl" (see figure 5.5).[47] People who lived most of their lives in British North

FIGURE 5.5. "Female Clothing Styles, Sierra Leone, 1805" in Francis B. Spilsbury, *Account of a Voyage to the Western Coast of Africa; Performed by His Majesty's Sloop Favourite, in the Year 1805* [...] (London: Richard Phillips, 1807).

American colonies might reasonably be expected to dress in ways that reflect that background. But during their time in Sierra Leone, it is likely that modifications, such as the wearing of a top hat, began to develop out of the totality of this group's experience.

Such attire contrasts with the representations of Temne women (see figure 5.6), who are shown wearing ankle-length cloth wrappers cinched at the waist, nude or partially nude from the waist up, with beaded jewelry hanging from their necks and adorning their hair. These were sartorial expressions of belonging and aspiration for different imagined futures that existed side by side in early Freetown. Several local rulers were visually represented wearing clothing associated with members of the European elite or military, such as in the engraving of the Sherbro ruler (figure 5.7). Spilsbury's 1805 travel account of Sierra Leone[48] describes meeting a Temne noble who went further than his counterpart in Sherbro by dressing from head to toe in the clothing of a British aristocrat, complete with stockings, ruffled shirt,

*Merchants, Maroons, Mahdis, and Migrants on the Upper Guinea Coast* ~ 161

FIGURE 5.6. "Temminee Wives, Sierra Leone, 1805," in Francis B. Spilsbury, *Account of a Voyage to the Western Coast of Africa; Performed by His Majesty's Sloop Favourite, in the Year 1805* [...] (London: Richard Phillips, 1807).

naval officer's coat with brass buttons, and a broad-brimmed hat. Spilsbury notes that the clothes were from Monmouth Street, an area of West London known for burgeoning slums, secondhand clothing shops, and meeting places for political balladeers and pamphleteers. It suggests how imported European-tailored garments could be repurposed in an African context to convey a distinct set of meanings.

The women accompanying the Temne noble are represented wearing ample lengths of cloth that might be imported India cotton prints, European imitations, or locally made cloths, adorned with some type of beaded necklace. The number of wives a wealthy man had was a key indicator of his status, but the quality, assortment, and public display of the women's clothing also added to his prestige. It is noteworthy that the local style of dress—a pagne wrapper and top cloth for adult women—appears to construct a gendered persona tied intimately to the local space, with local tastes represented, if not defined, by these women's choices. In contrast, the man's foreign attire, which seems to project a high-status English military officer, perhaps elevated him even above the actual English merchants with whom he traded.

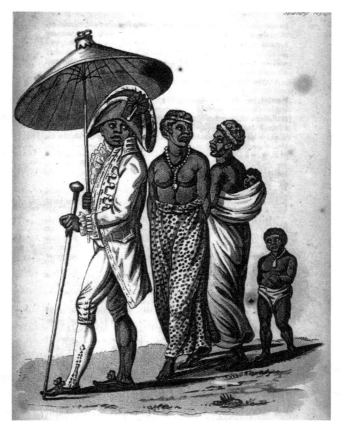

FIGURE 5.7. "A Negro King in Monmouth Street Clothes with His Wives and Children" in Francis B. Spilsbury, *Account of a Voyage to the Western Coast of Africa; Performed by His Majesty's Sloop Favourite, in the Year 1805* [...] (London: Richard Phillips, 1807).

In such a context, newcomers such as the Nova Scotians, individuals who originally fled to Canada from plantations in places like Virginia and South Carolina, effectively introduced their own riff on this process of claiming status through the appropriation of foreign clothing styles with their embrace of an aesthetic born of daily life in a British American colony. Neither were they all willing to remain solely in the British-controlled settlement of Freetown; some also circulated in riverine communities outside the colony and sometimes settled there, bringing with them their tastes for certain Western clothing styles.[49]

In 1795, the Sierra Leone Company sent Cooper to live in the Rio Pongo, where he built a trading factory named Freeport, which sat downriver from several major slave-trading settlements run by British merchants like John Ormond and Americans like John Holman, their Eurafrican children, and African families, clients, and enslaved laborers. It made some economic sense to be located near such settlements as Bangalan, Farenya, and Bakoro, which received caravans arriving from the Fuuta Jallon—even from as far north as the Gambia River—and also produced large amounts of rice,

*Merchants, Maroons, Mahdis, and Migrants on the Upper Guinea Coast* ~ 163

salt, and textiles that could be resold at Freetown. But as the company's agent at Freeport, Cooper also became a face of the company's bold move into this region, where there had long been profitable commerce, pushing its missionary agenda to end slave trading through diplomacy and to open missionary schools there. He faced distrust and hostility from slave traders with whom he sought to interact. Cooper regularly found himself in the position of being asked to purchase slaves or to redeem others from enslavement, but as the company's agent, he was constrained always to refuse to purchase human beings.[50]

In negotiating his way through difficult entanglements around slave trading, Cooper readily accommodated himself to other expectations of strangers and residents of the Rio Pongo. For instance, in securing permission to settle at Toke Keren,[51] Cooper ingratiated himself to his local African landlord, Mungo Kerefa, in the ways that were expected of newcomers with such requests: by making a customary gift of cloth, clothing, or another utilitarian object, especially if foreign or a luxury. Cooper gifted Kerefa an English-made hat and shirt that he reported back had greatly pleased the elder headman, who Cooper described as a man of around seventy years of age wearing a blue wrapper around his waist and a white tunic. Kerefa "acted like a father to me," Cooper reported to company officials, and had generously protected him in the face of hostility from some neighbors. Cooper wrote to the council of the Sierra Leone colony that he was optimistic about the possibilities for commerce in the Rio Pongo area. He notes that the people produced cloths woven from cotton they imported from the "Fula country" that could be resold elsewhere on the coast at a profit: "I wish that the high cloths may answer at Sierra Leone, for the purchase of these cloths have been greatly the means of establishing the factory and I have no doubt but that in a little time the company will find this a great place for trade. I am persuaded that it will save numbers from slavery."[52]

It is clear from sources such as this correspondence that many observers at the time—Cooper, the company, local African slave holders, and foreign slave traders alike—viewed cotton and cloth trading as a regular income producer and sought to develop their involvement with these commodities. The company responded by agreeing to support Cooper's effort as best they could, sending one of their members to assist him with setting up the factory and encouraging him to maintain his tenancy arrangements with the headman Kerefa and to purchase other available commodities, such as raw cotton and pepper, when prices were favorable.[53] In another letter from 1796, he wrote that during a seven-month lull in ships arriving on the Pongo to buy captive laborers, "The natives ... turned their slaves to the manufactory of strips of white cloth, which I bought in great quantity, neither did I hear of any dispute or wars in the country till a schooner had arrived from America and she was to carry two hundred slaves."[54]

Cooper's ongoing correspondence from the Rio Pongo to the council at Freetown reveals certain dynamics of the regional trade, such as the entanglements between slave trading and the "legitimate trade" that he and the company hoped to establish. Enslaved laborers, for example, were used as porters to carry the ivory, hides, wax, and other goods the company wanted to buy. Cooper described being aware that his purchase of ivory from a Fula caravan did little to diminish slave trading, as the caravan leader sold the human porters to a willing buyer a few villages away. He also notes how African slaveholders used such laborers to produce the "legitimate" commodities that the Sierra Leone Company most wanted to purchase.

Cooper's statements form part of an abolitionist discourse of the period that alleged a direct connection between internal wars and trader demand for enslaved people on the coast. This view was generally dismissive of the seriousness of internal dynamics around the struggle for religious and political hegemony in the Fuuta Jallon and its adjacent regions—framing it as little more than a primal lust for violence, power, and wealth. Most historians' treatment of these early efforts of the Sierra Leone Company to maintain a trading factory on the Rio Pongo understandably centers on its struggles with local foreign traders, who opposed its presence, and its eventual failure. Foreign traders and African traders such as the djula trader Mori Kanu[55] joined forces to undermine the company and were successful in turning local populations against it.

In addition to newcomers like Cooper, the Nova Scotians, and the Jamaican Maroons, Eurafrican traders and elites represented distinct constituencies purveying Western Christian clothing aesthetics. Of course, not all of these migrants embraced the antislavery worldview of the Sierra Leone Company even if they did accept in broad terms the religious and educational goals of the Church Missionary Society. As Mouser has detailed, a cohort of more than seventy children of Eurafrican traders and African elite families were educated in Liverpool, England, over several years before returning to the region.[56] Eurafrican traders took advantage of family linkages and opportunities in the Americas to send children to schools in Charleston, South Carolina; Havana, Cuba; and Matanzas, Cuba, for education, although this study has not found any evidence that elite Africans did so. Nevertheless, the mobility of Eurafrican traders, such as John Holman Jr., was deeply embedded in transnational, British Atlantic commercial flows even as their movements produced unique African Atlantic experiences specific to that historical conjuncture. Holman's life followed an atypical counterclockwise circumnavigation of the Atlantic, though it remained a path anchored in British networks. He was educated at Liverpool but later lived with his family in South Carolina for several years before finally returning to the Rio Pongo with an American-born "mulatto" wife and four children, who he enrolled in missionary schools there.[57] Holman was said to prefer the culture of the Rio Pongo to that of South Carolina, which is not surprising given the elevated social status he enjoyed in his West African birthplace. It is reasonable to surmise that having relocated to western Africa, the members of Holman's family, especially its American-born matriarch, dressed themselves with clothing and filled their home with objects that reflected their wealth and affiliations with the British and American Atlantic world. Their consumer and fashion choices would likely have found parallels with that of such prominent local figures as William Jellorum Fernandez, son of a prominent Luso-African family near Dominghia, and Jellorum Harrison, who had lived in Edinburgh, Scotland, and Central Asia before returning to the Rio Pongo. These was also a cohort of sophisticated, well-traveled, and educated Africans who were loosely aligned with some aspects of the missionaries' agenda but in a way that was distinct from that of Thomas Cooper and other migrants.

Upriver from Cooper was another major trading settlement on the Rio Pongo at Farenya, run by Nhara Bely, the daughter of a Luso-African trader and married to an American trader from South Carolina, Louis Styles Lightburn. The honorific *nhara* is a modification of the Portuguese *senhora*, or "lady," and thus locates Nhara Bely (who lived until 1880) in the coastal tradition of influential women merchants—from Gorée and Saint-Louis to Bathurst, Cacheu, and the Rio Pongo. Nhara Bely's full name, Elizabeth "Isabela" Bailey Gomez Lightburn, suggests not only her Luso-African heritage but also how by the nineteenth century some of these families had acquired British and American surnames through marriage to foreign merchants. Her grandfather, Emmanuel Gomez, settled in the Pongo region from Portuguese-speaking Bissau, where he married a local woman to facilitate his trading interests. In her time, Elizabeth married Lightburn, who relocated to Farenya in 1809, a year after the United States ban on slave trading took effect.

The Lightburns grew wealthy from slave trading, working in direct cross-purposes to people like Cooper and other officials of the Sierra Leone Company. Nhara Bely's role as a commercial intermediary was critical to the generation of their wealth, as much depended on her embeddedness in the social networks and practices of the region. As her business grew, Nhara Bely took on African clients. She allowed a migrant from the Konian region of the eastern savanna, Kanfory Mansa Conte, to settle in Farenya, where he distinguished himself as a cloth weaver and salt merchant.[58] By hosting a newcomer such as Conte, Nhara Bely gained a valuable addition to her town in a skilled laborer who produced income for himself and for her through his weaving. Conte came to control Nhara Bely's slave barracoon, which was in an area of a quarter of her town known as Balandougou, where he is said to have exercised "magical" powers to prevent the enslaved from running away. Nhara Bely was also said to have practiced forms of sorcery in exercising control over enslaved laborers and enemies alike. Such stories of magic and mystical powers likely masked the violence and cruelty that actually did the work of forcing captive people's compliance with their conditions in the barracoon. She took over the business completely after her husband's death in 1827.

She was not the only merchant woman at the head of a trading operation in the Guinea rivers. Betsy Heard, the daughter of an English man and an African woman, ran a trading post factory dealing in enslaved people and other commodities in the town of Bereira and became influential because of her relative wealth and connections with English traders. Heard had been educated for several years in Liverpool before returning to take over her father's enterprise. She was a friend to Fendan Dumbuya, the djula cloth trader, and a regular presence at Wonkifon, which was not far away. Heard had positioned herself as the person through whom foreign traders new to the region contacted local African headmen and rulers, and she had personal ties with the governor of the Sierra Leone Company. She impressed visitors from Freetown with the relative comforts of her home, outfitted with familiar English furnishings, linens, and tableware. Between her home furnishings and personal attire, which included the finest imported muslins, linens, and satin fabrics, Heard inscribed herself into the global circulation of these goods that moved across commercial networks connecting ports along the coastal perimeters of the Atlantic and Indian Oceans. But she was also renowned for her knowledge of local herbal medicines and sometimes appears in English sources under her local name, Calaminna,[59] a Mande-language name that translates as "learned one." This suggests the extensive local linkages of this woman, regarded simultaneously by British visitors as familiar with European customs in general and friendly to their interests in particular.

Such familiarity, however, sometimes bred discontent. One son of Fendan Dumbuya, Dala Modu, frequently dressed in English garments as he managed his commercial dealings along the coast. Modu was a key player in the nascent colony at Freetown during the early nineteenth century, witnessing the early struggles of its officials to enact an abolitionist ban on slave trading within the colony and eventually being expelled from it during a conflict with the colonial governor Thomas Ludlam.[60] An elite scion of a well-known regional merchant, Dala Modu moved through the world of coastal traders, men who spoke multiple African and European languages, who boasted of education and travel overseas, and who marked themselves physically by wearing the European clothing and accessories of the day.

Some of Dala Modu's views and actions of this period were preserved as part of a court record of a case brought against Ludlam, a governor of the Sierra Leone Company, who was later accused of violating British laws against slave trading. Dala Modu's testimony in this case was important because three years earlier Ludlam had expelled Modu from the colony in a dispute over alleged slave trading. Modu denied Ludlam's accusation of being engaged in slave trading, making the countercharge that it was Ludlam who was guilty of such activity. Nevertheless, he complied with Ludlam's demand to leave the colony by relocating with a group of his followers to the neighboring Bullom Shore, where he continued to be active in regional commerce until his death in 1841.

The record of the conflict between Modu and Ludlam offers important insight into initial efforts to enact an antislavery and slave-trading policy within the Sierra Leone colony, which was beset by a number of problems widely documented by historians that threatened its continued existence. At stake in the conflict between Modu and Ludlam was the outcome of a contest between divergent understandings of enslavement and of law governing the political control of space. From Modu's perspective, Governor Ludlam held himself to a different standard from the one he sought to impose on Modu, while Ludlam argued that Modu simply refused to reject slave trading as a practice, and in doing so, he undermined colonial authority.[61]

Their conflict, however, can also be read as a contest between masculinities articulated within a discourse of religion and honor performed as the embrace of specific symbols and objects of material culture particular to the context of early nineteenth-century Guinea and Sierra Leone. For Dala Modu, this was partially symbolized with the deliberate rejection of English clothing in favor of local attire reserved for Muslim scholars and successful warriors. If it follows that gender norms are historically constructed, then the incident seems to describe a process by which elite or hegemonic masculinity among Susu and perhaps other African men of the period was redefining itself in cultural terms as distinctly antiabolitionist, at least as expressed by the British Protestants of Freetown.

In his testimony, Dala Modu described an incident in which Governor Ludlam, in deciding the fate of a group of enslaved Africans brought ashore after the British had intercepted their vessel at sea, distributed them to settlers and other buyers for a fee of twenty dollars, including to a settler with whom Modu regularly traded. Modu claimed that during Ludlam's tenure, some of his wives had purchased slaves in Freetown by exchanging them for a quantity of brass manillas—indicating a failure of colonial officials to enforce the law against their own subjects. Yet Modu said that Freetown officials surveilled activities within his village in a bid to find evidence of his own slaveholding and trading.[62]

As headman of his town, Modu participated on a council of notables that judged violations of customary law. It was another such trial by country law that brought the conflict between the two men to a head. A man from Port Loko seeking justice for the murder of his brother carried the suspect's son (presumably the suspect himself could not be located) to be held for trial by Modu and a council of notables. The council was to decide the boy's fate by first determining whether his father had murdered the plaintiff's brother. When the boy was later sold to traders at Bance Island, Ludlam sent "a white man and a black man" named Warwick Francis to Modu "with a large sheet of paper written all over, and they read it to me and tried to explain it and told me that if I would acknowledge that I had bought the boy, I should not be brought to trial."[63]

Although Ludlam was purportedly upset that Modu had approved the boy's enslavement and sale, his response was effectively to escalate the conflict. His message was that Modu could avoid a worse outcome by coming to a Freetown church to be christened. This seemingly incongruous demand struck Modu as revealing what he believed to be Ludlam's true intentions, leading him to object in the most strenuous terms available to him. Modu appeared at the church, arriving with a group of followers and presenting himself in a manner that communicated that he did not take the charge lightly and that he rejected Ludlam's judgment. "I came there in the full dress of a Mohammedan chief with my gris-gris about me," Modu is said to have recounted during the later trial. "[I was wearing] the white turban which is the mark of an Imam and which none other may wear on high occasions."[64]

Modu was unrecognizable to some in Freetown who knew him but had never seen him presented this way. There is no eyewitness account of his dress, but it likely included a loose-fitting top garment—a *bubu, dloki,* or *lomasa*—that may have been embroidered, possibly bright white or alternatively dyed indigo, and worn with a cap and leather sandals. He also conceivably carried a sword, which was a common accessory, especially by notable men. The weight that Modu placed on his sartorial choice is underlined by the fact that he went on to narrate the lengthy process by which he earned the right to wear the turban in the eyes of regional leaders. He had done so by leading a successful military campaign against a fortified settlement of formerly enslaved people who had fled from their Susu captors to the Yanghekori mountains and lived independently there for years.[65] Modu had broken through the settlement's defensive wall, where as many as five other rulers had been unsuccessful. For this feat, he was awarded the white turban in a public ceremony and given the authority to settle disputes in the country. Such turbans may have been of locally woven cotton or imported linen, but their color and texture were meant to signal a "purity" of attachment and affiliation with Islamic values.

Although the title *imam* typically refers to a learned scholar or teacher, Modu's account shows that in coastal Guinea in this period, the title, as well as the white turban used to symbolize it, could be extended to those with acknowledged military accomplishments or services to a state. Local engagements with Islam are also suggested by the mention of gris-gris, or amulets, worn either as necklaces, bracelets, or anklets, or sewn directly onto Modu's garment, a practice not universally accepted in all Muslim communities in the region. Modu's behavior in the church must be read in the larger context of the ethnic fluidity practiced throughout the region, where flexibility of ethnic identification was common as a means for autochthonous communities to manage in-migration and trade. Modu would have been aware of this practice even as he seemed to acknowledge its limitations in his interactions with Freetown. By effectively ceding Freetown to British colonial officials and continuing his commercial enterprises on land he controlled politically, Modu was not foreclosing his participation in expanding trade but rather repositioning himself in relation to it.

Modu's testimony makes clear the ways in which his social status and wealth were entangled with enslavement and slave trading as well as with discourses of Islam and masculine power. Ludlam's charge had seemed to conflate antislavery with conversion to Christianity and to promote the adoption of a range of other cultural practices, such as attending church dressed in a particular way he deemed to be "civilized"—a notion that contains within it certain culturally informed and gendered ideas of honorable behavior. By going to trial at the church dressed as he did, Modu deployed his clothing to reassert an alternative masculine posture rooted in local norms and to reclaim sovereignty over his own body as a prelude to ultimately claiming it for himself and his followers in a separate settlement on Bullom Shore across the Sierra Leone estuary from Freetown.

With his sartorial protest inside the church, Modu seemed not only to question Ludlam's broad-brush characterization of slavery as an institution in Africa but also to reject Ludlam's alleged double standard in imposing rules on Africans and foreign settlers within space granted to the colony.

# 6 ～ Textures of a Changing Era

*Old Redcoats, Groundnuts, and Afro-Atlantic Missionaries, 1825–1850*

BY THE 1820s, Kankan was already an important urban center of the agricultural region of Bate, located three hundred fifty miles northeast of Freetown, Sierra Leone. Bate—"between two rivers" in Maninka—was the name of the fertile valley that extended south from the confluence of the Niger River and its branch with the Milo River. Maninka-speaking farmers of rice and fonio in the Bate occupied a geographically vital crossroads between the gold mines of Bure to the north and the Fulbe-led clerical state in the Fuuta Jallon to the south. Soninke Muslims founded the community in the late seventeenth century after fleeing drought conditions in their homeland of Diafunu, an old and important clerical town near the Sahara, and settling among Maninka-speaking rice farmers who were non-Muslims. The Soninke clerics who migrated to the Bate region were adherents of Suwarian Islam, named for al-Hajj Salim Suware, who preached tolerance, pacifism, study, and faith. Suware's teachings emphasized that it was for God, not human beings, to effect the conversion of non-Muslims to Islam, and his adherents therefore generally did not proselytize their faith, seeking instead to persuade by example, and rejected militant forms of jihad that used violence. Bate oral traditions recount that the children of the cleric Kaba Laye of Diafunu, Abdurahmane and Maramagbe Kaba, established a settlement and lived peaceably among non-Muslim farmers through bonds of intermarriage after a Muslim Kaba man married a non-Muslim Conde woman and through agreeing to live in separate villages.[1] Soninke settlers in Bate assimilated into local social structure even as they asserted their distinct religious identities. In time, they became speakers of Maninka and adopted a new title evocative of their new home, the Maninka-Mori.

Their pacifist project nearly collapsed under the assault of armies from neighboring non-Muslim communities that began mounting attacks against Bate in the 1770s, drawing them into a larger regional conflict between the Fula imamate. Armies from the Fuuta Jallon had led annual raids for captives in the Wasulu and other non-Muslim areas for many years. The leading clerical families of Kankan differed in opinion on the use of violence from their coreligionists in the Fuuta Jallon but nevertheless identified with and empathized with them as Muslims. Konde Birama of Sankaran built a temporary coalition of a larger fighting force of armies from Sankaran, Toron, and the Wasulu to confront both clerical states.[2] Konde Birama's siege forced many Bate villagers, including the clerical elites' families, to flee the Fula capital at Timbo, located about two hundred miles west. Birama's armies pursued the refugees and continued to advance into Fula territory all the way to Timbo, where they burned buildings, manuscript libraries, and a mosque. The clerical town of Fugumba was the first in the Fuuta Jallon to repel an attack from Birama's fighters, marking the beginning of the end for his advance. The Fuuta Jallon state followed this victory with a series of military campaigns that finally defeated Konde Birama in 1792, who, in the interim, had sent thousands of enslaved people to Atlantic ports near Sierra Leone and on the Guinea coast.

The circulation of cloth and the dynamics of dress trace complex, overlapping political economies between the savanna interior and the Atlantic coast during the early nineteenth century. Despite British abolition of the slave trade in 1807 and the efforts of British naval vessels conducting antislavery patrols of the coast, an illicit traffic in enslaved captives continued in the Rio Pongo into the 1850s.[3] Even as a new generation of European and American merchants flocked to the coastal rivers to develop new export crops of groundnuts and coffee, the success of these efforts proceeded unevenly and often still relied upon enslaved laborers. Missionaries became a more active presence in several coastal towns, setting up schools for children and holding church services. Among them were Afro-descendants, formerly enslaved migrants from Barbados and elsewhere around the Atlantic who settled in Freetown and the adjacent riverine areas of Guinea. Colonial officials at Freetown, Banjul, and Saint-Louis who sought to develop local agricultural farms to produce cash crops first turned to cotton, imagining they might enhance or replace local practices with more robust, profit-generating methods. But none of these endured as groundnuts became the export crop embraced by African farmers responding in entrepreneurial ways to colonial demand. How were social relations, both in an Islamizing savanna and in Atlantic port towns, constructed or renegotiated through the exchange of cloth or the practices of dress in this context?

In the first section of the chapter, I examine how certain forms of dress facilitated claims making and forms of mobility—but only conditionally and never completely—in trading centers between the coast and Kankan. Some of these connections were articulated in European travel accounts. René Caillié traveled to Timbuktu during these years, beginning on the Guinea coast at Rio Nunez before passing through the Fuuta Jallon, Kankan, and farther north. To smooth his passage, Caillié contrived a false identity for himself as the "Arab" son of an Egyptian, dressing himself in local clothing and participating in Muslim prayer to convince people of this invented story. Caillié's race manipulation was suffused with nineteenth-century orientalist tropes about Africans and Muslims. But these tropes also offer insight into regional perspectives in moments that contrast Caillié's own ideas about race and gender with the ideas of others he met.

I then offer a reading of slave trader Théodore Canot's account of the Rio Pongo, particularly of his ties with the Eurafrican trader John Ormond Jr. and the Muslim state at Timbo that highlight the gendered and racial dynamics along the coast, where the lives of Eurafrican commercial elites, African farmers, and itinerant European traders intersected in the early nineteenth century.

Finally, I look at French and British colonial efforts to take advantage of indigenous cotton cultivation to establish plantations of the cash crop at Saint-Louis and Freetown using wage labor as an alternative to enslaved labor, which is just one of the projects that were forerunners of the more direct colonial interventions that began to take shape by the mid-nineteenth century. Efforts to promote cotton plantations were rejected, however, by local farmers, who took up groundnut cultivation, which took off in the 1840s in Senegal and south to Guinea. The ability of local farmers to easily incorporate groundnut cultivation into established farming practices without interfering with the cultivation of staple food crops promoted its expansion across the region in the period up to 1850. Unlike cotton, groundnuts did not have a long history of cultivation and were not enmeshed in long-established social and cultural mores. But they did represent a commercial opportunity that many seized upon. Profits from this export crop in some areas eventually supported an even greater number of imported textiles than in earlier periods.

## CARAVANS OF CLOTH ACROSS THE SAVANNA AND PLATEAU ENTER THE ERA OF "LEGITIMATE TRADE"

The mobility of Fulbe and Maninka Muslim merchants and guides, or *silatigui* in Maninka, shaped the flow of textiles and other goods into Kankan, Timbo, and other market centers between the coast and savanna.[4] Some guides also shepherded much larger caravans of hundreds of people leaving Fuuta Jallon carrying loads of textiles, gold, cowhides, beeswax, ivory, and other goods. The guides (e.g., see figure 6.1) were valued for their knowledge of changing political conditions that might affect the safe movement of these caravans through the mountainous paths descending to the tropical coastal towns, such as Bangalan and Farenya on the Rio Pongo or Kakundy on the Rio Nunez. In the early nineteenth century, the clerical state at Timbo taxed and controlled the use of paths between the Fuuta Jallon plateau and the coast, taking steps to keep the paths open and safe for its commercial benefit.

Additionally, open paths were vital to the flow of information, surveillance, and control. Clerics at Timbo were kept informed about trade developments at coastal towns such as Kissi and Robaina, where they sent emissaries with correspondence in Arabic to clients on the Guinea rivers. The clerics also corresponded with the governors of the British colony at Sierra Leone, expressing their desire to maintain trade and objecting to Freetown's refusal of the slave trade.[5] In one letter, they indicate that their trade in captive laborers had become so important to the state's survival because, unlike other commodities they claimed, it generated enough income to purchase the weapons to arm its soldiers. They sought collaboration as equals with the British on the basis that they were both people of the Book, explaining that they did not enslave Muslims, only "kaffirs" who "know not the rights of God and still less the rights of men."[6]

Leaders of the clerical state prioritized acquiring weapons in pursuit of their political goals and argued that continuing the highly profitable traffic in captives—especially of persons deemed expendable—was the best way to pay for them. Cotton textiles remained a basic trade good animating this more volatile commerce with the coast, although their manufacture was not generally viewed as a viable potential alternative to slaving. This regional exchange of cotton woven in the plateau for coastal salt was in fact older than the Fulbe clerical state itself. In the sixteenth century, it was Susu merchants who were then the predominant population of the plateau, who led caravans bringing indigo dyestuffs and white cotton textiles along some of the same paths to exchange for salt and rice with Baga, Nalu, and Landuma communities on the coast.[7] By the nineteenth century, the

FIGURE 6.1. "Bokari, the Kaartan guide" in Major William Gray and Staff Surgeon Dochard, *Travels in Western Africa, in the Years 1818, 19, 20, and 21* [...] (London: J. Murray, 1825).

extensive in-migration of Fulbe Muslims from Maacina in the Niger River valley and those from Fuuta Tooro on the Senegal River valley converged to radically alter the demography and politics of what became known as Fuuta Jallon. It had not, however, fundamentally altered the symbiotic nature of exchanges between these two climatic regions.

In the Fuuta Jallon, dress was a key mode of the personal expression of various forms of Muslim belonging, but it also set social boundaries between Muslims and non-Muslims. Within the habitus of an expanding Islamic state, individuals, social groups, and communities defined themselves and their relations to one another in dynamic, historically contingent ways. Many Fula women, for example, resisted the politicized views of male clerical leaders by selectively adapting to Islamic principles when favorable to their interests. They refused the creation of harems, insisted on raising their own children, and often rejected wearing a veil—while still upholding other expectations of faithful Muslims (see figure 6.2).[8] Similarly, non-Muslim communities found ways to assert their independence from clerical dictates. Laing claims that Solimana residents visiting Timbo had dressed like Fulbe Muslims when allied politically with Timbo but had ceased to do so when relations soured between the two communities. Solimana women

FIGURE 6.2. "The Women at Timbo Drawing Water" in Théodore Canot and Brantz Mayer, *Captain Canot; or, Twenty Years of an African Slaver* [...] (New York: D. Appleton, 1854).

FIGURE 6.3. "Soolima Women Dancers" in Alexander Gordon Laing and Edward Sir Sabine. *Travels in the Timannee, Kooranko, and Soolima Countries, in Western Africa* (London: J. Murray, 1825).

had taken to wearing copious amounts of gold jewelry in their left ears both to distinguish themselves from Fula women and to announce their relative wealth (see figure 6.3).[9]

Caravans of enslaved porters transporting goods from Timbo and Labe in the Fuuta Jallon plateau, and even from Kankan to the northeast, walked for weeks to reach the trading settlements on the Atlantic coastal outlets of the Rio Pongo and the Rio Nunez. Kakundy, an old slaving port near Boke and about two hundred miles north of Freetown, had for decades been home to European, American, and Eurafrican merchants who trafficked thousands of captives across the Atlantic. In the wake of British abolition being enforced by the Royal Navy patrols of the coast, the overseas slave trade was largely choked off by the 1820s, and most merchants had turned to the production of the cash crops of coffee, cotton, and groundnuts as alternatives. This was the Kakundy into which René Caillié—an errant French sailor in his twenties from an impoverished background with only an elementary education but experience laboring on both sides of the Atlantic—arrived in 1827. He had seemingly followed the trend of French entrepreneurs migrating south from Gorée Island and mainland Senegal who, in pursuing new opportunities, went first to the British colony at Freetown. He worked for several months there at an indigo factory—one instance of how colonial enterprises of this period sought to insert themselves into local industry. He had come to Rio Nunez looking to join a caravan into the interior after the Geographic Society of Paris announced an award of ten thousand francs to "the first" European to reach and describe the famed city of Timbuktu. Caillié already had significant experience in Senegal having once walked from Saint-Louis to Dakar and spending six months living among the Brakna Moors north of the Senegal River. There, he studied the Quran with local marabouts, learned to read Arabic, and professed conversion to Islam.[10]

Caillié arrived in the Rio Nunez wearing clothing styled like that of the Brakna Moors and peddling a fake story about his background that he hoped would facilitate his movement through a region where many African authorities ostensibly did not allow European merchants to pass. He claimed to be an Arab who was captured by Napoleon's army in Egypt; then he was enslaved and brought by his slaveholder to Saint-Louis, where he was freed but left with few resources to return to his homeland.

Of course, Caillié's' pretense tells us more about his understanding and imagination of Islam, West Africa, and race than it does about the people he attempted to mislead. West Africans could readily distinguish between Europeans, Arabs, and Berber Arabs, no matter their attire—and a person's phenotype, or physical body, was an important but not always conclusive factor

*Textures of a Changing Era* ⁓ 177

in determining an individual's "race" or social category. In some instances, villagers cited behaviors such as his lack of generosity with gifts that revealed him as "a Christian" foreigner rather than who he claimed to be.[11]

Though Caillié met frequently with suspicion and challenges to his claims and agenda, his declaration of being a devout Muslim also gained him special benefits and favors in several instances. He was allowed to cross a river in the gold mining region of Bure without paying the customs duty usually imposed on travelers. The intervention of his guide Ibrahim, who vouched for Caillié's story, led villagers at Popoco to lavish attention and praise upon him as an "Arab" and "countryman of the Prophet" and attracted visits from local scholars and merchants who refused payment for basic provisions. Ultimately, Caillié was not the first European of this period to visit Timbuktu, as British major Gordon Laing, who had not bothered with the pretense of local dress or claim to Muslim identity, reached the city a year before Caillié began his journey, traveling in a caravan south from Tripoli across the Sahara. But Caillié's narrative suggests that West African discourses of race and social privilege—in which his light skin signified both foreignness and potential belonging to an elite class of Muslims—combined to allow him enough plausibility to reach Timbuktu from the south (and to continue onward across the Sahara to Tangier) when others had failed to do so.

Ibrahim, Caillié's guide, was the son of the headman at Cambaya and therefore a person with an elevated social status. Ibrahim traveled with his wife, who is described as cooking meals for them but is not named, which follows discursive and social conventions that extracted and invisibilized women's labor. Ibrahim was enmeshed in a series of patron-client relationships that included moments in which he effectively occupied the role of patron—beyond whatever his relationship with Caillié or another European partner may have been. He led the caravan, including Caillié, to his home village and fired several shots of his European musket to call the people of the village together to distribute gifts he had procured for them from Kakundy. To the old men of the local council, Ibrahim gave tobacco that had been folded into individual packets and made ready for distribution, possibly North American or Cuban in origin. He gave each of his three wives pieces of indigo-blue guinee cloth. Onlookers began to praise his generosity, shouting prayers for his well-being and prosperity as women danced in appreciation of Ibrahim. It is clear how Ibrahim's distribution of specific goods of high symbolic value and practical use to distinct constituencies animated a gendered and gerontocratic social order in towns such as Cambaya.

After a few days, Caillié left Cambaya without Ibrahim and his wife. He was led by a second guide, Lamfia, whose wife is also described as cooking

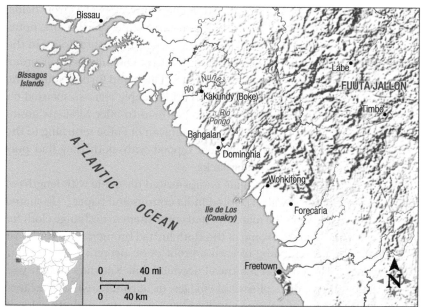

MAP 6.1. Map of coastal Guinea region showing towns along the riverine coast from Bissau to Freetown, and their proximity to the Fuuta Jallon. Map by Matt Johnson at Johnson Cartographic.

meals for them and also not named. In crossing the Fuuta Jallon plateau, Caillié and his company traversed a landscape where not only "the principal trade of the country is in salt and cotton cloth,"[12] he remarks, but one where warfare and slavery were rampant.

On their journey, the group passed several *ourunde*, or settlements of enslaved farmers, where fields of cotton, yam, cassava, and banana were planted. They crossed the Tinkisso River, where years before a Muslim scholar, Muhammad Kaba Saghanughu, was captured during a conflict, sold to slavers on the coast, and transported to Jamaica. Kaba Saghanughu was connected to one of the most scholarly families of western Africa and had been part of a larger internal diaspora of Qadiriyya Sufi. Enslaved in Jamaica, he penned an account in Arabic script that reflects his early Quranic school education in either the Fuuta Jallon or Bate region.[13] He also spoke of this background to Irish doctor and abolitionist Richard Robert Madden, who describes the ourunde controlled by Kaba Saghanughu's father: "His father was a substantial yeoman, possessing 140 slaves, several cows and horses, and grounds producing quantities of cotton, rice and provisions which he exchanged for European and other commodities brought from the coast by Higglers."[14]

*Textures of a Changing Era* ⁓ 179

Other eyewitness accounts mention the cultivation of cotton fields. Gaspard Mollien, traveling through the same area a few years before, notes how the expanse of cotton fields he encountered from Fuuta Tooro in the north, where fields were "surrounded by hedges, carefully kept in order, placed two feet asunder," to parts of the Fuuta Jallon and further south. The chief of one village in Bondu reported that his people were so focused on cotton cultivation that he had no lodging or food to offer Mollien's group of travelers.[15] He later mentions passing a caravan of Fulbe returning to the Fuuta Jallon with long, narrow baskets topped with cloth they had purchased in Bondu strapped to their backs.

Upon arrival at Kankan, Caillié compensated his guide with lengths of indigo guinee cloths as well as printed India cottons and paper.[16] He shared a room in town with a Fulbe man who had come there to exchange cloth for salt. Later, Caillié also sold some of the cloth he had brought from the coast at Kankan's market, claiming to earn a profit of 60 percent over its value at Rio Nunez.[17] He noted in his travel account that Kankan's wealth was supported by the produce of several villages, or ourundes, where enslaved laborers raised fields of cotton as well as yam, corn, rice, and other foods that fed the town's residents. When a marabout in town from Segu visited Caillié and offered benedictions to the unusual visitor, his hosts gifted the man with several lengths of a local cloth as a sign of respect.[18]

In the 1820s, Kankan was a town of about six thousand residents rebounding well after the previous years of warfare. Following Birama's defeat, Alfa Kabine, the son of a chief in Bate known as a learned, pious scholar and defender of the older Suwarian worldview, had returned with a group of followers from the Fuuta Jallon to rebuild. Kabine had set the community on a new trajectory, however, ending the decades of isolation prior to the conflict by attracting regional merchants and young male migrants to Kankan to settle permanently through marriages to local women. This approach, known locally as *nabaya,* meaning "welcome," not only strengthened Kankan by growing its population and increasing the town's economic activity but also acted as a mechanism the Maninka-Mori elites deployed to incorporate newcomers into their established hierarchy.

Kankan's markets attracted merchants and goods from such distant market centers as Segu, Jenne, and Kong, as well as Timbo, coastal Guinea, the Gambia River, Gajaaga, and even Saint-Louis on the Senegal River. Woven white cottons and local pottery from Wasulu once again flowed into market stalls at Kankan, as did a variety of goods from European merchants on the coast, such as varieties of muskets, gunpowder, European and Indian guinee cloth, Indian cotton prints, European woolens, and amber, coral, and glass beads.

Cotton textiles sent to Kankan from the Sankaran region to the southeast (parts of which had previously been at war with Bate) were prized market items with a reputation for high quality and beauty.[19] Sankaran weavers sold their manufactures to markets in the gold mining region of Bure to the northeast and used the gold they obtained from these sales to buy goods in neighboring regions closer to the coast, such as the Fuuta Jallon and Solimana to the southeast. Solimana consumers preferred cloth dyed very black after a local fashion that used "pitch water and iron ore" or dyed yellow from the bark of the nete tree.[20] They obtained such cloth, as well as flints, gunpowder, beads, and other goods from the Atlantic markets. They also obtained gold and horses from Sankaran.

At Kankan, the annual celebration of Tabaski drew crowds into the street for a procession and public speeches. A group of elderly men led the procession through town wearing short red cloaks trimmed at the neck with yellow thread meant to approximate gold and red caps. They carried large staffs as they chanted, "Allahu-akbar!" A series of officials on horseback followed, flanked by dozens of soldiers carrying shotguns walking on either side of the horses. Some onlookers lining the road wore outfits that consisted of a *dloki*, or a loose-fitting cotton tunic, trousers, and a pointed cap, all of the same material. Others donned headscarves and striped or indigo-dyed cotton pagnes or wrappers, some glistening, perhaps with starch. Some in the crowd are described as wearing European cloaks, jackets of various colors, and hats that had once belonged to English soldiers miles away on the coasts but that had circulated through local networks of commerce and exchange.[21]

The procession culminated with the arrival of Kankan's top cleric on horseback. It is said he wore a finely tailored, red military cloak with gold lace given to him personally by a British officer he met on a visit to the coast at Rio Nunez, possibly Major John Peddie, who had died before ever traveling inland.[22] No further details are offered, but this garment might possibly have been an alderman's gown or naval officer's cloak, although these generally were black. If the almaami at Kankan ever wore such a cloak, especially on such an important occasion, it suggests the garments did some of the seductive work of statecraft by materially incorporating a high-status garment from a powerful foreign partner, demonstrating an affiliation to this perceived power. Certainly, the Fuuta Jallon clerical state placed importance on its commercial and diplomatic ties with the British and other foreign merchants on the Atlantic coast. As an outer garment, the cloaks may easily have served to enhance the authority of the kusaaba and turban worn by the cleric. Both garments are visually similar to the burnoose worn by a figure of the almaami's status.

There are not many contemporaneous sources to confirm or expand upon what Caillié claimed to witness at the festival. But his testimony is suggestive not only of the reach of commercial goods imported on the coasts hundreds of miles away but also of a sense of a West African public both connected to global currents and sartorially expressive in dynamic ways. The clerical and political leaders of Kankan rebuilt their community after years of war by adopting a more inclusive posture toward the region's ethnic and social cleavages and by more deeply embedding their town into regional commerce. They preserved aspects of Kankan's unique Islamic theological tradition, which was distinct from that of the clerics at Timbo and Labe, by reconstituting it as a mixed urban center open to external influences.

## FROM THE RIVERS TO THE SEA: OLD PATTERNS MEET CHANGING TIMES ON THE RIO NUNEZ AND THE RIO PONGO

In the 1830s, a new economy was emerging from an influx of francophone migrants from Gorée and Saint-Louis into the Rio Nunez area. They were attracted by the commercial possibilities of farming groundnuts and coffee for export. They settled at the head of the river's estuary in a region dense with tropical mangroves whose diverse residents included predominantly non-Muslim Landuma, Nalu, and Baga farming communities as well as Muslim Susu, Fulbe, and Maninka-Mori migrants from the interior. The newcomers sought to gain favor with local chiefs and headmen to secure labor for their enterprises.

Slaving had long dominated commerce in these riverine settlements, with the Landuma especially active as intermediaries between foreign ships docking from the Atlantic and merchant caravans arriving from the Fuuta Jallon. The Landuma were subjects of the Fulbe Muslim clerical state to whom they paid annual tribute in addition to facilitating Fulbe caravan commerce. In the advent of the British abolition of Atlantic slave trading being enforced with naval patrols, they began to facilitate the commerce of French newcomers to the area.[23] The Rio Nunez was easily patrolled by British antislavery vessels because of its wide coastal outlet and relatively straight course inland. As a result, the Rio Nunez made the transition to only legal commodities faster and more decidedly than along the Rio Pongo to the south.

The Fulbe state protected the rice-growing Baga communities from the violence of slave raiding and trading because of their importance in producing salt, greatly in demand by their pastoralists for their cattle.[24] Textiles were deeply imbricated in this exchange between the coast and the plateau that had existed before the rise of the Fulbe state and continued even as a new colonial, extractive economy developed alongside it. Baga had long dressed themselves in textiles obtained through this trade with the plateau and adorned their bodies with palm oil they also produced for trade. Imported goods from Atlantic merchants expanded their repertoire of textiles used as wrappers covering the body. But the Baga, like a cross section of other African residents in the Rio Nunez, occasionally may have been seen wearing other imports, such as tailored breeches, a sailor's jacket, or a felted hat obtained from the market or in payment for labor.

Around the time that Caillié's caravan stopped in Cambaya with Ibrahim, an errant merchant seaman from the Ligurian coast of Italy found work a few hundred miles south of Kakundy/Boke on the Rio Pongo. Théophilus Conneau had sailed widely in the Atlantic and Mediterranean on the ships of multiple nations when he arrived at what was then a regional hot spot of ongoing illicit human trafficking—mostly supplying slave ships destined for Cuba. Several trading settlements along the Rio Pongo continued to provide captive laborers to slaving vessels in exchange for imported goods despite British attempts to abolish the trade. Vessels took advantage of the waterway's serpentine path, dense mangroves, and limited sight lines to evade British naval patrols. The trading families living scattered throughout the river's branches included British, Eurafrican, Euro-American, African diaspora, French, and other settlers who lived among predominantly Susu- and Baga-speaking villagers.

Eurafrican slave-trading merchant John Ormond Jr., then the most prominent merchant on the Rio Pongo, hired Conneau as a keeper for enslaved captives held in barracoons on his premises and as a storekeeper for his warehouse of imported and local textiles, leather hides, beads, mirrors, tobacco, and pipes. Having inherited a commercial operation from his father, Ormond periodically held thousands of captives trafficked in caravans from the interior who grew coffee and groundnuts on his land until they could be sold to arriving ships—many of which at that time were sailing to Cuba.[25] Conneau became known as Théodore Canot during the years Ormond introduced him to the business of slaving.

Born on the river to a Susu mother, educated in England, and having traveled around the Atlantic and Mediterranean, Ormond lived in a large compound protected by cannons at Bangalan, a settlement at the upper reaches of the Rio Pongo closest to caravan paths from the Fuuta Jallon. Like the dwelling places of many elites of the area, his home was likely built of stone and featured one or more piazzas, or covered outdoor seating areas to receive guests and commercial clients.[26] Inside it likely contained mahogany furniture, porcelain and pewter dishes, and imported cottons. Known as a *mangue* (chief) in the Susu language (and often mispronounced as "mongo"), Ormond derived status from his mother's lineage. But Mongo John was also a client of the clerical state in the Fuuta Jallon, whose caravan trade goods were a primary engine of the coastal economy. To conduct trade, he sent hired drummers and musicians to accompany caravans as large as seven hundred people arriving from the plateau into town, where negotiations unfolded over as many as three days. The protocol required coastal traders like Ormond not only to house and feed the caravan guide and leading merchants but to offer them gifts—such as cloth or other sample merchandise—to both open and close the trading process. It was important the gifts be sufficiently impressive to secure a reputation for generosity that would continue to attract caravans to his factory and not to any competitor.

Ormond's knowledge of local commercial protocol, his language skills in Susu, Fulbe, and English, and his cultural fluency marked him as a cosmopolitan Afro-Atlantic figure in the early nineteenth century. He was deeply embedded in the economy of transatlantic slaving, although he was not immune from the violence and precarity associated with it. Ormond had business relations in South Carolina and owned property in Havana, Cuba. By the time Canot showed up in his town around 1827, Ormond had traveled several times to Cuba, possibly aboard the same slaving vessels carrying captives he sold to his Spanish partners. Several of the métis, or Eurafrican, trading families along the Rio Pongo sent children overseas to study in Havana and Matanzas in Cuba, as well as in Charleston, South Carolina, and Liverpool, England.[27] In Cuba, Ormond once filed a claim in the Tribunal de Comercio in Havana for nonpayment of a debt against slave trader Antonio Escoto, who argued, unsuccessfully, that Ormond had no standing in court because he was a "black savage."[28] In the Rio Pongo, by contrast, he was regarded as a high-born, privileged elite. His influence extended to several towns throughout the area, where he had prosperous relatives. His property included a building inherited from his father being used as a school for the Church Missionary Society. Described as having multiple wives and as many as thirty concubines,[29] Ormond lived a life of profligate excess that included heavy drinking, extravagant meals, and entertaining. No description of his manner of dress has survived, but it is clear that he had access to a range of possibilities and that his choices likely reflected his travels and social status as well as his extensive cultural ties.

In Canot's account, Ormond's public-facing role as a leading trader and patriarch was mediated by several women within the household, who exercised considerable power over people and relationships in part through manipulating the distribution of goods, including cloth, to which they had privileged access. He recounts, for example, that not long after he began

FIGURE 6.4. Interior of a piazza in the *Illustrated London News* (October 25, 1856), vol. 29, p. 434. This figure illustrates what the homes looked like in Ormond's town.

working at the Bangalan storehouse, a woman of mature age confronted Canot there. The two had no shared language, but she nevertheless made it clear to him in Susu that access to the storehouse was actually to be controlled by her, not Ormond. As if to demonstrate her point, the woman demanded that Canot open a cloth chest "whence she immediately helped herself to several fathoms of calico" and threatened to drive him from the property if he informed Ormond of her activities.[30]

Mongo John's status as community leader and regional trader was predicated partly on his cosmopolitan background but also on the gendered politics of his polygynous household, which Canot's account sheds light on. That status fell under increasing pressure during the years Canot worked for him. He had in fact been feuding for decades with the British naval patrols, one of which burned several of his buildings to the ground in 1814 and continued to police and constrain his ability to sell captives to Atlantic-bound ships. He also fought with competing coastal traders in a series of violent conflicts as the Rio Pongo region struggled to adapt to the changing dynamics of the choking off of Atlantic slaving. He began to lose the support of the Fulbe state, which had plans to replace him as their primary coastal client.[31] Mongo John drank heavily in those years and began to lose control of his business, which suffered losses. He was irascible and violent toward his concubines. In 1833, Ormond died by suicide, shooting himself in the chest.

Canot, having learned the business from his Eurafrican patron, became a slave trader on his own. He describes how he ingratiated himself with the Fulbe state by paying a diplomatic visit to Timbo and presenting Almaami Ahmed de Bello with a garment he had commissioned from a local tailor in the Rio Pongo, "one of the most skillful artists on the river." A year after Ormond's death, a French court condemned Canot to five years in prison for slave trading in the Saloum region of Senegal. He was released with a commuted sentence a year later and abstained from slave trafficking for a while before again becoming active in the trade on the Gallinas/Kerefe River near the American colony of Liberia.

After decades as a slave trafficker in the Atlantic, Canot ended up in Baltimore, Maryland. In 1850, he wrote his recollection of his experiences in collaboration with editor Brantz Mayer. The pair aimed to benefit from public debates about slavery and the commercial success of Harriet Beecher Stowe's *Uncle Tom's Cabin*. Canot's work reads like an adventure tale crafted for an imagined young male reader for whom the narrator performs a white, imperial masculinist fantasy of both bravery and moral probity against an African backdrop. The racist and misogynist language the two men deployed to describe African women and men helped to construct and inform its readers' notions of racial and gender hierarchies, thus justifying both slavery and imperial expansion.

### COTTON AND GROUNDNUTS: COLONIAL CASH CROPS IN EARLY NINETEENTH-CENTURY WESTERN AFRICA

Administrators at both the French colony at Saint-Louis, Senegal, and the British colony at Freetown, Sierra Leone, viewed cotton agriculture as the potential basis of a colonial economy. Similar ventures had been tried previously several times without success going back to at least to the early eighteenth century. The new energy and interest in colonial agriculture in the 1820s emerged in the context of increased raw cotton production farmed by enslaved African Americans in the United States. The administrators hoped to compete by improving and expanding the scale of an already familiar West African export crop.

At Saint-Louis, French and Eurafrican habitants struggled to replace profits from a now defunct slave trade in the years after France regained colonial territory from Britain in 1817. Julien Schmaltz, the French officer sent to govern the colony, had spent time in Java, Bengal, and was briefly appointed governor of the sugar slave plantation economy of Guadeloupe in the Caribbean. He brought these experiences to his vision for a French colony in Senegal but arrived there only after surviving the disastrous 1816 shipwreck of *La Méduse,* in which hundreds perished.[32] In Senegal, Schmaltz imagined replacing slave trading with an agricultural economy of cotton and indigo estates owned by European and Eurafrican habitants and worked by African wage laborers.

These experiments on land ceded to France in the Waalo region upriver from Saint-Louis began in 1819 but had already run their course by 1830, when they were largely abandoned. Farms at Richard Tol, Koilel, Faf, and Dagana struggled to match French expectations for output, as unexpectedly difficult growing conditions limited the amount of cotton produced, and indigo crops raised near the banks of the Senegal River suffered from seasonal flooding of brackish water that ruined young plants.[33] The proprietors also failed to establish a workable system of wage or indentured labor. The French negotiants running these farms found the wages offered could not attract enough labor, as local farmers preferred to continue operating as seasonal traders to Saint-Louis. An even more decisive blow against the colonization scheme was the withdrawal of support by the local Wolof brak, who encouraged villagers to destroy the dikes built to control the flooding. At the same time, Trarza Moors from north of the river periodically raided both the French planters and the Wolof-speaking villagers, destroying crops and burning buildings on some farms. In 1833, the French governor at Saint-Louis sent military expeditions against the Trarza Moors to oppose their proposed unification with the Waalo chiefs through marriage, and the ensuing violence pulled the French into more direct intervention in regional politics and destroyed the viability of their already struggling colonial agricultural experiments.

Even as the cotton experiments in the Waalo faded, similar experiments were underway in Freetown and its surroundings, where members of the Church Missionary Society had introduced seeds of Sea Island cotton from the United States and were enthusiastic about the results. They advocated the development of these farms as a source of industry for liberated Africans, who could be guaranteed profitable sales of cotton with relatively modest investments of labor and time. They did so to counter the political claims of proslavery advocates in the British Parliament who sought to undermine the notion that a colony of free, wage-earning Africans might be a viable alternative to plantations in the Caribbean. So wrote William Fergusson, a surgeon with the Royal African Corps charged with caring for Africans rescued from slave ships and brought to Freetown, in an 1839 letter to the British politician and abolitionist Thomas Fowell Buxton.[34] Fergusson thought the governor of Sierra Leone should expand upon these experiments by setting aside land for three cotton farms of fifty acres each and that the land chosen should be near population centers to keep laborers from having to travel too far to reach them.

The liberated Africans populating Freetown at this time had acquired a reputation for being entrepreneurial, finding opportunities to engage in petty trading or to hire themselves out as common laborers, and many gradually became bigger traders who were able to access credit, earn more profit, and improve their living circumstances within a decade or two. The most successful among them were living in wood-frame houses on stone foundations and even in two-story stone houses with a covered porch and furnished with "mahogany chairs, tables, sofas, and four post bedsteads, pier glasses, floor cloths, and other articles indicative of domestic comfort and accumulating wealth."[35] Fergusson wrote to Buxton, trying to convince him of the entrepreneurial spirit of these Africans brought ashore from captured slaving vessels: "A leading feature in the character of the liberated Africans, as a body, is their great love of money." The hope was that the colony could tap this entrepreneurial behavior by demonstrating to new arrivals who were petty traders or common laborers that much money was to be made in producing cotton on government farms.

Meanwhile, the relative success and quick profits generated by cultivating groundnuts in the Guinea rivers area north of Freetown was quickly overtaking interest in the potential for cotton. Eurafrican habitants on Gorée Island were active in the early stages of this trade, as they owned canoes that traveled to ports on the mainland along the Gambia River and south on the coast to Sierra Leone. There, they picked up harvests of groundnuts to be brought to Gorée before shipment to France, where they were used to produce soap, wax, and machine oil. However, these habitant merchants soon found themselves marginalized by competition from metropolitan French companies whose larger organizations and vessels were more effective in transporting the export crops.

Some of the earliest French purchases of this crop occurred in 1833 and 1834[36] along the Gambia River. By 1841, exports had expanded in both directions along the coast to ports in Senegal and southward to Sierra Leone. The cultivation of groundnuts was more favorable in the light, sandy soils of northern Senegambia than in the Guinea rivers coast, which had much higher humidity. In the Guinea rivers, landlords cultivated the new crop using the labor of captives who could no longer be exported abroad. Cultivators found that groundnuts were easily integrated into established farming patterns, could be grown in fields of varying size, and quickly paid returns on the labor invested in planting it.[37] Édouard Bouët-Willaumez, then governor of Saint-Louis, reports that groundnut exports in the region between Cape Verde and Sierra Leone had more than quadrupled over four years, from fifteen hundred tons in 1842 to sixty-seven hundred tons in 1846.[38] He notes in particular that French vessels were active along the coast between the Rio Nunez and Sierra Leone, from which they returned directly to France, bypassing Gorée Island.[39] The combined advantages of metropolitan companies' transportation and the lack of interest in groundnuts from British competitors resulted in an intensified French commercial presence throughout the Senegambia and Upper Guinea coastal regions in this period.[40]

Bouët-Willaumez also observes that the rapid increase in groundnut exports from the region was accompanied by the increased importation of Asian- and French-manufactured goods, especially cotton textiles produced in Rouen: "There is cause to celebrate this growth of commerce that has taken over a branch of commerce so favorable to our navigation and our industry at the same time."[41] In West Africa, Rouen-manufactured textiles were selling at a higher price than Indian textiles, yet they still readily found buyers.[42] Cloth imports were especially sought after by Mandinka merchants in the Guinea rivers region north of Freetown, where French merchants trading groundnuts were gradually edging out earlier generations of English and Anglo-African merchants. Bouët-Willaumez theorizes that cloth sales could compensate for their inability to sell alcohol, another major French export, to "fervent Muslim sectarians." Two principal types of cloth sales were to be made in Africa, he expresses—fine cloths and trade cloths. Trade cloths, or common cloths, were used to purchase wood and grains, whereas items such as gold, ivory, and palm oil had to be purchased using fine cloths. The names of India-produced cloths are listed in both categories. The names of the fine luxury cloths he mentions suggest their global sources: Indian guinee cloths in indigo or white, "limeneas, tom-coffee, sucretons, satin-streap, glasgow-danes, siamoise, printanieres, nicanees, bandanna, taffetas, antipod-danes."[43]

In 1838, Bouët-Willaumez led the expedition of the ship *La Malouine* that traveled from Gorée to Gabon. He expanded French presence in the region by establishing trading outposts at Assinie and Grand Bassam in the Ivory Coast and Gabon. In 1842, the French monarch Louis Philippe signed a new ordinance governing the importation of Indian-made guinee cloths into Senegal. The ordinance was meant to advance the French commercial position in the gum trade by confirming the high quality of these originally sourced goods critical to consumers in this market. This commercial maneuver fell far short of its intended goal.[44] Still, it nonetheless suggests that cotton cloth and textiles remained a key arena of contact, exchange, and struggle in the increasing French and British interventions in African economies leading up to the establishment of colonial states in West Africa.

### NHARA BELY AND THE RIO PONGO LOSE THEIR INDEPENDENCE

Elizabeth Bailey Gomez Lightburn, Nhara Bely, outlived her cousin Mongo John Ormond Jr. by several decades. Her place at Farenya was only four miles upriver from his at Bangalan, and after his death, she continued in the old ways, receiving caravans from the plateau, working captive labor on coffee plantations, and occasionally selling some of her captives to vessels willing to try to outmaneuver British naval patrols. By the 1850s, Nhara Bely was already a wealthy woman. She had been born into a local elite family as the daughter of Emmanuel Gomez, a Luso-African merchant and chief at Bakia on the Rio Pongo, and Dominka Beli, a Susu woman, also of Bakia.[45] Her uncle was Jellorum Fernandez, the Luso-African village chief at Bouramaya, whose grandson Jellorum Harrison had traveled to Edinburgh, Scotland, where he converted to Christianity then joined a missionary expedition with Henry Brunton to central Asia.[46]

When she was younger, Nhara Bely had also spent some time in England, where she had been sent by her well-connected father to attend school. It had been the same with several of her relatives who were scattered in towns throughout the Rio Pongo area, like Ormond at Bangalan and Richard Wilkinson, a Christian convert who wanted to attract English-speaking missionaries to settle with him at nearby Fallanghia. She was said to consider herself more "African" because she never left the country again after her time in England, unlike her cousins who traveled more outside the continent.[47]

Elizabeth Gomez had already been working as a trader at Farenya when she married Styles Lightburn Jr., an American ship captain from South Carolina who had arrived in the Rio Pongo in 1809, soon after the United States abolished the slave trade. Their country-style marriage had elements of a commercial arrangement, as was customary. Into their union, Gomez brought land, laborers (*grumetes*), and enslaved people inherited from her father, as well as her connections and expertise as a cross-cultural commercial broker. Lightburn brought his skills and networks around the Atlantic. By the 1830s, after Mongo John had died, Lightburn had left the Rio Pongo permanently, leaving Nhara Bely to continue running the operation with one of their five children, his Eurafrican son and namesake, Styles Jr. Her *tata* (compound) covered a large area that included several buildings surrounded by a wall on one side and featured a clear view of the Rio Pongo from its elevated position.

She was living there in 1855 when two missionaries from the Caribbean arrived at Farenya, making their way up a jetty from the riverbank to the veranda where she stood waiting to receive her visitors. She greeted the men on veranda, surrounded by a few attendants and three of her young grandchildren, who were neatly dressed in European-tailored clothes. Bely was dressed in a cloth wrapper that covered her full body. She wore large gold jewelry, including a golden comb adorning her neatly styled hair.[48] She spoke English well but communicated with her Caribbean visitors through a Susu-language interpreter (e.g., see figure 6.5).[49]

The men were Reverend James Leacock, the son of a wealthy sugar plantation owner in Barbados, and John Henry Duport, an Afro-descendant man who had received primary and religious education on Saint Kitts. They were lead agents of the West Indian Mission to Rio Pongo that was conceived in the wake of the emancipation of enslaved people in the British Empire in

FIGURE 6.5. "Susu Women / Femmes Soussous" by Ernest Maurice Laumann in the Jean Blackwell Hutson Research and Reference Division, Schomburg Center for Research in Black Culture, New York Public Library Digital Collections.

*Textures of a Changing Era* ⟿ 191

1834. Leacock and other leaders of the West Indian Church imagined that formerly enslaved Barbadians might be effective proselytizers of the Gospel. Some imagined the resources and benefits produced from the spiritual and educational labor might constitute a form of "repayment" to West Africans "for slavery."[50]

When the men explained their reasons for coming, this concept must have struck Nhara Bely as false. She certainly would have been familiar with the missionaries' rationale, as it was virtually the same one advocated a generation earlier when the colony at Freetown was still in its earliest days. Like her cousin Mongo John, Bely was hostile and distrustful toward British colonial officers of the navy and of the colony at Freetown who pressured her to cease the slave trading that had made her wealth and that her partners in the Fuuta Jallon wished her and others to maintain. The British navy had reportedly raided her factory several times, destroying buildings and commercial goods. After one raid in 1841, she joined a lawsuit against the British government with French merchant Rene Valentin to recoup the cost of his merchandise destroyed in the attack.

At different periods, she was thought to have held several hundred to as many as six thousand captives in barracoons. They farmed rice and coffee for a season before Bely would find a buyer to load groups of them on to stealthy ships, which was the extent of her engagement with the new commerce. She was said to engage in spiritual practices so that her captives might better accept their condition. At the same time, she discouraged missionaries preaching in Farenya because of fear that her slaves might come to "look on her as their equal if they sat in the same church, and said the same prayers, and were partakers of the same hope."[51]

Bely was a mature African woman whose life had bridged the turn of a century and who had experienced a major transformation of her birth society and the wider world she depended upon for her high standard of living. Like women merchants on many parts of the coast from Senegal to Guinea, she had built a life for herself and children in a volatile, violent commercial world dominated by men, long-distance djula traders, clerical figures in the Fuuta Jallon, and a transnational, multiracial set of entrepreneurs, freebooters, refugees, missionaries, and abolitionists pursuing dreams of their own making. Through her charm, intelligence, and hard work she had become a nhara, having built her kinship and social networks amid a patriarchal culture she proved skilled at navigating. She made much of her ties to local customs and may have belonged to the Sande Society, a ritualistic initiation society controlled by women and found in Guinea, Sierra Leone, and Liberia.[52] Despite this, she was part of a coastal elite of hybrid cultural affect considered foreign by many other western Africans. She had seen much, but she was now witnessing events evolving in new directions away from some of the advantages she had always known and toward subordination in a starkly different colonial context. Bely eventually promised to allow the missionaries Leacock and Duport to preach in her town of Farenya.[53] But she ultimately declined to offer land to the West Indian Mission to build a church and school by saying it did not belong to her and such permission could be granted only by several Susu small landholders.[54]

British missionary expansion in the Rio Pongo occurred in a context where greater French commercial and military interventions were already underway, first at Rio Nunez but eventually continuing to encompass the Rio Pongo and parts of coastal Guinea.[55] Far to the north at Saint-Louis, then governor General Louis Faidherbe had launched military attacks against the Serer and the forces of Umar Tal, who were resisting French colonial expansion. Faidherbe then traveled south to the Rio Nunez and Rio Pongo, where he met with French merchants and attempted to sign treaties with African headmen such as Mathia Katty, Nhara Bely's neighbor and competitor on the river.[56] Later at Farenya, Faidherbe met Bely, who he estimated still commanded as many as two thousand enslaved laborers.[57]

The new midcentury added another layer to the overlapping histories of the commerce of enslavement, which had shaped many aspects of regional life for centuries. Built on a centuries-old transregional exchange of agricultural goods and products, like textiles that met basic human needs, a vast transatlantic slaving economy emerged from these practices. By the mid-nineteenth century, this commerce was being fed by a network of global suppliers equipped with transportation now powered by steam engines, protected with more lethal weapons, and supported by a more elaborate, state-backed financial system.

Nhara Bely converted to Christianity decades later in the 1870s, when she was in her eighties. It was said she was convinced to do so by a black man from Trinidad who had settled on the river in the years after Leacock and Duport.[58] Nhara Bely had done much to secure her descendants' well-being in the colonial society where French would become the new colonial language, sharing space with Susu, Maninka, and Fulbe. But the world she had known was slipping away. She died in 1880. Nhara Bely had lost ground.

# Conclusion

THIS BOOK has studied the social and cultural history of an expansive region that encompasses parts the Sahel as well as riverine and Atlantic coastal towns, from Saint-Louis, Senegal, to Freetown, Sierra Leone, and the temperate Fuuta Jallon plateau. It has done so through the lens of textiles and dress to foreground the historical experiences of western Africans themselves, in their considerable variety, during a period defined by global connections and regional transformation.

Beginning in the fifteenth century, but with increasing speed and impact from the seventeenth century onward, centuries-old traditions of textile crafting, use, and exchange across western Africa became entwined with networks connecting the region with parts of Europe, Asia, and the Americas. This book has added to the scholarship signaling the ways that western Africans, as consumers of imported textiles and other goods, shaped the region's integration into an emerging global economy. It has also highlighted that textiles were a key commodity in connecting western African economies to European commercial expansion from the late seventeenth century through the mid-nineteenth century—a fact that raises questions and implications distinct from those that emerge when focusing exclusively on Atlantic slave trading.

Although it has demonstrated how western Africans played into a larger dynamic of drawing populations on four continents into symbiotic and unequal relationships, this book has first and foremost sought to contend with the multiple and competing forces within the region itself. An important goal has been to use textiles to recognize and to account for the multiplicity of voices across this culturally and linguistically diverse region in a way that is in conversation with the historiography of empire, Atlantic slavery, and Islam in West Africa but is not limited by any of those frameworks. In doing so, the book demonstrates the region's variegated but shared history. Textiles allow historians to center the western African context, to do so through a variety of perspectives, and to query the significance of the often-cosmopolitan character of the lives of people encountered in the archive.

It was not just the signares who wore imported Indian chintz, muslins, and indigo guinees but also the laptots and pileuses who were employed in selling such goods on seasonal trips upriver and likely acquired some in the course of their itinerant labor. Across the region, elites drew on the symbolic power of imported cloth to uphold their social advantages by incorporating it into their attire, by storing it, or by distributing it as patronage to their clients. Textile samples pasted into the pattern books of European mercantile companies, and drawings of western Africans based on contemporary witnesses, suggest that people used these imported textiles both to animate existing forms of dress and to innovate new vernacular sartorial expressions.

From throughout the period, there are many archival examples of naval uniforms or accessories such as caps, boots, swords, and pistols passing on to the descendants of European soldiers who died in western Africa. At Kankan, the incorporation of British military uniforms into the dress of authority figures in a highly visible and symbolic occasion of Tabaski suggests how state or clerical officials appropriated foreign symbols of power.

The incorporation of foreign clothing as a statement of worldliness, prestige, and connection to global trends also appeared in other western African contexts. For example, a younger generation of Muslim merchants in coastal Guinea, such as Dala Modu Dumbuya, adopted English trousers, petticoats, jackets, cloaks, hats, and walking sticks. In the early days of the settlement at Freetown, these merchants donned such clothing as a sign of affiliation with their British trading partners—a phenomenon that historians have described as part of a wider British Atlantic material culture.[1] But in the context of western Africa during this period, it expressed African Muslim cosmopolitanism, of which traded British goods were only one part.

The Tabaski procession at Kankan and the sartorial expressions of coastal Guinean residents reflect the deep integration of African communities into a global circulation of goods and the ideas and political transformations of the period. Dala Modu's eventual rejection of English attire while he disputed with the English governor of Freetown reflects Ayuba Suleiman's use of clothing to assert himself as not only different but dignified when traveling in Britain as a formerly enslaved African man. Whether the voluminous kusaaba, white linen turbans, or fitted English breeches, clothing marked difference, but it was also a material expression of dynamics between people negotiating relationships with one another. This pattern was remarked upon by Laing, who noted how women in the Solimana region began to dress differently from the Fulbe of Fuuta Jallon once the two communities fell into conflict in the nineteenth century.[2]

These examples show that by paying attention to dress and materiality, scholars can reveal the specificity and nuance of diverse western African experiences and changing dynamics between people across this region. As an archive, or a vital element within the archive, dress records individual moments of self-assertion for a hoped-for belonging or, alternatively, as declarations of independence, dignity, and personal power. These sartorial expressions intertwined with a politics of place and connected to the wider economy of production and exchange. They highlighted the role of status across western Africa as a nonverbal, embodied expression of social relationships and power. Such dynamics certainly did not begin during the period of Atlantic commerce described in this book, but were gradually transformed through connections and entanglements with commercial networks dominated by European capital.

The lives of coastal merchants reveal how some of those dynamics unfolded. Nhara Bely (née Elizabeth Gomez) brought wealth and cultural and social capital into her marriage with the itinerant American slave trader Louis Styles Lightburn. She embodied a Luso-African heritage of transregional commerce and culture stretching back to the sixteenth century. Managing a sizable commercial operation first in Lightburn's absence, then later after his death, Nhara Bely spent years resisting the expansion of the British into the Rio Pongo because their abolitionist policies threatened her livelihood based on slave trading. When Nhara Bely died in 1879, British influence was only a memory in the Rio Pongo. But the region had instead come under French colonial control.

Nhara Bely is today remembered by many in Guinea-Conakry as a cultural heroine, a woman of ambition and courage. Her role in trafficking captives, however, is often excised from nationalist narratives that focus instead on the shrewdness which allowed her to accumulate wealth and power, and on her resistance to colonial rule. Yet women merchants like Nhara Bely appear in the archival record as more complicated figures who navigated the countervailing forces and contradictions of the societies in which they lived. In the eighteenth and nineteenth centuries, these women profited from the textile trade that grew in tandem with Atlantic slave trading and fed regional and local exchanges. In many instances they spun cotton threads along with young dependents or enslaved girls. The organization of this critically important labor within a household—in which senior women joined dependent girls in cleaning, carding, and spinning cotton threads—was similar across the region. Recognition of the scale of this work, along with an appreciation of the role of skilled women artisans in producing valuable indigo-dyed cloth, expands our historical view of the economic activity of women throughout western Africa.

What distinguished nharas on the coast, however, was clothing that announced their privileged access to foreign luxuries, their cultivation of taste derived from business with European and American merchants. Their careful curation of favored foreign textiles and accessories with local ones invented unique western African expressions of modernity. Their contributions have been lionized in popular discourse within the region. But although their alliances with foreign commercial partners generated wealth that they passed on to their descendants, the historical reality is that their commerce did little to improve the circumstances or general welfare of their communities. Rather, like Fendan Dumbuya and other men, these women accumulated power by embracing violence and domination and by building on social practices that legitimized enslavement and human trafficking. Yet they fiercely defended the independence of the communities (and the social positions they enjoyed within them) against colonial incursions. They embodied several contradictions: they were (sometimes ambivalent) anti-colonial figures who were also enslavers, multicultural women who were proudly African, and successful entrepreneurs who were gradually marginalized by commercial forces beyond their control.

Formerly enslaved migrants from the Americas settled into coastal communities of the Rio Pongo and other nearby rivers, but these settlements' transition away from a reliance on slave trading was slow. Primarily from British colonies such as Nova Scotia, Jamaica, and Barbados, they brought with them Anglo-Protestant habits of dress, material culture, and forms of worship that added to the already heterogeneous mix of people on the coast. New Afro-descendant settlers such as Thomas Cooper had to confront whatever hopes they might have had for a "return" to Africa amid the reality of surviving there within a social and economic system organized around slavery.

A remarkable continuity through the fragmentary record of African individuals discussed in this book was that their proximity to the harder realities of Atlantic slaving, even becoming enslaved themselves, did not seem to mitigate their commitment to certain forms of social hierarchy and domination. This seemed to be as true for the Bamana leaders of the Sahel and the clerics of the Fuuta Jallon as it was for Catin Jerome, Bibiana Vaz, Nhara Bely, Mongo John Ormond, Ayuba Diallo, Fendan Dumbuya, and Maram

Njaay. In each instance, individuals expressed a commitment to status and social hierarchy, and dress was often a primary means to display their status as elites who were socially distinct from those considered enslaveable. Their wealth included the accumulation of locally made and imported textiles in chests inside their homes. These textiles might be loaned to others for special occasions, transferred as inheritance to descendants, or, especially, worn in dramatic fashion. The stored cloths served as a form of valuable social capital; with time, theirs was a value not measured in price but in a narrative of lineage and belonging constructed through the materiality of the cloth itself. Kings, headmen, senior wives, signares, and nharas across the region all used cloth not only to consecrate kinship ties but also to support relationships with clients, dependents, and laborers.

At the other end of the social hierarchy, cotton farming, weaving, and textile trading were important for enslaved and self-emancipated people across the region. This was the case at Yanghekori in coastal Guinea, where a maroon community grew cotton to support themselves for more than the dozen years they lived independently of their Susu overlords.

The cultural richness and layered complexities of these plural and contested histories are not readily reducible to any single explanatory framework. In their multiple and competing voices, western Africans sought to advance their perceived material interests in ever-changing contexts.

One aim of this book has been to show that a wide variety of actors and circumstances across western Africa shaped this history. Cotton and textiles help reveal these individuals, because these goods impacted so many people's lives within the region. They also return attention to how the region's deep history of cotton cultivation, weaving, dyeing, and trading became entangled first with an Atlantic slaving economy connecting four continents, followed by a colonial economy that sought to render textile manufacture in western Africa obsolete.

This history is one in which western Africans pursued varied strategies of individual and group reinvention against a backdrop of environmental, economic, and political shifts. Fragments of this past are scarcely discernible across a vast archive of sources in different media located on several continents. However, the descriptive, visual, and physical evidence of how people expressed themselves sartorially in particular contexts, the fleeting evidence of self-fashioning, does reveal textures of human experience rooted in a historical western African context that avoid abstraction. This study has highlighted only some of the ways sources featuring textiles and dress—and the stories of inventiveness, manufacture, and commerce that they evoke—may help us to reimagine both past and future.

# Notes

### INTRODUCTION

1. Anne Raffenel, *Nouveau voyage dans le pays des nègres suivi d'études sur la colonie du Sénégal et de documents historiques, géographiques et scientifiques* (Paris: Napoléon Chaix et Cie, 1856), 82.
2. Raffenel, 82.
3. Anne Raffenel, *Voyage dans l'Afrique Occidentale: Comprenant l'exploration du Sénégal [. . .] Exécuté, en 1843 et 1844, par une commission composée de MM. Huard-Bessinières, Jamin, Raffenel, Peyre-Ferry et Pottin-Patterson* (Paris: A. Bertrand, 1846).
4. Louis-Édouard Bouët-Willaumez, *Commerce et traite des noirs aux côtes occidentales d'Afrique* (Paris: Imprimerie Nationale, 1848).
5. George E. Brooks, *Landlords and Strangers: Ecology, Society, and Trade in Western Africa, 1000–1630* (Boulder, CO: Westview Press, 1993); George E. Brooks, *Eurafricans in Western Africa: Commerce, Social Status, Gender and Religious Observance from the Sixteenth to the Eighteenth Century* (Athens: Ohio University Press, 2003).
6. Colleen E. Kriger, "Mapping the History of Cotton Textile Production in Precolonial West Africa," *African Economic History* 33 (2005): 87–116; Rita Bolland, *Tellem Textiles: Archaeological Finds from Burial Caves in Mali's Bandiagara Cliff* (Amsterdam: Tropenmuseum, 1991); Bernhard Gardi, ed., *Woven Beauty: The Art of West African Textiles* (Basel: Museum der Kulturen; Christoph Meiran Verlag, 2009).
7. Michael A. Gomez, *African Dominion: A New History of Empire in Early and Medieval West Africa* (Princeton, NJ: Princeton University Press, 2018), 35; J. F. P. Hopkins and Nehemia Levtzion, *Corpus of Early Arabic Sources for West African History* (Princeton, NJ: Markus Wiener Publishers, 2000).
8. Boubacar Barry, *Senegambia and the Atlantic Slave Trade*, African Studies 92 (New York: Cambridge University Press, 1998).
9. Brooks, *Landlords and Strangers*; Brooks, *Eurafricans in Western Africa*.
10. Barry, *Senegambia and the Atlantic Slave Trade*.
11. Barry.

12. JoAnn McGregor, Heather Akou, and Nicola Stylianou, eds., *Creating African Fashion Histories: Politics, Museums, and Sartorial Practices* (Bloomington: Indiana University Press, 2022); Sylviane Jacquemin, *Objets des mers du sud: Histoire des collections océaniennes dans les musées et établissements parisiens, XVIIIème–XXème siècles, Mémoire de l'École du Louvre* (Paris: École du Louvre, 1991); Charlotte Nicklas and Annebella Pollen, eds., *Dress History: New Directions in Theory and Practice* (London: Bloomsbury Academic, 2015); Jean Marie Allman, ed., *Fashioning Africa: Power and the Politics of Dress* (Bloomington: Indiana University Press, 2004).
13. Fernand Braudel, "Costume and Fashion," in *Capitalism and Material Life, 1400–1800* (London: Weidenfeld and Nicolson, 1973), 228.
14. Braudel.
15. Georg Simmel, *Fashion* (N.p.: 1904), 137.
16. Deborah Posel and Ilana Van Wyk, "Thinking with Veblen: Case Studies from Africa's Past and Present," in *Conspicuous Consumption in Africa*, ed. Deborah Posel and Ilana Van Wyk (Johannesburg: Wits University Press, 2019), 1–21.
17. Mary Ellen Roach and Joanne Bubolz Eicher, eds., *Dress, Adornment, and the Social Order* (New York: Wiley, 1965).
18. Sonja Magnavita, "The Oldest Textiles from the Sub-Saharan West Africa: Woolen Facts from Kissi, Burkina Faso," *Journal of African Archaeology* 6 (2008): 243–57; S. S. Murray, "Medieval Cotton and Wheat Finds in the Middle Niger Delta (Mali)," in *Fields of Change: Progress in African Archaeobotany*, ed. René Cappers (Groningen, the Netherlands: Groningen University Library, 2007), 43–52; Renée Boser-Sarivaxévanis, *West African Textiles and Garments: From the Museum Für Völkerkunde Basel* (Minneapolis: University of Minnesota, 1980).
19. Gardi, *Woven Beauty;* Annette Schmidt and Rogier Bedaux, "Oldest Archaeological Evidence of Weaving in West Africa," in Gardi, *Woven Beauty,* 58–59; Colleen E. Kriger, *Cloth in West African History,* African Archaeology Series (Lanham, MD: AltaMira Press, 2006); Kriger, "Mapping the History"; Philip James Shea, "The Development of an Export Oriented Dyed Cloth Industry in Kano Emirate in the Nineteenth Century" (PhD diss., University of Wisconsin–Madison, 1975); Sarah C. Brett-Smith, *The Silence of the Women: Bamana Mud Cloths* (Milan: 5 Continents Editions, 2014); Elisha P. Renne, *Cloth That Does Not Die: The Meaning of Cloth in Bùnú Social Life* (Seattle: University of Washington Press, 1995).
20. Brooks, *Eurafricans in Western Africa;* Philip J. Havik, *Silences and Soundbytes: The Gendered Dynamics of Trade and Brokerage in the Pre-colonial Guinea Bissau Region* (Münster: LIT, 2004); Colleen Kriger, *Making Money: Life, Death, and Early Modern Trade on Africa's Guinea Coast* (Athens: Ohio University Press, 2017); Lorelle D. Semley, "Signares before Citizens," in *To Be Free and French: Citizenship in France's Atlantic Empire* (Cambridge: Cambridge University Press, 2017), 69–112.
21. A. G. Hopkins, *An Economic History of West Africa* (London: Longman, 1973); Philip D. Curtin, *Economic Change in Precolonial Africa: Senegambia in the*

*Era of the Slave Trade* (Madison: University of Wisconsin Press, 1975); Joseph E. Inikori, *Africans and the Industrial Revolution in England: A Study in International Trade and Economic Development* (Cambridge: Cambridge University Press, 2002); Joseph E. Inikori, "Slavery and the Revolution in Cotton Textile Production in England," *Social Science History* 13, no. 4 (1989): 343–79.

22. Marion Johnson, "Cloth Strips and History," *West African Journal of Archaeology* 7 (1977): 169–78; Marion Johnson, "Cloth as Money: The Cloth Strip Currencies of Africa," *Textile History* 11, no. 1 (1980): 193–202; Marion Johnson, "Technology, Competition and African Crafts," in *The Imperial Impact: Studies in the Economic History of Africa and India*, ed. Clive Dewey and A. G. Hopkins (London: Athlone Press, 1978).

23. Beverly Lemire and Giorgio Riello, *Dressing Global Bodies: The Political Power of Dress in World History* (London: Routledge, 2020); Victoria L Rovine, *African Fashion, Global Style: Histories, Innovations, and Ideas You Can Wear* (Bloomington: Indiana University Press, 2015); Laura Fair, "Remaking Fashion in the Paris of the Indian Ocean: Dress, Performance, and the Cultural Construction of a Cosmopolitan Zanzibari Identity," in Allman, *Fashioning Africa*, 13–30; Jean Comaroff, "The Empire's Old Clothes: Fashioning the Colonial Subject," in *Cross-Cultural Consumption: Global Markets, Local Realities*, ed. David Howes (London: Routledge, 1996), 19–38; Judith A. Byfield, *The Bluest Hands: A Social and Economic History of Women Dyers in Abeokuta (Nigeria), 1890–1940* (Portsmouth, NH: Heinemann; Oxford: James Currey, 2002).

24. Antoinette Burton, "The Body in/as World History," in *A Companion to World History*, ed. Douglas Northrup (Malden, MA: Wiley, 2015), 272–84.

25. Rudolph T. Ware III, *The Walking Qur'an: Islamic Education, Embodied Knowledge, and History in West Africa* (Chapel Hill: University of North Carolina Press, 2014).

26. George E. Brooks, "Artists' Depiction of Senegalese Signares: Insights concerning French Racist and Sexist Attitudes in the Nineteenth Century," *Genève-Afrique: Acta Africana Genève-Afrique* 18, no. 1 (1980): 75–89.

27. Havik, *Silences and Soundbytes*.

28. Brooks, *Eurafricans in Western Africa*; Havik, *Silences and Soundbytes*; Kriger, *Making Money*; Semley, "Signares before Citizens."

29. Barbara Cooper, "Oral Sources and the Challenge of African History," in *Writing African History*, ed. John Phillips (Rochester, NY: University of Rochester Press, 2005), 191–215; Ralph A. Austen, ed., *In Search of Sunjata: The Mande Oral Epic as History, Literature and Performance* (Bloomington: Indiana University Press, 1999); Donald R. Wright, *Oral Traditions from the Gambia*, Papers in International Studies, Africa Series, no. 37/38 (Athens: Ohio University Center for International Studies, Africa Program, 1979); Emily Lynn Osborn, *Our New Husbands Are Here: Households, Gender, and Politics in a West African State from the Slave Trade to Colonial Rule* (Athens: Ohio University Press, 2011).

30. Assan Sarr, *Islam, Power, and Dependency in the Gambia River Basin: The Politics of Land Control, 1790–1940* (Rochester, NY: University of Rochester Press, 2016).
31. Gomez, *African Dominion*, 63.
32. Robert S. DuPlessis, *The Material Atlantic: Clothing, Commerce, and Colonization in the Atlantic World, 1650–1800* (Cambridge: Cambridge University Press, 2016).
33. Joseph C. Miller, "Beyond Blacks, Bondage, and Blame: Why a Multi-centric World History Needs Africa," *Historically Speaking* 6, no. 2 (2004): 7–11.
34. Mary Louise Pratt, *Imperial Eyes: Travel Writing and Transculturation* (London: Routledge, 2008).
35. Pratt, 7.
36. Cécile Fromont, "Foreign Cloth, Local Habits: Clothing, Regalia, and the Art of Conversion in the Early Modern Kingdom of Kongo," *Anais do Museu Paulista: História e Cultura Material* 25, no. 2 (2017): 11–31.
37. Anne Gerritsen and Giorgio Riello, eds., *Writing Material Culture History* (London: Bloomsbury Academic Press, 2015).
38. Lisa Lowe, *The Intimacies of Four Continents* (Durham, NC: Duke University Press, 2015).
39. Joseph C. Miller, "History and Africa / Africa and History," *American Historical Review* 104, no. 1 (1999): 1–32.
40. Jean-Louis Triaud, "*Haut-Sénégal-Niger*, un modèle 'positiviste'? De la coutume à l'histoire: Maurice Delafosse et l'invention de l'histoire africaine," in *Maurice Delafosse: Entre orientalisme et ethnographie; L'itinéraire d'un africaniste, 1870–1926* (Paris: Maisonneuve et Larose, 1998), 210–32; Miller, "History and Africa."
41. Kevin C. MacDonald, "'A Chacun Son Bambara' encore une fois: History, Archeology and Bambara Origins," in *Ethnic Ambiguity and the African Past: Materiality, History, and the Shaping of Cultural Identities* (Walnut Creek, CA: Left Coast Press, 2015), 119–44; Maria Grosz-Ngaté, "Power and Knowledge: The Representation of the Mande World in the Works of Park, Caillié, Monteil, and Delafosse (Pouvoir et savoir: La représentation du monde mandé dans les oeuvres de Park, Caillié, Monteil et Delafosse)," *Cahiers d'Etudes Africaines* 28, no. 111/112 (1988): 485–511.
42. Eric Porter, "Imagining Africa, Reimagining the World," in *The Problem of the Future World: W. E. B. Du Bois and the Race Concept at Midcentury* (Durham, NC: Duke University Press, 2010), 103–44; Miller, "History and Africa."
43. Eric Eustace Williams, *Capitalism and Slavery* (Temecula, CA: Textbook Publishers, 2003); Joseph E. Inikori and Stanley L. Engerman, eds., *The Atlantic Slave Trade: Effects on Economies, Societies, and Peoples in Africa, the Americas, and Europe* (Durham, NC: Duke University Press, 2007). My choice to lowercase the terms *black* and *white* reflects my own historical analysis of these terms over time rather than contemporary discourse about race in the United States.

44. Kriger, *Making Money*, 47.
45. Jean M. Allman, "#HerskovitsMustFall? A Meditation on Whiteness, African Studies, and the Unfinished Business of 1968," *African Studies Review* 62, no. 3 (September 2019): 6–39.
46. Porter, "Imagining Africa"; Penny M. Von Eschen, *Race against Empire: Black Americans and Anticolonialism, 1937–1957* (Ithaca, NY: Cornell University Press, 1997).
47. Omar Gueye, "African History and Global History: Revisiting Paradigms," in *Global History, Globally: Research and Practice around the World*, ed. Sven Beckert and Dominic Sachsenmaier (London: Bloomsbury Academic, 2018), 83–108; Babacar Fall, "Ly, Abdoulaye," in *Dictionary of African Biography*, ed. Henry Louis Gates Jr. and Emmanuel Akyeampong (Oxford: Oxford University Press, 2011).
48. J. D. Fage, "Slavery and the Slave Trade in the Context of West African History," *Journal of African History* 10, no. 3 (1969): 393–404; Walter Rodney, *How Europe Underdeveloped Africa* (Washington, DC: Howard University Press, 1974); Curtin, *Economic Change in Precolonial Africa;* John K. Thornton, *Africa and Africans in the Making of the Atlantic World, 1400–1800*, 2nd ed., expanded (New York: Cambridge University Press, 1998).
49. Immanuel Wallerstein, *The Modern World-System I: Capitalist Agriculture and the Origins of the European World-Economy in the Sixteenth Century* (New York: Academic Press, 1974).
50. Inikori, "Slavery and the Revolution"; Inikori, *Africans and the Industrial Revolution in England*.
51. Richard Reid, "Past and Presentism: The 'Precolonial' and the Foreshortening of African History," *Journal of African History* 52, no. 2 (2011): 135–55.
52. Jemima Pierre, "Race across the Atlantic . . . and Back: Theorizing Africa and/in the Diaspora," in *The Predicament of Blackness: Postcolonial Ghana and the Politics of Race* (Chicago: University of Chicago Press, 2012), 185–216.
53. Kazuo Kobayashi, *Indian Cotton Textiles in West Africa: African Agency, Consumer Demand and the Making of the Global Economy, 1750–1850*, Cambridge Imperial and Post-colonial Studies Series (Cham: Palgrave Macmillan, 2019); Toby Green and Neil Gower, *A Fistful of Shells: West Africa from the Rise of the Slave Trade to the Age of Revolution* (London: Penguin Random House, 2020).
54. Simon Gikandi, "Unspeakable Events: Slavery and White Self-Fashioning," in *Slavery and the Culture of Taste* (Princeton, NJ: Princeton University Press, 2014), 97–144.
55. Toby Green, *The Rise of the Trans-Atlantic Slave Trade in Western Africa, 1300–1589* (Cambridge: Cambridge University Press, 2011), 20.
56. Green, 32–68.
57. Gomez, *African Dominion*, 53.
58. Bruce S. Hall, *A History of Race in Muslim West Africa, 1600–1960* (Cambridge: Cambridge University Press, 2011), 22.

59. Mohammed Bashir Salau, *Plantation Slavery in the Sokoto Caliphate: A Historical and Comparative Study* (Rochester, NY: University of Rochester Press, 2018).
60. James L. A. Webb Jr., *Desert Frontier: Ecological and Economic Change along the Western Sahel, 1600–1850* (Madison: University of Wisconsin Press, 1995).
61. Ghislaine Lydon, *On Trans-Saharan Trails: Islamic Law, Trade Networks, and Cross-Cultural Exchange in Nineteenth-Century Western Africa* (New York: Cambridge University Press, 2009), 6; John O. Hunwick, *Timbuktu and the Songhay Empire: Al-Sa'di's "Ta'rīkh al-sūdān" down to 1613 and Other Contemporary Documents* (Leiden: Brill, 1999), 2, n. 3.
62. Gomez, *African Dominion;* Hall, *A History of Race.*
63. Cedric J. Robinson, *Black Marxism: The Making of the Black Radical Tradition* (Chapel Hill: University of North Carolina Press, 2000).
64. Gikandi, "Unspeakable Events."
65. Philip D. Curtin, *The Image of Africa: British Ideas and Action, 1780–1850* (Madison: University of Wisconsin Press, 1964); Pierre, "Race across the Atlantic."
66. Beverly Lemire, *Global Trade and the Transformation of Consumer Cultures: The Material World Remade, c. 1500–1820* (Cambridge: Cambridge University Press, 2018); Trevor R. Getz, *Cosmopolitan Africa, c.1700–1875* (New York: Oxford University Press, 2013); Ifeoma Kiddoe Nwankwo, *Black Cosmopolitanism: Racial Consciousness and Transnational Identity in the Nineteenth-Century Americas* (Philadelphia: University of Pennsylvania Press, 2014); Jeremy Prestholdt, "Africa and the Global Lives of Things," in *Oxford Handbook of the History of Consumption,* ed. Frank Trentmann (Oxford: Oxford University Press, 2012), 85–108.
67. Raffenel, *Nouveau voyage,* 234.
68. Green and Gower, *A Fistful of Shells.*
69. David Robinson, *The Holy War of Umar Tal: The Western Sudan in the Mid-nineteenth Century* (New York: Clarendon Press, an imprint of Oxford University Press, 1985); Paul E. Lovejoy, *Jihād in West Africa during the Age of Revolutions* (Athens: Ohio University Press, 2016).
70. A person born in Africa of both African and European parents or ancestry.
71. Roger Pasquier, "Un explorateur senegalais: Leopold Panet, 1819–1859," *African Historical Studies* 2, no. 2 (1969): 307–17.
72. Pasquier, "Un explorateur senegalais."
73. Raffenel, *Nouveau voyage.*
74. Raffenel, 224.
75. Raffenel, 224.

CHAPTER 1: TWELVE MEASURES OF NEW CLOTH AND A MAGNIFICENT BUBU

1. Jeli Mamary Kouyate, "Sonsan of Kaarta," oral historical narrative recorded by David Conrad in Kolokani, Mali, August 19, 1975. Conrad provided a translated transcript of the recording to the author.

2. Moussa Sow, *L'État de Ségou et ses chefferies aux XVIIIe et XIXe siècles: Côté cour, côté jardin*, Études culturelles (Pessac, France: Presses universitaires de Bordeaux, 2021), 273.
3. Kevin C. MacDonald, "'A Chacun son Bambara' encore une fois: History, Archeology and Bambara Origins," in *Ethnic Ambiguity and the African Past: Materiality, History, and the Shaping of Cultural Identities*, ed. François G. Richard and Kevin C. MacDonald (Walnut Creek, CA: Left Coast Press, 2015), 119–44; Bethwell A. Ogot, ed., *Africa from the Sixteenth to the Eighteenth Century*, abridged ed., vol. 5, *General History of Africa* (Oxford: James Currey, 1999), 158.
4. Emily Lynn Osborn, *Our New Husbands Are Here: Households, Gender, and Politics in a West African State from the Slave Trade to Colonial Rule* (Athens: Ohio University Press, 2011), 25.
5. Mustafa Alloush et al., *Écrire la guerre au Fouta-Djalon: Récits en vers arabes d'expéditions militaires au xixe siècle* (Paris: Guethner, 2023); Maladho Diallo, *Histoire du Fouta Djallon* (Paris: L'Harmattan, 2002).
6. Charles Monteil, *Le coton chez les noirs*, Publications du Comité d'études historiques et scientifiques de l'Afrique occidentale française, vol. 4 (Paris: E. Larose, 1927), 66.
7. Tavy Aherne, "Gudhe Ngara: Exploring the Dynamics of the Creation, Use and Trade in Guinea's Indigo Cloths" (PhD diss., Indiana University, 2000); René Caillié, *Travels through Central Africa to Timbuctoo and across the Great Desert, to Morocco, Performed in the Years 1824–1828* (New York: Cambridge University Press, 2013).
8. E. J. Hobsbawm and T. O. Ranger, *The Invention of Tradition* (Cambridge: Cambridge University Press, 1983); Jean Bazin, "A chacun son Bambara," in *Au coeur de l'ethnie: Ethnies, tribalisme et État en Afrique*, ed. Jean-Loup Amselle and Elikia M'Bokolo (Paris: La Découverte, 2005), 87–127; MacDonald, "A Chacun son Bambara"; Peter Caron, "'Of a Nation Which the Others Do Not Understand': Bambara Slaves and African Ethnicity in Colonial Louisiana, 1718–60," in *Routes to Slavery*, ed. David Eltis and David Richardson (Abingdon, UK: Routledge, 1997), 104–27.
9. Bazin, "A chacun son Bambara"; MacDonald, "A Chacun son Bambara."
10. Tal Tamari, "Bambara," in *Oxford African American Studies Center*, online ed., Oxford University Press, article published online September 30, 2012, https://oxfordaasc.com/.
11. Paul Clammer, *Black Crown: Henry Christophe, the Haitian Revolution and the Caribbean's Forgotten Kingdom* (London: Hurst, 2023); Frédéric Mocadel, *1755 au Galam et à l'Île Bourbon: L'odyssée de Niama, "des portes de l'or aux plantations de café"* (Sainte-Marie, Réunion: Azalées Éditions, 2006); Gwendolyn Midlo Hall, *Africans in Colonial Louisiana: The Development of Afro-Creole Culture in the Eighteenth Century* (Baton Rouge: Louisiana State University Press, 1992).
12. John O. Hunwick, *Timbuktu and the Songhay Empire: Al-Sa'di's "Ta'rīkh al-sūdān" down to 1613 and Other Contemporary Documents* (Leiden: Brill,

1999), 193; Ahmad ibn Ahmad Baba, *Mi'rāj Al-Ṣu'ūd: Ahmad Baba's Replies on Slavery*, ed. John O. Hunwick and Fatima Harrak, al-Ṭab'ah 1, Manshūrāt Ma'had Al-Dirāsāt al-Afrīqīyah, Nuṣūs Wa-Wathā'iq 7 (Rabaṭ: Publications of the Institute of African Studies, 2000).
13. Michael A. Gomez, *African Dominion: A New History of Empire in Early and Medieval West Africa* (Princeton, NJ: Princeton University Press, 2019), 304; Timothy Cleaveland, "Ahmad Baba Al-Timbukti and His Islamic Critique of Racial Slavery in the Maghrib," *Journal of North African Studies* 20, no. 1 (January 2015): 42–64.
14. Hunwick, *Timbuktu and the Songhay Empire*, 193.
15. Hunwick, 2n3, 193.
16. Hunwick, 149.
17. Paul Marty, *Les chroniques de Oualata et de Nema (Soudan Francais): Extrait de la Revue des Etudes Islamiques annee 1927* (Paris: Librairie Orientaliste Paul Geuthner, 1927), 565, 568.
18. Bruce S. Hall, *A History of Race in Muslim West Africa, 1600–1960* (Cambridge: Cambridge University Press, 2011); Gomez, *African Dominion*.
19. Hall, *A History of Race*; Gomez, *African Dominion*; Ghislaine Lydon, "Writing Trans-Saharan History: Methods, Sources and Interpretations across the African Divide," *Journal of North African Studies* 10, no. 3/4 (2005): 293–324; James L. A. Webb Jr., *Desert Frontier: Ecological and Economic Change along the Western Sahel, 1600–1850* (Madison: University of Wisconsin Press, 1995).
20. Gomez, *African Dominion*, 50–57; Hall, *A History of Race*; Mohammed Bashir Salau, *Plantation Slavery in the Sokoto Caliphate: A Historical and Comparative Study* (Rochester, NY: University of Rochester Press, 2018).
21. Kouyate, "Sonsan of Kaarta."
22. Kouyate.
23. Kouyate.
24. Kouyate.
25. Anne Raffenel, *Nouveau voyage dans le pays des nègres suivi d'études sur la colonie du Sénégal et de documents historiques, géographiques et scientifiques* (Paris: Napoléon Chaix et Cie, 1856), 233. Translation mine.
26. Mungo Park, *Travels in the Interior Districts of Africa*, ed. Kate Ferguson Marsters (Durham, NC: Duke University Press, 2000), 235.
27. Toby Green and Neil Gower, *A Fistful of Shells: West Africa from the Rise of the Slave Trade to the Age of Revolution* (London: Penguin Random House, 2020), 421–24.
28. Bernhard Gardi and Michelle Gilbert, "*Arkilla, Kaasa,* and *Nsaa*: The Many Influences of Wool Textiles from the Niger Bend in West Africa," *Textile Museum Journal* 48 (2021): 24–53; Colleen Kriger, "Mapping the History of Cotton Textile Production in Precolonial West Africa," *African Economic History* 33 (2005): 87–116.
29. Bernhard Gardi, ed., *Woven Beauty: The Art of West African Textiles* (Basel: Museum der Kulturen; Christoph Meiran Verlag, 2009), exhibition catalog.

30. Aboubakar Fofana, "Beyond the Blueness: The Light and Dark Shades of Aboubakar Fofana's Indigo," with Johanna Macnaughtan, *Tatter*, no. 3 (n.d.), https://tatter.org/issues/articles/beyond-the-blueness.
31. Sarah C. Brett-Smith, *The Silence of the Women: Bamanan Mud Cloths* (Milan: 5 Continents Editions, 2014).
32. Quote in section heading comes from G. Adam, *Légendes historiques du pays de Nioro (Sahel)* (Paris: A. Challamel, 1904).
33. Colleen Kriger, "Robes of the Sokoto Caliphate," *African Arts* 21, no. 3 (1988): 52.
34. Philip D. Curtin, *Economic Change in Precolonial Africa: Senegambia in the Era of the Slave Trade* (Madison: University of Wisconsin Press, 1975), 69; Hall, *A History of Race*, 62–63; Bernhard Gardi and Museum der Kulturen Basel, eds., *Le boubou—c'est chic: Les boubous du Mali et d'autres pays de l'Afrique de l'Ouest* (Basel: Museum der Kulturen Basel; Christoph Meiran Verlag, 2000), exhibition catalog, 109.
35. Webb, *Desert Frontier*, 17.
36. Géraldine Barron, "Le Musée de Marine du Louvre: Un Musée des techniques?," *Artefact* 5, no. 5 (2017): 143–62.
37. "Inventaire Duhamel Dumonceau (Jusqu'au No. 1272 et Louis Phillipe)," Archives du Musée du Quai Branly-Jacques Chirac: D004864, 1830, Musée de Marine du Louvre.
38. Gardi and Museum der Kulturen Basel, *Le boubou c'est chic;* Alisa LaGamma, "From the Rise of Songhay to the Fall of Segu," in *Sahel: Art and Empires on the Shores of the Sahara* (New York: Metropolitan Museum of Art; New Haven, CT: Yale University Press, 2020), exhibition catalog, 219–49.
39. "Inventaire Duhamel Dumonceau."
40. Felwine Sarr and Bénédicte Savoy, *Restituer le patrimoine africain* ([Paris?]: Philippe Rey / Seuil, 2019).
41. Adam, *Légendes historiques*.
42. There may be minor stylistic differences between what has been termed a *boubou* and a *kusaaba* in particular regions. However, my analysis uses these terms interchangeably to describe the large, tailored, often embroidered upper garment common to the region.
43. Adam, 487–89.
44. Philip D. Curtin, "The Western Juula in the Eighteenth Century" (paper presented at the International Conference on Manding Studies, 1972); Marie Perinbam, "The Julas in Western Sudanese History: Long-Distance Traders and Developers of Resources," in *West African Culture Dynamics: Archaeological and Historical Perspectives*, ed. B. K. Swartz and Raymond E. Dumett (The Hague: De Gruyter, 1980); Ivor Wilks, "The Juula and the Expansion of Islam into the Forest," in The History of Islam in Africa, ed. Nehemia and Randall Lee Pouwels Levtzion (Oxford: Cape Town: Ohio University Press, 2000).
45. Adam, *Légendes historiques*, 487–89.
46. Adam, 487–89.

47. Marty, *Les chroniques de Oualata*.
48. Charles Victor Monteil, *Les Bambara du Segou et du Kaarta: Étude historique, ethnographique et littéraire d'une peuplade du Soudan Français* (Paris: Larose, 1960), 52.
49. Laurence Douny, "Wild Silk Indigo Wrappers of Dogon of Mali: An Ethnography of Materials Efficacy and Design," in *The Social Life of Materials*, ed. Adam Drazin and Susanne Küchler (London: Bloomsbury, 2015), 101–18; Laurence Douny, "The Material Agency of West African Wild Silk: An Ethnographic Exploration into Marka-Dafing Conceptions of Sheen," *Japanese Review of Cultural Anthropology* 21, no. 1 (2020): 291–313; Gardi and Museum der Kulturen Basel, *Le boubou c'est chic*.
50. Raffenel, *Nouveau voyage*, 373.
51. Confirmation of this gruesome act does not appear in written or archaeological sources. Oral accounts of the city of Jenne do mention a similar incident where an autochthonous girl was said to have been buried in a wall to protect the town and guarantee its prosperity.
52. Raffenel, *Nouveau voyage*.
53. Robert Arnaud, "La singuliere legende des Soninkes: Traditions orales sur le royaume de Koumbi et sur divers autres royaumes soudanais," in *L'Islam et la politique musulmane française en Afrique occidentale française* (Paris: Comité de l'Afrique française, 1912), 182.
54. Kouyate, "Sonsan of Kaarta."
55. Kouyate.
56. Kouyate.
57. Peter Linebaugh, *The London Hanged: Crime and Civil Society in the Eighteenth Century* (Cambridge: Cambridge University Press, 1993); T. C. McCaskie, *State and Society in Pre-colonial Asante* (Cambridge: Cambridge University Press, 1995); Linda M. Heywood and John K. Thornton, "Kongo and Dahomey, 1660–1815: African Political Leadership in the Era of the Slave Trade and Its Impact on the Formation of African Identity in Brazil," in *Soundings in Atlantic History: Latent Structures and Intellectual Currents, 1500–1830*, ed. Bernard Bailyn and Patricia L. Denault (Cambridge, MA: Harvard University Press, 2009), 86–111.
58. Vincent Brown, *The Reaper's Garden: Death and Power in the World of Atlantic Slavery* (Cambridge, MA: Harvard University Press, 2008).

CHAPTER 2: COTTON CLOTH IN WESTERN AFRICA

1. A. Teixeira da Mota, "Un document nouveau pour l'histoire des Peuls au Sénégal pendant les XVème et XVIème siècles," in *Boletim Cultural da Guiné Portuguesa* (Lisbon: Junta de Investigações do Ultramar, 1969).
2. Yves Person, "States and Peoples of Senegambia and Upper Guinea," *General History of Africa, ed. J. F. Ade Ajayi, vol. 6, Africa in the Nineteenth Century until the 1880s* (Paris: Unesco; Oxford: Heinemann; Berkeley: University of California Press, 1989), 636–61; George E. Brooks, *Landlords and Strangers:*

*Ecology, Society, and Trade in Western Africa, 1000–1630* (Boulder, CO: Westview Press, 1993).
3. Brooks, *Landlords and Strangers*.
4. Mota, "Un document nouveau."
5. Toby Green, *The Rise of the Trans-Atlantic Slave Trade in Western Africa, 1300–1589* (Cambridge: Cambridge University Press, 2011).
6. Toby Green, "Africa and the Price Revolution: Currency Imports and Socioeconomic Change in West and West-Central Africa During the Seventeenth Century," *Journal of African History* 57, no. 1 (2016): 1–24.
7. John Vogt, "Notes on the Portuguese Cloth Trade in West Africa, 1480–1540," *International Journal of African Historical Studies* 8, no. 4 (1975): 623–51; Green, *Rise of the Trans-Atlantic Slave Trade*, 72.
8. Colleen E. Kriger, "Guinea Cloth: Production and Consumption of Cotton Textiles before and during the Atlantic Slave Trade," in *The Spinning World: A Global History of Cotton Textiles, 1200–1850*, ed. Giorgio Riello (New York: Oxford University Press, 2009).
9. Carlos F. Liberato, "Money, Cloth-Currency, Monopoly, and Slave Trade in the River of Guiné and the Cape Verde Islands, 1755–1777," in *Money in Africa*, ed. Catherine Eagleton, Harcourt Fuller, and John Perkins (London: British Museum, 2009), 9–19.
10. Colleen E. Kriger, *Making Money: Life, Death, and Early Modern Trade on Africa's Guinea Coast* (Athens: Ohio University Press, 2017); George E. Brooks, *Eurafricans in Western Africa: Commerce, Social Status, Gender and Religious Observance from the Sixteenth to the Eighteenth Century* (Athens: Ohio University Press, 2003), 62–63; Carlos F. Liberato, "Money, Cloth-Currency, Monopoly, and Slave Trade in the River of Guiné and the Cape Verde Islands, 1755–1777," in *Money in Africa*, ed. Catherine Eagleton, Harcourt Fuller, and John Perkins (London: British Museum, 2009), 9–19.
11. Labelle Prussin, "Judaic Threads in the West African Tapestry: No More Forever?," *Art Bulletin* 88, no. 2 (2006): 328–53.
12. Liberato, "Money, Cloth-Currency, Monopoly, and Slave Trade," 13.
13. Philip J. Havik, *Silences and Soundbytes: The Gendered Dynamics of Trade and Brokerage in the Pre-colonial Guinea Bissau Region* (Münster: LIT, 2004); André Donelha and A. Teixeira da Mota, *Descrição da Serra Leoa e dos rios de Guiné do Cabo Verde, 1625* (Lisboa: Junta de Investigações Científicas do Ultramar, 1977); Green, *Rise of the Trans-Atlantic Slave Trade*.
14. Peter Mark, *"Portuguese" Style and Luso-African Identity: Precolonial Senegambia, Sixteenth–Nineteenth Centuries* (Bloomington: Indiana University Press, 2002); Green, *Rise of the Trans-Atlantic Slave Trade*.
15. Linda A. Newson, "The Slave-Trading Accounts of Manoel Batista Peres, 1613–1619: Double-Entry Bookkeeping in Cloth Money," *Accounting History* 18, no. 3 (2013): 343–65; Toby Green, "Beyond an Imperial Atlantic: Trajectories of Africans from Upper Guinea and West-Central Africa in the Early Atlantic World," *Past and Present*, no. 230 (2016): 91–122.

16. Newson, "Slave-Trading Accounts."
17. Mark, *"Portuguese" Style and Luso-African Identity.*
18. Green, *Rise of the Trans-Atlantic Slave Trade*, 45; Martin A. Klein, "Defensive Strategies: Wasulu, Masina, and the Slave Trade," in *Fighting the Slave Trade: West African Strategies*, ed. Sylviane A. Diouf (Athens: Ohio University Press; Oxford: James Currey, 2003).
19. Peter Mark, "'Portuguese' Architecture and Luso-African Identity in Senegambia and Guinea, 1730–1890," *History in Africa* 23 (1996): 179–96. Portudal is a place-name that evolved from the Portuguese-language original Porto d'Ale, or Port of Ale.
20. André Brue, "Voyage of the Sieur Brue to Bissau and Bissagos," in *A New and Complete Collection of Voyages and Travels: Containing All That Have Been Remarkable from the Earliest Period to the Present Time* [. . .], ed. John Hamilton Moore (London, 1780), 2 vols., 449.
21. Brue, 447.
22. Brue, 140.
23. Winifred Faye Galloway, "A History of Wuli from the Thirteenth to the Nineteenth Century" (PhD diss., Indiana University, 1975).
24. Colleen Kriger, "Mapping the History of Cotton Textile Production in Precolonial West Africa," *African Economic History* 33 (2005): 87–116.
25. Newson, "Slave-Trading Accounts."
26. Newson.
27. In this instance, the satigi was the uncle of Gaspar Vaz, whom I discuss later.
28. Donelha and Mota, *Descrição da Serra Leoa.*
29. Donelha and Mota.
30. Peter Mark, "Constructing Identity: Sixteenth- and Seventeenth-Century Architecture in the Gambia-Geba Region and the Articulation of Luso-African Ethnicity," *History in Africa* 22 (1995): 307–27.
31. Donelha and Mota, *Descrição da Serra Leoa.*
32. Toby Green and Neil Gower, *A Fistful of Shells: West Africa from the Rise of the Slave Trade to the Age of Revolution* (London: Penguin Random House, 2020), 421–24.
33. Green, "Africa and the Price Revolution"; Prasannan Parthasarathi, *The Transition to a Colonial Economy: Weavers, Merchants and Kings in South India, 1720–1800* (Cambridge: Cambridge University Press, 2001); Joseph Calder Miller, *Way of Death: Merchant Capitalism and the Angolan Slave Trade, 1730–1830* (Madison: University of Wisconsin Press, 1988).
34. Green and Gower, *Fistful of Shells*, 15.
35. Green and Gower, 89.
36. Richard Jobson, *The Golden Trade: or, A Discouery of the Riuer Gambra and the Golden Trade of the Aethiopians: Also the Commerce with a Great Blacke Merchant Called Buckor Sano and His Report of the Houses Couered with Gold and Other Strange Obseruations for the Good of Our Owne Countrey* [. . .] (London, 1623), 88.

37. Francis Moore, *Travels into the Inland Parts of Africa: Containing a Description of the Several Nations for the Space of Six Hundred Miles up the River Gambia; Their Trade, Habits, Customs, Language, Manners, Religion and Government* [...] (London, 1738), 25.
38. Boubacar Barry, *Senegambia and the Atlantic Slave Trade*, African Studies 92 (Cambridge: Cambridge University Press, 1998), 19.
39. André Alvares d'Almada et al., *Brief Treatise on the Rivers of Guinea* (Liverpool: Department of History, University of Liverpool, 1984), 107.
40. José da Silva Horta, "Evidence for a Luso-African Identity in 'Portuguese' Accounts on 'Guinea of Cape Verde' (Sixteenth-Seventeenth Centuries)," *History in Africa* 27 (2000): 99–130.
41. Galloway, "A History of Wuli."
42. Donelha and Mota, *Descrição da Serra Leoa*.
43. Donelha and Mota.
44. Donelha and Mota, 149.
45. Donelha and Mota.
46. Donelha and Mota.
47. Green, *Rise of the Trans-Atlantic Slave Trade*, 113.
48. Cécile Fromont, "Foreign Cloth, Local Habits: Clothing, Regalia, and the Art of Conversion in the Early Modern Kingdom of Kongo," *Anais do Museu Paulista: História e Cultura Material* 25, no. 2 (2017): 11–31; Hildi Hendrickson, ed., *Clothing and Difference: Embodied Identities in Colonial and Postcolonial Africa* (Durham, NC: Duke University Press, 1996).
49. André Delcourt, *La France et les établissements français au Sénégal entre 1713 et 1763: La Compagnie des Indes et le Sénégal; La guerre de la gomme* (Dakar: Institut Français d'Afrique Noir, 1952), 108–9; Ibrahima Seck, "The French Discovery of Senegal: Premises for a Policy of Selective Assimilation," in *Brokers of Change: Atlantic Commerce and Cultures in Precolonial Western Africa*, ed. Toby Green (New York: Oxford University Press / British Academy, 2012), 149–70.
50. C 739, "Andre Brue, memoire a La Compagnie Royal du Senegal, 29 Juin 1702," Departement du Senegal, 1702, Archives départementales de Loire-Atlantique, France (hereafter cited as ANOM).
51. Olfert Dapper, *Description de l'Afrique: Contenant les noms, la situation & les confins de toutes ses parties, leurs rivières, leurs villes & leurs habitations, leurs plantes & leurs animaux, les moeurs, les coûtumes, la langue, les richesses, la religion & le gouvernement de ses peoples* [...] (Amsterdam: Chez Wolfgang, Waesberge, Boom and van Someren, 1686), 240.
52. Linda A. Newson and Susie Minchin, *From Capture to Sale: The Portuguese Slave Trade to Spanish South America in the Early Seventeenth Century*, Atlantic World 12 (Leiden: Brill, 2007); Colleen Kriger, "The Importance of Mande Textiles in the African Side of the Atlantic Trade, ca. 1680–1710," *Mande Studies* 11 (2009): 1–21.
53. Kriger, *Making Money*.

54. Newson and Minchin, *From Capture to Sale*.
55. Green, "Beyond an Imperial Atlantic"; Philip D. Curtin, *Economic Change in Precolonial Africa: Senegambia in the Era of the Slave Trade* (Madison: University of Wisconsin Press, 1975).
56. C 739, "Andre Brue, memoire."
57. Nize Izabel de Moraes, "Le commerce des tissus à la Petite Côte au XVIIe siècle (Sénégambie)," *Notes Africaines* 139 (1973): 72n1.
58. Green, "Beyond an Imperial Atlantic," 106.
59. Green, "Beyond an Imperial Atlantic."
60. Jutta Wimmler, *The Sun King's Atlantic: Drugs, Demons and Dyestuffs in the Atlantic World, 1640–1730*, The Atlantic World 33 (Leiden: Brill, 2017), 44.
61. James L. A. Webb, "The Trade in Gum Arabic: Prelude to French Conquest in Senegal," *Journal of African History* 26, no. 2/3 (1985): 149–68.
62. Wimmler, *Sun King's Atlantic*, 44–45.
63. Webb, "The Trade in Gum Arabic"; Wimmler, *The Sun King's Atlantic*.
64. Kazuo Kobayashi, *Indian Cotton Textiles in West Africa: African Agency, Consumer Demand and the Making of the Global Economy, 1750–1850* (Cham: Palgrave Macmillan, 2019).
65. Wimmler, *Sun King's Atlantic*, 40.
66. Beverly Lemire, "Revising the Historical Narrative: India, Europe and the Cotton Trade, c. 1300–1800," in *The Spinning World: A Global History of Cotton Textiles, 1200–1850*, Pasold Studies in Textile History 16, ed. Giorgio Riello and Prasannan Parthasarathi (Oxford: Oxford University Press, 2009), 205–26.
67. Joseph Jerome Brennig, "The Textile Trade of Seventeenth-Century Northern Coromandel: A Study of a Pre-modern Asian Export Industry" (PhD diss., University of Wisconsin–Madison, 1975), 42.
68. Felicia Gottman, "French-Asian Connections: The Compagnies des Indes, France's Eastern Trade, and New Directions in Historical Scholarship," *Historical Journal* 56, no. 2 (2013): 537–52; Jonathan P. Eacott, "Making an Imperial Compromise: The Calico Acts, the Atlantic Colonies, and the Structure of the British Empire," *William and Mary Quarterly*, 3rd ser., 69, no. 4 (October 2012): 731–62.
69. Kobayashi, *Indian Cotton Textiles*; Giorgio Riello, *Cotton: The Fabric That Made the Modern World* (Cambridge: Cambridge University Press, 2013).
70. Michel Jajolet de La Courbe and Prosper Cultru, *Premier voyage du Sieur de La Courbe fait a la coste d'Afrique en 1685* (Paris: Édouard Champion; Émile Larose, 1913), 170.
71. La Courbe and Cultru, *Premier voyage*, 172.
72. Howard French, "Capitalism's Big Jolt," in *Born in Blackness: Africa and the Making of the Modern World* (New York: Liveright Publishing, 2022), 208–24.
73. Green, "Africa and the Price Revolution"; Linda A. Newson and Susie Minchin, "A Bureaucratic Business," in *From Capture to Sale: The Portuguese*

*Slave Trade to Spanish South America in the Early Seventeenth Century,* Atlantic World 12 (Leiden: Brill, 2007).
74. António Carreira, *Mandingas da Guiné Portuguesa,* Memórias 4 (Lisbon: Centro de Estudos da Guiné Portuguesa, 1947).
75. C6/8, "Memoire sur le commerce de Guinee," 1724, ANOM.
76. Newson and Minchin, "A Bureaucratic Business."
77. Robin Blackburn, *The Making of New World Slavery: From the Baroque to the Modern, 1492–1800* (London: Verso, 1997), 294.
78. Graziano Krätli and Ghislaine Lydon, eds., *The Trans-Saharan Book Trade: Manuscript Culture, Arabic Literacy and Intellectual History in Muslim Africa,* Library of the Written Word 8 (Leiden: Brill, 2011); Michael A. Gomez, *African Dominion: A New History of Empire in Early and Medieval West Africa* (Princeton, NJ: Princeton University Press, 2018); Bruce S. Hall, *A History of Race in Muslim West Africa, 1600–1960* (Cambridge: Cambridge University Press, 2011); Chouki El Hamel, *Black Morocco: A History of Slavery, Race, and Islam* (Cambridge: Cambridge University Press, 2013).
79. Gomez, *African Dominion;* Rudolph T. Ware III, "Slavery in Islamic Africa, 1400–1800," in vol. 3 of *The Cambridge World History of Slavery,* ed. David Eltis and Stanley L. Engerman (Cambridge: Cambridge University Press, 2011), 47–80.
80. Green, *Rise of the Trans-Atlantic Slave Trade,* 62.
81. Paul Lovejoy, *Jihād in West Africa during the Age of Revolutions* (Athens: Ohio University Press, 2016); Rudolph T. Ware, *The Walking Qur'an: Islamic Education, Embodied Knowledge, and History in West Africa* (Chapel Hill: University of North Carolina Press, 2014); James F. Searing, "Islam, Slavery and Jihad in West Africa," *HIC3 History Compass* 4, no. 5 (2006): 761–79; Barry, *Senegambia and the Atlantic Slave Trade.*
82. Boubacar Barry, *The Kingdom of Waalo: Senegal before the Conquest* (New York: Diasporic Africa Press, 2012), 67–87; Curtin, *Economic Change in Precolonial Africa.*
83. Barry, *Senegambia and the Atlantic Slave Trade;* Lovejoy, *Jihād in West Africa;* Michael A. Gomez, *Pragmatism in the Age of Jihad: The Precolonial State of Bundu,* African Studies Series 75 (Cambridge: Cambridge University Press, 1992).
84. This French-backed victory of a traditional aristocracy over Muslim reformers had lasting impact in Senegal. The struggle inspired subsequent waves of Islamic reform that swept the region in the 1770s and 1860s and entrenched a small group aligned with the interests of the Euro-Atlantic world against those of the region's majority populations. Barry, *Kingdom of Waalo;* Lovejoy, *Jihād in West Africa.*
85. La Courbe and Cultru, *Premier voyage,* 142–43.
86. Barry, *Kingdom of Waalo,* 95.
87. La Courbe and Cultru, *Premier voyage,* 179.
88. La Courbe and Cultru.

89. La Courbe and Cultru, 160.
90. J. Daget and Z. Ligers, "Une ancienne industrie malienne: Les pipes en terre," *Bulletin de l'Institut Francais d'Afrique Noir,* sèrie B: Sciences humaines, 24b, no. ½ (1962): 12–53.
91. La Courbe and Cultru, *Premier voyage.*
92. La Courbe and Cultru.
93. La Courbe and Cultru.
94. James F. Searing, "The Seven Years' War in West Africa: The End of Company Rule and the Emergence of the *Habitants,*" in *The Seven Years' War: Global Views,* ed. Mark H. Danley and Patrick J. Speelman (Leiden: Brill, 2012), 271–72.
95. Jean-Baptiste Labat, *Nouvelle relation de l'Afrique Occidentale: Contenant une description exacte du Sénégal & des pais situés entre de Cap-Blanc & La Rivière de Serrelionne, Jusqu'a plus de 300. lieuës* [...] (Paris: G. Cavelier, 1728), part III, 7.
96. La Courbe and Cultru, *Premier voyage.*
97. La Courbe and Cultru, 28. Emphasis mine.
98. Seck, "French Discovery of Senegal."
99. La Courbe and Cultru, *Premier voyage.*
100. La Courbe and Cultru.
101. Seck, "French Discovery of Senegal," 157.
102. La Courbe and Cultru, *Premier voyage.*
103. La Courbe and Cultru, 26 note.
104. Philip J. Havik, "Gendering the Black Atlantic: Women's Agency in Coastal Trade Settlements in the Guinea Bissau Region," in *Women in Port: Gendering Communities, Economies, and Social Networks in Atlantic Port Cities, 1500–1800,* ed. Douglas Catterall and Jodi Campbell (Boston: Brill, 2012), 315–56.
105. Havik, *Silences and Soundbytes.*
106. Havik.
107. Brooks, *Landlords and Strangers.*
108. Peter Mark and José da Silva Horta, "Two Early Seventeenth-Century Sephardic Communities on Senegal's Petite Côte," *History in Africa* 31 (2004): 231–56.
109. Peter Mark and José da Silva Horta.
110. Moraes, "Le commerce des tissus."
111. Moore, *Travels into the Inland Parts of Africa.*
112. Barry, *Senegambia and the Atlantic Slave Trade.*

CHAPTER 3: CENTERING THE SAHEL
IN THE EARLY EIGHTEENTH CENTURY

1. Frédéric Mocadel, *1755 au Galam et à l'Île Bourbon: L'odyssée de Niama, "des portes de l'or aux plantations de café"* (Sainte-Marie, Réunion: Azalées Éditions, 2006).

2. Mocadel.
3. James F. Searing, *West African Slavery and Atlantic Commerce: The Senegal River Valley, 1700–1860* (Cambridge: Cambridge University Press, 1993); Aissata Kane Lo, *De la Signare à la Diriyanké sénégalaise: Trajectoires féminines et visions partagées* (Dakar: L'Harmattan Senegal, 2014), 115–28.
4. Bernhard Gardi, ed., *Woven Beauty: The Art of West African Textiles* (Basel: Museum der Kulturen: Christoph Meiran Verlag, 2009), exhibition catalog.
5. Jutta Wimmler, *The Sun King's Atlantic: Drugs, Demons and Dyestuffs in the Atlantic World, 1640–1730,* The Atlantic World 33 (Leiden: Brill, 2017).
6. Wimmler, *The Sun King's Atlantic.*
7. Gwendolyn Midlo Hall, *Africans in Colonial Louisiana: The Development of Afro-Creole Culture in the Eighteenth Century* (Baton Rouge: Louisiana State University Press, 1992).
8. J. F. P. Hopkins and Nehemia Levtzion, *Corpus of Early Arabic Sources for West African History* (Princeton, NJ: Markus Wiener, 2000), 78, 107.
9. Michael A. Gomez, *African Dominion: A New History of Empire in Early and Medieval West Africa* (Princeton, NJ: Princeton University Press, 2018); Hopkins and Levtzion, *Corpus of Early Arabic Sources.*
10. Ibrahima Thiaw, "Atlantic Impacts on Inland Senegambia: French Penetration and African Initiatives in Eighteenth- and Nineteenth-Century Gajaaga and Bundu (Upper Senegal River)," in *Power and Landscape in Atlantic West Africa: Archaeological Perspectives,* ed. J. Cameron Monroe and Akinwumi Ogundiran (New York: Cambridge University Press, 2012), 49–77.
11. Abdoulaye Bathily, *Les portes de l'or: Le royaume de Galam (Sénégal) de l'ère musulmane au temps des négriers, VIIIe–XVIIIe siècle* (Paris: L'Harmattan, 1989).
12. Joseph Pruneau, *Mémoire sur le commerce de la concession du Sénégal, 1752,* ed. Charles Becker (Kaolack: CNRS, 1983).
13. Richard L. Roberts, "West Africa and the Pondicherry Textile Industry," in *Cloth and Commerce: Textiles in Colonial India,* ed. Tirthankar Roy (New Delhi: SAGE, 1996), 142–74; Kobayashi, *Indian Cotton Textiles in West Africa: African Agency, Consumer Demand and the Making of the Global Economy, 1750–1850* (Cham: Palgrave Macmillan, 2019).
14. Claude Boucard, Philip D. Curtin, and Jean Boulègue, "Relation de Bamboue (1729)," *Bulletin de l'Institut Fondamental d'Afrique Noir, sèrie B: Sciences humaines,* 36 (1974): 246–75.
15. C6/10, "Galam Census," 1732, Archives National d'Outre-Mer, Aix-en-Provence, France (hereafter cited as ANOM).
16. C6/10.
17. C6/10.
18. Mary Terrall, "African Indigo in the French Atlantic: Michel Adanson's Encounter with Senegal," *Isis* 114 (2023): 2.
19. Charles Monteil, *Le coton chez les noirs,* Publications du Comité d'études historiques et scientifiques de l'Afrique occidentale française, vol. 4 (Paris:

E. Larose, 1927), 68; Bernhard Gardi and Michelle Gilbert, "*Arkilla, Kaasa,* and *Nsaa:* The Many Influences of Wool Textiles from the Niger Bend in West Africa," *Textile Museum Journal* 48 (2021): 24–53.

20. Colleen E. Kriger, "Black Cloth: Status and Identity in Islamic West Africa, 1500–1900," in *The Cambridge Global History of Fashion*, vol. 1, *From Antiquity to the Nineteenth Century*, ed. Christopher Breward, Beverly Lemire, and Giorgio Riello (Cambridge: Cambridge University Press, 2023), 445–71.
21. Michael A. Gomez, *Pragmatism in the Age of Jihad: The Precolonial State of Bundu*, African Studies Series 75 (Cambridge: Cambridge University Press, 1992).
22. Lovejoy, *Jihād in West Africa during the Age of Revolutions* (Athens: Ohio University Press, 2016).
23. C6/11, "Lettre," juin 1736, ANOM.
24. C882, "Toile Bleue de Rouen Pour Guinee et Droit de Traite Sur Le Coton et Laine," 1767, f.268, Archives départementales de Loire-Atlantique, Nantes, France.
25. C6/11.
26. Paul Naylor and Marion Wallace, "Author of His Own Fate? The Eighteenth-Century Writings of Ayuba Sulayman Diallo," *Journal of African History* 60, no. 3 (November 2019): 343–77.
27. Boucard, Curtin, and Boulègue, "Relation de Bamboue (1729)," 255.
28. Philip D. Curtin, *Economic Change in Precolonial Africa: Senegambia in the Era of the Slave Trade* (Madison: University of Wisconsin Press, 1975), 89–90.
29. Thomas Bluett, *Some Memoirs of the Life of Job: The Son of Solomon the High Priest of Boonda in Africa, Who Was a Slave about Two Years in Maryland, and Afterwards Being Brought to England, Was Set Free and Sent to His Native Land* [. . .] (London, 1734), 14–15.
30. Naylor and Wallace, "Author of His Own Fate?"
31. Naylor and Wallace.

CHAPTER 4: THE POLITICS OF DRESS AT SAINT-LOUIS DURING AN AGE OF ISLAMIC REVOLUTION, 1785–1815

1. Documents on the Sloop *Swallow,* 1776, Arnold Family Business Papers, John Carter Brown Library, Providence, RI.
2. The term, meaning "residents," referred initially to people living in stone or masonry houses near the European fort, which was known as *l'habitation;* later, it applied more generally to the descendants of these people and to those who earned enough wealth to enter an elite social class.
3. Sloop *Swallow.*
4. James F. Searing, *West African Slavery and Atlantic Commerce: The Senegal River Valley, 1700–1860* (Cambridge: Cambridge University Press, 1993), 165.
5. Aissata Kane Lo, *De la Signare à la Diriyanké sénégalaise: Trajectoires féminines et visions partagees* (Dakar: L'Harmattan Senegal, 2014), 115–28;

Jessica Marie Johnson, "Tastemakers: Intimacy, Slavery, and Power in Senegambia," in *Wicked Flesh: Black Women, Intimacy, and Freedom in the Atlantic World* (Philadelphia: University of Pennsylvania Press, 2020).
6. G. Thilmans, "L'église oubliée de Saint-Louis du Sénégal," *Outre-Mers* 93, no. 350 (2006): 193–236.
7. Pierre Lintingre, *Voyages du sieur de Glicourt à la côte occidentale d'Afrique pendant les années 1778 et 1779* (Dakar: Afrique Documents, 1966).
8. C6/15, "Lettre Du Sieur Thevenot Maire Du Senegal a Mr Le Ch De Menager Gouverneur de Goree," August 29, 1766, ANOM.
9. Hilary Jones, *The Métis of Senegal: Urban Life and Politics in French West Africa* (Bloomington: Indiana University Press, 2013).
10. Michael A. Gomez, *African Dominion: A New History of Empire in Early and Medieval West Africa* (Princeton, NJ: Princeton University Press, 2018), 240–42; Boubacar Barry, *Senegambia and the Atlantic Slave Trade*, African Studies Series 92 (Cambridge: Cambridge University Press, 1998), 7–8.
11. Lovejoy, *Jihād in West Africa during the Age of Revolutions* (Athens: Ohio University Press, 2016).
12. Karen Amanda Sackur, "The Development of Creole Society and Culture in Saint-Louis and Gorée, 1719–1817" (PhD diss., University of London, 1999), 131–33.
13. Dominique Harcourt Lamiral, *L'Affrique et le peuple affriquain, Considérés sous tous leurs rapports avec notre commerce & nos colonies* [...] (Paris: Dessenne, 1789), 43.
14. Jones, *Métis of Senegal*, 37.
15. Philip D. Curtin, *The Image of Africa: British Ideas and Action, 1780–1850* (Madison: University of Wisconsin Press, 1964), 28–55.
16. Laura Fair, "Remaking Fashion in the Paris of the Indian Ocean: Dress, Performance, and the Cultural Construction of a Cosmopolitan Zanzibari Identity," in *Fashioning Africa: Power and the Politics of Dress*, ed. Jean Allman (Bloomington: Indiana University Press, 2004), 13–30.
17. Simon Gikandi, *Slavery and the Culture of Taste* (Princeton, NJ: Princeton University Press, 2014), 99–100.
18. Lorelle D. Semley, "Signares before Citizens," in *To Be Free and French: Citizenship in France's Atlantic Empire* (Cambridge: Cambridge University Press, 2017), 69–112; Jones, *Métis of Senegal*.
19. Semley, "Signares before Citizens," 94.
20. Lamiral, *L'Affrique et le peuple affriquain*, 119.
21. Lamiral, 120.
22. Lamiral, 121.
23. Lamiral, 183.
24. Bruce S. Hall, *A History of Race in Muslim West Africa, 1600–1960* (Cambridge: Cambridge University Press, 2011).
25. Searing, *West African Slavery and Atlantic Commerce*.

26. Searing.
27. M. Saugnier and François Bessire, *Relations de plusieurs voyages à la côte d'Afrique, à Maroc, au Sénégal, à Gorée, à Galam* (Saint-Étienne: L'Université de Saint-Étienne, 2005), 214–15.
28. 117S 173, "Manuscript of Albert Merle on Senegal Commerce 1719–1830," 1787, Archives Municipales de Bordeaux, ANOM.
29. Saugnier and Bessire, *Relations de plusieurs voyages*.
30. Beverly Lemire, *Global Trade and the Transformation of Consumer Cultures: The Material World Remade, c. 1500–1820* (Cambridge: Cambridge University Press, 2018).
31. Saugnier and Bessire, *Relations de plusieurs voyages*.
32. Colleen E. Kriger, "Guinea Cloth: Production and Consumption of Cotton Textiles before and during the Atlantic Slave Trade," in *The Spinning World: A Global History of Cotton Textiles, 1200–1850*, ed. Giorgio Riello (New York: Oxford University Press, 2009); Kazuo Kobayashi, *Indian Cotton Textiles in West Africa: African Agency, Consumer Demand and the Making of the Global Economy, 1750–1850* (Cham: Palgrave Macmillan, 2019).
33. Richard L. Roberts, *Two Worlds of Cotton: Colonialism and the Regional Economy in the French Soudan, 1800–1946* (Stanford, CA: Stanford University Press, 1996); Kobayashi, *Indian Cotton Textiles in West Africa*.
34. C6–19, Durand, "Etat Des Depenses Locales Au Senegal," 1786, ANOM.
35. P. D. Boilat, *Esquisses sénégalaises* (Paris: Karthala, 1984), 445.
36. Boilat, 8.
37. Jacques Grasset de Saint-Sauveur, *Encyclopédie des voyages: Contenant l'abrégé historique [...]* ([Paris], 1796).
38. Rudolph T. Ware III, *The Walking Qur'an: Islamic Education, Embodied Knowledge, and History in West Africa* (Chapel Hill: University of North Carolina Press, 2014).
39. Ware.
40. Barry, *Senegambia and the Atlantic Slave Trade*, 103.
41. David Robinson, "The Islamic Revolution of Futa Toro," *International Journal of African Historical Studies* 8, no. 2 (1975): 185–221.
42. Jean Boulègue, *Les royaumes wolof dans l'espace sénégambien: XIIIe–XVIIIe siècle* (Paris: Karthala, 2013), 445.
43. Barry, *Senegambia and the Atlantic Slave Trade*; Philip D. Curtin, *Economic Change in Precolonial Africa: Senegambia in the Era of the Slave Trade* (Madison: University of Wisconsin Press, 1975).
44. Mungo Park, *Travels in the Interior Districts of Africa*, ed. Kate Ferguson Marsters (Durham, NC: Duke University Press, 2000), 341; Ware, *Walking Qur'an*, 134.
45. CO 267/29, "Maxwell Report on Senegal to HM Commissioner on Investigating Africa's Forts and Settlements (Barry/Waalo)," 1805, The National Archives, UK.

## CHAPTER 5: MERCHANTS, MAROONS, MAHDIS, AND MIGRANTS ON THE UPPER GUINEA COAST, 1795-1825

1. Adam Afzelius, *Sierra Leone Journal 1795–1796*, ed. Alexander Peter Kup, Studia Ethnographica Upsaliensia 27 (Uppsala: Inst. för allm. och jämförande etnografi, 1967), 107.
2. James Watt, *Journal of James Watt: Expedition to Timbo, Capital of the Fula Empire in 1794*, with an introduction and ed. Bruce L. Mouser (Madison: African Studies Program, University of Wisconsin–Madison, 1994), 48.
3. Watt.
4. Watt, 50.
5. Paul E. Lovejoy, *Jihād in West Africa during the Age of Revolutions* (Athens: Ohio University Press, 2016), 41–42; Boubacar Barry, *Senegambia and the Atlantic Slave Trade*, African Studies Series 92 (Cambridge: Cambridge University Press, 1998), 92–103.
6. Bruce L. Mouser, "Insurrection as Socioeconomic Change: Three Rebellions in Guinea/Sierra Leone in the Eighteenth Century," in *The Powerful Presence of the Past: Integration and Conflict along the Upper Guinea Coast*, ed. Jacqueline Knörr and Wilson Trajano Filho (Leiden: Brill, 2010), 55–73; Martin A. Klein, "Defensive Strategies: Wasulu, Masina, and the Slave Trade," in *Fighting the Slave Trade: West African Strategies*, ed. Sylviane A. Diouf (Athens: Ohio University Press; Oxford: James Currey, 2003), 62–78.
7. Barry, *Senegambia and the Atlantic Slave Trade*, 122.
8. Bruce L. Mouser, "Origins of the Church Missionary Society Accommodation to Imperial Policy: The Sierra Leone Quagmire and the Closing of the Susu Mission, 1804–17," *Journal of Religion in Africa* 39, no. 4 (2009): 375–402.
9. Author interview of Almamy Daouda Toure at Forecaria, Guinea, March 2013.
10. This idea of the Guinean coast as a savanna hinterland reorients it to the African world, in contrast to Atlantic historians who conceive of it as a frontier or periphery of that world.
11. Richard Bright, Alexander Smith, and Brian O'Beirne, *Guinea Journals: Journeys into Guinea-Conakry during the Sierra Leone Phase, 1800–1821*, ed. Bruce L. Mouser (Washington, DC: University Press of America, 1979), 87.
12. Bright, Smith, and O'Beirne, 31–98; George E. Brooks and Bruce L. Mouser, "An 1804 Slaving Contract Signed in Arabic Script from the Upper Guinea Coast," *History in Africa* 14 (1987): 341–48.
13. Bright, Smith, and O'Beirne, *Guinea Journals*.
14. Brooks and Mouser, "An 1804 Slaving Contract."
15. Bright, Smith, and O'Beirne, *Guinea Journals*.
16. Bruce L. Mouser, "The 1805 Forékariah Conference: A Case of Political Intrigue, Economic Advantage, Network Building," *History in Africa* 25 (1998): 219–62.
17. Mouser.

18. Samuel Abraham Walker, *Missions in Western Africa, among the Soosoos, Bulloms, Etc.: Being the First Undertaken by the Church Missionary Society for Africa and the East (1845)* (Dublin: W. Curry, Jun., 1845), 211.
19. Walker, 81.
20. "Bonne Amitié," Jean Amant (Captain), Voyage ID number 31959, Honfleur, Sierra Leone Estuary, Les Cayes, 1787, Transatlantic Slave Trade Database, https://www.slavevoyages.org/voyage/database.
21. "Account Book for La Bonne Amitie," n.d., Musée du Vieux Honfleur.
22. Afzelius, *Sierra Leone Journal*, 140.
23. Afzelius, 140.
24. BL 12.131, Sierra Leone, "Mr Watts Journal to Furry Canaba's 31 January & 11 February 1795," British Library, London.
25. BL 12.131, Sierra Leone, "Mr Gray's Journal," British Library, London; and BL 12.131, "Mr Watts Journal to Furry Canaba's 31 January & 11 February 1795."
26. BL 12.131, "Mr Gray's Journal"; and BL 12.131, "Mr Watts Journal to Furry Canaba's 31 January & 11 February 1795."
27. BL 12.131, "Mr Gray's Journal"; and BL 12.131, "Mr Watts Journal to Furry Canaba's 31 January & 11 February 1795."
28. Hannah More and Henry W. Weston, *The Black Prince: A True Story; Being an Account of the Life and Death of Naimbanna, an African King's Son, Who Arrived in England in the Year 1791, and Set Sail on His Return in June 1793* (Philadelphia: B. & J. Johnson, 1800).
29. BL 12.131, "Mr Gray's Journal"; and BL 12.131, "Mr Watts Journal to Furry Canaba's 31 January & 11 February 1795."
30. Lovejoy, *Jihād in West Africa*, 42.
31. Lovejoy.
32. Lovejoy.
33. Thomas Masterman Winterbottom, *An Account of the Native Africans in the Neighbourhood of Sierra Leone: To Which Is Added, an Account of the Present State of Medicine among Them* (London: C. Whittingham, 1803), 246–50.
34. Winterbottom, 246–50.
35. Bruce L. Mouser, "Insurrection as Socioeconomic Change."
36. Afzelius, *Sierra Leone Journal*.
37. Alexander Gordon Laing and Edward Sabine, *Travels in the Timannee, Kooranko, and Soolima Countries, in Western Africa* (London: J. Murray, 1825), 405.
38. Suzanne Schwarz, *"A Just and Honourable Commerce": Abolitionist Experimentation in Sierra Leone in the Late Eighteenth and Early Nineteenth Centuries* (London: Hakluyt Society, 2014), 24.
39. Schwarz.
40. Bright, Smith, and O'Beirne, *Guinea Journals*.
41. Lamin O. Sanneh, *Abolitionists Abroad: American Blacks and the Making of Modern West Africa* (Cambridge, MA: Harvard University Press, 1999).
42. Sanneh.

43. Kevin G. Lowther, *The African American Odyssey of John Kizell: A South Carolina Slave Returns to Fight the Slave Trade in His African Homeland* (Columbia: University of South Carolina Press, 2012).
44. Afzelius, *Sierra Leone Journal*, 95.
45. Mary Louise Clifford, *From Slavery to Freetown: Black Loyalists after the American Revolution* (Jefferson, NC: McFarland, 2006), 184–85.
46. *Africa Redeemed: Or, The Means of Her Relief Illustrated by the Growth and Prospects of Liberia* (London: James Nisbet, 1851).
47. F. B. Spilsbury, *Account of a Voyage to the Western Coast of Africa: Performed by His Majesty's Sloop Favourite, in the Year 1805* [...] (London: R. Phillips, 1807), 10.
48. Spilsbury, *Account of a Voyage*.
49. Spilsbury, *Account of a Voyage*.
50. Afzelius, *Sierra Leone Journal*, 103.
51. CO 270/3 TNA, "Letter from Buckle to Cooper," *Sierra Leone Original Correspondence*, May 25, 1795, The National Archives, UK (hereafter cited as TNA).
52. CO 270/3 TNA, "Resolutions of Council at Sierra Leone Correspondence," 1794–1796, TNA.
53. CO 270/4 TNA, "Sierra Leone Council Records," 1796–1798, TNA.
54. CO 270/4 TNA, "Sierra Leone Council Records," 47.
55. Mouser, "The 1805 Forékariah Conference."
56. Bruce L. Mouser, "African Academy—Clapham 1799–1806," *History of Education* 33, no. 1 (2004): 87–103.
57. Jacqueline Knörr and Christoph Kohl, eds., *The Upper Guinea Coast in Global Perspective*, Integration and Conflict Studies 12 (New York: Berghahn, 2016), 21–40.
58. Mamady Diallo, "Implantation coloniale à travers les vestiges au Rio Pongo" (PhD diss., Université Polytechnique de Conakry, 1971).
59. Afzelius, *Sierra Leone Journal*.
60. Alice Bellagamba, "The Expulsion of Dala Modu," in *African Voices on Slavery and the Slave Trade*, ed. Alice Bellagamba, Sandra E. Greene, and Martin A. Klein, vol. 1 (Cambridge: Cambridge University Press, 2013), 334–42.
61. Bellagamba.
62. Bellagamba.
63. Bellagamba, 338.
64. Bellagamba, 339.
65. Bruce L. Mouser, "Rebellion, Marronage and Jihād: Strategies of Resistance to Slavery on the Sierra Leone Coast, c. 1783–1796," *Journal of African History* 48, no. 1 (2007): 27.

CHAPTER 6: TEXTURES OF A CHANGING ERA

1. Jan Jansen, "When Marrying a Muslim: The Social Code of Political Elites in the Western Sudan, c. 1600–c. 1850," *Journal of African History* 57, no. 1

(2016): 25; Emily Lynn Osborn, *Our New Husbands Are Here: Households, Gender, and Politics in a West African State from the Slave Trade to Colonial Rule* (Athens: Ohio University Press, 2011).
2. Lansiné Kaba, "Islam, Society and Politics in Pre-colonial Baté, Guinea," *Bulletin de l'Institut Fondamental d'Afrique Noire,* sèrie B: Sciences humaines, 35, no. 2 (1973): 323–44; C. Magbaily Fyle, *The Solima Yalunka Kingdom: Precolonial Politics, Economics and Society* (Freetown, Sierra Leone: Nyakon, 1979).
3. Odile Goerg, *Commerce et colonisation en Guinée, 1850–1913* (Paris: L'Harmattan, 1986); Bruce L. Mouser, "Lightbourn Family of Farenya, Rio Pongo," *Mande Studies* 13 (2011): 21–90.
4. Bruce L. Mouser, "'Walking Caravans' of Nineteenth Century Fuuta Jaloo, Western Africa," *Mande Studies* 12 (2010): 19–104.
5. CO 268/8 TNA, "Three Letters of Imam of Foota Jaloo of 1810 Translated by J. Perronet Thomps, Capt of 17th Light Dragoons and Formerly Governor of Sierra Leone," 1810, TNA.
6. CO 268/8 TNA.
7. Edda L. Fields-Black, *Deep Roots: Rice Farmers in West Africa and the African Diaspora* (Bloomington: Indiana University Press, 2008), 46–47.
8. Saidou Mohamed N'Daou, "Dress, Social Change, and the (Re)Construction of Identity in Guinea (Nineteenth Century to Present)," *Mande Studies* 23 (2021): 99.
9. Alexander Gordon Laing and Edward Sabine, *Travels in the Timannee, Kooranko, and Soolima Countries, in Western Africa* (London: J. Murray, 1825), 359.
10. Maria Grosz-Ngaté, "Power and Knowledge: The Representation of the Mande World in the Works of Park, Caillié, Monteil, and Delafosse (Pouvoir et savoir: La représentation du monde mandé dans les oeuvres de Park, Caillié, Monteil et Delafosse)," *Cahiers d'Etudes Africaines* 28 (1988): 485–511.
11. René Caillié and M. Jomard, *Travels through Central Africa to Timbuctoo: And across the Great Desert, to Morocco; Performed in the Years 1824–1828* (London: H. Colburn and R. Bentley, 1830), 214.
12. Caillié and Jomard, 223.
13. Paul E. Lovejoy, *Jihād in West Africa during the Age of Revolutions* (Athens: Ohio University Press, 2016); Paul E. Lovejoy, *Slavery on the Frontiers of Islam* (Princeton, NJ: Markus Wiener, 2004).
14. Richard Robert Madden, *A Twelvemonth's Residence in the West Indies, during the Transition from Slavery to Apprenticeship: With Incidental Notices of the State of Society, Prospects, and Natural Resources of Jamaica and Other Islands* (London: J. Cochrane; A. J. Valpy, 1835), 197.
15. Gaspard Théodore Mollien et al., *Travels in the Interior of Africa, to the Sources of the Senegal and Gambia: Performed by Command of the French Government, in the Year 1818* (London: H. Colburn, 1820), 181.
16. Caillié and Jomard, *Travels through Central Africa,* 256.

17. Caillié and Jomard, 262.
18. Caillié and Jomard, 269.
19. Laing and Sabine, *Travels in the Timannee*, 81.
20. Laing and Sabine, 359.
21. Caillié and Jomard, *Travels through Central Africa*, 267.
22. The British officer referenced is likely Brevet-Major John Peddie, who died in 1817 before undertaking a major caravan expedition to the Fuuta Jallon.
23. Leland Conley Barrows, "General Faidherbe, the Maurel and Prom Company, and French Expansion in Senegal" (PhD diss., University of California, Los Angeles, 1974), 553.
24. Fields-Black, *Deep Roots*, 66.
25. Bruce L. Mouser, "Théophilus Conneau: The Saga of a Tale," *History in Africa* 6 (1979): 97–107, https://doi.org/10.2307/3171742; Bruce L. Mouser, *American Colony on the Rio Pongo: The War of 1812, the Slave Trade, and the Proposed Settlement of African Americans, 1810–1830* (Trenton, NJ: Africa World Press, 2013).
26. (RHO) 721.12 r. 19, "A Letter to Thomas Fowell Buxton . . . on the Character of the Liberated Africans at Sierra Leone, and on the Cultivation of Cotton in That Colony," 1839, Bodleian Library, University of Oxford (hereafter BLUO).
27. Mouser, *American Colony*, 52.
28. Mouser, 45.
29. Théodore Canot, *A Slaver's Log Book, or 20 Years' Residence in Africa: The Original Manuscript* (Englewood Cliffs, NJ: Prentice Hall, 1976).
30. Canot.
31. Canot, 224; Mouser, "Walking Caravans."
32. Richard L. Roberts, *Two Worlds of Cotton: Colonialism and the Regional Economy in the French Soudan, 1800–1946* (Stanford, CA: Stanford University Press, 1996); Richard L. Roberts, "West Africa and the Pondicherry Textile Industry," in *Cloth and Commerce: Textiles in Colonial India*, ed. Tirthankar Roy (New Delhi: SAGE, 1996), 142–74; Georges Hardy, *La mise en valeur du Sénégal de 1817 à 1854* (Paris: É. Larose, 1921).
33. Georges Perrottet, "Rapport general sur les divers essais de culture particulierement des Indigoferes Anil et Emargine qui ont eu lieu au Senegal pendant les annees 1825–1829," Archival, Dakar, 1R 26/158, Senegal National Archives.
34. William Fergusson, *A Letter to Thomas Fowell Buxton . . . on the Character of the Liberated Africans at Sierra Leone, and on the Cultivation of Cotton in That Colony* (London: Green, 1839), Oxford (RHO) 721.12 r. 19, Bodleian Library, University of Oxford.
35. Fergusson, 11.
36. Goerg, *Commerce et colonisation;* Martin A. Klein, "Slaves, Gum, and Peanuts: Adaptation to the End of the Slave Trade in Senegal, 1817–48," *William and Mary Quarterly*, 3rd ser., 66, no. 4 (October 1, 2009): 895–914.
37. Goerg, *Commerce et colonisation*, 41.

38. Louis-Édouard Bouët-Willaumez, *Commerce et traite des noirs aux côtes occidentales d'Afrique* (Paris: Imprimerie Nationale, 1848).
39. Bouët-Willaumez, 52.
40. Goerg, *Commerce et colonisation*, 43.
41. Bouët-Willaumez, *Commerce et traite des noirs*, 52.
42. Bouët-Willaumez, 56.
43. Bouët-Willaumez.
44. Kazuo Kobayashi, *Indian Cotton Textiles in West Africa: African Agency, Consumer Demand and the Making of the Global Economy, 1750–1850* (Cham: Palgrave Macmillan, 2019); Richard Roberts, "Guinée Cloth: Linked Transformations within France's Empire in the Nineteenth Century," *Cahiers d'Etudes Africaines* 32 (1992): 597–627.
45. Mamady Diallo, "Implantation coloniale à travers les vestiges au Rio Pongo" (PhD diss., Université Polytechnique de Conakry, 1971); Mouser, "Lightbourn Family."
46. Mouser, *American Colony*.
47. Mouser, "Lightbourn Family of Farenya, Rio Pongo."
48. A. H. Barrow, *Fifty Years in Western Africa: Being a Record of the Work of the West Indian Church on the Banks of the Rio Pongo* (London: Society for Promoting Christian Knowledge, 1900), 58.
49. Barrow, 59.
50. Barrow, 10–11.
51. Bakary Gibba, "The West Indian Mission to West Africa: The Rio Pongas Mission, 1850–1963" (PhD diss., University of Toronto, 2011), 80.
52. Debra Newman Ham, "The Role of African American Women in the Founding of Liberia," in *Global Dimensions of the African Diaspora*, ed. Joseph E. Harris (Washington, DC: Howard University Press, 1993); E. Frances White, *Sierra Leone's Settler Women Traders: Women on the Afro-European Frontier* (Ann Arbor: University of Michigan Press, 1987).
53. Barrow, 57.
54. "Half Yearly Report of the West Indian Church Association, Pongas Mission. SPG Western Africa," Barbados, 1859, SPG CC/AFW-2, BLUO.
55. Gibba, "West Indian Mission to West Africa."
56. Barrows, "General Faidherbe"; Gibba, "The West Indian Mission."
57. Goerg, *Commerce et colonization*.
58. Barrow, *Fifty Years in Western Africa*.

CONCLUSION

1. John Styles and Amanda Vickery, *Gender, Taste, and Material Culture in Britain and North America, 1700–1830* (New Haven, CT: Yale Center for British Art, 2006).
2. Alexander Gordon Laing and Edward Sir Sabine, *Travels in the Timannee, Kooranko, and Soolima Countries, in Western Africa* (London: J. Murray, 1825), 359–60.

# Bibliography

### ARCHIVAL SOURCES

"Account Book for La Bonne Amitie." N.d. Musée du Vieux Honfleur.
Archives National d'Outre-Mer, Aix-en-Provence, France (ANOM)
  117S 173. "Manuscript of Albert Merle on Senegal Commerce 1719–1830," 1787.
  Archives Municipales de Bordeaux.
  ANOM C6/8. "Memoire sur le commerce de Guinee." 1724.
  ANOM C6/9. Levens, Sieur. "Compte Rendu Du Sieur Levens," July 10, 1725.
  ANOM C6/10. "Galam Census," 1732.
  ANOM C6/11. "Lettre," June 1736.
  ANOM C6/15. "Lettre Du Sieur Thevenot Maire Du Senegal a Mr Le Ch De Menager Gouverneur de Goree," August 29, 1766.
  ANOM C6/18.
  ANOM C6-19.
  Brue, André. "Departement Du Senegal 29 Juin 1702," n.d.
  ———. "Memoire a La Compagnie Royal du Senegal," June 29, 1702.
  C 739. "Andre Brue, memoire a La Compagnie Royal du Senegal, 29 Juin 1702." Departement du Senegal, 1702. Archives départementales de Loire-Atlantique, France.
Bodleian Library, University of Oxford (BLUO)
  Fergusson, William. *A Letter to Thomas Fowell Buxton . . . on the Character of the Liberated Africans at Sierra Leone, and on the Cultivation of Cotton in That Colony.* London: Green, 1839. Oxford (RHO) 721.12 r. 19.
"Half Yearly Report of the West Indian Church Association, Pongas Mission. SPG Western Africa." Barbados, 1859. SPG CC/AFW-2.
(RHO) 721.12 r. 19. "A Letter to Thomas Fowell Buxton . . . on the Character of the Liberated Africans at Sierra Leone, and on the Cultivation of Cotton in That Colony," 1839.
BL 12.131, Sierra Leone, British Library, London
C882. "Toile Bleue de Rouen Pour Guinee et Droit de Traite Sur Le Coton et Laine." 1767, f.268, Archives départementales de Loire-Atlantique, Nantes, France.

"Inventaire Duhamel Dumonceau (Jusqu'au No. 1272 et Louis Phillipe)." Archives du Musée du Quai Branly-Jacques Chirac: D004864, 1830. Musée de Marine du Louvre.

Kouyate, Jeli Mamary. "Sonsan of Kaarta." Oral historical narrative recorded by David Conrad in Kolokani, Mali, August 19, 1975. Conrad provided a translated transcript of the recording to the author.

Senegal National Archives

Sloop *Swallow*. Documents. Arnold Family Business Papers, 1776. John Carter Brown Library, Providence, RI.

The National Archives, United Kingdom (TNA)
12.131, Sierra Leone. "Letter Addressed to the Chairman of the Sierra Leone Company by the Rev. Mr. Thomas Clarkson," n.d.
Company of Royal Adventurers of England Trading with Africa and Successors: Records (T70)
India Office Library, MSS EUR D. 624/2. "The Memorial of Sargent, Chambers and Co.," 1801 1800.
Records of the Colonial Office (CO)

### DISSERTATIONS

Aherne, Tavy. "*Gudhe Ngara: Exploring the Dynamics of the Creation, Use and Trade in Guinea's Indigo Cloths.*" PhD diss., Indiana University, 2000.

Barrows, Leland Conley. "General Faidherbe, the Maurel and Prom Company, and French Expansion in Senegal." PhD diss., University of California, Los Angeles, 1974.

Brennig, Joseph Jerome. "The Textile Trade of Seventeenth-Century Northern Coromandel: A Study of a Pre-modern Asian Export Industry." PhD diss., University of Wisconsin–Madison, 1975.

Diallo, Mamady. "Implantation coloniale à travers les vestiges au Rio Pongo." PhD diss., Université Polytechnique de Conakry, 1971.

Galloway, Winifred Faye. "A History of Wuli from the Thirteenth to the Nineteenth Century." PhD diss., Indiana University, 1975.

Gibba, Bakary. "The West Indian Mission to West Africa: The Rio Pongas Mission, 1850–1963." PhD diss., University of Toronto, 2011.

Sackur, Karen Amanda. "The Development of Creole Society and Culture in Saint-Louis and Gorée, 1719–1817." PhD diss., University of London, 1999.

Shea, Philip James. "The Development of an Export Oriented Dyed Cloth Industry in Kano Emirate in the Nineteenth Century." PhD diss., University of Wisconsin–Madison, 1975.

### PUBLISHED SOURCES

Adam, G. *Légendes historiques du pays de Nioro (Sahel)*. Paris: A. Challamel, 1904.

*Africa Redeemed: Or, The Means of Her Relief Illustrated by the Growth and Prospects of Liberia*. London: James Nisbet, 1851.

Afzelius, Adam. *Sierra Leone Journal 1795–1796*, edited by Alexander Peter Kup. Studia Ethnographica Upsaliensia 27. Uppsala: Inst. för allm. och jämförande etnografi, 1967.

——. "#HerskovitsMustFall? A Meditation on Whiteness, African Studies, and the Unfinished Business of 1968." *African Studies Review* 62, no. 3 (September 2019): 6–39.

Arnaud, Robert. "La singuliere legende des Soninkes: Traditions orales sur le royaume de Koumbi et sur divers autres royaumes soudanais." In *L'Islam et la politique musulmane française en Afrique occidentale française*. Paris: Comité de l'Afrique française, 1912.

Austen, Ralph A., ed. *In Search of Sunjata: The Mande Oral Epic as History, Literature and Performance*. Bloomington: Indiana University Press, 1999.

Baba, Ahmad ibn Ahmad. *Mi'rāj Al-Ṣu'ūd: Ahmad Baba's Replies on Slavery*. Edited by John O. Hunwick and Fatima Harrak. Al-Ṭab'ah 1, Manshūrāt Ma'had Al-Dirāsāt al-Afrīqīyah, Nuṣūṣ Wa-Wathā'iq 7. Rabaṭ: Publications of the Institute of African Studies, 2000.

Bah, El Hadj Thierno Mamadou. *Histoire du Fouta-Djallon, Tome I. Des origines à la pénétration coloniale*. Paris: L'Harmattan, 2008.

Barron, Géraldine. "Le Musée de Marine du Louvre: Un Musée des techniques?" *Artefact* 5, no. 5 (2017): 143–62.

Barrow, A. H. *Fifty Years in Western Africa: Being a Record of the Work of the West Indian Church on the Banks of the Rio Pongo*. London: Society for Promoting Christian Knowledge, 1900.

Barry, Boubacar. *The Kingdom of Waalo: Senegal before the Conquest*. New York: Diasporic Africa Press, 2012.

——. *Senegambia and the Atlantic Slave Trade*. African Studies 92. Cambridge: Cambridge University Press, 1998.

Bashir Salau, Mohammed. *Plantation Slavery in the Sokoto Caliphate: A Historical and Comparative Study*. Rochester, NY: University of Rochester Press, 2018.

Bathily, Abdoulaye. *Les portes de l'or: Le royaume de Galam (Sénégal) de l'ère musulmane au temps des négriers (VIIIe–XVIIIe siècle)*. Paris: L'Harmattan, 1989.

Bazin, Jean. "A chacun son Bambara." In *Au coeur de l'ethnie: Ethnies, tribalisme et État en Afrique*, edited by Jean-Loup Amselle and Elikia M'Bokolo, 87–127. Paris: La Découverte, 2005.

Bellagamba, Alice. "The Expulsion of Dala Modu." In *African Voices on Slavery and the Slave Trade*, edited by Alice Bellagamba, Sandra E. Greene, and Martin A. Klein, 334–42. Vol. 1. Cambridge: Cambridge University Press, 2013.

Blackburn, Robin. *The Making of New World Slavery: From the Baroque to the Modern, 1492–1800*. London: Verso, 1997.

Bluett, Thomas. *Some Memoirs of the Life of Job: The Son of Solomon the High Priest of Boonda in Africa, Who Was a Slave about Two Years in Maryland, and Afterwards Being Brought to England, Was Set Free and Sent to His Native Land [. . .]*. London, 1734.

Boilat, P. D. *Esquisses sénégalaises*. Paris: Karthala, 1984.

Bolland, Rita. *Tellem Textiles: Archaeological Finds from Burial Caves in Mali's Bandiagara Cliff*. Amsterdam: Tropenmuseum, 1991.

Boser-Sarivaxévanis, Renée. *West African Textiles and Garments: From the Museum Für Völkerkunde Basel.* Minneapolis: University of Minnesota, 1980.
Boucard, Claude, Philip D. Curtin, and Jean Boulègue. "Relation de Bamboue (1729)." *Bulletin de l'Institut Fondamental d'Afrique Noir, sèrie B: Sciences humaines,* 36 (1974): 246–75.
Bouët-Willaumez, Louis-Édouard. *Commerce et traite des noirs aux côtes occidentales d'Afrique.* Paris: Imprimerie Nationale, 1848.
Boulègue, Jean. *Les royaumes wolof dans l'espace sénégambien (XIIIe–XVIIIe siècle).* Paris: Karthala, 2013.
Braudel, Fernand. *Capitalism and Material Life, 1400–1800.* London: Weidenfeld and Nicolson, 1973.
Brett-Smith, Sarah C. *The Silence of the Women: Bamana Mud Cloths.* Milan: 5 Continents Editions, 2014.
Bright, Richard, Alexander Smith, and Brian O'Beirne. *Guinea Journals: Journeys into Guinea-Conakry during the Sierra Leone Phase, 1800–1821,* edited by Bruce L. Mouser. Washington, DC: University Press of America, 1979.
Brooks, George E. "Artists' Depiction of Senegalese Signares: Insights concerning French Racist and Sexist Attitudes in the Nineteenth Century." *Genève-Afrique: Acta Africana* 18, no. 1 (1980): 75–89.
———. *Eurafricans in Western Africa: Contested Arenas of Commerce, Social Status, Gender, and Religious Observance from the Sixteenth to the Eighteenth Century.* Athens: Ohio University Press, 2003.
———. *Landlords and Strangers: Ecology, Society, and Trade in Western Africa, 1000–1630.* Boulder, CO: Westview Press, 1993.
Brooks, George E., and Bruce L. Mouser. "An 1804 Slaving Contract Signed in Arabic Script from the Upper Guinea Coast." *History in Africa* 14 (1987): 341–48.
Brown, Vincent. *The Reaper's Garden: Death and Power in the World of Atlantic Slavery.* Cambridge, MA: Harvard University Press, 2008.
Brue, André. "Voyage of the Sieur Brue to Bissau and Bissagos." In *A New and Complete Collection of Voyages and Travels: Containing All That Have Been Remarkable from the Earliest Period to the Present Time* [...], edited by John Hamilton Moore, 2 vols. (viii, 592, [2], 593–1172, 11, [9]p.), plates. London, 1780.
Burton, Antoinette. "The Body in/as World History." In *A Companion to World History,* edited by Douglas Northrup, 272–84. Malden, MA: Wiley, 2015.
Byfield, Judith A. *The Bluest Hands: A Social and Economic History of Women Dyers in Abeokuta (Nigeria), 1890–1940.* Portsmouth, NH: Heinemann; Oxford: James Currey, 2002.
Caillié, René. *Travels through Central Africa to Timbuctoo and across the Great Desert, to Morocco, Performed in the Years 1824–1828.* New York: Cambridge University Press, 2013.
Caillié, René, and M. Jomard. *Travels through Central Africa to Timbuctoo; And across the Great Desert, to Morocco; Performed in the Years 1824–1828.* London: H. Colburn and R. Bentley, 1830.

Canot, Théodore. *A Slaver's Log Book, or 20 Years' Residence in Africa: The Original Manuscript by Captain Theophilus Conneau.* Englewood Cliffs, NJ: Prentice Hall, 1976.

Caron, Peter. "'Of a Nation Which the Others Do Not Understand': Bambara Slaves and African Ethnicity in Colonial Louisiana, 1718–60." In *Routes to Slavery: Direction, Ethnicity and Mortality in the Atlantic Slave Trade,* edited by David Eltis and David Richardson, 104–27. Abingdon, UK: Routledge, 1997.

Carreira, António. *Mandingas da Guiné Portuguesa.* Memórias 4. Lisbon: Centro de Estudos da Guiné Portuguesa, 1947.

Clammer, Paul. *Black Crown: Henry Christophe, the Haitian Revolution and the Caribbean's Forgotten Kingdom.* London: Hurst, 2023.

Cleaveland, Timothy. "Ahmad Baba Al-Timbukti and His Islamic Critique of Racial Slavery in the Maghrib." *Journal of North African Studies* 20, no. 1 (January 2015): 42–64.

Clifford, Mary Louise. *From Slavery to Freetown: Black Loyalists after the American Revolution.* Jefferson, NC: McFarland, 2006.

Comaroff, Jean. "The Empire's Old Clothes: Fashioning the Colonial Subject." In *Cross-Cultural Consumption: Global Markets, Local Realities,* edited by David Howes, 19–38. London: Routledge, 1996.

Cooper, Barbara. "Oral Sources and the Challenge of African History." In *Writing African History,* ed. John Phillips, 191–215. Rochester, NY: University of Rochester Press, 2005.

Curtin, Philip D. *Economic Change in Precolonial Africa: Senegambia in the Era of the Slave Trade.* Madison: University of Wisconsin Press, 1975.

———. *The Image of Africa: British Ideas and Action, 1780–1850.* Madison: University of Wisconsin Press, 1964.

———. "The Western Juula in the Eighteenth Century." Paper presented at the International Conference on Manding Studies, 1972.

Daget, J., and Z. Ligers. "Une ancienne industrie malienne: Les pipes en terre." *Bulletin de l'Institut Français d'Afrique Noir,* sèrie B: Sciences humaines, 24b, no. 1/2 (1962): 12–53.

d'Almada, André Alvares, A. Teixeira da Mota, P. E. H. Hair, and Jean Boulègue. *Brief Treatise on the Rivers of Guinea.* Liverpool: Department of History, University of Liverpool, 1984.

Dapper, Olfert. *Description de l'Afrique: Contenant les noms, la situation & les confins de toutes ses parties, leurs rivières, leurs villes & leurs habitations, leurs plantes & leurs animaux, les moeurs, les coûtumes, la langue, les richesses, la religion & le gouvernement de ses peoples [. . .].* Amsterdam: Chez Wolfgang, Waesberge, Boom and van Someren, 1686.

Delcourt, André. *La France et les établissements français au Sénégal entre 1713 et 1763: La Compagnie des Indes et le Sénégal; La guerre de la gomme.* Dakar: Institut Français d'Afrique Noir, 1952.

Diallo, Maladho. *Histoire du Fouta Djallon.* Paris: L'Harmattan, 2002.

Donelha, André, and A. Teixeira da Mota. *Descrição da Serra Leoa e dos rios de Guiné do Cabo Verde, 1625*. Lisboa: Junta de Investigações Científicas do Ultramar, 1977.

Douny, Laurence. "The Material Agency of West African Wild Silk: An Ethnographic Exploration into Marka-Dafing Conceptions of Sheen." *Japanese Review of Cultural Anthropology* 21, no. 1 (2020): 291–313.

——. "Wild Silk Indigo Wrappers of Dogon of Mali: An Ethnography of Materials Efficacy and Design." In *The Social Life of Materials*, edited by Adam Drazin and Susanne Küchler, 101–18. London: Bloomsbury, 2015.

DuPlessis, Robert S. *The Material Atlantic: Clothing, Commerce, and Colonization in the Atlantic World, 1650–1800*. Cambridge: Cambridge University Press, 2016.

Eacott, Jonathan P. "Making an Imperial Compromise: The Calico Acts, the Atlantic Colonies, and the Structure of the British Empire." *William and Mary Quarterly*, 3rd ser., 69, no. 4 (October 2012): 731–62.

El Hamel, Chouki. *Black Morocco: A History of Slavery, Race, and Islam*. Cambridge: Cambridge University Press, 2013.

Fage, J. D. "Slavery and the Slave Trade in the Context of West African History." *Journal of African History* 10, no. 3 (1969): 393–404.

Fair, Laura. "Remaking Fashion in the Paris of the Indian Ocean: Dress, Performance, and the Cultural Construction of a Cosmopolitan Zanzibari Identity." In *Fashioning Africa: Power and the Politics of Dress*, edited by Jean Allman, 13–30. Bloomington: Indiana University Press, 2004.

Fall, Babacar. "Ly, Abdoulaye." In *Dictionary of African Biography*, edited by Henry Louis Gates Jr. and Emmanuel Akyeampong. Oxford: Oxford University Press, 2011.

Fields-Black, Edda L. *Deep Roots: Rice Farmers in West Africa and the African Diaspora*. Bloomington: Indiana University Press, 2008.

Fofana, Aboubakar. "Beyond the Blueness: The Light and Dark Shades of Aboubakar Fofana's Indigo." With Johanna Macnaughtan. *Tatter*, no. 3 (n.d.). https://tatter.org/issues/articles/beyond-the-blueness.

French, Howard. "Capitalism's Big Jolt." In *Born in Blackness: Africa and the Making of the Modern World*, 208–24. New York: Liveright Publishing, 2022.

Fromont, Cécile. "Foreign Cloth, Local Habits: Clothing, Regalia, and the Art of Conversion in the Early Modern Kingdom of Kongo." *Anais do Museu Paulista: História e Cultura Material* 25, no. 2 (2017): 11–31.

Fyle, C. Magbaily. *The Solima Yalunka Kingdom: Pre-colonial Politics, Economics and Society*. Freetown, Sierra Leone: Nyakon, 1979.

Gardi, Bernhard, ed. *Woven Beauty: The Art of West African Textiles*. Basel: Museum der Kulturen; Christoph Meiran Verlag, 2009. Exhibition catalog.

Gardi, Bernhard, and Michelle Gilbert. "*Arkilla, Kaasa,* and *Nsaa:* The Many Influences of Wool Textiles from the Niger Bend in West Africa." *Textile Museum Journal* 48 (2021): 24–53.

Gardi, Bernhard, and Museum der Kulturen Basel, eds. *Le boubou—c'est chic: Les boubous du Mali et d'autres pays de l'Afrique de l'Ouest*. Basel: Museum der Kulturen Basel; Christoph Meiran Verlag, 2000. Exhibition catalog.

Gerritsen, Anne, and Giorgio Riello, eds. *Writing Material Culture History*. London: Bloomsbury Academic Press, 2015.
Getz, Trevor R. *Cosmopolitan Africa, c.1700–1875*. New York: Oxford University Press, 2013.
Gikandi, Simon. *Slavery and the Culture of Taste*. Princeton, NJ: Princeton University Press, 2014.
Goerg, Odile. *Commerce et colonisation en Guinée, 1850–1913*. Paris: L'Harmattan, 1986.
Gomez, Michael A. *African Dominion: A New History of Empire in Early and Medieval West Africa*. Princeton, NJ: Princeton University Press, 2018.
———. *Pragmatism in the Age of Jihad: The Precolonial State of Bundu*. African Studies Series 75. Cambridge: Cambridge University Press, 1992.
Gottman, Felicia. "French-Asian Connections: The Compagnies des Indes, France's Eastern Trade, and New Directions in Historical Scholarship." *Historical Journal* 56, no. 2 (2013): 537–52.
Green, Toby. "Africa and the Price Revolution: Currency Imports and Socioeconomic Change in West and West-Central Africa during the Seventeenth Century." *Journal of African History* 57, no. 1 (2016): 1–24.
———. "Beyond an Imperial Atlantic: Trajectories of Africans from Upper Guinea and West-Central Africa in the Early Atlantic World." *Past and Present*, no. 230 (2016): 91–122.
———. *The Rise of the Trans-Atlantic Slave Trade in Western Africa, 1300–1589*. Cambridge: Cambridge University Press, 2011.
Green, Toby, and Neil Gower. *A Fistful of Shells: West Africa from the Rise of the Slave Trade to the Age of Revolution*. London: Penguin Random House, 2020.
Grosz-Ngaté, Maria. "Power and Knowledge: The Representation of the Mande World in the Works of Park, Caillié, Monteil, and Delafosse (Pouvoir et savoir: La représentation du monde mandé dans les oeuvres de Park, Caillié, Monteil et Delafosse)." *Cahiers d'Etudes Africaines* 28, no. 111/112 (1988): 485–511.
Gueye, Omar. "African History and Global History: Revisiting Paradigms." In *Global History, Globally: Research and Practice around the World*, edited by Sven Beckert and Dominic Sachsenmaier, 83–108. London: Bloomsbury Academic, 2018.
Hall, Bruce S. *A History of Race in Muslim West Africa, 1600–1960*. Cambridge: Cambridge University Press, 2011.
Hall, Gwendolyn Midlo. *Africans in Colonial Louisiana: The Development of Afro-Creole Culture in the Eighteenth Century*. Baton Rouge: Louisiana State University Press, 1992.
Ham, Debra Newman. "The Role of African American Women in the Founding of Liberia." In *Global Dimensions of the African Diaspora*, edited by Joseph E. Harris. Washington, DC: Howard University Press, 1993.
Hardy, Georges. *La mise en valeur du Sénégal de 1817 à 1854*. Paris: É. Larose, 1921.
Havik, Philip J. "Gendering the Black Atlantic: Women's Agency in Coastal Trade Settlements in the Guinea Bissau Region." In *Women in Port:*

*Gendering Communities, Economies, and Social Networks in Atlantic Port Cities, 1500–1800*, edited by Douglas Catterall and Jodi Campbell, 315–56. Boston: Brill, 2012.

———. *Silences and Soundbytes: The Gendered Dynamics of Trade and Brokerage in the Pre-colonial Guinea Bissau Region*. Münster: LIT Verlag, 2004.

Hendrickson, Hildi, ed. *Clothing and Difference: Embodied Identities in Colonial and Post-colonial Africa*. Durham, NC: Duke University Press, 1996.

Heywood, Linda M., and John K. Thornton. "Kongo and Dahomey, 1660–1815: African Political Leadership in the Era of the Slave Trade and Its Impact on the Formation of African Identity in Brazil." In *Soundings in Atlantic History: Latent Structures and Intellectual Currents, 1500–1830*, edited by Bernard Bailyn and Patricia L. Denault, 86–111. Cambridge, MA: Harvard University Press, 2009.

Hobsbawm, E. J., and T. O. Ranger. *The Invention of Tradition*. Cambridge: Cambridge University Press, 1983.

Hopkins, A. G. *An Economic History of West Africa*. London: Longman, 1973.

Hopkins, J. F. P., and Nehemia Levtzion. *Corpus of Early Arabic Sources for West African History*. Princeton, NJ: Markus Wiener, 2000.

Hunwick, John O. *Timbuktu and the Songhay Empire: Al-Sa'di's "Ta'rīkh al-sūdān" down to 1613 and Other Contemporary Documents*. Leiden: Brill, 1999.

Inikori, Joseph E. *Africans and the Industrial Revolution in England: A Study in International Trade and Economic Development*. Cambridge: Cambridge University Press, 2002.

———. "Slavery and the Revolution in Cotton Textile Production in England." *Social Science History* 13, no. 4 (1989): 343–79.

Jacquemin, Sylviane. *Objets des mers du sud: Histoire des collections océaniennes dans les musées et établissements parisiens, XVIIIème–XXème siècles, Mémoire de l'École du Louvre*. Paris: École du Louvre, 1991.

Jansen, Jan. "When Marrying a Muslim: The Social Code of Political Elites in the Western Sudan, c. 1600–c. 1850." *Journal of African History* 57, no. 1 (2016): 25–45.

Jobson, Richard. *The Golden Trade: or, A Discouery of the Riuer Gambra, and the Golden Trade of the Aethiopians: Also, the Commerce with a Great Blacke Merchant Called Buckor Sano and His Report of the Houses Couered with Gold and Other Strange Obseruations for the Good of Our Owne Countrey [...]*. London, 1623.

Johnson, Jessica Marie. "Tastemakers: Intimacy, Slavery, and Power in Senegambia." In *Wicked Flesh: Black Women, Intimacy, and Freedom in the Atlantic World*. Philadelphia: University of Pennsylvania Press, 2020.

Johnson, Marion. "Cloth as Money: The Cloth Strip Currencies of Africa." *Textile History* 11, no. 1 (1980): 193–202.

———. "Cloth Strips and History." *West African Journal of Archaeology* 7 (1977): 169–78.

———. "Technology, Competition and African Crafts." In *The Imperial Impact: Studies in the Economic History of Africa and India*, edited by Clive Dewey and A. G. Hopkins. London: Athlone Press, 1978.

Jones, Hilary. *The Métis of Senegal: Urban Life and Politics in French West Africa*. Bloomington: Indiana University Press, 2013.

Kaba, Lansiné. "Islam, Society and Politics in Pre-colonial Baté, Guinea." *Bulletin de l'Institut Fondamental d'Afrique Noire,* sèrie B: Sciences humaines, 35, no. 2 (1973): 323–44.

Klein, Martin A. "Defensive Strategies: Wasulu, Masina, and the Slave Trade." In *Fighting the Slave Trade: West African Strategies,* edited by Sylviane A. Diouf, 62–78. Athens: Ohio University Press; Oxford: James Currey, 2003.

———. "Slaves, Gum, and Peanuts: Adaptation to the End of the Slave Trade in Senegal, 1817–48." *William and Mary Quarterly,* 3rd ser., 66, no. 4 (October 1, 2009): 895–914.

Knörr, Jacqueline, and Christoph Kohl, eds. *The Upper Guinea Coast in Global Perspective.* Integration and Conflict Studies 12. New York: Berghahn, 2016.

Kobayashi, Kazuo. *Indian Cotton Textiles in West Africa: African Agency, Consumer Demand and the Making of the Global Economy, 1750–1850.* Cham: Palgrave Macmillan, 2019.

Krätli, Graziano, and Ghislaine Lydon, eds. *The Trans-Saharan Book Trade: Manuscript Culture, Arabic Literacy and Intellectual History in Muslim Africa.* Library of the Written Word 8. Leiden: Brill, 2011.

Kriger, Colleen E. "Black Cloth: Status and Identity in Islamic West Africa, 1500–1900." In *From Antiquity to the Nineteenth Century,* edited by Christopher Breward, Beverly Lemire, and Giorgio Riello, 445–71. Vol. 1 of *The Cambridge Global History of Fashion.* Cambridge: Cambridge University Press, 2023.

———. *Cloth in West African History.* African Archaeology Series. Lanham, MD: AltaMira Press, 2006.

———. "Guinea Cloth: Production and Consumption of Cotton Textiles before and during the Atlantic Slave Trade." In *The Spinning World: A Global History of Cotton Textiles, 1200–1850,* edited by Giorgio Riello, 105–26. New York: Oxford University Press, 2009.

———. "The Importance of Mande Textiles in the African Side of the Atlantic Trade, ca. 1680–1710." *Mande Studies* 11 (2009): 1–21.

———. *Making Money: Life, Death, and Early Modern Trade on Africa's Guinea Coast.* Athens: Ohio University Press, 2017.

———. "Mapping the History of Cotton Textile Production in Precolonial West Africa." *African Economic History* 33 (2005): 87–116.

———. "Robes of the Sokoto Caliphate." *African Arts* 21, no. 3 (May 1988): 52–57, 78–79, 85–86.

———. "Textile Production and Gender in the Sokoto Caliphate." *Journal of African History* 34 (1993): 361–401.

Labat, Jean-Baptiste. *Nouvelle relation de l'Afrique occidentale: Contenant une description exacte du Senegal & des païs situes entre de Cap-Blanc & la Riviere de Serrelionne, jusqu'à plus de 300. lieuës* [...]. Paris: G. Cavelier, 1728.

La Courbe, Michel Jajolet de, and Prosper Cultru. *Premier voyage du Sieur de La Courbe fait a la coste d'Afrique en 1685.* Paris: Édouard Champion; Émile Larose, 1913.

LaGamma, Alisa. "From the Rise of Songhay to the Fall of Segu." In *Sahel: Art and Empires on the Shores of the Sahara*, 219–49. New York: Metropolitan Museum of Art; New Haven, CT: Yale University Press, 2020. Exhibition catalog.

Laing, Alexander Gordon, and Edward Sabine. *Travels in the Timannee, Kooranko, and Soolima Countries, in Western Africa*. London: J. Murray, 1825.

Lamiral, Dominique Harcourt. *L'Affrique et le peuple affriquain, Considérés sous tous leurs rapports avec notre commerce & nos colonies* [...]. Paris: Dessenne, 1789.

Lemire, Beverly. *Global Trade and the Transformation of Consumer Cultures: The Material World Remade, c.1500–1820*. Cambridge: Cambridge University Press, 2018.

———. "Revising the Historical Narrative: India, Europe and the Cotton Trade, c. 1300–1800." In *The Spinning World: A Global History of Cotton Textiles, 1200–1850*, Pasold Studies in Textile History 16, edited by Giorgio Riello and Prasannan Parthasarathi, 205–26. Oxford: Oxford University Press, 2009.

Lemire, Beverly, and Giorgio Riello. *Dressing Global Bodies: The Political Power of Dress in World History*. London: Routledge, 2020.

Liberato, Carlos F. "Money, Cloth-Currency, Monopoly, and Slave Trade in the River of Guiné and the Cape Verde Islands, 1755–1777." In *Money in Africa*, edited by Catherine Eagleton, Harcourt Fuller, and John Perkins, 9–19. London: British Museum, 2009.

Linebaugh, Peter. *The London Hanged: Crime and Civil Society in the Eighteenth Century*. Cambridge: Cambridge University Press, 1993.

Lintingre, Pierre. *Voyages du sieur de Glicourt à la côte occidentale d'Afrique pendant les années 1778 et 1779*. Dakar: Afrique Documents, 1966.

Lo, Aissata Kane. *De la Signare à la Diriyanké sénégalaise: Trajectoires féminines et visions partagées*. Dakar: L'Harmattan Senegal, 2014.

Lovejoy, Paul E. *Jihād in West Africa during the Age of Revolutions*. Athens: Ohio University Press, 2016.

———, ed. *Slavery on the Frontiers of Islam*. Princeton, NJ: Markus Wiener, 2004.

Lowe, Lisa. *The Intimacies of Four Continents*. Durham, NC: Duke University Press, 2015.

Lowther, Kevin G. *The African American Odyssey of John Kizell: A South Carolina Slave Returns to Fight the Slave Trade in His African Homeland*. Columbia: University of South Carolina Press, 2012.

Lydon, Ghislaine. *On Trans-Saharan Trails: Islamic Law, Trade Networks, and Cross-Cultural Exchange in Nineteenth-Century Western Africa*. New York: Cambridge University Press, 2009.

———. "Writing Trans-Saharan History: Methods, Sources and Interpretations across the African Divide." *Journal of North African Studies* 10, no. 3/4 (2005): 293–324.

MacDonald, Kevin C. "'A Chacun son Bambara,' encore une fois: History, Archeology and Bambara Origins." In *Ethnic Ambiguity and the African Past: Materiality, History, and the Shaping of Cultural Identities*, edited by François G. Richard and Kevin C. MacDonald, 119–44. Walnut Creek, CA: Left Coast Press, 2015.

Madden, Richard Robert. *A Twelvemonth's Residence in the West Indies, during the Transition from Slavery to Apprenticeship; With Incidental Notice of the State of Society, Prospects, and Natural Resources of Jamaica and Other Islands.* London: J. Cochrane; A. J. Valpy, 1835.

Magnavita, Sonja. "The Oldest Textiles from the Sub-Saharan West Africa: Woolen Facts from Kissi, Burkina Faso." *Journal of African Archaeology* 6 (2008): 243–57.

Mark, Peter. "Constructing Identity: Sixteenth- and Seventeenth-Century Architecture in the Gambia-Geba Region and the Articulation of Luso-African Ethnicity." *History in Africa* 22 (1995): 307–27.

———. "'Portuguese' Architecture and Luso-African Identity in Senegambia and Guinea, 1730–1890." *History in Africa* 23 (1996): 179–96.

———. *"Portuguese" Style and Luso-African Identity: Precolonial Senegambia, Sixteenth–Nineteenth Centuries.* Bloomington: Indiana University Press, 2002.

Mark, Peter, and José da Silva Horta. "Two Early Seventeenth-Century Sephardic Communities on Senegal's Petite Côte." *History in Africa* 31 (2004): 231–56.

Marty, Paul. *Les chroniques de Oualata et de Nema (Soudan Français): Extrait de la Revue des Etudes Islamiques annee 1927.* Paris: Librairie Orientaliste Paul Geuthner, 1927.

McCaskie, T. C. *State and Society in Pre-colonial Asante.* Cambridge: Cambridge University Press, 1995.

McGregor, JoAnn, Heather Akou, and Nicola Stylianou, eds. *Creating African Fashion Histories: Politics, Museums, and Sartorial Practices.* Bloomington: Indiana University Press, 2022.

Miller, Joseph Calder. "Beyond Blacks, Bondage, and Blame: Why a Multi-centric World History Needs Africa." *Historically Speaking* 6, no. 2 (2004): 7–11.

———. *Way of Death: Merchant Capitalism and the Angolan Slave Trade, 1730–1830.* Madison: University of Wisconsin Press, 1988.

Mocadel, Frédéric. *1755 au Galam et à l'Île Bourbon: L'odyssée de Niama, "des portes de l'or aux plantations de café."* Sainte-Marie, Réunion: Azalées Éditions, 2006.

Mollien, Gaspard Théodore comte de. *Travels in the Interior of Africa, to the Sources of the Senegal and Gambia: Performed by Command of the French Government, in the Year 1818.* London: H. Colburn, 1820.

Monteil, Charles. *Le coton chez les noirs.* Publications du Comité d'études historiques et scientifiques de l'Afrique occidentale française, vol. 4. Paris: E. Larose, 1927.

Monteil, Charles Victor. *Les Bambara du Segou et du Kaarta: Étude historique, ethnographique et littéraire d'une peuplade du Soudan Français.* Paris: Larose, 1960.

Moore, Francis. *Travels into the Inland Parts of Africa: Containing a Description of the Several Nations for the Space of Six Hundred Miles up the River Gambia; Their Trade, Habits, Customs, Language, Manners, Religion and Government* [...]. London, 1738.

Moraes, Nize Izabel de. "Le commerce des tissus à la Petite Côte au XVIIe siècle (Sénégambie)." *Notes Africaines* 139 (1973): 71–75.

More, Hannah, and Henry W. Weston. *The Black Prince: A True Story; Being an Account of the Life and Death of Naimbanna, an African King's Son, Who Arrived in England in the Year 1791, and Set Sail on His Return in June 1793*. Philadelphia: B. & J. Johnson, 1800.

Mota, A. Teixeira da. "Un document nouveau pour l'histoire des Peuls au Sénégal pendant les XVème et XVIème siècles." *Boletim Cultural da Guiné Portuguesa*. Lisbon: Junta de Investigações do Ultramar, 1969.

Mouser, Bruce L. "African Academy—Clapham 1799–1806." *History of Education* 33, no. 1 (2004): 87–103.

———. *American Colony on the Rio Pongo: The War of 1812, the Slave Trade, and the Proposed Settlement of African Americans, 1810–1830*. Trenton, NJ: Africa World Press, 2013.

———. "The 1805 Forékariah Conference: A Case of Political Intrigue, Economic Advantage, Network Building." *History in Africa* 25 (1998): 219–62.

———. "Insurrection as Socioeconomic Change: Three Rebellions in Guinea/Sierra Leone in the Eighteenth Century." In *The Powerful Presence of the Past: Integration and Conflict along the Upper Guinea Coast*, edited by Jacqueline Knörr and Wilson Trajano Filho, 55–73. Leiden: Brill, 2010.

———. "Lightbourn Family of Farenya, Rio Pongo." *Mande Studies* 13 (2011): 21–90.

———. "Origins of the Church Missionary Society Accommodation to Imperial Policy: The Sierra Leone Quagmire and the Closing of the Susu Mission, 1804–17." *Journal of Religion in Africa* 39, no. 4 (2009): 375–402.

———. "Rebellion, Marronage and Jihād: Strategies of Resistance to Slavery on the Sierra Leone Coast, c. 1783–1796." *Journal of African History* 48, no. 1 (2007): 27–44.

———. "Théophilus Conneau: The Saga of a Tale." *History in Africa* 6 (1979): 97–107.

———. "'Walking Caravans' of Nineteenth Century Fuuta Jaloo, Western Africa." *Mande Studies* 12 (2010): 19–104.

Murray, S. S. "Medieval Cotton and Wheat Finds in the Middle Niger Delta (Mali)." In *Fields of Change: Progress in African Archaeobotany*, edited by René Cappers, 43–52. Groningen, the Netherlands: Groningen University Library, 2007.

Naylor, Paul, and Marion Wallace. "Author of His Own Fate? The Eighteenth-Century Writings of Ayuba Sulayman Diallo." *Journal of African History* 60, no. 3 (November 2019): 343–77.

N'Daou, Saidou Mohamed. "Dress, Social Change, and the (Re)Construction of Identity in Guinea (Nineteenth Century to Present)." *Mande Studies* 23 (2021): 85–115. https://doi.org/10.2979/mande.23.1.07.

Newson, Linda A. "The Slave-Trading Accounts of Manoel Batista Peres, 1613–1619: Double-Entry Bookkeeping in Cloth Money." *Accounting History* 18, no. 3 (2013): 343–65.

Newson, Linda A., and Susie Minchin. *From Capture to Sale: The Portuguese Slave Trade to Spanish South America in the Early Seventeenth Century*. Atlantic World 12. Leiden: Brill, 2007.

Nicklas, Charlotte, and Annebella Pollen, eds. *Dress History: New Directions in Theory and Practice*. London: Bloomsbury Academic, 2015.

Nwankwo, Ifeoma Kiddoe. *Black Cosmopolitanism: Racial Consciousness and Transnational Identity in the Nineteenth-Century Americas*. Philadelphia: University of Pennsylvania Press, 2014.
Ogot, Bethwell A., ed. *Africa from the Sixteenth to the Eighteenth Century*. Abridged ed. Vol. 5 of *General History of Africa*. Oxford: James Currey, 1999.
Osborn, Emily Lynn. *Our New Husbands Are Here: Households, Gender, and Politics in a West African State from the Slave Trade to Colonial Rule*. Athens: Ohio University Press, 2011.
Park, Mungo. *Travels in the Interior Districts of Africa*. Edited by Kate Ferguson Marsters. Durham, NC: Duke University Press, 2000.
Parthasarathi, Prasannan. *The Transition to a Colonial Economy: Weavers, Merchants and Kings in South India, 1720–1800*. Cambridge: Cambridge University Press, 2001.
Pasquier, Roger. "Un explorateur senegalais: Leopold Panet, 1819–1859." *African Historical Studies* 2, no. 2 (1969): 307–17.
Perinbam, Marie. "'Animist'/Islamized Imaging in the Western Sudan: The Fulbe's 'Bambara' in the Bamako Region, c. 1700–c. 1900." In *Peuls et Mandingues: Dialectique des constructions identitaires*, edited by Mirjam de Bruijn and Han Van Dijk, 101–28. Paris: Karthala; Leyden: Afrika-Studiecentrum, 1997.
———. "The Julas in Western Sudanese History: Long-Distance Traders and Developers of Resources." In *West African Culture Dynamics: Archaeological and Historical Perspectives*, edited by B. K. Swartz and Raymond E. Dumett, 455–76. The Hague: De Gruyter, 1980.
Person, Yves. "States and Peoples of Senegambia and Upper Guinea." *Africa in the Nineteenth Century until the 1880s*. Vol. 6 of *General History of Africa*, edited by J. F. Ade Ajayi, 636–61. Paris: Unesco; Oxford: Heinemann; Berkeley: University of California Press, 1989.
Pierre, Jemima. "Race across the Atlantic . . . and Back: Theorizing Africa and/in the Diaspora." In *The Predicament of Blackness: Postcolonial Ghana and the Politics of Race*, 185–216. Chicago: University of Chicago Press, 2012.
Porter, Eric. "Imagining Africa, Reimagining the World." In *The Problem of the Future World: W. E. B. Du Bois and the Race Concept at Midcentury*, 103–44. Durham, NC: Duke University Press, 2010.
Posel, Deborah, and Ilana Van Wyk. "Thinking with Veblen: Case Studies from Africa's Past and Present." In *Conspicuous Consumption in Africa*, edited by Deborah Posel and Ilana Van Wyk, 1–21. Johannesburg: Wits University Press, 2019.
Pratt, Mary Louise. *Imperial Eyes: Travel Writing and Transculturation*. London: Routledge, 2008.
Prestholdt, Jeremy. "Africa and the Global Lives of Things." In *The Oxford Handbook of the History of Consumption*, edited by Frank Trentmann, 85–108. Oxford: Oxford University Press, 2012.
———. *Domesticating the World: African Consumerism and the Genealogies of Globalization*. California World History Library 6. Berkeley: University of California Press, 2008.

Pruneau, Joseph. *Mémoire sur le commerce de la concession du Sénégal, 1752.* Edited by Charles Becker. Kaolack: CNRS, 1983.

Prussin, Labelle. "Judaic Threads in the West African Tapestry: No More Forever?" *Art Bulletin* 88, no. 2 (2006): 328–53.

Raffenel, Anne. *Nouveau voyage dans le pays des nègres, suivi d'études sur la colonie du Sénégal et de documents historiques, géographiques et scientifiques.* Paris: Napoléon Chaix et Cie, 1856.

———. *Voyage dans l'Afrique Occidentale: Comprenant l'exploration du Sénégal [. . .] Exécuté, en 1843 et 1844, par une commission composée de MM. Huard-Bessinières, Jamin, Raffenel, Peyre-Ferry et Pottin-Patterson.* Paris: A. Bertrand, 1846.

Reid, Richard. "Past and Presentism: The 'Precolonial' and the Foreshortening of African History." *Journal of African History* 52, no. 2 (2011): 135–55.

Renne, Elisha P. *Cloth That Does Not Die: The Meaning of Cloth in Bùnú Social Life.* Seattle: University of Washington Press, 1995.

Riello, Giorgio. *Cotton: The Fabric That Made the Modern World.* Cambridge: Cambridge University Press, 2013.

Roach, Mary Ellen, and Joanne Bubolz Eicher, eds. *Dress, Adornment, and the Social Order.* New York: Wiley, 1965.

Roberts, Richard L. "Guinée Cloth: Linked Transformations within France's Empire in the Nineteenth Century." *Cahiers d'Etudes Africaines* 32 (1992): 597–627.

———. *Two Worlds of Cotton: Colonialism and the Regional Economy in the French Soudan, 1800–1946.* Stanford, CA: Stanford University Press, 1996.

———. "West Africa and the Pondicherry Textile Industry." In *Cloth and Commerce: Textiles in Colonial India,* edited by Tirthankar Roy, 142–74. New Delhi: SAGE, 1996.

Robinson, Cedric J. *Black Marxism: The Making of the Black Radical Tradition.* Chapel Hill, NC: University of North Carolina Press, 2000.

Robinson, David. *The Holy War of Umar Tal: The Western Sudan in the Mid-nineteenth Century.* New York: Clarendon Press, an imprint of Oxford University Press, 1985.

———. "The Islamic Revolution of Futa Toro." *International Journal of African Historical Studies* 8, no. 2 (1975): 185–221.

Rovine, Victoria L. *African Fashion, Global Style: Histories, Innovations, and Ideas You Can Wear.* Bloomington: Indiana University Press, 2015.

Saint-Sauveur, Jacques Grasset de. *Encyclopédie des voyages: Contenant l'abrégé historique [. . .].* [Paris], 1796.

Sanneh, Lamin O. *Abolitionists Abroad: American Blacks and the Making of Modern West Africa.* Cambridge, MA: Harvard University Press, 1999.

Sarr, Assan. *Islam, Power, and Dependency in the Gambia River Basin: The Politics of Land Control, 1790–1940.* Rochester, NY: University of Rochester Press, 2016.

Sarr, Felwine, and Bénédicte Savoy. *Restituer le patrimoine africain.* [Paris?]: Philippe Rey / Seuil, 2019.

Saugnier, M., and François Bessire. *Relations de plusieurs voyages à la côte d'Afrique, à Maroc, au Sénégal, à Gorée, à Galam.* Saint-Étienne: L'Université de Saint-Étienne, 2005.

Schmidt, Annette, and Rogier Bedaux. "Oldest Archaeological Evidence of Weaving in West Africa." In Gardi, *Woven Beuaty*, 58–59.

Schwarz, Suzanne. *"A Just and Honourable Commerce": Abolitionist Experimentation in Sierra Leone in the Late Eighteenth and Early Nineteenth Centuries*. London: Hakluyt Society, 2014.

Searing, James F. "Islam, Slavery and Jihad in West Africa." *HIC3 History Compass* 4, no. 5 (2006): 761–79.

———. "The Seven Years' War in West Africa: The End of Company Rule and the Emergence of the *Habitants*." In *The Seven Years' War: Global Views*, edited by Mark H. Danley and Patrick J. Speelman, 263–91. Leiden: Brill, 2012.

———. *West African Slavery and Atlantic Commerce: The Senegal River Valley, 1700–1860*. Cambridge: Cambridge University Press, 1993.

Seck, Ibrahima. "The French Discovery of Senegal: Premises for a Policy of Selective Assimilation." In *Brokers of Change: Atlantic Commerce and Cultures in Precolonial Western Africa*, edited by Toby Green, 149–70. New York: Oxford University Press / British Academy, 2012.

Semley, Lorelle D. "Signares before Citizens." In *To Be Free and French: Citizenship in France's Atlantic Empire*, 69–112. Cambridge: Cambridge University Press, 2017.

———. *To Be Free and French: Citizenship in France's Atlantic Empire*. Cambridge: Cambridge University Press, 2017.

Silva Horta, José da. "Evidence for a Luso-African Identity in 'Portuguese' Accounts on 'Guinea of Cape Verde' (Sixteenth-Seventeenth Centuries)." *History in Africa* 27 (2000): 99–130.

Simmel, Georg. *Fashion*. N.p.: 1904.

Sow, Moussa. *L'État de Ségou et ses chefferies aux XVIIIe et XIXe siècles: Côté cour, côté jardin*. Études culturelles. Pessac, France: Presses universitaires de Bordeaux, 2021.

Spilsbury, F. B. *Account of a Voyage to the Western Coast of Africa: Performed by His Majesty's Sloop Favourite, in the Year 1805* [. . .]. London: R. Phillips, 1807.

Styles, John, and Amanda Vickery. *Gender, Taste, and Material Culture in Britain and North America, 1700–1830*. New Haven, CT: Yale Center for British Art, 2006.

Tamari, Tal. "Bambara." In *Oxford African American Studies Center*. Online ed. Oxford University Press. Article published online September 30, 2012. https://oxfordaasc.com/.

Tauxier, Louis. *Histoire des Bambara*. Paris: P. Geuthner, 1942.

Terrall, Mary. "African Indigo in the French Atlantic: Michel Adanson's Encounter with Senegal." *Isis* 114 (2023): https://doi.org/10.1086/723496.

Thiaw, Ibrahima. "Atlantic Impacts on Inland Senegambia: French Penetration and African Initiatives in Eighteenth- and Nineteenth-Century Gajaaga and Bundu (Upper Senegal River)." In *Power and Landscape in Atlantic West Africa: Archaeological Perspectives*, edited by J. Cameron Monroe and Akinwumi Ogundiran, 49–77. New York: Cambridge University Press, 2012.

Thilmans, G. "L'église oubliée de Saint-Louis du Sénégal." *Outre-Mers* 93, no. 350 (2006): 193–236.
Thornton, John K. *Africa and Africans in the Making of the Atlantic World, 1400–1800*. 2nd ed., expanded. New York: Cambridge University Press, 1998.
Triaud, Jean-Louis. "*Haut-Sénégal-Niger*, un modèle 'positiviste'? De la coutume à l'histoire: Maurice Delafosse et l'invention de l'histoire africaine." In *Maurice Delafosse: Entre orientalisme et ethnographie; L'itinéraire d'un africaniste, 1870–1926*. Paris: Maisonneuve et Larose, 1998.
Vogt, John. "Notes on the Portuguese Cloth Trade in West Africa, 1480–1540." *International Journal of African Historical Studies* 8, no. 4 (1975): 623–51.
Von Eschen, Penny M. *Race against Empire: Black Americans and Anticolonialism, 1937–1957*. Ithaca, NY: Cornell University Press, 1997.
Walker, Samuel Abraham. *Missions in Western Africa, among the Soosoos, Bulloms, Etc.: Being the First Undertaken by the Church Missionary Society for Africa and the East (1845)*. Dublin: W. Curry, Jun., 1845.
Wallerstein, Immanuel. *The Modern World-System I: Capitalist Agriculture and the Origins of the European World-Economy in the Sixteenth Century*. New York: Academic Press, 1974.
Ware, Rudolph T., III. "Slavery in Islamic Africa, 1400–1800." In vol. 3 of *The Cambridge World History of Slavery*, edited by David Eltis and Stanley L. Engerman, 47–80. Cambridge: Cambridge University Press, 2011.
———. *The Walking Qur'an: Islamic Education, Embodied Knowledge, and History in West Africa*. Chapel Hill: University of North Carolina Press, 2014.
Watt, James. *Journal of James Watt: Expedition to Timbo, Capital of the Fula Empire in 1794*. With an introduction and edited by Bruce L. Mouser. Madison: African Studies Program, University of Wisconsin–Madison, 1994.
Webb, James L. A., Jr. *Desert Frontier: Ecological and Economic Change along the Western Sahel, 1600–1850*. Madison: University of Wisconsin Press, 1995.
———. "The Trade in Gum Arabic: Prelude to French Conquest in Senegal." *Journal of African History* 26, no. 2/3 (1985): 149–68.
White, E. Frances. *Sierra Leone's Settler Women Traders: Women on the Afro-European Frontier*. Ann Arbor: University of Michigan Press, 1987.
Williams, Eric Eustace. *Capitalism and Slavery*. Temecula, CA: Textbook Publishers, 2003.
Wimmler, Jutta. *The Sun King's Atlantic: Drugs, Demons and Dyestuffs in the Atlantic World, 1640–1730*. The Atlantic World 33. Leiden: Brill, 2017.
Winterbottom, Thomas Masterman. *An Account of the Native Africans in the Neighbourhood of Sierra Leone: To Which Is Added, an Account of the Present State of Medicine among Them*. London: C. Whittingham, 1803.
Wright, Donald R. *Oral Traditions from the Gambia*. Papers in International Studies, Africa Series, no. 37/38. Athens: Ohio University Center for International Studies, Africa Program, 1979.

# Index

Page numbers in *italics* indicate figures.

Abdurahmane, 171
Accra, 16
African consumers, 15, 102, 111, 151; contingent agency of, 112; demand cloths from Pondicherry, 130; quality of dyed cloth and, 129–30; in Sahel, 92
African diaspora, 14, 183
African dyers, 124
African elites, 153, 157; in coastal Saint-Louis, 23; consumption and dress of, 158–70; cultural pluralism practiced by, 137
African farmers, 173
Africanists, 17
African Muslims, 141; communities, 9; cosmopolitanism, 195; European discourse, 156; high social standing, 106; intellectuals, 31; politics of dress, 141; traders, 5; traditions, 106. *See also* Muslim(s)
African pluralism, 3
African textiles and clothing, 6–13
*Africa Redeemed* (Couber), 159, *160*
Afro-Atlantic figure, 184
Afro-descendants, 172, 191, 197
Afzelius, Adam, 151
agency, 18
*ajami*, 28, 38
Al-Bakri, 2, 62
Albreda, 96
alderman's gown, *155*
al-Din. *See* Nasir al-Din
Alentejo textiles, 59
Algeria, 25
Alichandora (king of Trarza Moors), 35
al-Idrisi, 94
Alimana, Tunka, 90, 98–99; female pawn for, 98–99; of Makrana, 98; as political ruler, 90; protest by, 91
*almaami* (imam), 134
Almada, André, 66
al-Sa'di, Abd al-Rahman ibn. *See* Sa'di, Abd al-Rahman ibn al-
American merchants, 139, 172, 177
American Revolution, 145, 159
Amselle, Jean-Loup, 17
Amsterdam, 60
Anglo-African merchants, 189
Anglo-Protestants, 197
anti-blackness, 141
anticolonial figures, 197
anticolonialism, 141
anticolonial project, 16
antislavery, 141, 170; British naval vessels and, 172, 182; within Sierra Leone colony, 168; and Sierra Leone Company's aims, 159, 165
Arabization, cultural, 76
Arabo-Berber, 38; chief, 122; communities, 124; merchants, 104
Arabs, 43, 178; merchants and clerics in Walata, 43; pastoralist communities in Sahara, 38; travelers, 2, 19, 94
Arguin, 83
Arnaud, Robert, 48
artisanal industry, 94
*arunku*, 148
Asante, 52
Assinie, 189
Atlantic commerce, 34, 88, 196; economy of Sahel and, 55; expansion of, 55–56, 112; impact of, assessing, 75; renewed commercial ties to, 85
Atlanticist, 17

241

Atlas Mountains, 41
Awlil, 94
Azemmour, 58

Baba, Ahmad, 36, 37
*baftas*, 58
Baga, 23, 148; community, 174; dress in, 182–83
Bahamas, 110
*bajutapeaux*, 150
Bakel, 1, 5; as French military and commercial garrison fort, 1; Raffenel's procurement of packhorse and donkeys at, 24–25
Bakia, 190
Bakoro, 163
Bakri, Al-. *See* Al-Bakri
Balandougou, 167
Balmaure, 90
Baltimore, 186
Bamako, 27
Bamana, 127
Bamana Kaarta, 31, 55, 56; emergence of, 54; and exchange of goods, 59; warrior elite of, 96
Bamana Massasi of Kaarta, 100
Bamanan, 3, 24, 28–32, 48; caravan routes, 22; communities, 29–30; on De l'Isle's map, 36; early kingdoms, 31–32; farmers, 40, 43, 49, 50; fondness for beer, 40; local Arabic sources of, 22; polities of Kaarta and Segu, 31; royal lineage, 33; self-fashioning, 31; textile production and consumption, 41–42. *See also* Bambara
Bamanan Kaarta, 10, 32; Kulubali clan, 25; Nioro, 27; oral traditional account of, 20
Bamanankan language, 1, 36, 41
Bamanan language, 44
Bamanaya, 39, 42, 46; Bamanan self-fashioning via, 31; celebratory assertions of, 28; facets of, 46
Bambara, 31, 35, *35*, 36–38, *41*, 43, 44, *50*, 98. *See also* Bamanan
Bambara, Pemba, 98
Bambuk, 35, 92, 101, 103, 108; gold mines of, 37, 54, 68, 89, 96; landscape of, 89; mining region, 97, 104, 148; neighboring communities in, 103
Bance Island, 153, 159, 169
Bandiagara Escarpment, 2, 8, 40–41
Bangalan, 163, 174; conversion to Christianity, 190; storehouse, 185

Banjul, 146, 147; colonial officials at, 172–73
*bantan* cloths, 70
*barafulas*, 70, 72
Barbados, 172, 197
Barrakunda, 36
Barry, Boubacar, 3, 135
Bate, 147, 171–72, 179
Bathily: conflicts with Fulbe clerics, 89; lineage of Soninke, 95
Bazin, Jean, 17
beer, 40
Beledugu, 27
Bellay, Julien du, 75
Bello, Almaami Ahmed de, 186
Bely, Nhara, 5–6, 166–67, 190–93; commercial intermediary, role as, 166; conversion to Christianity, 193; cross-cultural diplomacy, 5; death, 196; marriage, 196; slave barracoon, 167; transregional commerce, 5
Benin, 70
Benna, 148, 157
Berber-Arab: aristocracies in Waalo, 88, 177; merchants, 71, 72
Berbers, 38, 43
Ber Caaka, 56, 80
*Bidan* (white), 19–20, 38
Bijagos Islands, 61
*bila*, 46
*Bilad-al-Sudan*, 19
Birama, Konde, 145, 172, 180
Bissau, 5, 23, 59, 166
black Loyalists, 142, 145
blackness, 19–21; internal Islamic discourse of, 19
blankets, 33
*bogolan* cloths, 41
"Bokari, the Kaartan guide," *175*
Boke, 183
Bondu, 180
*bonya*, 156
Borno, 37
Botte, Roger, 17
Boucard, Claude, 101
Bouët-Willaumez, Édouard, 189
Bowie, James, 153
Bozo, 36
*brak* (king), 56
Brakna Moors, 177
Braudel, Fernand, 7
Bray, Gabriel, 131, *131*
Brazzaville, 70
*bretagnes*, 150

Bright, Richard, 158
British merchants, 36, 139, 152, 163
British North America, enslavement in, 106
British Protestants, 168
Brooks, George, 10
Brown, Vincent, 52
Brue, André, 11, 60–61, 85
Brunton, Henry, 190
*bubu*, 169
Buffon, Comte de, 124
Bukooy, 137
Bullom Shore, 144, 168, 170
Bundu, 3, 98, 104, 149; Boulebane in, *105;* dyed-textiles production in, 92; male weavers in, 108; merchant women in, 101; women dyers in, 101, 108; women's labor in, 92
Bure, 178
Burton, Antoinette, 9
Buxton, Thomas Fowell, 187, 188
Byfield, Judith, 9

Cacheu, 5, 70, 72, 99; governor of, 82; Indian cotton cloth in, 60; Kriston community of, 81; and marriage to African women, 59; Pepel community of, 81
Caillié, René, 173, 177–83; arrival at Kankan, 180; arrival in Rio Nunez, 177; crossing of Fuuta Jallon, 179; departure from Cambaya, 178–79; Muslim, declaration of being, 178
Calaminna, 167
Cambaya, 178, 183
Cannaba, Fury, 142, 152–56
Canot, Théodore, 173, 183, 184–86
Capatches River, 157
Cape Verde, 57–60, 189; cloths, 122; enslaved people and labor, 59; mobile merchants and traders, 56; slave-produced cotton textiles, 58; trade of goods, 59
capitalism: European, 111; global (*see* global capitalism); racial, 21
*Capitalism and Slavery* (Williams), 15
*captifs de case*, 127
*captifs de traite*, 127
Caribbean, 96; colonial capitals, 15; Dominica, 144; French Caribbean, 68, 71; Guadeloupe, 186–87; Indian cottons, 102; indigo plantations, 68; Saint-Domingue, 94, 138; slave plantations, 71, 127, 144; slavery, 15; sugar plantations, 15

Cartagena, 70
Catholics, 116; French, 116; Portuguese, 58, 66; social order, 66
*ceddo* soldiers, 86, 136
Charleston, 5, 159, 165, 184
Charles X (king), 43
*chasselas*, 150
chinaware, 149
Church Missionary Society, 149, 184, 187; goals of, 165; members of, 187; Sierra Leone Company supported by, 145–46
Cisse, 147
civil rights movement, 15
Clarkson, Thomas, 124, 136
clerical communities, 65; of Diafunu, 33; in Kayor, 136
cloth as currency, 73–77
Code Noir, 90
coffeehouses (in London), 18
Cold War, 15, 17
color revolution, 72
Companhia de Cacheu, 82
Conakry, 147, 148
Congress of Vienna in 1815, 138
Conneau, Théophilus, 183
conspicuous consumption, 8
contact zone, 12
Conte, Kanfory Mansa, 166–67
Cooper, Thomas, 139–43, 197; and base in Dominghia, 142–43; and Freeport, 139, 163; refugees of, 140; sent to Rio Pongo, 163–64; settled near Rio Pongo, 145; and story of three women, 140–41
cosmopolitanism: African Muslim, 195; at Sahel, 115–25; at Saint-Louis, 119; of Senegal River valley, 137–38
"Costume of the Gambia," *147*
Couber, Kong, 159
*coudees*, 101
"Coussave or Blouse N'ajate Sego," *42*
cowries, 22
creolization, 19, 132
Cuba, 183, 184
cultural pluralism: heterogeneous population and, 82; practiced by African elites, 137; *signares* associated with, 118; tradition of tolerance for, 138
Curtin, Philip, 8, 17

Dafe, 147
Dagana, 187

Index ~ 243

Dahomey, 52
Dakar School, 16
*damiya*, 44
*dammel* (king), 136
*dampe*, 34, 44
Dangasago, 157
Dar-al-Islam, 108
Darwin, Charles, 7
David, Pierre, 103–4
Dawud, Askiya, 37
Deenanke, 51
Delafosse, Maurice, 14
de l'Isle, Guillaume, 44; "Map of French Africa or of Senegal," 35; maps of West Africa, *34, 35*, 35–36
Denyanke, 117, 135
*dhiata*, 131
Dia (city), 8
Diafunu, 36, 171; Soninke communities in, 33
"Diai Boukari," *135*
Diallo, Ayuba Sulayman, 104–8, 195, 197; ambushed by group of Maninka, 105; arrested by French, 92; back in Bundu, 106; letters, 104; literacy in Arabic, 105; personal biography, 104–5; portrait, 106, *107;* trade in humans and textiles, 92
Diarra, Ngolo, 33
Dike, Kenneth Onwuka, 16
Din, al-. *See* Nasir al-Din
Diop, Cheikh Anta, 16
Ditwaller, Cuiba Sione, 114
*djeliw*, 49
*djula* merchants, 65, 95, 96
*djula* traders, 57; cotton clothing, 62; networks of Mande, 70
*dloki*, 169, 181
*dloki ba*, 44, 47
Dogon, 47
Dominghia, 141
Domingue, Claude, 97
Donelha, André, 63, 73
Dor, Borom, 98
*Dress, Adornment, and the Social Order* (Eicher and Roach), 8
Du Bois, W. E. B., 15
Dumbuya, Dala Modu, 148, 149, 150, 167–70, 195
Dumbuya, Fendan, 23–24, 142, 148–51, 154, 157, 158, 167, 197
Duport, John Henry, 191, 193
Durand, Jean-Baptiste, 121

East Indian Company, 102
Edinburgh, 166, 190
Edo, 94
Egypt, 131; merchants traveling from, 21–22; Napoleon's army in, 177
Eicher, Joanne Bubolz, 8
embroidery, 43–44, 53, 78, 146
*Encyclopédie des voyages* (Saint-Sauveur), 12, 131
equestrian figure from Mali, *29*
Eurafrican habitants, 111, 186; cotton and indigo estates owned by, 187; on Gorée Island, 188; on Saint-Louis, 115, 186; and urban slavery and slave trading, 115
Eurafrican merchants, 139, 177; in Dominghia, 143; in Kakundy, 177; slave-owning class of, 146; women, 146
Eurafrican traders, 165
Euro-African elites, 23, 141
Euro-Americans, 19–20, 183
European Christians, 106, 118; politics of dress, 141; trafficking in captives, 98
European mercantile, 2, 8, 23, 115, 177
European merchants, 18
European textile industry, 71
European travelers, 21, 101, 111

*faama*, 33
Faf, 187
Fage, John, 17
Faidherbe, Louis, 193
Fal, Lat Sukaabe, 83
Faleme River, 35, 89, 90, 96, 103
Faleme River valley: eastern, map of, *93;* southern stretches of, French withdrawal from, 97
Fallanghia, 190
Fara Kumba, 77
Farenya, 163, 174, 190–91; missionaries preaching in, 192, 193; trading settlement on, 166
*fataro*, 62
female pawn, 90–91
"Femme Bambara," *41*
Fergusson, William, 187–88
Fernandes, Pero, 55
Fernandez, William Jellorum, 166, 190
Fez, 58
fonio, 40
Ford, David, 152
Forecaria, 147
Fort Saint Joseph, 90–91, 92, 93; French East India Company's construction,

244 — Index

96; population inside, seasonal growth of, 97–98; world inside, 98
Fouta, 44
*Fragment of Ancient Chronicles of Oualata*, 37
France: enslaved labor and American colonies, 75; gestures of diplomacy, 96–97; *indiennes*, 138; reliance on manufacturing at Pondicherry, 130; textile manufacturing, 109; trading concession at Saint-Louis, 103
Francis, Warwick, 169
Freeport, 139, 163
Freetown, 21, 140, 145, 147, 153, 192; British colony at, 144, 159, 186; British Protestants in, 168; colonial officials at, 172–73; cotton cultivation at, 173; Dala Modu moved to, 149; Dumbuya's trade with, 149–50; European commercial exchanges, 21; Nova Scotians in, 160; and refusal of slave trade, 174; settlers at, 24; trading groundnuts in, 189
French East India Company, 92; agents in Gajaaga, 96–97; construction of Fort Saint Joseph, 96; cotton cloth imported to Saint-Louis, 102; directors, 106–7; headquarters, 102; payment of extant *tunka*, 96; textiles transported to West Africa, 96
French Enlightenment, 91
French merchants, 57, 91; based on Cape Verde, 57; exporting and importing cloth, 111; La Courbe, 73, 77–81; new colonial state, 118; new generation, 138; trading groundnuts, 189; treaties with African headmen, 193; Valentin, 192
French Royal Academy of Science, 90
French Senegal Company, 121, 130
Fromont, Cécile, 12
Fula Coundingi, 157
Fulbe, 1, 48, 174, 182, 186, 193; civilizing discourse, 76; clerical revolution, 135–36; clerics, 89, 96, 140; cultural interplay with Manden, 70; marabouts, 100; Muslim clerics and merchants, 51, 92, 116; Muslims, 28, 33, 182; notables, 144–45; pastoralists, 33; soldiers at Fuuta Tooro, 129; weavers, 43, 44; women, 124
Fuuta Jallon Mountains, 2, 3, 35, 117, 137, 145, 148, 173, 192; armies from, 172; caravans of cloth across, 174–82; ceremonial customs from, 135; clerical state in, 140, 171, 181; cotton cultivation in, 34; Fugumba in, 172; Fulbe of, 196; highlands of, 35, 140; religious and political hegemony in, 165
Fuuta Tooro, 44, 98, 101, 116, 129, 138, 149, 175, 180; clerics, 117; Denyanke rule of, 51, 117; Tukulor of, 9; warrior aristocracies in, 77
Gajaaga, 43, 96, 100, 101, 116, 118, 130, 180; commercial expansion, 96–97; dyed-textiles production, 99; enslaved captives at, exchange of, 129; *Galam* referring to, 44; indigo and cotton production in, 92, 94; Lamiral voyage to, 127; Makrana, town in, 90; Moorish cavalry's raiding of, 90; mosque and place of assembly in, *95;* Pelays as ruler in, 97; Sahelian girls from, 90–91; Saugnier's journey to, 129; social and religious politics of, 92; Soninke *tunka* of, 98; textiles or clothing in, 95–96; as transregional entrepôt, 100–101; women laborers in, 89–94
*gala* (indigo), 41
Galam, 44
*gala yiri* (divine plant), 41
Gallinas, 186
Gambia, 2, 10
Gambia River, 36, 96, 104, 163, 180, 188
Gao, 37
Genevieve, Marie. *See* Niama
Geoffroy, Jean-Baptiste, 90
Geographic Society of Paris, 177
Georgia, 158
Ghana, 2, 33, 45, 116; Sahelian empires of, 14; savannas from, 10
Ghana Empire, 43
Gikandi, Simon, 18, 119
global capitalism: emergence of, 112–13; history of, 74; imperial, 2
Goa, 60
Gomes, Ambrosio, 82
Gomez, Emmanuel, 166, 190
Gomez, Michael, 11
Gorée Island, 12, 24, 59, 189; Cape Verdean cloths in, 122; coastal settlements of, 36; coastal trading posts from, 96; commerce conducted in, 96; European commercial exchanges, 21; French colony on, 126; French entrepreneurs' migration from, 177

*Index* ~ 245

gourds, 49
Grand Bassam, 189
Gray, John, 152, 153, 154
Green, Toby, 18–19, 22
Gregoire, Abbe Henri, 124
groundnuts, 186–90
*grumetes,* 190
Guadeloupe, 186–87
Guemou, 33, 40
"Guerrier de l'Isle de Saint Louis," *133*
Guibe, Boubou Birame, 114
Guinea, 2, 10, 139–70, 168; clerics of, 9; coastal, 140, 141, 142, 146, 172, *179;* coastal societies in, 152; commercial towns of, 146; Conakry as sprawling city in, 148; Mandinka populations in, 76; map of, *142, 179;* rivers flowing to coast of, 140; textiles arrived in, 144
Guinea, Upper, 12
Guinea-Bissau, 2, 11, 70; enslaved people purchased in, 62; tropical coastal region of, 11; women traders in, 10
*guinees,* 9, 25, 40, 96, 128, 129

Haitian Revolution, 150
Hall, Bruce, 19, 125
Hansberry, William Leo, 15
Harrison, Jellorum, 166, 190
Hassaniya Arabs, 1, 77, 117
Hassaniya language, 20
Hausa, 94
Havana, 165, 184
Havik, Philip, 10
Heard, Betsy, 167
Hejaz, 39–40
Herskovits, Melville, 16
*History of the Upper Guinea Coast, 1545–1800* (Rodney), 16–17
Holman, John, Jr., 163, 165–66
"Homme Bambara," *41*
Honfleur, 150
Hopkins, Antony, 8, 17
Hull, Thomas, 104

Ibadan School, 16
Idrisi, al-. *See* al-Idrisi
Iles de Los, 148, 149; European traders, 150
imam, 104, 134, 135, 169, 170, 172
imperialism, 14; free trade, 21
India, 21; *bafta* cottons, 102; chintz and muslin cotton, 121; indigo-dyed cotton cloth, 117; indigo-dyed *guinee* cloths, 150; weavers, 96

Indian cottons, 130; French ban on, 72, 102; imitation, 102; importance of, 103; popularity of, 72; value of, 22; by West African weavers and dyers, 129
Indian Ocean, 21, 96, 111, 167; commerce, 7, 22, 115; demands for labor, 109; Horn of Africa, 24; Isle de Bourbon, 103; perimeters, 23, 64, 83, 167; *pieza de India,* 74–75; ports, 36, 92, 167; trade networks, 60, 80
*indiennage* industry, 102
*indiennes,* 138
indigo: cultivation in western Sahel, 94; production in Gajaaga, 92; skilled dyers, 100
indigo cloths, 71; in Gajaaga, 94; regional demand for, 92; women laborers' production of, 92
indigo cottons, 23, *42,* 101–3; African, 101; and cloth economy of Sahel, 93–101; garment, *71;* Indian, 25, 72, 102; *kusaaba,* 31; production of, 91
indigo-dyed cottons: African-made cloths, 11; *baftas,* 58; *barafulas,* 70; cloths from India, 71, 72, 73; demand, 72; *guinees,* 9, 40, 96; *panos pretos,* 58; *salampores,* 96
indigo dyeing industry: at Abeokuta, 9; active, 101
*Indigofera tinctoria,* 100
indigo *guinees,* 128, 129–30, 195
indigo textiles, 28, 73, 92
Industrial Revolution (Britain), 15
Inikori, Joseph, 8; enslaved African laborers, 17
intercropping, 48–51
*Isatis tinctoria,* 94
Islam, 36–40, 156; believers vs. nonbelievers, 76; conversion, 37; discourse of race and blackness, 19; hegemonic status, 38, 39; history in Sahel, 19, 50; influence, 138; Suwarian Islam, 171. *See also* Muslim(s)
Islamic reform: during Atlantic revolutions, 134–37; and enslavement of Muslims, 111; movement, 96; political dynamics of, 111; Quranic schools during, 101; in Senegal River valley, 117; and sociopolitical alliances, 96; in western Sahel, 117
Isle de Bourbon (Réunion), 36, 90, 103

Jacques, Tell Birama, 114
Jallonke, 33
Jamaica, 52, 179, 197

Jamaican Maroons, 165
*janjon*, 49
Jara, Pierre, 97
Java, 186
Jay, Lamine, 106
Jegi, Samba Gelaajo, 105
Jenne, 29, 36, 37, 129; Bamanan fighters attack, 49–50; market centers at, 180; Quranic school at, 46
Jerome, Catin, 90, 91, 197; return to Saint-Louis, 98
*jinnamagha*, 49
*jinnamuso*, 49
Joao III (Portuguese king), 54
Jobson, Richard, 65
John, Mongo, 184, 185, 192
Johnson, Marion, 8, 17
*joussab*, 44
*jula*, 46

Kaarta, 22–42; Bamana Massasi of, 100; Bamanan polity of, 4–5, 31; cloth in, 51–53; and conflict with Segu, 46; cotton and weaving in, 52; emergence of, 33; finding, 33–42; Guemou as capital of, 40; historical roots of, 27; location of, 5; military force of, 25; origin story of, 22, 27–28; rise of, 38; sources related to, 25; traditional oral sources for, 38–39, 45; traffic in, 43
Kaarta, Bamanan, 10
*kaasa*, 33–34
Kaba, Maramagbe, 171
Kabine, Alfa, 180
"kaffirs," 174
Kagoro, 36
Kajoor: warrior aristocracies in, 77; women in, 79, 80
Kajoor-Bawol state, 83
Kakundy, 174, 177, 183
Kalabari Ijo, 8
Kamaranka, 152
Kan, Abdul Qadir, 51, 117, 134–37, 145; enslavement of Muslims, 134; French and habitant vessels blocked, 117; social agenda, 134; Torodbe reform movement, 117–18; trade with Saint-Louis, 134; Tukulor state, 117
Kan, Almaami, 136
Kankan, *142*, 147, 171–74, 177, 180–82; Caillié's arrival at, 180; cotton cultivation in, 34; Maninka-Mori of, 9; Tabaski procession at, 181, 195

Kano, 37
Kanu, Mori, 165
Kassang, 59
Katty, Mathia, 193
Kayor, 3; and attempt to boycott French trade, 136; *dammel* as ruler of, 136; Quranic schools in, 134
Kerefa, Mungo, 139, 164
Kerefe River, 186
Khasso, 98, 103
Khaybar, 39–40
Kissi, 148, 174
Kizell, John, 159
Kobayashi, Kazuo, 18
Koilel, 187
Koita, Soro Silamakan, 26–28, 39
Kokki, 136
Koli Tengela, 54; diplomacy with Mamadou II, 55; Fulbe followers, 116–17
Kolokani, 27
Kondeah, 157
Kong, 180
*koso wolani*, 44
Koulikoro, 40
Kouyate, Djeli Mamary, 10, 11, 22, 26–28, 38; Kaarta origin story, 27–28; Maraka women, account of, 39; narrative of Sonsan Kulubali, 53; oral account of early Kaarta, 32; oral tradition, 31, 48, 53
Kriger, Colleen, 8, 9
Kriol, 59
Kriolu language, 19, 88
Kugha, 94
Kulubali, Bakari, 46
Kulubali, BaSana, 45, 46
Kulubali, Dekoro, 46–48, 52
Kulubali, Fulakoro, 45, 46
Kulubali, Mamari Biton, 38, 45–47
Kulubali, Sonsan, 26, 27, 32, 33, 48; character of, 48; cultural dexterity of, 49; Kouyate's narrative of, 40, 53; lineage descendants of, 46; Maraka and, 50; Maraka jinn's advice to, 49; oral tradition of, 39, 53; revolt led by, 51; rise of, 28; Sonsanna named after, 38
Kumbi Saleh, 43
Kuranko, 151
*kusaaba*, 6, 42–45, 181; in Maninka, 42; preserved in Paris museum, 22–23, 31

Labe, 177; clerics at, 182
*La Bonne Amitié* (vessel), 150

Index 247

*La Compagnie du Sénégal* (Ly), 16
La Courbe, Michel Jajolet de, 73, 77–81; Leydy, account of, 73; Maram Njaay, account of, 77–80; meeting with royal lineage at Waalo, 77; women's role in cloth production and trading, 56
Laing, Gordon, 157, 175, 178, 196
Lake Debo, 33
*La Méduse*, 187
Lamfia, 178
Lamiral, Dominique, 118–25, 127, 137
*lançados*, 59
Landuma, 174, 182
La Poupiere, 90, 98
*lappato bi*, 111, 125
*laptots*, 23, 43, 111, 126–29
Laye, Kaba, 171
Leacock, James, 191–93
Leclerc, Georges-Louis, 124
legitimate trade, 174–82
Les Cayes, 150
Liberia, 186
*libre* status, 97
Lightburn, Louis Styles, 5, 166, 196
Lima, 70
*limeneas*, 150
Limhajib Berbers, 43
Lisboa, Diogo Rodrigues de, 60
Liverpool, 165, 167
*livres*, 96
*lomanca*, 43
*lomasa*, 44, 169
London: black Loyalists in, 145; migrants to Sierra Leone from, 158–59
Louis XIV, 35
Lowe, Lisa, 14
Ludlam, Thomas, 168–70
Luso-Africans: architectural styles, 63; merchants, 57, 66; partners, 60; *tangama* merchants, 66; traders, 5, 70
Ly, Abdoulaye, 16
Lydon, Ghislaine, 20

Maacina, 40, 116; Fulbe Muslims from, in-migration of, 175; *kaasa* produced in, 33–34; textile weaving practices brought from, 33–34
Macaulay, Zachary, 144, 152
Maghreb, 131
Mahdi, 151, 156
Mahdist reforms, 151–56
*maître de langue*, 24
maize, 49, 99

*majus*, 37
Makrana, 90
Maldives, 21
Maliguia, 151
Mali or Mali Empire, 14; borders of, 4; breakup of, 22; Dogon region of, 8; equestrian figure from, *29;* hegemony of, 33; influence of, 54–55; Mamadou II and, 54; Middle Niger valley during, 28–29; rulers of, 54; Tambaoura Escarpment in, 104; terra-cotta sculptures from, 28–30, *29;* western, 2
Mamadou II: diplomacy with Koli Tengela, 55; messages to Joao III, 54
Mambee, 157
Mande blacksmiths, 54, 60
Mande language, 167
Manden: cultural interplay with Fulbe, 70; culture, 55; language, 54–55, 70; *pagnes*, 101
"Manding Man," *112*
Mandingo clothes, 151
Mandinka merchants, 189
*ma ngalaba yiri* (the Creator), 41
*mangue*, 183
Maninka, 172, 193; of Bambuk, 103; clerics of coastal Guinea, 9; Diallo ambushed by, 105; *kusaaba* as name of robe in, 42; *silatigui* in, 174; slaveholders, 157
Maninka-Mori, 172; elites, 180; Kankan, 9; migrants, 182
*mansa*, 54
"Man with Walking Stick," *132*
marabouts, 45–46, 63, 77, 86, 97, 100, 119–21, *120*, 180
Maraka, 28, 34, 48–51; chief of, 39; jinn, 49; women, 39
Maray, 158
Marka-Dafin, 47
maroons, 141, 157, 198
Marx, Karl, 7
Massasi, 46
Matanzas, 165, 184
material culture, 13
Maurel and Prom Company, 24
Mauritania, 35; Arguin in, 83; borders of, 4; coasts of, 83, 94; contemporary, 35; Quranic schools in, 134; salt deposit in, 94
Mauritius (Isle de France), 90
Maxwell, Charles, 137
Mayer, Brantz, 186
*mboube*, 131

Mecca, 40
Medina, 40
Mediterranean North Africa, 51
Meillassoux, Claude, 17
Middle Niger valley, 28
millet, 40, 99
Milo River, 33, 171
Minianka, 36
Mississippi, 110
Moctar, Ahmet, 129
Modu, Dala, 167–70
Mollien, Gaspard, 180
Monmouth Street, 162
Monteil, Charles, 14
Moore, Francis, 83
Moorish Spain, 2
Moors, 40, 79
Mopti, 29
Morocco, 41, 121; indigo trafficked to markets in, 41; New Christian emigrants from, 58
Musée du Quai Branly, 42
Muslim(s), 37–38, 100, 126, 134, 156; in Bamanan-led Kaarta, 36; civilizing discourse of, 76; cosmopolitans, 142–51; discursive tradition of, 31; enslavement of, 111, 134; marabouts, 121; merchants, 117, 141, 157, 174; notables, 141, 142–51; political elites, 100; slavery and abolition, 117–18; societies, 9; Soninke, 171. *See also* Islam

*nabaya,* 180
Naimbanna, John, 153
Nalu, 35; community, 174; non-Muslim, 182
Nantes, 102; center of *indiennage* industry, 102; textile manufacturers, 102, 130
Napoleonic Wars, 118
Nasir al-Din: death of, 72, 77; Islamic reform movement led by, 96; raids on villagers criticized by, 77
Naval Museum, 43, 44
Ndar. *See* Saint-Louis
Ndumbe, Matar, 136
*neganepeaux,* 150
"Negres de Bondu," 109
Negro cloth, 106
"Negro King in Monmouth Street Clothes with His Wives and Children, A," 163
Neteko, 104; Bundu merchants traveled to, 104; French fort at, 97
New Orleans, 36

Newport, 110
New Spain, 70
*ngoni* lute, 27, 73
*nhara,* 166
Niama, 89–90, 96, 108; captured during fratricidal warfare, 90; enslaved to East India Company, 90
*nicanies,* 150
Niger delta, 3, 8; textiles exchanged for palm oil in, 16
Nigeria, 94; garments and textiles from, 9; Ibadan in, 16; textiles and dress in, 8
Niger River, 30, 33, 95, 129, 171, 175; Segu on, 44
Nioro, 27, 33, 36
Njaay, Maram, 56, 77–80, 87, 197–98
Nova Scotia, 159, 197; black Loyalists in, 145; British vessels to, 159
Nyouman, Massa, 98

Ormond, John, Jr., 163, 173, 183–86, 190; death, 186; language skills, 184; local commercial protocol, knowledge of, 184; public-facing role, 184–85
Ormond, Mongo John, 197
Oualata, 43
*ourunde,* 179

*pagnes,* 101, 122
*pagnes de Maures* (Moorish cloth), 79–80
*Pallas* (ship), 131
Panet, Leopold, 24
*panos,* 62, 70
*panos de obra,* 58–59
*panos de terra,* 58
*panos pretos,* 58
Paris, 44, 138; museum vault in, 45
Park, Mungo, 40, 136
Patungwa, 152
pawn, 90, 91
*peça da India,* 74
Peddie, John, 181
Pelays, Jacques, 97, 103, 104, 107
Perez, Manuel Bautista, 60, 72
Peters, Frank, 159
piazzas, 183, 185
Pierre, Jemima, 17
*pierres a fusil,* 150
*pieza de India,* 23, 73–77
*pileuses,* 137
plantation slavery, 14, 18; in the Americas, 18; scholarship on, 19; in Sokoto Caliphate, 19

*Index* 〜 249

Pondicherry, 96; connections between colonial outposts in, 8–9; dyed indigo cottons woven at, 102; French reliance on manufacturing at, 130; *guinees,* 9
Popoco, 178
Port Loko, 169
Portudal, 59
Portugal: Christian emigrants, 58; Pero Fernandes sent to Mali, 55; relationship with Mali, 54–55; rulers, 54
Portuguese Catholics, 58, 66
Pratt, Mary Louise, 12
"precolonial" periods, 13–14
"Pretre sacrificateur," *132*
"Products of Industry," 43
proslavery advocates, 187
Protestants, 168, 197

Quran, 105, 134, 177
Quranic schools, 9, 43, 100–101, 134, 136, 179

race: Euro-American Atlantic discourse, 20–21; internal Islamic discourse, 19
Raffenel, Anne, 1, 2, 24, 40, 47, 48; cowries and imported metals, account of, 22; mission to cross Sahel, 25; travel account, 15
Revolutionary War, 159
Richardson, David, 17
Richard Tol, 187
*riche etoffe* (fine cloth), 47
Rio Nunez, 59, 181, 182–86, 193; African residents around, 182; Atlantic coastal outlets of, 177; coastal geography of, 143; coastal towns on, 174; Guinea coast at, 5, 140, 173; selling cloth around, 180
Rio Pongo, 5, 21, 59, 139, 166, 172, 174, 182–86, 193; Atlantic coastal outlets of, 177; British missionary expansion in, 193; commerce in, 164; Cooper's correspondence from, 165; Nalu on, 35; strangers and residents of, 164; trading settlements along, 183; West Indian Mission to, 191–92, 193
*Rise of the Trans-Atlantic Slave Trade in Western Africa, 1300–1589, The* (Green), 18–19
River Seine, 42
Roach, Mary Ellen, 8
Robaina, 153, 174
Roberts, Richard, 8–9
Robinson, Cedric, 21
Rodney, Walter, 16, 17

Rodrigues de Lisboa, Diogo, 104, 108
Rouen, 102, 130; cloth from, dye quality of, 103; "Siamoise" cloths from, 150
Royal African Company, 104, 108
Royal African Corps, 187
Royal Navy, 177
Rufisque, 59
Ryan, Jack, 152

Sa'di, Abd al-Rahman ibn al-, 36; *Tarikh al-Sudan,* 37
Sadu, Almaami, 140, 145
Safi, 58
Saghanughu, Muhammad Kaba, 179
Sahara, 19, 41, 111; caravans, 1, 115; clay pipes for smoke, 78; currency, 51; Moors, 40, 79; traditional commercial ties, 51; trans-Saharan commerce, 43, 45, 54, 137, 148
Sahel, the, 2, 14, 18; Bamanan states of, 3, 34; "blackness" in, 19; clay pipes for smoke in, 78; commodity exchanges from, 198; cosmopolitanism in, 115–25; and cotton cloths from India, 21; dynamics in, 108–9; in early eighteenth century, 89–109; French and British commerce in, 91; golden age of, 15; historians of Islam in, 19; indigo cotton cloth economy of, 93–101; indigo cultivation in, 94, 99–100; inland markets of, 11; Islamic histories of, 108; Islamic reform in, 117; map of, *31;* political and economic instability in, 89, 92; precarity in, 89–91; race and blackness in, 19; reddish scrublands of, 95; western, 94; women's labor in, 93–101
Saint-Domingue: enslaved plantation laborers on, 94; as French overseas colony, 36; "indigoterie" (indigo works) in, 71; after Napoleon's defeat, 138
Saint-Louis, 1, 12, 36, 110–38, 147; Cape Verdean cloths in, 122; clothing of merchant women at, 5; as coastal trading post, 96; colonial officials at, 172–73; cosmopolitanisms of, 119, 137–38; cotton cultivation at, 173; cultural interaction in, 18; culture influenced by *laptots,* 111; Eurafrican Catholic society of, 113; Euro-Christian commercial center at, 134; European commercial exchanges at, 21; French colonial administrators at, 186; French trading concession at, 103; habitants and

textiles in, 115–25; marabouts in, *120;* politics of dress in, 110–38; seasonal traders in, 187; *signares* in, 10, 118–23, *120, 123;* taste for fashion in, 132; women's labor in, 98–99
Saint Paul's Cathedral, 153
Saint-Sauveur, Jacques Grasset de, 12, 131–32
*salampores,* 96
Salau, Mohammed Bashir, 19
Saloum, 186
Sande Society, 192
Sangare, Alou, 49
Sangare, Duba, 49–51, 53
Sanghe, 25
Sankaran, 172, 181
Sano, Buckor, 65
sartorial hybridity, 142, 151–58
*satigi* (governor), 63
Saugnier, M., 128, 129, 130
savannas, 10, 49; caravans of cloth across, 174–82; eastern, 147
Schmaltz, Julien, 186–87
Scipio, Charles, 128–31
Sea Island cotton, 187
Segu, 10, 30, 43, 47–48, 180; army from, 38; Bamanan polity of, 31; and conflict with Kaarta, 46; emergence of, 33; origins of, 22; piling of adorned bodies at, 52; traditional oral sources for, 38–39, 45; traffic in, 43
Senegal, 137; borders, 4; Dakar, 16; dress regimes, 5; French colonial administrators, 186; French entrepreneurs' migration, 177; Gajaaga, 5; gold and captive laborers, 92; Saint-Louis, 5; Saloum, 186
Senegal Company, 85; André Brue, 60; Jean-Baptiste Durand, 121; Julien du Bellay, 75; 1786 memo, 130
Senegal River valley, 24, 54, 96, 109, 111, 175, 187; cosmopolitanisms in, 137–38; cotton and indigo cultivation in, 94; floodplains of, 94, 95; Islamic reform in, 117; land-resource conflicts, 20; map of, *114;* map of eastern, *93;* sailors as sellers and consumers along, 125–33; slave trading along, 111; Soninke-led polities of, 3; stratified ethnic groups along, 127; traffic in, 43
Senegambia, 12, 83, 188; cloth currencies in, 62; coastal and riverine villages in, 59–60; coast of, 58, 147; European capitalism in, 111; French commercial presence in, 189; indigo *guinees* imported to, 129–30; low-wage laborers in, 110–11; Mandinka populations in, 76; market centers in, 57; market towns in, 56
*senhora,* 166
Senufo, 36
Sephardic Jewish refugees, 58
Serakhule, 129
Serer, 193
settler colonialism, 14
Seven Years' War, 72
Sherbro Island, 159
Siamoise cloths, 150
Sierra Leone, 2, 3, 17, 54, 59, 69, 81, 96, 139, 168, 174, 186, 189; antislavery within, 168; coastal, 18, 59–60, 142, 172; Forecaria in, 147; map of, *144,* 157; and migrants from London, 158–59; Nova Scotian settlers at, 160; textiles and dress in, 151
Sierra Leone Company, 166, 167; antislavery aims of, 159, 165; Church Missionary Society supported by, 145–46; Cooper sent to Rio Pongo by, 163–64; governor of, 167–68; independent partners of, 149; land rented to, 139; "legitimate" commodities and, 165; officials of, 146; and trading factory on Rio Pongo, 165
Sierra Leone Cooperative Society, 159
*signares,* 18, 115; cultural fluidity of, 137; enslaved labor of, 119; Muslim marabouts' relationship with, 121; religious and cultural pluralism of, 118; in Saint-Louis, 10, 118–23, *120, 123*
*silatigui,* 174
Silla, 94
Simmel, Georg, 7
slave trading, 21, 55, 91–92, 110–19, 143, 153–54, 163, 186–87, 192; in Bambuk, 96; ban on, 24, 134, 139, 166, 167, 182; Bely and, 196; British abolition of, 182; Canot and, 186; Congress of Vienna in 1815 and, 138; early expansion of, 30; and Fulbe followers of Koli Tengela, 116–17; and *History of the Upper Guinea Coast, 1545–1800,* 16–17; Lightburns and, 166; Ludlam and, 168; and missionary agenda of Coopery, 164–65; Modu and, 168, 170; political economy and, 46, 56, 140; transatlantic, 17, 20–21, 102, 146, 150, 182, 185, 193, 194–97

Index ~ 251

Sloane, Hans, 105–6
sofa, 188
Sokoto Caliphate, 117; nineteenth-century cloth industry in, 8; plantation slavery in, 19
Soliman, Francois, 97
Solimana, 149, 157, 181, 196; residents visiting Timbo, 175–77
Somono, 36
Songhay, 14
Songhay Empire, 14, 37, 54
Soninke, 1, 36, 43, 51, 127, 171; Bathily lineage, 95; city of Dia, 40; civilizing discourse, 76; clerics, 171; Diafunu, 33; elites, 90, 92, 95; *lomanca*, 43; marabouts, 97; settlers in Bate, 172; *tunka*, 100; weavers, 43, 44
Soninke-lineage elites, 92
Sonsanna, 38, 45, 46, 51
"Soolima Women Dancers," 176
sorghum, 99
*soro*, 51
Soumah, 147
South Carolina, 159, 163, 166, 184
Sow, Moussa, 28
Spencer, Herbert, 7
Spilsbury, Francis, 160, 161
spinners, 99
state making, 42–48
Stowe, Harriet Beecher, 186
strip cloths: loom-patterned, 34; white cotton, 74; woven, 122
Sudan (black), 20, 38
Sufi, Qadirriyya, 179
Sunjata Keita, 11
Susu, 9, 23, 149, 168, 170, 174, 182, 185, 193; lineage head, 148; masculinity, 168; slaveholders, 157–58
Susu language, 183, 184, 191
"Susu Women / Femmes Soussous," 191
Suware, al-Hajj Salim, 171
Suwarian Islam, 171
*Swallow* (vessel), 113; captured in 1776, 116; sailors, 110, 115
Switzerland, 150
Sy, Malik, 100–101, 104

Takrur, 94
*tama*, 51
Tambaakundaa, 130
Tambaoura Escarpment, 104
*tangomas/tungumas*, 66
*Tarikh al-Sudan* (al-Sa'di), 37

*tata*, 95
Tauxier, Louis, 14, 47
*tefe*, 95
"Temminee Wives, Sierra Leone, 1805," 162
Temne: chief, 149, 159; noble, 161, 162; women, attire of, 161
Temne women, 161, 162
Tengela, Koli, 116–17
Terray, Emmanuel, 17
*Theory of the Leisure Class, The* (Veblen), 7–8
Theresa, Maria, 138
Timbo, 140, 141, 145, 157, 173–74, 177, 180; Canot's diplomatic visit to, 186; clerics at, 174, 182; infrastructure of, 145; Solimana residents visiting, 175–77; wealth and authority in, 145
Timbuktu, 36, 129, 177, 178; Moroccan invasion, 37
Tinkisso River, 179
*toiles*, 90
*toiles baftas*, 102
*toiles noires*, 70
Toke Keren, 164
Tom, King, 149
*ton mansa*, 46
Torodbe movement, 104, 117–18, 134, 136
Toron, 172
Toure, Daouda, 147
Town of Runaway Slaves, 157
Trab al-Bidan (Land of the Whites), 20
*Trade and Politics in the Niger Delta, 1830–1885* (Dike), 16
transatlantic slave trade / trading, 102, 146, 150, 182, 185, 193, 194–97; Africa, impact on, 17; European-language documents, 20–21; historical debates, 17
trans-Saharan commerce, 137, 148; Ghana Empire, 43; Mamari Biton Kulubali, 45; trade in gold, 54
Trarza Moors, 187
Tripoli, 178
Tuabo, 96
Tukulor of Fuuta Tooro, 9
*tungumas*, 59
Tunka Alimana of Makrana, 98
Tuwat, 37

Umar Tal, al-Hadj, 24, 193
*Uncle Tom's Cabin* (Stowe), 186
"Uniformes des Corps des Laptots de Goree," 126

Upper Guinea, 12
urban slavery, 115

Valentin, Rene, 192
Vaz, Gaspar, 66, 67, 73, 82, 87
Vaz, Na Bibiana, 81, 99, 197
Veblen, Thorstein, 7–8
Vietnam, 25
Virginia, 159, 163

Waalo, 56, 187; goldsmiths of, 78; La Courbe's visit to, 78; local warrior aristocracies in, 77; Muslim migrants' villages in, 126; women in, 77–81
Walata merchants, 37–38, 43
Walker, Tamara, 12
Walker, Tom, 152
Walla, 152
Walo, Madoune, 114
Wanqara, 94
Ware, Rudolph, 9, 134
War of the Marabouts, 85
Wasulu, 23, 145, 172, 180
Watt, James, 144–45, 152, 153, 154
weaving, 8, 28, 33, 59, 78; Bamanan artisans and, 41; on Cape Verde, 58; cotton, 30, 62; in Kaarta, 52; in Kouyate's oral tradition, 22; physical evidence of, 2
Webb, James, 19
western Africa, 3–5; "creole" society in, 19; Eurafrican women in, 18; free trade in, 81–86; Fuuta Jallon plateau in, 4;
geographical diversity of, 3–4; map of, *4;* race and blackness in, 21; reinvention in, 12–13
West Indian Church, 192
West Indian Mission, 191, 193
West Indian missionaries, 24
West Indies, 150
Wilkinson, Richard, 190
Williams, Eric, 15, 17
Williams, Thomas, 148
Wimmler, Jutta, 72
*wolo* cottons, 89
Wolof, 44, 85, 127, 187; aristocracy, 85, 88; cloth traders, 83; interactions with Moors, 79; naming practices, 119; society and *signares,* 121; women, 79, 118
Wolof language, 1, 3, 44, 97, 111, 118, 125, 136
"Woman in Senegal," *132*
women as agents in western Africa, 77–81
"Women at Timbo Drawing Water, The," *176*
Woney, Pa, 152
Wonkifon, 143, 148, 149, 150, 151, 157, 158, 167
World War II, 16
Woulada, 147
Wuuli, 59; Cape Verdean cloth in, 61–62
Wynter, Sylvia, 75

Yanghekori, 142, 157–58, 170
Yaye, Madame, 114
Yelimane, 33
Yoruba, 94

Index ~ 253

Printed and bound by CPI Group (UK) Ltd, Croydon, CR0 4YY
01/12/2024
14602661-0001